D0889994

Published under the auspices of

The Center for Japanese and Korean Studies

University of California, Berkeley

THE LAST PHASE
OF THE
EAST ASIAN WORLD ORDER

THE LAST PHASE
OF THE
EAST ASIAN WORLD ORDER

Korea, Japan, and the Chinese Empire,
1860–1882

KEY-HIUK KIM

University of California Press / Berkeley, Los Angeles, London

University of California Press
Berkeley and Los Angeles, California
University of California Press, Ltd.
London, England
© 1980 by
The Regents of the University of California
ISBN 0-520-03556-9
Library of Congress Catalog Card Number: 77-83106
Printed in the United States of America

1   2   3   4   5   6   7   8   9

To the memory of my elder brother,
Key-Dal Kim.

Contents

Foreword

The present study by Professor K. H. Kim is exemplary as diplomatic history in that it examines the policies of three East Asian countries with a thorough knowledge of the language of each, making possible mastery of the diverse sources. It is also institutional history, since the author's aim is to define the traditional system under which East Asian states conducted their mutual relations, a system which could perhaps best be described as a world order of its own and which was undergoing fundamental changes in the roughly two decades' time dealt with in this book. Although the author is too modest to make the claim, the book also serves to isolate two basic considerations in the making of a country's foreign policy—the strategic needs for its security and the more intangible factor often described vaguely as cultural, in fact involving the ideas and outlook of the policy-makers as well as the sentiments of the domestic political groups with which they had to contend.

Professor Kim's contributions begin with the title of his book. He has chosen the phrase East Asian world order to describe relations among several components of this area in the historical epoch that ended in the late-nineteenth century. The world order that prevailed in East Asia in the Ming-Ch'ing period was dominated by the tribute system centered in China. Whatever the realities of power and of commerce, there had been a large constellation of political entities all over Asia that dispatched, at longer or shorter intervals, respectful tribute missions to Peking. Within the geographical confines of East Asia, the spread of Chinese language, culture, and ideology to Korea, Vietnam, the Liu-ch'iu Islands, and Japan made these countries look to China as the source of civilization. Yet there were limits to

China's claim to be the suzerain of the civilized world. Although Japan had sent many tribute missions to the Ming court during the Ashikaga period, this practice was discontinued totally during the isolation of the Tokugawa period. It was not just the Shinto clergy who insisted that the Japanese monarch, whatever his actual power, had a status at least as divine as that of the Chinese emperor. Japanese disregard for the imperial authority in Peking is seen in Hideyoshi's attempt to invade the Middle Kingdom itself through Korea and in the Satsuma daimyo's success, after 1609, in making the Liu-ch'iuan king regularly pay tribute, borne by a royal prince, to Kagoshima and to Edo. Satsuma annexed the northern islands of Liu-ch'iu (or Ryūkyū, according to Japanese pronunciation); the kingdom that comprised the southern islands, with its capital on Okinawa, was put under tight Satsuma control. "Foreign relations, overseas trade, and military affairs were controlled by the Satsuma government; general laws and domestic policies were left to the Ryūkyū king and his advisers. Satsuma declared in 1624, however, that judicial cases that involved the death penalty or exile should be referred to Satsuma for final decision, and in 1627 it was decreed that new laws or changes of customs . . . must be approved by *han* officials."[1]

During the Ch'ing dynasty there were, therefore, two claimants to suzerainty in the world of East Asia. In contrast to Japan's relations with Ryūkyū, however, China exercised far less control over Korea or Vietnam. China also regarded Liu-ch'iu as a tributary since, despite its allegiance to Japan, the archipelago kingdom continued to send tribute missions to Peking regularly. China enjoyed ceremonial submission from these states—the sending of tribute missions, the acceptance of Chinese investiture whenever a new king ascended the throne, the observance of proper forms in official communications. But it was assumed that these vassal states were in practice virtually independent in the conduct of foreign relations as well as of internal affairs. Except dur-

[1]Robert K. Sakai, "The Ryūkyū Islands as a Fief of Satsuma," in John K. Fairbank, ed., *The Chinese World Order*, 120.

ing the prescribed short visits by Ch'ing envoys, usually for the investiture of a new king or queen, there were not to be any Ch'ing officials on the soil of Korea, Liu-ch'iu, or Vietnam—in clear contrast to the Satsuma *han*'s "resident magistrates" and "inspectors" stationed on Okinawa.

It was not just benevolence, of course, that determined Ch'ing non-interference in the affairs of its tributaries. On rare occasions when a serious situation arose in a tributary that seemed to threaten the stability of the Chinese border, as in the case of the Tâyson rebellion in Vietnam in 1787– 90, the likelihood of Ch'ing military intervention was not ruled out.[2] Nonetheless, a tributary was not the same as a protectorate. Korea and Vietnam—to say nothing of Liu- ch'iu—lay in the geographical area which the Ch'ing gov- ernment at the time did not deem it necessary to rule even indirectly. Ritualistic observances and regulated commercial contacts were, from China's standpoint, all that were neces- sary to ensure stability in such peripheral areas. The rela- tionship between China and these actually autonomous kingdoms was, however, clearly hierarchical—as was indeed Japan's relationship with Ryūkyū. As Professor Kim em- phasizes, such hierarchical relationships, albeit in many cases limited to mere ritual, constituted the unifying princi- ple of the interstate system in Asia. It was this concept of superiority and inferiority that East Asian states found so difficult to discard when, beginning in the mid–nineteenth century, they were confronted by the coercive power of Western nations representing the very different ideology of a community of equal sovereign states—the imperialistic practices of these states notwithstanding.

A basic contribution of Professor Kim's wide-ranging study lies in the attention that it draws to the case of Korea, which longer than any other Asian country avoided or pro- hibited contact with Western powers. In status only a vassal

---

[2]In 1788 the Ch'ing sent a small military force to Hanoi after Vietnamese rebels drove the king of the Lê dynasty from his capital. The Ch'ing force was disas- trously defeated and Peking accepted, in 1790, the tribute mission of Nguyên Huê, the rebel king now legitimized.

to the Chinese suzerain, Korea, which enjoyed autonomy in the conduct of its foreign relations, nonetheless long remained isolated from the new community of nations which China itself had joined. Comparing China's diplomatic record in the 1860s with that of Korea, Mary C. Wright posed the question: "If inadaptability is used to characterize China, what word is left for Korea?"[3] Professor Kim now offers a word: "exclusionism," by which he means an even more restrictive policy in foreign affairs than the seclusion of Tokugawa Japan. The roots of Korea's "exclusionism" are traced to its long history, which bequeathed a deep distrust of foreigners—including Japanese, Manchus, and Europeans. Korea's ruling elite was, to be sure, deeply steeped in Neo-Confucian teaching and found it comfortable to honor Korea's ceremonial obligations to the Son of Heaven in Peking. But up till the late 1870s it was loath to have contact with any country besides China. It was ironic that in the end it was China itself, along with Japan, that brought about Korea's entry into the Western community of nations.

The guardian of Korea's exclusionism was none other than its *yangban* class—the lineages enjoying hereditary status, from whose ranks government officials emerged. Because the institution of kingship was weak in Korea's aristocratic society, the king was often manipulated to suit the ideas and interests of the powerful *yangban* families. Foreign trade was disdained; hence Korea's lack of enthusiasm for relations with the Japanese. Even after 1609, when Korea resumed relations with Japan by an agreement in the spirit of neighborly friendship, the Koreans would not allow envoys from the shogunate to visit their country, although up to 1811 Korea did send twelve "communication missions" to the shogunate. The Japanese could trade with Korea through Tsushima, but even the Tsushima daimyo, who was granted a seal by Seoul signifying a sub-tributary status, could send envoys to visit only Pusan, where they were con-

[3]Mary C. Wright, "The Adaptability of Ch'ing Diplomacy: The Case of Korea," *Journal of Asian Studies,* 17.3 (May 1958), 364.

fined to restricted quarters. Indeed, the Koreans were distrustful even of the Manchus, to whose court in Peking they regularly dispatched annual tributary envoys. The savage Manchu wars against Korea, in the period before the Ch'ing conquest of China, were not forgotten by the Korean elite. In the early eighteenth century, after Ming loyalists had all but disappeared in China, the Korean king and his courtiers had secret shrines built in the palace grounds in honor of the Ming. This behavior indicates at least an ideological exclusion of the Manchus—separating their role as China's reigning dynasty from the cherished Chinese cultural heritage.

Long before European ships first appeared in Korean waters in the 1830s, many Koreans harbored a grudge against the West. According to present knowledge, Catholicism gained converts in Korea during the eighteenth century simply through the influence of books in Chinese which had been produced by Jesuit missionaries. By 1795, when the first Chinese Catholic priest is known to have been smuggled into the peninsula, there were already Korean commoners—and even certain *yangban* out of power—who had converted to Christianity. Massacres of Christians began in 1801, but the Christian community survived and even grew, especially after the 1830s when French priests entered the country secretly. By the early 1860s, at a time of large-scale popular revolts, Christianity was gaining strength rapidly and was regarded as a dangerous source of heterodoxy. It was against this background of a threat to the Korean aristocrats' culture that the famed Taewŏn'gun (Yi Ha-ŭng) received his first training in statecraft. As de facto ruler in the crucial period 1864–1873, he was determined to perpetuate Korea's exclusionist policy.

The Taewŏn'gun was a remarkable reformer of a conservative kind, seeking to bolster the decaying Yi dynasty by reducing the *yangban* power and strengthening the royal prerogative. But when the French sent a few naval vessels to attack Korea in 1866, and the Americans did so in 1871, he was with the *yangban* in pursuing the extermination of

heterodoxy by war against the "barbarians." The Europeans
and Americans were identified with the Korean Christians,
who were massacred as the invaders were repulsed. In Professor Kim's words, the French and American expeditions
strengthened the "militant cultural chauvinism" in Korea in
the 1870s. As he also aptly observes, this cultural
chauvinism, together with the meager information on the
wider world that came to the attention of Korean policy-
makers, resulted in the latter's over-confidence regarding
Korea's ability to deal with the Western threat. It seems that
as late as 1870 all the Korean court knew about the Western
nations had come from Wei Yüan's *Hai-kuo t'u-chih* (Illustrated gazetteer of the maritime countries, first published in
1844, enlarged and re-issued in 1847 and 1852). The
Taewŏn'gun, for all his acumen, does not seem to have fully
grasped the gravity of Russian activities east of the Ussuri or
that of the developments in bakumatsu and early Meiji Japan. In a proud, self-contained society, the easy victories
over the small French and American expeditions merely
added to Korea's over-confidence regarding its own military
strength. It remained for the Japanese to shake this confidence by a formidable display of naval power in 1875–1876.
King Kojong had meanwhile begun his personal rule and
gradually steered his government toward a rapprochement
with Japan. In February 1876 Korea signed the Treaty of
Kanghwa, opening two additional ports besides Pusan to
Japanese trade and granting the Japanese consular jurisdiction in these ports.

Professor Kim's study is not concerned with comparing
the opening of Korea with corresponding events in Japan
and China. It is concerned, however, with how in the same
two decades 1860–1882 Japan and China acted diplomati-
cally to meet their own needs for security and to bolster
their own positions in the new international system they had
joined. It is the author's provocative contention that, even as
the new Japan strove to adopt Western ideas and technology, its ancient claim of superiority, which had deep cultural
roots, was also strongly asserted. It was, in the author's

phrase, an era of "Restoration diplomacy." For, along with the restoration of imperial rule in Japan, there was also a revival of the age-old myth of Japan's overlordship over Korea. Japan not only strove for equality with the Western powers. In its relations with its East Asian neighbors, it wanted a superior position and used its treaty with Korea to advance this aim.

Japan's expansionist impulse, as Professor Kim also emphasizes, must be explained partly by the country's strategic needs—especially the potential threat from Russia that was perceived even in the 1860s. *Sei-Kan ron* (the proposal to invade Korea) of the early Meiji period had, moreover, become virtually a domestic political issue, cherished especially by the disgruntled samurai longing for military ventures. Their clamor for action, as the author has carefully documented, was often held in check by such rational statesmen as Ōkubo Toshimichi. Yet it must be recognized that there was an ideological component even in the politics of realism—in the domestic political milieu in which such statesmen as Ōkubo worked. The historian need not subscribe to the theory of a Japanese "expansionist" plot to accept the fact that ideology constituted a factor in the early Meiji political equation.

In the background of *sei-Kan* ideology was, of course, the warrior spirit, so different from the ethos of the *yangban* class in Korea or that of the literati-officials in China. Among the most vocal proponents of Japanese action to "chastise" Korea were such former samurai as Saigō Takamori and his Satsuma followers, men who had pursued military careers and who, in the battles that made possible the transition to the Meiji era, had rapidly learned Western techniques of warfare. In early 1873, before those imperial councilors who advocated an invasion of Korea were frustrated and resigned from the government, Japan's national conscription law had been promulgated. The martial spirit was to be disseminated more widely. Among the oligarchs that controlled Meiji foreign policy in the following decades, former warriors, sensitive to Japan's military needs, remained dominant. While Shinto-based support for the emperor continued to be inculcated, the Ministry of War, employing foreign advisors, pushed forward military reforms that were to provide the teeth for Japan's foreign policy. In the years between the invasion of Taiwan in 1874 and the establishment of a legation in Seoul in 1880, Japan's new ambitions in East Asia were backed by warriors equipped with Western arms as well as with an ancient mystique.

While Japan's response to Perry was eventually expansionism, China, which for centuries had claimed to be the suzerain of the world, was now reduced to depending on the treaty system initiated by the West to maintain its own security—at least the security of the Ch'ing dynasty.[4] As early as 1867, moreover, as Professor Kim's evidence shows, such statesmen as Prince Kung and Wen-hsiang had already perceived the potential threat that Japan posed to China's strategically important tributary. China plainly had to do something to meet its new international situation. For various reasons, the resources that China needed for the build-up of its military strength were difficult to muster in this period. But on the diplomatic front it was not entirely helpless.

Like the Meiji leaders, Ch'ing policy-makers in the 1860s and 1870s were fully aware of the possibility of further foreign encroachment. Unlike the Japanese, who came to link Japan's security with the need for expansion, China's problem was chiefly defensive; it was well enough if further

[4]When China first accepted the Sino-Western treaty system after the Opium War, the Ch'ing officials had merely found the treaty provisions tolerable from the standpoint of imperial institutions. Joseph Fletcher argues convincingly that the Central Asian precedent of a Ch'ing commercial accord with Kokand (1835) provided a model for the treaty provisions conceded in 1842–1844 for the coastal ports. See *The Cambridge History of China*, vol. 10, 375–385. After the second coastal treaty settlement of 1858–1860, Ch'ing statesmen found certain stipulations of the new treaties to be onerous, e.g., regarding missionary activities. Nonetheless the Ch'ing court also found the treaties to redound to China's advantage. The British and the French helped repulse Taiping invasion of Shanghai in 1860 and 1862. Moreover, the fact that China had entered treaty relations with a number of Western powers gave the impression that the ambitions of any one of them had been thereby moderated.

wars could be avoided and if its own territory could be kept
intact. To avoid wars, Prince Kung and Wen-hsiang, the ar-
chitects of the Ch'ing side of the so-called cooperative policy, saw no better way than to abide by the provisions of the
Sino-Western treaties, which could at least restrain Western
activities to some extent. Around the time of the Tientsin
Massacre (1870), the anti-foreignism that had been building
up in the empire found powerful advocates in Prince Ch'un
and a few newly arisen Han Chinese officials. But Prince
Kung's influence was still weighty enough to allow such
pragmatic officials as Tseng Kuo-fan and Li Hung-chang an
important voice in foreign policy.

The Chinese, whose sense of superiority was supposed to
be the strongest, were not entirely reluctant to yield their
claim of being superior. Li Hung-chang, who negotiated the
first Sino-Japanese treaty (1871), was satisfied with the
equality accorded by the treaty to China and Japan. Justifying this view by saying that Japan had not really been China's tributary "since the Yüan dynasty," Li even agreed to
granting consular jurisdiction to the Japanese in China as
well as to the Chinese in Japan, although he rejected Japan's
demand for trading rights in China's interior and for a
most-favored–nation clause. With equal disregard for ancient institutions, both the Tsungli Yamen and Li were willing to forego Chinese suzerainty over Liu-ch'iu when this
claim was challenged by Japanese action, beginning with the
expedition to Taiwan in 1874 ostensibly undertaken on behalf of Ryūkyū to seek redress for its sailors murdered
there.[5] After Japan officially annexed Ryūkyū in early 1879,
a furor was aroused among the literati-officials in Peking
critical of the government's passivity. But the real outlet for
China's "muscular Confucianism" was not in maritime Asia

[5] Liu-ch'iu was not referred to explicitly in the Sino-Japanese agreement of October 1874 conceding Japan its claims for redress. But in 1875 the Ch'ing government took no action after Japan prohibited Liu-ch'iu tribute missions to China.
Envoys from Liu-ch'iu who came to Peking to seek aid were given little attention.
The subsequent declarations made by the Ch'ing government, between 1878 and
1881, reasserting China's suzerainty over Liu-ch'iu, were inspired, at least partly,
by the need to defend the principle of tributary relations in order to protect
Korea.

but in the highlands and deserts of Inner Asia. The Ch'ing
dynasty's greatest military undertaking in the 1870s was the
recovery of land lost to the Chinese- and Turkic-speaking
Muslims in the large expanse from Shensi to Sinkiang. As
hostile powers closed in on the Ch'ing empire, it was the
perceived strategic importance of a given area that determined the priorities of Ch'ing defense efforts.

China's concern for Korea in the late 1870s is to be understood in this light. For, with its proximity to Manchuria
and to Peking itself, Korea was—now that Russia had extended its power to Vladivostok and Japan was rapidly
adopting Western arms—more than ever China's protective
"shield". The strategy China now tried was to persuade
Korea to open itself to Western diplomatic and commercial
contact—what Professor Kim aptly describes as the "treaty
system policy." This was a strategy only broadly comparable
to *i-i chih-i* (using barbarians to check barbarians), practiced
by dynasties of the past in their dealings with Inner Asian
peoples who either threatened or had penetrated the Middle Kingdom's frontier. Specifically, China's new strategy
called for Korea's entering into treaty relations not only
with Japan but also with the Western powers, which in turn
would encourage these nations to develop commercial interests in the peninsula. Korea, it was hoped, could thus be
protected by a treaty system just as China itself had been. In
late 1876, the same year that Japan coerced Korea into accepting the Treaty of Kanghwa, Li Hung-chang resumed an
intermittent correspondence with a Korean elder statesman
on the advisability of making treaties with Western powers.
In August 1879, after Japan had annexed Ryūkyū, Peking
entrusted the responsibility for Korea to Li. A little more
than a year later, the Korean government acquiesced in the
establishment of the Japanese legation in Seoul, partly because some of King Kojong's advisors began to listen to
Chinese advice.

The United States happened to be the first Western
power to conclude a treaty with Korea. But this was not a
feat comparable to Perry's, for it was with Li Hung-chang at

Tientsin that Commodore Robert W. Shufeldt negotiated. When the treaty was signed at Inch'ŏn by the Korean plenipotentiary in May 1882, a Chinese official who accompanied Shufeldt there was also on the scene. Prompted by Li, a British admiral came to Inch'ŏn only five days later, and a German envoy arrived in June. The American, British, and German treaties, identical in content, stipulated that each contracting party would extend aid and good offices should the other be treated "unjustly or oppressively" by a third party. The treaties may otherwise be taken as evidence of China's quest for redressing, albeit vicariously, the more onerous features of the Sino-Western treaties. Korea was to enjoy tariff autonomy and the opium trade was prohibited. Extraterritoriality was granted, but its abolition was promised pending judicial reforms in Korea.

Whatever the merits of these treaties, their provenance signified Chinese interference with the autonomy of Korea. Li Hung-chang had in effect taken over the conduct of Korea's foreign policy. But China was soon to depart from the tradition of non-interference to an even greater extent. Less than two months after the signing of the Shufeldt treaty, there was a riot among the troops in Seoul. The rioters, apparently instigated by the Taewŏn'gun (then living in retirement), attempted to murder Queen Min, Kojong's manipulative consort. The soldiers also burned down the Japanese legation, and on August 3 a cable from the Chinese legation at Tokyo reached Tientsin, reporting that the Japanese had dispatched warships carrying 1,400 men to Korea. Li Hung-chang was away on mourning leave, but Chang Shu-sheng, Li's temporary replacement, immediately alerted the commander of the Peiyang squadron and instructed an army commander in Shantung province (which was closest to Korea by the sea route) to have 2,000 troops ready for a ship-borne expedition. On August 7, Chang's memorial recommending the expedition was approved by the throne, and two days later Admiral Ting Ju-ch'ang and Ma Chien-chung, the official who had accompanied Shufeldt to Korea, departed from Chefoo with three

European-built warships, arriving at Inch'ŏn on the night of the 10th. General Wu Ch'ang-ch'ing and his 2,000 troops, carried by five Chinese steamships, reached Korea on August 20, in time to save Seoul from possible retaliatory action by the Japanese forces that had arrived meanwhile. Also on August 20, Japanese Minister Hanabusa had an audience with King Kojong, presenting harsh demands to be met within three days. Ma, the Chinese official, now intervened with the Japanese, counseling a peaceful settlement. Impressed by the display of Chinese military and naval power, the Japanese decided to press only for indemnities and additional commercial advantages and to await opportunities in the future.

Ma and General Wu now made a blatant move in the name of Chinese suzerainty. The Taewŏn'gun, who was accused by most of King Kojong's courtiers of opposing the new treaties, had again risen to power in the wake of the soldiers' riot. On August 26 he was abducted and brought by warship to Tientsin. Korea was again ruled by the king and his queen—but General Wu and two thousand Chinese troops remained in Seoul.

Since China had generally been pursuing a policy of accommodation toward Western powers and Japan, it is remarkable that, when the stability and security of Korea were at stake, such vigorous action was undertaken. In the early 1880s China was clearly not entirely devoid of military capacity. Nor were the Chinese completely ineffective in their use of Western military equipment—warships to display in Korean harbors and telegraph lines to communicate between Tientsin and Shanghai, the principal shipping center. Governor-General Chang Shu-sheng's quick action was backed by a court fully aware of Korea's importance to the defense of north China and was especially appreciated by the literati-officials who had lamented Japan's formal annexation of Liu-ch'iu three years before. The decision to have General Wu Ch'ang-ch'ing's 2,000 troops stay in Korea indicated that in some circumstances China also could be expansionist—China's claims as Korea's ritualistic suzerain being now extended to facilitate action taken for China's own defense needs.

This essay is a tribute to a very good book. It is hoped that these remarks may serve to point out certain assumptions implicit in Professor Kim's scheme of analysis—in particular, the concern for national safety present in every country and the cultural predilections from which no society can be free. Behind the events and policies discussed in this book were the policy-makers of Korea, Japan, and China, those of each country being inspired by their respective needs and distinctive ethos.

It is Professor Kim's principal purpose to observe the way in which the policies of the three countries interacted and thereby brought about distinct changes in the East Asian world order. The hierarchical heritage in international relations was unfortunately to remain, even as Korea was ushered into the new world of rival sovereign states. Professor Kim's work is a remarkably well wrought synthesis of diplomatic and institutional history. It treats with acuity and impartiality the extensive relevant sources of all three countries involved. It invites us to explore the range of apparent differences and similarities within the several geographical and cultural components of East Asia, politically isolated at some times and at others interlocked.

Kwang-Ching Liu

Preface

The middle decades of the nineteenth century saw profound disturbances in the existing world order in East Asia as a result of new waves of Western expansion. The changes on the international scene in the northwestern Pacific region cannot, however, be ascribed to Western diplomatic, economic, or military action alone. The rise of Meiji Japan, stimulated partly by the impact of the West, presented an immediate challenge to the position of supremacy that China had held over the East Asian world since early times. The subsequent disintegration and ultimate demise of the traditional world order in East Asia was as much a result of an emerging rivalry between China and Japan as of the broad cultural conflict between the East and the West. No other event better illustrates this than the transition of Korea from a tributary state of the Ch'ing empire to a member of the modern world community.

While it was the "opening" of China and Japan that started far-reaching and revolutionary changes in international relations in East Asia in modern times, it was to a large degree the indigenous heritage and tradition that determined the shape and course of these changes. Similarly, while Western powers such as France and the United States provided the original impetus for opening the "hermit kingdom," it was China and Japan that played decisive roles in ending its isolation from the outside world. Therefore, although interaction between China, Japan, and Korea must be studied in the context of the new international environment in East Asia created by the arrival of the West, policies and actions themselves can be understood fully only in the context of the domestic background of each country.

Major works have been published in Western languages on Chinese, Japanese, and Korean policies concerning the opening of Korea. A pioneering work is M. Frederick Nelson's *Korea and the Old Orders in Eastern Asia* (1945). Nelson's study provides a starting point for an inquiry into the nature of the Sino-Korean tributary relations as they existed in the mid-nineteenth century; it covers in broad strokes the entire history of Sino-Korean relations from the earliest times. In his seminal study, *The Japanese Seizure of Korea, 1868–1910* (1960), Hilary Conroy provides an imaginative and valuable analysis of Meiji Japanese policy toward Korea in the framework of a universal problem of great significance, conflict between realism and idealism in international relations. The Korean background for the same period is cogently examined in C. I. Eugene Kim and Han-Kyo Kim, *Korea and the Politics of Imperialism, 1876–1910* (1967). A valuable study of Chinese policy toward Korea for the decade that saw the opening of Korea to Western nations is Frederick Foo Chien, *The Opening of Korea: A Study of Chinese Diplomacy, 1876–1885* (1967). A work by Martina Deuchler, *Confucian Gentlemen and Barbarian Envoys: The Opening of Korea, 1875–1885* (1977), offers an excellent analysis of Korea's reactions and response to new pressures from Japan and the West.

Each of these works is a valuable study, but none of them answers the question: How did the policies and actions of China and Japan bringing Korea into the international community affect the existing world order in East Asia? It is with this question that the present volume is chiefly concerned. My inquiry is mainly institutional in nature and multinational in perspective. I have examined the transition of Korea's international position as a representative part of the process whereby the dualistic world order—the last phase of the traditional world order—created in East Asia by the introduction of the Western international system was brought to an end.

In the course of examining the policies of China, Japan, and Korea, three salient points have emerged: the role of tradition in policy-making, the correlation between domestic politics and foreign policy, and the interaction among the policies and actions of the three countries. Although tradition at any given time may have weighed more heavily in one country than in others, its influence was universal and persistent. I have found Meiji Japan's initial policy toward its East Asian neighbors no less traditional than that of China or even Korea—its zeal for reform and modernization notwithstanding.

In order to gain deeper understanding of the policies of each country, I deemed it necessary to probe into the domestic cultural and political background of policy-making. With regard to Japan, my findings generally support Conroy's theme of realism versus idealism in early Meiji policy toward Korea. However, I put greater emphasis on Japan's domestic problems and their relationship to persistent expansionist sentiment in that country in the bakumatsu and early Meiji periods. In addition to inspirations provided by the West, early schism within the emerging oligarchy was a principal factor behind Japan's actions with regard to Korea and Taiwan in the early Meiji period.

Finally, in order to show the gradual and often subtle changes that led to the ultimate demise of the traditional world order in East Asia, I considered it necessary to study not only the policies of each of the principal countries involved but interaction among them. As my research progressed, it became clear that the policy of China could not be fully understood without a careful, chronological analysis of the actions Japan and Korea were taking. Although policies changed from month to month, the basic overall pattern was one of challenge and response.

The present study was first conceived as a doctoral dissertation in history at the University of California at Davis. I wish to express my heartfelt gratitude to members of my dissertation committee: Professor Kwang-Ching Liu, the late Professor Richard J. Miller, and Professor Don C. Price of the Department of History, University of California, Davis, and Professor Hilary Conroy of the Department of History, University of Pennsylvania. From the beginning,

Professor Liu, chairman of the committee, has given me inspiration and guidance without which this study would not have been completed. In addition to scrutinizing the dissertation, Professor Miller gave warm and unfailing moral support, which sustained my often-flagging spirit. My lasting regret is that the present volume will appear in print too late for him to see it. I have benefited greatly from Professor Price's thoughtful advice and comment. My special thanks go to Professor Conroy, who, having consented to be an outside member of the committee, read the manuscript at various stages of its preparation and offered valuable advice and warm encouragement. Finally, I wish to thank Professor Immanuel C. Y. Hsü of the University of California at Santa Barbara and Professor James B. Palais of the University of Washington for their incisive comments and valuable suggestions. I also warmly thank Ms. Gayle Bacon and Ms. Barbara Beckman of the Department of Anthropology, University of California, Davis, for typing the manuscript.

K. H. K.

Davis, California

Abbreviations
Used in Notes

CJHK *Ch'ing-chi Chung-Jih-Han kuan-hsi shih-liao*
CKCJ *Ch'ing Kuang-hsü ch'ao Chung-Jih chiao-she shih-liao*
CWS *Chosŏn wangjo sillok*
ISN-KJ *Ilsŏngnok: Kojong p'yŏn*
IWSM-TC *Ch'ou-pan i-wu shih-mo: T'ung-chih ch'ao*
IWSM-TK *Ch'ou-pan i-wu shih-mo: Tao-kuang ch'ao*
KHOM *Ku Han'guk oegyo munsŏ*
KJS *Kojong Sunjong Sillok: Kojong sillok*
LWCK Li Hung-chang, *Li Wen-chung-kung ch'üan-shu*
NGB *Nihon gaikō bunsho*
TNS Tabohashi Kiyoshi, *Kindai Nissen kankei no kenkyū*

Dates

Dates are by year, month, and day of the king's reign. KJS, 10/2/10 indicates the 10th day of the second month of King Kojong's 10th reign year.

CHAPTER I

Korea in Traditional East Asia

Until the great inroads of Western power and influence in the nineteenth century, East Asia was a self-contained world, the home of the venerable Chinese civilization that had been little affected by the dynamic, expanding civilization of the modern West. From the earliest times China, with its continental locus, vast size, and wealth, and especially its superior culture, had been the center of this world. This historical reality, combined with the ancient notion of universal kingship and the Confucian concept of a preordained hierarchy in the universe and among men, gave rise to a perception of the world as a universal empire (*t'ien-hsia*) presided over by the Son of Heaven (the Chinese emperor) from the Middle Kingdom (China). As Chinese cultural and political influence spread, the people of such adjacent lands as Korea, Japan, and Vietnam accepted this sinocentric world view. Acknowledging Chinese titular superiority and cultural leadership, they emulated China in developing their own political, social, and cultural institutions. The subsequent history of East Asia served to confirm the view that China was the center of the world, the suzerain of all lands and peoples on earth, and the fountainhead of culture and enlightenment.[1]

In the Confucian world order as conceived by the ancient Chinese there existed a close unity of man, nature, and so-

---

1. For the traditional Chinese view of the world, see John K. Fairbank, ed., *The Chinese World Order;* M. Frederick Nelson, *Korea and the Old Orders in Eastern Asia,* 3–20; Abe Takeo, *Chūgokujin no tenka kannen* (The Chinese concept of the world).

ciety. The notion of the sovereignty of individual states or nations was alien to the universal hierarchy that theoretically embraced the entire world, at the center of which stood China, supreme in moral authority and cultural grandeur. Relations between China, the Middle Kingdom, and the "lesser" states and nations, all of which were theoretically tributaries of China, were to be governed by the same Confucian rules of propriety (*li*) that regulated familial and social relations within China—namely, relations between father and son, ruler and official, husband and wife, elder and younger brother, and friend and friend. The analogy between relations among men and those among states and nations was given an institutional expression in a scheme of interstate relations known as the tribute system of the Chinese empire. Until it was supplanted by the Western system of international relations in the late nineteenth century, the tribute system governed relations between China on the one hand and non-Chinese states and peoples on the other. It also provided the basis upon which non-Chinese states in East Asia conducted their relations with one another, and served as the model for such states in organizing relations with the peoples of their own peripheral regions. The system thus was the symbol and institutional framework of the sinocentric Confucian world order that for centuries flourished in East Asia and adjacent lands until modern times.[2]

Geography, culture, and history combined to give Korea a unique place within this East Asian world order. Through long and close cultural and political ties with China, Korea became the most Confucian of all East Asian societies outside the Chinese heartland. It was probably the first major non-Chinese state to acknowledge Chinese suzerainty and

2. For the origins and history of the Chinese tribute system, see John K. Fairbank and S. Y. Teng, "On the Ch'ing Tributary System," *Harvard Journal of Asiatic Studies* 6 (1941), 135–246; Ying-shih Yü, *Trade and Expansion in Han China*, 36–64. For examples of tributary or semi-tributary relations between non-Chinese states and their peripheral regions in East Asia, see Robert K. Sakai, "The Ryūkyū Islands as a Fief of Satsuma," in Fairbank, ed., *The Chinese World Order*, 112–134; Alexander B. Woodside, *Vietnam and the Chinese Model*, 235–294.

certainly the last one to renounce it formally. Embracing the sinocentric view of the world wholeheartedly, the Koreans historically regarded their country's close ties with China as a mark of distinction and remained loyal and submissive to the Middle Kingdom. Many Chinese rulers considered the peninsular state as their model tributary and traditionally accorded it the foremost place within their empire.[3]

Korea also derived importance from its pivotal geographical position that lay astride the main crossroads of culture, trade, and war among the major fonts of power in East Asia. Its control was deemed a matter of great importance by those seeking the mastery of the Chinese continent or hegemony in East Asia. Japanese rulers such as Hideyoshi and his latter-day heirs regarded the peninsula as the first bridgehead they must secure if they were to fulfill their dream of continental expansion. Many dynasties and regimes in China, especially those with their principal base of political or military power in the north, considered Korea a shield protecting the eastern flank of their empire and sought to control or keep it within the Chinese orbit.[4]

In the middle of the nineteenth century, the sinocentric world order that China had historically maintained in East Asia faced two grave challenges, one external and the other internal. The former was the massive intrusion of Western power and the latter was the rise of modern Japan. After decades of trade, diplomacy, war, and proselytizing, the Western powers succeeded, by the early 1860s, in imposing upon China, Japan, and the rest of East Asia their system of international relations based on the concept of the equal sovereignty of all states. Only Korea, the "hermit of the East," remained outside this newly introduced Western in-

3. For the history of Sino-Korean tributary relations, see Nelson, *Korea and the Old Orders*, 21–297; Chun (Chŏn) Hae-jong, *Han-Chung kwan'gyesa yŏn'gu* (Studies on the history of Sino-Korean relations), 26–58. For Ch'ing-Korean tributary relations, see Kim Sŏng-ch'il, "Yŏnhaeng sogo" (A short study of the missions to Peking), *Yŏksa hakpo* 12 (May 1960), 1–79; Chun Hae-jong, "Sino-Korean Tributary Relations during the Ch'ing Period," in Fairbank, ed., *The Chinese World Order*, 90–111; Chang Ts'un-wu, *Ch'ing-Han tsung-fan mou-i, 1637–1894* (Sino-Korean tributary trade, 1637–1894).

4. David I. Steinberg, *Korea: Nexus of East Asia*, 1–5.

ternational system. Closely following upon this revolutionary change in the East Asian international scene was the
emergence of Meiji Japan with a growing interest in continental East Asia and a zeal for reform and Westernization.
Korea became an immediate object of Japan's new interest
and diplomacy in East Asia. During the decades that followed the opening of China and Japan, Korea became the
institutional keystone of the East Asian world order that
China tried to preserve. It also became a symbol of the traditional supremacy which China was determined to maintain
in East Asia in the face of the Western and Japanese challenges. Korea's eventual incorporation into the Western international system in the early 1880s, along with the French
seizure of Vietnam, marked the effective end both of the
old world order and of Chinese supremacy in East Asia.

The present study concentrates on Korea's transition
from a tributary of the Chinese empire to a member of the
modern international community as an event of pivotal historical significance among the vast changes that occurred in
East Asian international relations between the early 1860s
and the early 1880s—an event that symbolized the broad
East-West cultural conflict and the emerging Sino-Japanese
rivalry in East Asia. The book begins with an analysis of
Korea's traditional relations with China and Japan—the two
neighbors which were to play principal roles in the modern
transformation of its foreign relations—and of the relevant
domestic background of Korea. Such an analysis enables us
to better appraise Korea's reactions and responses to threats
as well as to opportunities presented by Western intrusion
and Japanese pressure.

TRIBUTARY RELATIONS WITH CHINA

Korea entered into tributary relations with China early in its
history. It was, however, not until the early fifteenth
century—the early decades of both Ming China and Yi
Korea—that Sino-Korean tributary relations attained full
institutional maturity. Yi Sŏng-gye, the founder of the Yi

dynasty (1392–1910), seized the throne with the support of a rising Confucian scholar-official class, which had become disenchanted with the decrepit Koryŏ (Wang) dynasty dominated by a corrupt Buddhist aristocracy allied with the Mongols. Having suppressed Buddhism, which had been the dominant influence in society and government during the preceding dynasty, Yi proclaimed Neo-Confucianism the ideological orthodoxy of his regime. He and his heirs proceeded to transform Korea into a model Confucian state by creating new political, social, and cultural institutions closely patterned on those of Sung and Ming China. Thoroughly Confucian in education and outlook, the ruling elite of Yi Korea believed as firmly as did its Chinese counterpart that the world was a universal empire centered on China.

The rulers of Yi Korea apparently regarded the rise of the Ming as a restoration of the proper Confucian order in China and the world after the Mongol "aberration." Readily acknowledging Ming suzerainty, they adopted the celebrated doctrine of *sadae* ("serving the superior") as the fundamental principle guiding their kingdom's relations with China.[5] Despite certain disagreements and discord that marred the initial Ming-Korean relations, Korea quickly became the model and most important Ming tributary. The transition from Ming to Ch'ing China in the first half of the seventeenth century caused a deep trauma in Sino-Korean relations.[6] After the Manchu conquest of China, however,

5. On early Ming-Korean relations, see Hugh D. Walker, "The Yi-Ming Rapprochement" (Ph.D. dissert., University of California, Los Angeles, 1971); Sin Sŏk-ho, "Chosŏn wangjo kaeguk tangsi ŭi tae-Myŏng kwan'gye" (Relations with the Ming at the time of founding the Yi dynasty), *Kuksasang ŭi chemunje* 1 (1959), 93–134; Kim Yong-gi, "Chosŏn ch'ogi ŭi tae-Myŏng chogong kwan'gye ko" (A study of tributary relations with the Ming in the early Yi period), *Pusandae nonmunjip* 14 (1972), 131–182.

6. For Ming-Manchu-Korean relations in the early seventeenth century, see Yi Pyŏng-do, "Kwanghaegun ŭi tae-Hugŭm chŏngch'aek" (Prince Kwanghae's policy toward the Manchus), *Kuksasang ŭi chemunje* 1 (1959), 135–175; Inaba Iwakichi, *Kōkaikun jidai no Man-Sen kankei* (Manchu-Korean relations during Prince Kwanghae's reign); Chang Ts'un-wu, "Ch'ing-Han kuan-hsi, 1636–1644" (Ch'ing-Korean relations, 1636–1644), pt. 1, *Ku-kung wen-hsien* 4.1 (December 1972), 15–37; pt. 2, *ibid.* 4.2 (March 1973), 15–35.

the pattern of harmonious relations that had obtained between the two countries during the Ming period was soon restored. From that time until the late nineteenth century, when Korea ultimately renounced its tributary ties with China, it remained steadfastly loyal and submissive and faithfully discharged all its tributary obligations to China.

CHINA'S CEREMONIAL SUZERAINTY

Sino-Korean relations during the Ch'ing period consisted of the exchange of ceremonial envoys, symbolic observances, and an attendant trade between the two countries. Korea's most important duty under the tribute system was to send tributary envoys to China whenever the occasion demanded. During most of the Ch'ing period it sent one regular embassy to China every year, usually at the time of the winter solstice. In addition, Korea sent numerous special embassies and missions on various occasions—such as the accession or death of an emperor or other events of special importance in China, or when the Korean court wished to report the accession or death of a king or other important events, or when it wished to request investiture for a king or queen. During 245 years from 1637 to 1881, a total of 435 special embassies and missions were sent to China.[7]

Whenever it sent an embassy, regular or special, to China, the Korean court presented a tribute of local products to the Ch'ing court. In return, the latter bestowed gifts upon members of the Korean royal family and principal members of its tributary embassy. When a Korean ruler came to the throne, he was to request investiture from the Chinese emperor. Upon receiving such a request, the emperor dispatched edict-bearing envoys to Korea to confer upon the Korean ruler an imperial patent of appointment formally designating him as "king of Korea," and the Korean ruler personally greeted the envoys outside the city wall of his

7. Kim Sŏng-ch'il, "Yŏnhaeng sogo," 7–13; Chun, "Sino-Korean Tributary Relations," 90–96.

capital and prostrated himself when the imperial edict was read to him. Investiture was also granted to the Korean queen and heir-designate to the throne. As a symbolic act of submission Korea used the Chinese calendar. All Korean documents going to China, including the king's communications to the presidents of the Board of Rites—the highest Ch'ing officials with whom he was allowed to communicate—were dated by the year title of the reigning Chinese emperor.[8]

Each Korean embassy carried a certain amount of silver and merchandise to trade for Chinese goods on behalf of the Korean court and government. In addition, members of an embassy were allowed to take a fixed amount of silver and merchandise to conduct their own private trade. While in Peking, they were allowed to sell their merchandise and buy Chinese goods at a designated market place. Also, fairs were held at regular intervals at three places along the Korean-Manchurian border, where Chinese and Korean merchants engaged in barter trade under government supervision.[9]

Since relations between China and Korea were considered analogous to those between father and son or between elder and younger brother, they imposed on both parties moral rather than legal obligations. Such obligations, it was believed, could be best fulfilled if each party behaved toward the other strictly in accordance with the rules of proper conduct between superior and inferior. The two countries therefore exchanged envoys primarily to perform ceremonial rituals and symbolic acts that embodied such rules. Although the trade between the two countries was of considerable importance, it was regarded as incidental in nature. Even material exchanges such as the presentation

8. George M. McCune, "Korean Relations with China and Japan, 1800–1864" (Ph.D. dissert., University of California, Berkeley, 1941), 233–239.
9. Chang Ts'un-wu, *Ch'ing-Han tsung-fan mou-i,* is the most comprehensive study of the Sino-Korean trade during the Ch'ing period. See also, Kim Sŏng-ch'il, "Yŏnhaeng sogo," 27–46; McCune, "Korean Relations," 96–123; Chun, "Sino-Korean Tributary Relations," 107–109.

of Korean tribute and the bestowal of Chinese gifts were viewed primarily in terms of their moral or symbolic significance rather than in those of their material value.[10]

The fact that Sino-Korean relations during the Ch'ing period consisted chiefly of ceremonial exchanges and symbolic observances suggests that, while China's titular superiority and authority as suzerain were absolute in theory, in practice its suzerainty over Korea seldom extended beyond the realm of ceremonial diplomacy. For all practical intents and purposes, Korea was completely independent in the management of its own affairs.

KOREAN AUTONOMY UNDER THE TRIBUTE SYSTEM

Although China and Korea regularly and frequently exchanged envoys, the two countries hardly ever conferred concerning each other's internal or external affairs. The primary functions of the regular Korean embassy were to deliver Korea's annual tribute to the Ch'ing court and to participate in court ceremonies in Peking marking the winter solstice and New Year. Special Korean embassies performed similar ceremonial duties on other occasions, such as the accession or wedding of an emperor. Few of these embassies ever engaged in substantive diplomatic negotiations or political discussions. Edict-bearing envoys were the only Ch'ing officials to set foot in Korea; their mission was almost invariably to bring the imperial patent of appointment for a Korean king or queen. Their brief sojourn in the Korean capital was devoted entirely to ceremonial and entertainment activities.[11]

The institution of investiture, a feature of the tribute system that could have easily become a tool of political leverage, was never so used by China. With few exceptions, all Korean requests for investiture were routinely granted.

10. Fairbank and Teng, "The Ch'ing Tributary System," 140–144; McCune, "Korean Relations," 232–240.

11. For the activities of Korean embassies in Peking, see Gari Ledyard, "Korean Travelers in China over Four Hundred Years," *Occasional Papers on Korea* 2 (March 1974), 1–42. For the activities of Chinese embassies in Seoul, see McCune, "Korean Relations," 58–68.

Even more significantly, while investiture from the Son of Heaven was regarded as the final step in the legitimization of the rule of a Korean monarch, it neither created nor materially enhanced his authority as ruler. He was a ruler in name as well as in fact even without it.[12] The king's memorials to the emperor, while always reverential and submissive in tone, never mentioned Korean domestic questions. Nor did the emperor's edicts, always ritualistic in content, ever touch upon Korean internal issues. In external as in internal affairs, Korea was fully autonomous, free to maintain relations with any country so long as such relations did not conflict with its tributary obligations to China. Throughout the Ch'ing period Korea maintained diplomatic and commercial relations with Tokugawa Japan with little Chinese supervision or interference.[13]

It was neither China's intention nor its normal practice under the tribute system to interfere in or to assume responsibility for Korean affairs, internal or external. Nor was Korea, its ceremonial submission to China notwithstanding, ever willing to accept Chinese interference in its affairs. Non-interference was the basic principle and norm of Chinese policy toward Korea during the Ch'ing period. Korea remained master in its own house, functioning as a fully independent state in fact, if indeed not in name as well.

TRADE, CULTURE, AND SECURITY

Whatever their theoretical basis or moral justification, Sino-Korean relations would not have been as stable as they were, especially during the Ch'ing period, when anti-Manchu sentiment persisted in Korea, unless there had been sufficient practical benefits accruing from them for both countries. One source of such benefit was obviously trade between the two countries.

12. McCune, "Korean Relations," 237–238.
13. Under the terms of Korean surrender to the Ch'ing, Korea was authorized to trade with Japan and instructed to induce Japan to send tribute to the Ch'ing court. See Nakamura Hidetaka, *Nissen kankeishi no kenkyū* (Studies on the history of Japanese-Korean relations), vol. 3, 500–502.

As has been mentioned, every Korean tributary embassy took a certain amount of silver and merchandise— approximately 8,000 taels in value—to China to pay for Chinese goods purchased for the Korean court and government. In addition, members of the embassy took 2,000 taels each in silver or merchandise to conduct their own trade, ostensibly to supplement "insufficient" travel funds furnished by the government. In 1787 members of one embassy took a total of 80,000 taels in silver and merchandise, mostly Korean ginseng. Since an average of two to three Korean embassies visited China each year during the Ch'ing period, the volume of this trade was considerable, at least from the Korean standpoint. In addition, an average of some 45,000 taels' worth of Korean goods was traded for certain Manchurian products at the government-supervised trade fairs at the Korean-Manchurian border every year.[14]

While the trade with China was regarded as an important source of revenue by some Korean government agencies, neither the Korean nor the Chinese government as a whole seems to have greatly profitted from it. This would be true even if the exchange of Korean tribute and Chinese gifts were regarded as part of the overall Sino-Korean trade. Although the total value of Korean tribute exceeded that of Chinese gifts by some 80,000 taels every year, the figure did not represent a net gain for the Chinese government, for it spent at least an equal amount to support the visiting Korean embassy personnel.[15]

There is little doubt, however, that the Peking trade was highly lucrative for certain members of officialdom and some merchants in both countries, especially members of the Korean embassy, whose expenses during their trip to and from China were borne entirely by either the Korean or the Chinese government. Lured by the prospect of sure

14. See n. 9.
15. Kim Sŏng-ch'il, "Yŏnhaeng sogo," 76; Chun, "Sino-Korean Tributary Relations," 107. On the China trade being an important source of revenue for some Korean government agencies, see Chang Ts'un-wu, *Ch'ing-Han tsung-fan mou-i,* 87–89.

profit, many Korean merchants and even smugglers were said to have gone to China every year, disguised as personal servants or attendants of official members of an embassy or mission. Some Chinese merchants in Peking were said to have amassed fortunes from their monopoly of Korean trade. Certain Chinese officials and runners, particularly those in charge of the Korean hostelry in Peking under its Manchu director, partook of the profit from this trade.[16] If the Peking trade was chiefly for the benefit of the Koreans, the border trade fairs were organized mainly for the benefit of the local Manchu bannermen wishing to obtain daily necessities from Korea. The Koreans complained that they suffered net losses every year because they were responsible for provisioning the visiting Chinese merchants and officials and that they were forced to barter superior Korean goods for inferior Manchurian products at fixed rates of exchange.[17]

Although viewed as incidental in nature and unimportant in theory, Sino-Korean trade under the tribute system developed networks of vested bureaucratic and commercial interest in both countries. This seems to have contributed to the durable and stable relations between the two countries during the Ch'ing period.

There were other important practical benefits for both countries under the tribute system. What appeared to be merely ceremonial and symbolic ties offered tangible and intangible practical benefits of considerable political, cultural, and security value. Politically, since Korea was the most Confucian society in East Asia outside the Chinese heartland, its allegiance, however obtained, must have been useful to the Manchu rulers in the early Ch'ing period in

16. For an overall evaluation of the benefits of the Ch'ing-Korean trade, see Chang Ts'un-wu, *Ch'ing-Han tsung-fan mou-i*, 223–235. See also McCune, "Korean Relations," 48–50; Chun, "Sino-Korean Tributary Relations," 107; Ledyard, "Korean Travelers," 11, 21–22.

17. Kim Chong-wŏn, "Cho-Chung sangmin suryuk muyŏk changjŏng e taehayŏ" (On Korean-Chinese private maritime and overland trade regulations), *Yŏksa hakpo* 32 (December 1966), 136.

their efforts to consolidate their rule in China and to enhance their imperial authority in the East Asian world. Although Korea's political or diplomatic value to the Ch'ing
declined subsequently, it became important again in the
mid-nineteenth century as the Chinese empire faced challenges to its traditional authority in East Asia from Western
powers and Japan.

For Korea the importance of stable relations with China
can hardly be exaggerated. Lacking the cosmic symbols and
attributes that made the Chinese emperor the Son of
Heaven, the Korean ruler needed investiture from the
former as the ultimate symbol of legitimacy. Although his
power as ruler was neither derived from nor materially enhanced by the Chinese investiture, the lack of it could not
but adversely affect his prestige in the eyes of his officials
and subjects in a Confucian society such as Yi Korea. While
his status as vassal of the Chinese emperor put certain
theoretical limits upon his authority as ruler, it also lent
prestige to his position and enhanced its security, especially
in times of domestic unrest or uncertainty. Some scholars
attribute the relative longevity of dynasties in Korean history to their tributary ties with the Middle Kingdom.[18]

Culturally, close ties with China were invaluable to Korea.
It was the splendor of Chinese culture, not the lure of its
commerce, that had historically attracted the Koreans to
China. Appointment as members of a tributary embassy to
China was a coveted assignment, usually made on the basis
of scholarly achievement and literary talent. Frequent and
often extended visits to China by men of learning and literary skill assured Korea of a constant stream of information
and knowledge concerning the latest intellectual trends in
China. Since a visit to China provided an opportunity to
broaden one's education and intellectual outlook, members
of the tributary embassies often took their sons or nephews
with them to China. While in China, they eagerly sought

18. For a study of the effect of Sino-Korean tributary relations upon Korean
dynasties, see Chun Hae-jong, *Tong'a munhwa ŭi pigyosajŏk yŏn'gu* (Comparative historical studies on East Asian culture), 2–20.

personal contact and friendship with prominent Chinese
scholars.[19] Their favorite pastime in Peking was to ransack
its bookstores—books being a major item that they took
home from China. Most of them wrote voluminous diaries
during their trip to China, which were no doubt read by
their families, relatives, and friends.

In the days when Korean scholarship was dominated
completely by Sung Learning, some of these men introduced Han Learning to Korea, which led to the rise of a
new school known as Practical Learning (*sirhak*) in Korea in
the eighteenth century.[20] Even more remarkably, it was the
Christian tracts brought home from China by some of these
men which led to the growth and spread of Christianity in
the late eighteenth century.[21] In the mid-nineteenth century
Koreans gained their first hazy glimpse of the Western
world through books brought home from China by members of the tributary embassies—books such as Wei Yüan's
Hai-kuo t'u-chih (an illustrated gazetteer of maritime countries).[22] Throughout the centuries of Korean seclusion the
annual pilgrimages to Peking, Celestial Capital and cultural
mecca of the East Asian world, evolved into an indispensable cultural and educational institution for the Korean intellectual elite.

Less tangible but extremely important were the benefits
enjoyed by both Chinese and Koreans in the area of security
under the tribute system. Throughout history Korea by it-

19. Ledyard, "Korean Travelers," 6–28. For a study of fraternization and
cooperation between Chinese and Korean scholars during the Ch'ing period, see
Fujitsuka Rin, *Shinchō bunka tōden no kenkyū* (A study of the transmission of Ch'ing
culture to Korea). For Chinese cultural influence on Korea during the Ch'ing
period, see Chang Ts'un-wu, "Ch'ing-tai Chung-kuo tui Chao-hsien wen-hua chih
ying-hsiang" (Chinese cultural influence on Korea during the Ch'ing period), *Bulletin of the Institute of Modern History, Academia Sinica* 4.2 (December 1974), 551–599.
20. Kang Chae-ŏn (Kyō Zai-gen), *Chōsen kindaishi kenkyū* (Studies on modern
Korean history), 1–61; Fujitsuka, *Shinchō bunka tōden*, 61–79; Chun Hae-jong,
Tong'a munhwa, 65–72.
21. On the introduction of Christian tracts in Korea, see Ch'oe Sŏg-u, "Ch'ŏnjugyo ŭi suyong" (Acceptance of Catholicism), in Ch'oe Yŏng-hŭi, et al., eds.,
Han'guksa (History of Korea), vol. 14, 88–123; Yamaguchi Masayuki, *Chōsen Seikyō
shi* (A history of Christianity in Korea), 37–69.
22. Yi Kwang-yin, *Han'guk kaehwasa yŏn'gu* (Studies on the history of modernization in Korea), 26–34.

self has never been a threat to China or Japan. But in the hands of an actual or potential enemy, the peninsula could pose a serious threat to both China and Japan. Korea played an important role in the ill-fated Mongol invasions of Japan in the late thirteenth century. It was largely the fear of Japanese control of the peninsula that drove the Ming to the point of military and financial exhaustion in defending it from Japanese invaders in the 1590s. The Manchus found it necessary to invade the peninsula twice to secure its control before their campaigns against the Ming. Because of Korea's relative military weakness, one may wonder if it could have materially contributed to the security of China. Any such doubt, however, may be quickly dispelled by simply speculating on what might have happened had Korea cooperated with, instead of resisting, Hideyoshi when he asked for free passage for his forces through the peninsula for an invasion of China.[23] Korea's strategic importance was a major factor behind the shift in Ch'ing policy from punitive exploitation to relative tolerance immediately after the Manchu conquest of China. It became a major factor again in the calculations of Chinese policy-makers in the late nineteenth century as China faced Western and Japanese threats.

The guarantee of Chinese protection, implied or otherwise, was indispensable to Korea for its security in times of external threat. This was amply demonstrated by the massive Ming assistance that enabled the Koreans to withstand the Hideyoshi invasions. During most of the Ch'ing period tributary obligations to China continued to impose a considerable financial burden upon Korea. It was, however, undoubtedly less costly than the greater burden of national defense, which Korea would have been forced to carry had it been left without a reasonable prospect of Chinese aid in times of foreign invasion. Dependence on Chinese assistance seems to have been a factor that partly explains Yi Korea's failure to maintain an adequate military establish-

23. On Korean-Japanese negotiations preceding the Hideyoshi invasions, see Nakamura, *Nissen kankeishi*, vol. 2, 75–91.

ment even after such national catastrophes as the Japanese invasions of the 1590s. Under the protective shield of Ch'ing power, Korea lived in peace and security for more than two centuries. During the 1860s and 1870s, the possibility of Chinese military intervention was a factor that had to be weighed by both the proponents and opponents of *sei-Kan ron* ("proposal for the conquest of Korea") in Japan.

"NEIGHBORLY RELATIONS" WITH TOKUGAWA JAPAN

In contrast to its tributary relations with China, Korea's relations with Japan were traditionally defined as "neighborly relations" (*kyorin*). Although relations between the two countries date from much earlier, in the fifteenth century a firm pattern of relations was established that was to continue during the Tokugawa period. In 1404—a year after the ruler of Yi Korea had received formal Ming investiture for the first time—Yoshimitsu, the third Ashikaga shogun, received Ming investiture as "king of Japan." The identical status assigned to the rulers of Yi Korea and Ashikaga Japan under the Ming tribute system seems to have facilitated the establishment of formal relations between the two neighbors on the basis of "equality" within the "restored" Confucian world order in East Asia.[24] Despite intermittent Japanese piracy that plagued the Korean coast, official relations continued between the two countries through the fifteenth and sixteenth centuries until they were disrupted by the Japanese invasion of Korea in 1592. Shortly after the establishment of the Tokugawa shogunate in Japan at the turn of the seventeenth century, formal relations were restored between the two countries under a trade agreement signed in 1609.[25] This was to remain the sole legal basis for

24. *Ibid.*, vol. 2, 10–27.
25. On negotiations leading to the signing of the 1609 agreement, see *ibid.*, vol. 3, 253–300; Tanaka Takeo, *Chūsei taigai kankei shi* (A history of foreign relations during the middle ages), 235–268; Miyake Hidetoshi, "Tokugawa seiken shokai no Chōsen shinshi" (The first Korean embassy to the Tokugawa regime), *Chōsen gakuhō* 82 (January 1977), 101–132.

Japanese-Korean relations until 1876. Under the agreement, Korea conducted relations with Japan on two levels: with the bakufu or the central government and with the domain (*han*) of Tsushima.

CEREMONIAL DIPLOMACY: RELATIONS WITH THE BAKUFU

Nominally, Korea's relations with the bakufu took precedence over its relations with Tsushima. In practice, however, the former were limited to infrequent visits to Edo (Tokyo), the seat of the bakufu, by Korean embassies and the exchange of messages and gifts between the Korean monarch and the Tokugawa shogun on ceremonial occasions. During the seventeenth and eighteenth centuries a total of eleven Korean embassies visited Edo. In 1811 a Korean embassy went to Tsushima to meet with the shogun's emissaries from Edo. Thereafter the practice was discontinued because the Korean government and the bakufu could not agree on where and how Korean envoys should be received in Japan in the future; direct contact between the two ceased altogether.[26]

Korea sent embassies to Edo at irregular intervals, usually to congratulate a new shogun on his accession. The embassies were led by chief envoys bearing the title of "communication envoy" (*t'ongsinsa*). Their principal functions were to carry the Korean ruler's messages and gifts to the shogun and to take home the latter's replies and gifts. Regarding the shogun as the sovereign ruler of Japan as they had the Ashikaga shogun before, the Koreans at first addressed him as "king of Japan" (*Nihon kokuō* in Japanese; *Ilbon kugwang* in Korean). Uneasy over the use of the particular title for the shogun, the bakufu used it only reluctantly in communications to Korea, at the insistence of the Koreans.[27]

26. For details concerning the Korean embassies to Edo, see Nakamura, *Nissen kankeishi*, vol. 3, 481–497; George M. McCune, "The Exchange of Envoys between Korea and Japan during the Tokugawa Period," *Far Eastern Quarterly* 5.3 (May 1946), 308–325.

27. The bakufu at first used no specific title for the shogun in its messages to Korea, but later accepted the title "king" at Korean insistence. See *Haehaeng ch'ongjae* (Collected accounts of maritime missions), vol. 2, 98–99, 156, 158–160, 167, 264. The volume contains diaries written by the early Korean envoys to Edo.

The title was subsequently changed to "great prince" (*taikun* in Japanese; *taegun* in Korean) at Japanese request. Although the title "king" was briefly restored in the early eighteenth century, thereafter the shogun was always addressed as "great prince."[28] Whatever title was used, the Korean king and the Tokugawa shogun treated each other as equals; the gifts they exchanged were fixed in amount and considered equal in value. While members of the Korean embassy were in Japan, all their expenses were borne by the Japanese authorities.

Although the Tokugawa bakufu expected to send envoys to Seoul as had the Ashikaga bakufu, the Korean government refused to permit any Japanese representative to come beyond Pusan, the traditional Japanese entrepôt in Korea. Moreover, the Korean government insisted that the bakufu conduct all business with Korea through the medium of Tsushima, which had acted as the intermediary between the two countries during the Ashikaga period. Accordingly, throughout the Tokugawa period, the bakufu was obliged to transact its business either through the visiting Korean embassy in Edo or through Tsushima, whose daimyo (hereditary lord) was designated as the shogun's agent in the management of Korean affairs.[29]

Relations between the Korean government and the bakufu were thus limited in scope and purely ceremonial in nature and practice. There were no substantive relations such as trade between the two. Absence of trade may well have been a negative factor that caused both governments to terminate direct contact in the early nineteenth century.

Tsushima: A Tokugawa Feudatory and a Korean Semi-Tributary

A small insular domain in the Korean Strait, Tsushima had historically maintained close ties with the peninsula. Its

28. On the Japanese-Korean dispute over the shogun's title, see Ronald P. Toby, "Korean-Japanese Diplomacy in 1711: Sukchong's Court and the Shogun's Title," *Chōsen gakuhō* 74 (January 1975), 231–256; Nakamura, *Nissen kankeishi*, vol. 3, 306–308.

29. McCune, "Exchange of Envoys," 316–317.

hereditary ruler was one of the feudal barons of southwestern Japan who had been granted official titles or seals from
the Korean court in the early Yi period. The recipients of
such titles or seals put themselves in a semi-tributary relationship with the Korean court and were awarded in return
certain diplomatic and commercial privileges in Korea. The
arrangement, a modified version of the tribute system
common in interstate relations in traditional East Asia, had
been instituted originally by the Korean government as a
device to check Japanese piracy. It was revived with minor
modifications under the 1609 Trade Agreement. During
the following centuries Japanese holders of Korean titles
and seals, except the daimyo and certain hereditary officials
of Tsushima, terminated their ties with Korea. At Tsushima's request, the Korean government transferred some of
their privileges to Tsushima. By the late eighteenth century
Tsushima had acquired a complete monopoly of diplomacy
and trade with Korea.[30]

Korea sent missions to Tsushima at irregular and infrequent intervals, on such occasions as the accession of a
daimyo or when it wished to investigate conditions on the
island. Between 1800 and 1864, only eight Korean missions
visited Tsushima. Averaging forty men, these missions were
led by minor officials and remained on the island only
briefly. They did not engage in trade during their
sojourn.[31]

In contrast, Tsushima sent numerous envoys to Korea
every year. These belonged to three major categories: (1)
those sent by the Tsushima daimyo in his capacity as the
shogun's agent; (2) those sent by him in his own capacity as
the ruler of the insular domain; and (3) those sent by him
and other hereditary Tsushima officials in their capacity as
holders of Korean titles or seals. In whatever capacity the
Tsushima daimyo acted, the highest Korean official with
whom he was allowed to communicate was the vice minister

30. On Tsushima's monopoly of the Korean trade, see Nakamura, *Nissen kankeishi*, vol. 3, 228–240.
    31. McCune, "Exchange of Envoys," 318–319.

of rites. In his communications to Korea—which were
dated by the year title of the reigning Chinese emperor—
the Tsushima daimyo was required to use the official seal
given to him by the Korean court.[32]

When the Tsushima daimyo or other hereditary officials
sent envoys to Korea, they presented a token tribute to the
Korean court. In return they were awarded generous grants
of grain and other Korean products. They were also allowed to send a certain number of ships with trading goods,
as specified in the 1609 Trade Agreement. In addition to
regular envoys authorized under the agreement, Tsushima
sent numerous special envoys and messengers under various pretexts. In fact Tsushima used every conceivable device to send as many envoys and trading ships to Korea as
possible; the number of officials, merchants, and sailors visiting Korea exceeded 1,000 a year.

The visiting Tsushima Japanese were not allowed to
travel beyond Pusan. Moreover, they were confined within
the premises of a factory maintained there by the Korean
government. Known as Japan House (*Waegwan*), this was a
large walled enclosure containing offices, residences, ware-
houses, and market places. The Korean government spent
3,000 bags of rice a year to provision the visiting Japanese.
While the Korean authorities were responsible for the physical maintenance and security of the factory, a Japanese factor and his staff permanently stationed there by the
Tsushima government were responsible for its day-to-day
management. Trading was in the form of barter: ginseng,
rice, soybeans, and other Korean products were traded for
copper, lead, dyewood, and other Japanese goods at fixed
rates of exchange.[33]

Japanese-Korean relations during the Tokugawa period
were thus conducted in a triangular fashion, with Tsushima
acting as the intermediary. The insular domain's geographical location between the two countries and its dual status as
a feudatory of Tokugawa Japan and a semitributary of Yi

32. *Ibid.*, 319–320.
33. Nakamura, *Nissen kankeishi*, vol. 3, 322–332.

Korea enabled it for centuries to perform that role to the satisfaction of all parties concerned. With the centralization of political authority in Japan and the introduction of the Western concept of international relations in the middle of the nineteenth century, Tsushima's role became anachronistic. Yet both Korea and Tsushima, each for its own reasons, preferred to continue traditional practice, thereby creating impediments to the establishment of new relations between the two countries.

CONTRACTUAL RELATIONSHIP AND EQUALITY

Unlike its relations with China, which were considered familial in nature and obligation, Korea's relations with Japan were regarded as purely contractual in nature and origin. With their ingrained Confucian views, the rulers of Yi Korea regarded their country as tied to China by a natural or familial bond that could be broken under very few circumstances. The rulers did not, however, see a similar bond between their country and Japan. Nor was there an imperative political reason or cultural need for Korea to maintain close ties with Japan. On the contrary, historical experience had convinced the Koreans that the Japanese were treacherous and untrustworthy. Therefore, the Koreans insisted that Japan and Korea conduct their relations with each other on the basis of agreements spelling out mutual commitments and obligations. Throughout the Tokugawa period the Koreans resisted Japanese attempts to change or depart from rules and procedures established under the 1609 Trade Agreement. Early in the nineteenth century, when the bakufu wished to change the site and procedures for receiving Korean envoys in Japan, the Korean government regarded this as a breach of faith on the part of Japan and as sufficient ground for terminating its embassies to Japan.[34]

In contrast with the clear titular distinction that marked Sino-Korean relations, the most important principle govern-

---

34. For a detailed study of the Japanese-Korean dispute over the reception of Korean envoys, see Tabohashi Kiyoshi, *Kindai Nissen kankei no kenkyū* (Studies on modern Japanese-Korean relations) (hereafter cited as TNS), vol. 2, 639–894.

ing Japanese-Korean relations was titular equality. While Korea was free to maintain relations with Japan, its tributary obligations to China dictated that it could not and should not accord Japan the same status as China. Moreover, having traditionally enjoyed favored relations with the Middle Kingdom and having historically played the role of transmitter of Chinese culture to Japan, the Koreans tended to regard themselves as culturally superior to the Japanese. It was therefore inconceivable to them that Japan could be anything more than an equal of their own country in a sinocentric world hierarchy. The Tokugawa rulers understood and accepted the Korean position. Unlike Hideyoshi, they had no ambition for continental conquest or expansion. They tacitly acknowledged Chinese supremacy and cultural leadership in the East Asian world.[35]

POLITICAL PRESTIGE, TRADE, AND SECURITY

Japanese-Korean relations as organized under the 1609 Trade Agreement admirably met the needs of all parties concerned: political prestige for the bakufu, trade for Tsushima, and national security for Korea. In establishing formal relations with Korea, the early Tokugawa rulers were interested primarily in the political prestige such relations would bring to their new regime at home. The visits of Korean embassies with pomp and ceremony provided tangible evidence of their prestige abroad and thereby served to enhance their domestic authority. In their calculations the symbolic value of such embassies far outweighed whatever cost their reception might entail, especially in view of the fact that the bulk of such cost was borne, not by the bakufu, but by the individual domains through which the Korean embassies traveled to and from Edo.[36] With the consolida-

35. Nakamura, *Nissen kankeishi,* vol. 3, 476–479; Tanaka Takeo, "Sakoku seiritsuki Nitchō kankei no seikaku" (The nature of Japanese-Korean relations during the development of the national seclusion policy), *Chōsen gakuhō* 34 (January 1965), 55–56.
36. For an example of how domains (*han*) were required to support visiting Korean embassies, see Kobayashi Shigeru, "Tokugawa jidai ni okeru Chōsen tsūshinshi no jogō mondai" (The question of local support for the Korean communication embassies during the Tokugawa period), *Chōsen gakuhō* 43 (May 1967), 49–82.

tion of their rule, the political or symbolic value of such embassies to the Tokugawa rulers declined. By the early nineteenth century they became a burden as both the bakufu and the domains faced growing financial difficulties. This was the principal reason for the bakufu's decision to terminate direct contact with Korea.[37]

For Tsushima, the importance of stable and uninterrupted relations with Korea could hardly be exaggerated. Without largess from Korea and the profit from trade, it would have been virtually impossible for the small insular domain to survive economically. It was Tsushima that took the initiative in restoring relations between the two countries immediately after the withdrawal of the Japanese invasion forces in 1598. In the ensuing negotiations, the island's desperate need for an early peace and the resumption of trade with Korea caused its officials to doctor messages exchanged between the Korean government and the bakufu in order to facilitate agreement.[38] After the Meiji Restoration in Japan some two and a half centuries later, Tsushima was to face a similar predicament in its effort to retain its traditional intermediary role between the two countries as a means of protecting its commercial interests.

In the period of uneasy peace that followed the withdrawal of the Japanese forces from the peninsula in 1598, war-ravaged Korea remained grievously weak and lived in fear of renewed Japanese aggression. The rise of the Manchus as a formidable military power in the north posed a grave threat to Ming China and Korea. This seemed to preclude the possibility of effective Ming aid to Korea in the event of a new Japanese invasion. In the circumstances, reconciliation with Japan, however distasteful, became a necessity for Korea, especially after the withdrawal of the Ming expeditionary forces from the peninsula. Dictated by this imperative need for security, the Korean government

37. TNS, vol. 2, 880–891.
38. Nakamura, *Nissen kankeishi*, vol. 3, 266–267. The Korean government was aware that bakufu messages had been doctored by Tsushima officials. See *Haehaeng ch'ongjae*, vol. 2, 49.

felt compelled to reach an accord with Japan, even though the accord had undesirable features such as the sending of envoys to Edo, which gave the appearance of submission.[39] In practical terms, however, it was not an entirely unsatisfactory arrangement, for it gave Korea a direct opportunity to learn of Japanese intentions and plans for the future. It was almost solely for reasons of security that Korea agreed to restore, albeit on a reduced scale, trade with Tsushima. While the Tsushima trade was hardly profitable, it was useful to Korea in terms of national security, for it was the sole incentive that would keep Tsushima faithful and submissive to Korea.

In organizing new relations with Tokugawa Japan, Korea acted from a position of weakness vis-à-vis the bakufu but from one of strength vis-à-vis Tsushima. It was natural, therefore, that the Korean government preferred to deal with Tsushima, which it could dominate as a semi-tributary and suppliant. Hence its insistence that the bakufu conduct business with Korea through Tsushima. As a result, throughout the Tokugawa period Korea generally held the position of the superior and dominant party in conducting relations with Japan. When the bakufu decided to terminate direct contact with Korea, leaving the management of Korean affairs entirely in the hands of Tsushima, the Korean government probably welcomed the decision, which strengthened its position of dominance over Tsushima. Probably the decision was not unwelcome to Tsushima, for its monopoly of diplomacy and trade with Korea would be strengthened.

THE JAPANESE IMPERIAL INSTITUTION

Although Tokugawa Japan maintained no formal ties with China and remained outside the Chinese tribute system, for all intents and purposes it was as much a part of the Chinese world as Ashikaga Japan had been. The To-

39. On the circumstances leading to the Korean government's decision to restore formal ties with Japan, see Miyake, "Chōsen shinshi;" Nakamura, *Nissen kankeishi*, vol. 3, 476–504.

kugawa rulers took a position toward China that was essentially the same as that of the Ashikaga rulers, many of
whom had received formal investiture from the Ming court
as "king of Japan." The bakufu maintained commercial relations with China through Nagasaki. Institutionally Japan
was linked, though indirectly and informally, to China by its
relations with Korea and the kingdom of Liu-ch'iu. The
celebrated Tokugawa seclusion policy (*sakoku*) was not intended to cut Japan off from the rest of East Asia, but
mainly to insulate it from Christianity and to strengthen the
bakufu's monopoly of foreign trade.[40]

There was an obscure but highly significant element in
Tokugawa Japan which probably would have blocked any
serious attempt formally to incorporate Japan into the
Chinese tribute system: the indigenous imperial institution.
Though politically impotent for centuries, the mikado remained the de jure sovereign of the land. While the shogun
was in fact a hereditary ruler with dictatorial powers based
on military conquest, in theory he ruled by right of the authority delegated to him by the emperor. Those Ashikaga
shogun who received Ming investiture had been criticized
by the court nobility, the Shinto clergy, and other loyalist
elements in Japan. Fear of similar criticism was one of the
reasons behind the decision of the Tokugawa rulers not to
seek formal ties with China.[41]

Japan's indigenous imperial institution had even more
serious diplomatic implications for Korea. It sustained the
belief widely held in Japan that early Korean kingdoms
such as Paekche and Silla (Kudara and Shiragi, in Japanese)

40. On the Tokugawa bakufu's attitude toward China, see Nakamura, *Nissen
kankeishi*, vol. 3, 477–478. For major studies on *sakoku*, see Watsuji Tetsurō, *Sakoku*
(National seclusion) (1951), Ebisawa Arimichi, *Nihon Kirishitan shi* (A history of the
early Christians in Japan) (1966); Iwao Seiichi, *Sakoku* (National seclusion) (1966);
Kobori Keiichirō. *Sakoku no shisō* (The concept of national seclusion) (1974); Asao
Naohiro, *Sakoku* (National seclusion) (1975); Ronald P. Toby, "Reopening the
Question of *Sakoku*," *Journal of Japanese Studies* 3.2 (Summer 1977), 323–363.
41. For criticism against the Ashikaga shogun, see Nakamura, *Nissen kankeishi*,
vol. 2, 32. Tokugawa officials opposing formal relations with China argued that
since both China and Japan had "emperors" who were equal in status, Japan could
not enter into tributary relations with China. See *Haehaeng ch'ongjae*, vol. 2, 55.

were tributaries of Yamato Japan.[42] Of more importance, technically this put the Korean ruler below the Japanese emperor in titular precedence, and this was a serious matter in traditional East Asia, where status was all important in the conduct of relations. Since the shogun acted with full authority in the conduct of relations with Korea during the Tokugawa period, his theoretical status at home did not create problems in Japanese-Korean relations. But the Koreans were not unaware of the disturbing implications of the presence of an indigenous imperial institution in Japan. Yi Ik, an eighteenth-century scholar with remarkable insight into Japanese culture and society, expressed concern that a restoration of the imperial rule in Japan could create difficult problems for Korea in its relations with Japan.[43] Within a century Yi's fear became a reality: a dispute over titular precedence between the rulers of the two countries became a major obstacle to the establishment of new relations after the Meiji Restoration.

ROOTS OF KOREAN EXCLUSIONISM

Even in the Confucian world of traditional East Asia, where order and tranquility were to be ensured by the moral example and cultural leadership of the Middle Kingdom and by the voluntary submission of the "lesser" states and peoples, a universal gap persisted between theory and practice, between ideal and reality. Struggles for the mastery of the Chinese continent and hegemony in East Asia were frequent and fierce. When such struggles occurred, they often embroiled Korea, the pivot of East Asia, control of which was deemed important—if not essential—by all contestants. Korea has suffered the misfortune of being an unwitting object of rivalry and a focal point of conflict between opposing southern and northern continental forces or between contending continental and maritime powers in East

42. Nakamura, *Nissen kankeishi*, vol. 2, 318–319.
43. Yi Ik, *Sŏngho sasŏl* (Miscellaneous essays of Yi Ik), vol. 1, 602; Nakamura, *Nissen kankeishi*, vol. 3, 314–317.

Asia. Beginning with the establishment of the Han colonies in the north at the end of the second century B.C., the Korean peninsula has been subjected to invasions and conquests by various continental forces seeking mastery of the Chinese continent. In the second half of the thirteenth century the Mongol conquerors made Korea the springboard for their unsuccessful invasions of Japan. During the last decade of the sixteenth century it became the scene of another major continental-maritime power confrontation, when Toyotomi Hideyoshi invaded the peninsula with the professed aim of conquering China. Destruction of the peninsula begun by the Japanese was carried further a generation later by the Manchus in two invasions, a prelude to their conquest of China in a classic southern-northern continental power contest.

Deeply scarred by historical experience, the Koreans developed profound distrust of their neighbors and drastically reduced their contacts with both China and Japan in the seventeenth century. The result was a form of national seclusion that was tighter and more restrictive than the seclusion policy of Tokugawa Japan.

AMBIVALENCE TOWARD CH'ING CHINA

Despite the close and generally harmonious relations between China and Korea, a degree of ambivalence persisted in the Korean attitude toward China during the Ch'ing period. Seemingly contrary to the historical affinity of Korea with China, this was due largely to traumatic experience with the Manchus in the early Ch'ing period.

The Jurchen tribes of southeastern Manchuria, who were to become the unified Manchu nation in the early seventeenth century, had maintained semi-tributary ties with the Korean court for centuries. Following the founding of their own state of Ch'ing in southern Manchuria in the second decade of the seventeenth century, the Manchus invaded Korea twice—in 1627 and 1636—to secure control of the peninsula in preparation for their planned conquest of China. The invaders pillaged the country and perpetrated wanton atrocities, including kidnapping women and children for ransom. They forced Korea to renounce its tributary ties with the Ming and to accept vassalage to the Ch'ing. To meet their needs in an impending showdown struggle against the Ming, the Manchus also exacted, in the name of tribute, harsh indemnities from a Korea that had not yet recovered from the devastating Japanese invasions a generation earlier. The victors were the people who until recently had acknowledged semi-vassalage to Korea, and this added insult to injury for the Koreans. Memory of the Ming assistance during the Japanese invasions, still fresh in the minds of the Koreans, apparently intensified their hatred of the Manchus.[44]

With the Manchu conquest of China, a marked shift occurred in Ch'ing policy toward Korea, which was apparently calculated to restore the traditional pattern of harmonious suzerain-vassal relations between the two countries. Many Korean hostages, including two royal princes who had been held by the Manchus since 1637, were released. The number of tributary embassies Korea was required to send to the Ch'ing court each year was reduced from three to one, along with reductions in the amount and variety of tribute.[45] Still, certain features of Ch'ing-Korean relations retained the punitive and exploitative character of the original Manchu exactions.

Despite several reductions after the mid-seventeenth century, the amount of fixed annual Korean tribute remained substantial in the mid-nineteenth century. It included thousands of rolls of paper, hundreds of furs, thousands of bolts of silk and linen, and thousands of bolts of cotton cloth. Every year the total value of Korean tribute to the Ch'ing court was almost ten times that of Chinese imperial gifts to members of the Korean royal family. For two and a half centuries Korea was not once exempted from tribute

44. On the Manchu invasions, see Sin Ki-sŏk, *Hanmal oegyosa yŏn'gu* (Studies on the history of late Yi Korean foreign relations), 1–43; Yi Sang-baek, *Han'guksa kŭnse hugi p'yŏn* (History of Korea: late modern period), 87–107.

45. Kim Sŏng-ch'il, "Yŏnhaeng sogo," 30–32; Chun, "Sino-Korean Tributary Relations," 102–103.

payment, even in times of national emergency such as
famine, flood, or rebellion. Although the number of
Chinese embassies visiting Korea declined in the nineteenth
century, their visits continued to impose a financial burden
on the Korean government, chronically plagued by a shortage of revenues. The visit of one Chinese embassy cost
Korea 230,000 taels, or roughly one-sixth of the combined
annual expenditures of its central government agencies.[46]

All this no doubt contributed to the survival of Ming
loyalism among the Koreans, who never quite ceased to regard Manchu rule in China as an anomaly. After his accession in 1649 and until his death in 1659, King Hyojong,
who had spent eight years as a Manchu hostage, plotted a
war of revenge against the Manchus. In 1704—when the
Ming loyalist cause was all but dead in China—King Sukchong built a secret shrine to the Ming within his palace and
named it the Taebodan (the Altar of Great Retribution). In
1717 disciples of Song Si-yŏl, an eminent scholar-official
who had been Hyojong's tutor and assisted him with his secret war plans against the Manchus, built a shrine to the
Ming called the Mandongmyo (the Eastern Shrine to the
Wan-li emperor). Disregarding the pledge to use the Ch'ing
calendar, many Koreans continued to date their writings
with the reign title of the last Ming ruler (Ch'ung-cheng).
The tributary mission to China, which had been referred to
as "going to court" (*ch'ao-t'ien* in Chinese; *choch'ŏn* in Korean) during the Ming period, was simply called the "mission to Peking" (*Yen-hsing* in Chinese; *Yŏnhaeng* in Korean).
"Revere the Ming and resist the Ch'ing" (*sung-Myŏng pan-
Ch'ŏng*) became a national slogan to which the Korean officials and literati rallied.[47]

Aware of this persistent Korean recalcitrance, the Ch'ing
rulers imposed severe restrictions on intercourse between
the two countries, apparently to prevent possible contact between the Ming loyalists in China and the pro-Ming Koreans. Except for the exchange of ceremonial envoys and

46. Chun, "Sino-Korean Tributary Relations," 103–106.
47. On the Taebodan and the Mandongmyo, see James B. Palais, *Politics and
Policy in Traditional Korea*, 119–120; on anti-Manchu sentiment, see *ibid.*, 124–125.

attendant trade, there was no officially sanctioned contact between the two countries. During travel in China, members of the Korean embassy were escorted along a prescribed land route between the Korean border and Peking with no detour permitted. While in Peking, too, their movement was controlled closely. Contact with Han Chinese officials was discouraged, if not forbidden, except on official business. A three-hundred-mile palisade was maintained along the Korean-Manchurian border to check illegal border traffic. Maritime travel between China and Korea was forbidden.[48]

Although originally imposed by the Manchus, these restrictions came to reflect more and more the Korean desire to maintain as much physical isolation from China as practical. While the Ch'ing authorities gradually relaxed controls over the movement of visiting Koreans in Peking,[49] the Korean government continued to cloister the Ch'ing envoys in a mansion in Seoul with no outside contact. Subsequently the Korean government added new restrictions by outlawing fishing on the high seas and the disclosure of any domestic information to outsiders by Koreans.[50]

China broadened its diplomatic and trade relations with Western powers in the 1860s; Korea viewed the move with strong disapproval and suspicion. Influenced by deep-seated anti-Manchu sentiment, most Korean officials believed that the "deplorable" state of affairs in China had been brought about by the depravity of Manchu leaders such as Prince Kung. Korea was determined not to follow China's lead in entering into relations with the Western "barbarians."

DISTRUST OF JAPAN

Korea's predilection for isolation was even more pronounced toward Tokugawa Japan. While agreeing reluc-

48. On Korean-Manchu border regulations, see McCune, "Korean Relations," 69–72. On restrictions on the movement of Korean embassy personnel in China, see Ledyard, "Korean Travelers," 11–14.

49. Ledyard, "Korean Travelers," 13–14.

50. Han Woo-keun (U-gŭn), *Han'guk kaehanggi ŭi sang'ŏp yŏn'gu* (A study of commerce in Korea during the period of opening ports), 23; Martina Deuchler, *Confucian Gentlemen and Barbarian Envoys*, 4.

tantly to send envoys to Edo, the Korean government
refused to receive bakufu envoys. Although relations with
Tsushima were more extensive, they were rigidly controlled.
Visiting Japanese were confined to the prison-like factory at
Pusan and were not permitted to leave its premises. While
the Tokugawa bakufu maintained a policy that severely restricted contact with the outside world, the policy was neither
intended for nor applied to Korea. The restrictions on intercourse between Japan and Korea during the Tokugawa
period thus reflected chiefly the Korean desire for a minimum of contact with Japan.

In contrast to their traditional eagerness to maintain close
ties with China, the Koreans had been aloof toward Japan.
Basically this was due to their belief that they had little to
gain from Japan, either culturally or materially. More immediately, it stemmed from deep distrust of Japan. There
was little in the history of relations between the two countries that endeared Japan to the Koreans. From the mid-
fourteenth century Japanese pirates had continually rav-
aged the Korean coast. The unification of Japan under
Hideyoshi in the late sixteenth century spelled even greater
catastrophe for Korea. Partly to satisfy the hardened warriors still thirsting for fortune and glory and partly to fulfill his own insatiable ambitions for conquest, Hideyoshi
launched a large-scale invasion in 1592, and for the next
seven years the invaders wreaked death and destruction
upon the peninsula, until their withdrawal after Hideyoshi's
death in 1598.[51] Although the Koreans agreed to restore
normal relations with Japan shortly thereafter, they never
ceased to regard the Japanese as marauders whom they
should never trust and with whom they should have as little
contact as necessary.[52]

Japan began to show a growing interest in and aggressiveness toward Korea and the neighboring Asian continent
in the 1860s and 1870s, and this increased Korean distrust
of the Japanese. With cultural chauvinism hardened by cen-

51. On the Hideyoshi invasions, see Nakamura, *Nissen kankeishi,* vol. 2. 71–288.
52. McCune, "Korean Relations," 259.

turies of isolation, the Koreans regarded Japan's efforts to adopt Western ideas and institutions as evidence of Japanese depravity and barbarity. The Koreans' lingering resentment against the Manchus made them disapprove of China's dealings with the West, and their even deeper distrust of the Japanese predisposed them more firmly against Japan's Westernization activities. Apart from these twin causes of Korea's seclusion, which in the course of time had acquired the sanctity of tradition that could not be easily discarded, there were other factors that gave rise to militant exclusionism in Korea in the middle and late nineteenth century.

DOMESTIC UNREST AND THE SPREAD OF CHRISTIANITY

Yi Korea was an aristocratic society with a weak monarchy. As a vassal of the Chinese emperor, the Korean king could not claim absolute authority. This theoretical limitation on his authority, however, was not nearly as great as the political restraint exercised upon him by the country's Confucian ruling class, called the *yangban* (the civil and military classes). Composed of powerful lineages with hereditary aristocratic status and concomitant political and social privileges, the *yangban* monopolized access to the civil and military bureaucracy. Their political power was reinforced by the Confucian precept that enjoined the ruler to honor virtuous officials. Though an absolute monarch in theory, generally the Yi king could not act alone, without the consent of his ministers and high officials. Collectively they were a jealous guardian of *yangban* power. As James B. Palais defines it, Yi Korea was a society governed jointly by a weak monarchy and a strong aristocracy, which, while often mutually antagonistic, generally supported each other in a symbiotic relationship.[53]

The weakness of the throne appears to have been one of the major factors that gave free rein to the rampant strife

53. Palais, *Traditional Korea*, 9–12. On *yangban* restraint on royal power, see Pow-key Sohn (Son Po-gi), "Power versus Status: The Role of Ideology during the Early Yi Dynasty," *Tongbang hakchi* 10 (December 1969), 209–253.

among *yangban* factions, the most debilitating evil of Yi Korean society and government. From the late sixteenth century the court and government were embroiled constantly in virulent power struggles in which factions and splinter groups fought one another with a vengence. During the last quarter of the eighteenth century, however, the country gained a degree of political stability under an able and enlightened ruler, King Chŏngjo. As a result of his efforts to reconcile the feuding factions, the strife was brought under control; members of factions long out of power, particularly the *Namin* (the Southerners), were brought into the government.[54] Chŏngjo died in 1800.

The new king, Sunjo, was eleven *sui* old. A regency was established under Queen Dowager Kim, the widow of King Yŏngjo, whose male relatives belonged to a new factional coalition called the *Pyŏkp'a*. Under her patronage, the *Pyŏkp'a* gained ascendancy; factional strife resumed briefly between the *Pyŏkp'a* and another coalition, the *Sip'a*. But the reins of government soon fell into the hands of Kim Cho-sun, Sunjo's former tutor to whom the late king had entrusted the guardianship of his young heir. Kim Cho-sun, a member of the influential Andong Kim clan, installed his own daughter as the queen for the boy king and took over the control of the government by placing his own family members in important posts. This marked the beginning of the "rule of the consort clans"—domination of the court and government by the male relatives of the queen. During the next sixty years, until the end of 1863, two powerful consort clans, the Andong Kims and the P'ung'yang Chos, ruled the country.[55]

The period of the rule of the consort clans was marked by misgovernment and bureaucratic corruption. Nepotism and favoritism, already common in a society where fam-

54. Palais, *Traditional Korea*, 46–50. On Yi Korean factionalism, see Edwin O. Reischauer and John K. Fairbank, *East Asia: The Great Tradition*, 437–444; Han Woo-keun, *The History of Korea*, 298–303; Sŏng Nak-hun, "Han'guk tangjaeng sa" (A history of Korean factionalism), in *Han'guk munhwasa taegye* (Grand outline of Korean cultural history), vol. 2, 220–390.

55. On the consort clans, see Yi Sang-baek, *Han'guksa kŭnse hugi*, 43–46.

ily and clan loyalty were often put above loyalty to state, determined important official appointments. They also influenced the outcome of government examinations. Corruption and inefficiency in the central government were surpassed only by such practices in local administration. The provincial governors, military district commanders, and county magistrates, many of whom obtained their posts either by personal or family connections or by bribery, often were more interested in return on their investments than in discharging their official duties. They were aided by petty local officials and runners who, with their administrative know-how and knowledge of local affairs, became indispensable partners in organized peculation.

Misgovernment and official corruption further aggravated the hardships of the people caused by the worsening socio-economic conditions. Frequent natural calamities such as famine, flood, and epidemic disease caused more hardships. An inevitable result of all this was the progressive alienation of the populace from the regime. Ominous signs began to appear early in the nineteenth century and continued to multiply. In 1812 a major rebellion, led by a disgruntled former examination candidate, broke out in the northwestern province of P'yŏng'an; it took the government nearly half a year to suppress it. Other disturbances and uprisings followed during the next decades, reaching crisis proportions in the early 1860s.[56] The deepening social disorder and economic hardship were no doubt partly responsible for the spread of Christianity and the rise of a native religion called Tonghak (Eastern Learning) in the mid-nineteenth century.[57]

Christianity seeped into Korea through the medium of written words. From the mid-seventeenth century Chinese works on Western religion and science were taken home by

56. *Ibid.,* 364–372; Yi Sŏn-gŭn, *Han'guksa ch'oegŭnse p'yŏn* (History of Korea: most recent period), 36–90; Ching Young Choe, *The Rule of the Taewŏn'gun, 1864–1873,* 24–31.

57. On Tonghak, see Benjamin B. Weems, *Reform, Rebellion, and the Heavenly Way;* Han Woo-keun, *Tonghangnan kiin e kwanhan yŏn'gu* (A study of the causes of the Tonghak rebellion).

members of the Korean tributary embassies that visited Peking. For a century these works were studied by a small number of Korean scholars who took a purely academic interest in them. But by the mid-eighteenth century, the Christian teachings began to attract a small following among the commoners. During Chŏngjo's reign (1776–1800) some *yangban,* mostly members of the *Namin* out of power, embraced the faith. Although Christianity was officially proscribed in 1785, under Chŏngjo's tolerant rule Christians continued to enjoy relative freedom. In 1795 Chou Wen-mu (James Chou), a Chinese Roman Catholic priest, entered the country secretly in response to a repeated appeal from the native converts. The church membership grew steadily.[58]

When the *Pyŏkp'a* gained brief ascendancy following Chŏngjo's death, the fortunes of the church suddenly changed. Since some members of the opposition *Sip'a* were Catholics, the *Pyŏkp'a* combined its political attacks on the *Sip'a* with charges of heresy. The fledgling Korean Catholic church was thus unwittingly embroiled in the maelstrom of Korean domestic politics; this spelled the end of its religious freedom. The first major anti-Catholic purge came within a year, in 1801. During this time a fateful incident occurred that was to have far-reaching consequences, not only for Christianity in Korea but for the country's future relations with the West.

In October 1801, when government investigators arrested a prominent Catholic named Hwang Sa-yŏng, they found among his possessions a letter addressed to the French bishop in Peking. It was to be delivered by a convert who was scheduled to go to Peking that fall as interpreter for a tributary embassy. Its contents shocked the authorities. After describing in detail the fate that had befallen the Korean church, Hwang proposed startling measures, including a message from the Pope to the Chinese emperor, request-

58. For the history of the Catholic church in Korea, see Yi Nŭng-hwa, *Chosŏn Kidokkyo kŭp oegyo sa* (A history of Christianity and foreign relations in Korea); Yu Hong-nyŏl, *Han'guk Ch'ŏnjugyohoe sa* (A history of the Roman Catholic Church in Korea); Yamaguchi, *Chōsen Seikyō shi.*

ing that the latter command the king of Korea to grant freedom of worship to all Catholics in his kingdom; the establishment of a Chinese garrison in northern Korea, where a Ch'ing imperial prince would be stationed to oversee the Korean court and government; and dispatching one hundred Western ships with 50,000 to 60,000 men to exact a guarantee of freedom and safety for all Christians in Korea from the king of Korea. What Hwang proposed was not merely protection for the Korean Christians, but a virtual takeover of the country by China with Western military support.[59]

Hwang's proposal confirmed the Korean authorities' worst suspicions about Christianity. The Roman Catholic church was not merely propagating a heterodox faith that was fundamentally incompatible with the Confucian precepts and principles, upon which the kingdom's sociopolitical order was founded, but it seemed to be engaged in a sinister scheme to seize the whole country either by internal subversion or by force. That Hwang was a bright aristocratic youth with impeccable credentials, a member of the ruling elite, was doubly shocking to the authorities. The incident instantly transformed what might have been a minor incident into a wholesale massacre of Christians. Some three hundred converts were executed, and hundreds of others were imprisoned or exiled.[60] The gravity with which the Korean government viewed the affair is seen in the fact that it dispatched a special mission to Peking to report the matter to the Chinese authorities.[61]

The decimated Roman Catholic Church slowly rebuilt itself in Korea. In 1831 Korea was detached from the jurisdiction of the Bishop of Peking and made an independent diocese. In 1836 Pierre P. Maubant, a French priest, entered Korea secretly to become the first Western missionary on

59. Yamaguchi, *Chōsen Seikyō shi*, 233–260.
60. *Ibid.*, 82–125; Yi Sang-baek, *Han'guksa kǔnse hugi*, 320–325.
61. *Chosǒn wangjo sillok* (the veritable record of the Yi dynasty) (hereafter cited as CWS), *Sunjo sillok* (the veritable record of Sunjo), 3.47a–48a; Yamaguchi, *Chōsen Seikyō shi*, 132–141.

Korean soil. Two French missionaries, Jacques H. Chastand and Joseph Imbert, followed in 1837. Through the efforts of these men, the church membership gradually increased, reportedly reaching 9,000 in 1838.

Authorities soon learned of the presence of foreign priests in the country. This coincided with the ascendancy of the P'ung'yang Chos, who were traditionally hostile to Christianity. In October 1839, King Hŏnjong issued an edict reaffirming the existing ban on Christianity and reiterating the "evils" of its teachings. In another major purge, seventy-eight Catholics, including the three French priests, were executed in the capital region.[62] News of the execution was slow to reach the outside world.

In 1845 Kim Tae-gŏn (Andrew Kim), the first Korean Catholic priest trained in Macao, returned home with two French priests, Bishop Jean Ferreol and Father Henri Daveluy. In June 1846 Father Kim was arrested by the authorities while exploring a maritime communication route to China. Two months later, in August, Rear Admiral Cécille of the French navy arrived on the Korean west coast with three warships to investigate the 1839 execution of the French missionaries. Immediately after sending a letter of inquiry to Seoul, in which he stated that he would return the following year for a reply, the admiral left Korea.[63] The Korean authorities were convinced, however, that there was a connection between Father Kim's activities and the arrival of French warships. They promptly executed Father Kim and eight converts.[64] Return of the French warships the following summer further convinced the Korean authorities of the existence of a conspiracy between the French and the native converts.

Hŏnjong died in 1849 without leaving an heir. The new king, Ch'ŏljong, came to the throne from a cadet branch of the royal house, which had earlier been condemned for al-

62. Yamaguchi, *Chōsen Seikyō shi*, 144–145.
63. CWS, *Hŏnjong sillok* (the veritable record of Hŏnjong), 13.9b–12b; Mary C. Wright, "The Adaptability of Ch'ing Diplomacy," *Journal of Asian Studies* 17.3 (May 1958), 375; Yi Sang-baek, *Han'guksa kŭnse hugi,* 405–408.
64. Yamaguchi, *Chōsen Seikyō shi,* 144.

leged treason. His accession was engineered chiefly by the Andong Kims solely for the continuation of their own power. During Ch'ŏljong's reign official persecution of the Christians gradually ceased. This did not, however, signify a change in official policy. Rather, two factors seem to have been responsible for official acquiescence to Catholic proselytizing. One was the fact that the Andong Kims were traditionally tolerant of Christianity. The other was the fact that Ch'ŏljong's mother and grandmother, both of whom were converts to the Roman Catholic faith, had been put to death during the 1801 purge. At any rate, despite the continuing ban on Christianity, more French missionaries were smuggled into the country, bringing their total number to twelve by the early 1860s. They carried out their activities quite openly; the church membership reportedly reached 23,000 by the end of 1865.[65]

The spread of Christianity along with mounting social disorder and popular unrest in Korea, combined with a growing Western threat from abroad, engendered a deep sense of crisis among the Korean officials and literati. They saw in Christianity an alien faith that challenged their country's socio-political order, and they were convinced that the Roman Catholic Church was a tool of the French government, bent on seizing Korea either by internal subversion or by military force. The suspicions of the Korean authorities seemed to be confirmed by illegal proselytizing by the French missionaries in their midst, the native converts' liaison with church authorities in China and their repeated appeals for French assistance, and by the arrival of French warships in apparent response to the appeal. This, combined with Neo-Confucian cultural chauvinism and ignorance of the outside world, produced a militant exclusionist doctrine known as *wijŏng ch'ŏksa* ("defend the orthodox and reject the heterodox").[66] In a manner reminiscent of the re-

65. Yi Nŭng-hwa, *Chosŏn Kidokkyo*, 180–182; Han Woo-keun, *History of Korea*, 348–349.

66. On the *wijŏng ch'ŏksa* doctrine, see Ch'oe Ch'ang-gyu, "Ch'ŏksaron kwa kŭ sŏngkyŏk" (The *ch'ŏksa* doctrine and its nature), in Ch'oe Yŏng-hŭi, et al., eds, *Han'guksa* (History of Korea), vol. 16, 288–314.

sponse of the rulers of Tokugawa Japan to Christianity some two centuries before, the mid-nineteenth-century Korean ruling class was determined to stamp out Christianity and to exclude totally the Westerners from their land in order to protect their own country and to save civilization in East Asia.

CHAPTER II

Rising Western Pressure on Korea

Western expansionism reached a high point in East Asia in the early 1860s. By then, nearly all the countries of this region had been opened to Western trade and diplomacy. In China the treaty system, inaugurated in 1842 with the signing of the Treaty of Nanking after the Opium War, was consummated in 1860 with the signing of the Peking Conventions at the conclusion of the Anglo-French War against China. Japan, opened by Commodore Matthew C. Perry of the United States Navy in 1854, signed commercial treaties with the United States, Great Britain, France, Russia, and its former trading partner, Holland, in 1858. Russia acquired the vast eastern coastal regions of Siberia by treaty with China in 1860. France was moving step by step toward the colonization of Vietnam and other parts of Indochina. Korea, alone among the major East Asian countries, remained inaccessible to the Westerners. The "hermit of the East" clung firmly to its centuries-old policy of seclusion.

With the opening of China and Japan and with Russian expansion touching its northeastern frontier, the hermit kingdom was no longer to be left undisturbed. External pressure for its opening, intermittent in the past, grew stronger and more persistent. In the 1860s, Russia, France, and the United States began attempts to open the kingdom to Western trade and proselytism. These early Western efforts resulted in Korean armed clashes with Western powers, with France in 1866 and with the United States in 1871.

CATHOLIC PURGES AND THE
FRENCH INVASION

The first Western ship to approach Korea to trade was the
Lord Amherst of the British East India Company, which visited the west coast of the peninsula in 1832. It was turned
away by local authorities, who said that it was against the law
to engage in foreign commerce. In 1845 the British warship
Samarang, commanded by Captain Sir Edward Belcher, visited Cheju Island and some southern Korean ports on a
surveying mission. Belcher made inquiries into the possibility of trade. But he, too, was told that Korea, as a tributary
of China, had neither the authority nor the desire to trade
with foreign countries. Both incidents were reported to the
Ch'ing Board of Rites. On the latter occasion, the Korean
government requested that the Chinese authorities "instruct" the British in Hong Kong to refrain from sending
any more ships to Korea. Approving the Korean position,
Peking obliged. Accordingly, Ch'i-ying, the imperial commissioner in charge of relations with Westerners at the
Chinese trade ports, explained Korea's unique position to
the British: "It [Korea] could not be opened to trade by
China, for it was not a part of China; it could not open itself
to trade, for it was not independent."[1]

An incident that could have led to a serious Korean-
Western confrontation occurred in 1846–1847. As has been
mentioned, French Admiral Cécille visited Korea in August
1846 to initiate an inquiry into the 1839 execution of
French missionaries by the Korean authorities. The following August, Captain Lapierre of the French navy returned
with two warships to demand satisfaction for the "murders"
of the French subjects. He argued that the Chinese emperor's edict of 1844, guaranteeing toleration of Christians
in all Chinese territories, applied to Korea. The Koreans,
however, rejected his argument, maintaining that the execution of the French priests had been justified since they had

---

1. On the *Lord Amherst's* visit, see CWS, *Sunjo sillok,* 32.27b–30b; on the
Samarang's visit, see CWS, *Hŏnjong sillok,* 12.5a–b.

entered Korea illegally and engaged in the dissemination of a proscribed alien faith. Unfortunately for the French, their ships ran aground and sank. The Koreans treated the ship-wrecked French sailors with kindness and repatriated them to China aboard British vessels.[2]

Before leaving Korea, Lapierre sent a letter to Korea's chief minister. Expressing the hope that Korea would follow the Chinese example in establishing friendly relations with France and in tolerating Christianity, Lapierre emphasized that a treaty with France would be to Korea's advantage in case Korea became involved in a war with a third power. Lest the French come back again, the Korean government sent a detailed report of the execution of the missionaries and the visits of Cécille and Lapierre to the Ch'ing Board of Rites. It asked the Chinese authorities to instruct the governor-general at Canton to dissuade the French from returning to Korea.[3]

Nearly a decade later, a little-known incident indicated lingering French interest in Korea. In the summer of 1856, Admiral Guerin, Commander of the French Indochina Fleet, conducted a month-long reconnaissance of the Korean west coast under orders from Paris. In his report, Guerin predicted that Korea would soon fall prey to foreign aggression. He argued that Russia was encroaching upon Korea by taking advantage of China's decline and that France should seize the peninsula before another power did.[4]

The 1860s began with an event that was as shocking to the Koreans as it was to the Chinese: in October 1860, Anglo-French forces captured and pillaged the imperial capital of Peking. The incident had a powerful impact upon the Koreans, who for centuries had lived in security under the

2. Mary C. Wright, "The Adaptability of Ch'ing Diplomacy," *Journal of Asian Studies* 17.3 (May 1958), 375–376; Yi Sang-baek, *Han'guksa kŭnse hugi p'yŏn*, 408–410.

3. CWS, *Hŏnjong sillok*, 14.8b. For the Korean report to China, see *Ch'ou-pan i-wu shih-mo: Tao-kuang ch'ao* (The complete account of the management of barbarian affairs: the Tao-kuang reign) (hereafter cited as IWSM-TK), 78.24b–26a.

4. Ch'oe Sŏg-u, "Pyŏng'in yang'yo sogo" (A short study of the 1866 Western invasion), *Yŏksa hakpo* 30 (April 1966), 109–110.

shelter of Ch'ing power. China's defeat in the Opium War and the subsequent outbreak of the Taiping Rebellion, disturbing as they were, did not unduly shake Korea's faith in the might of the Manchu dynasty. Anglo-French occupation of Tientsin, however, alarmed the Koreans. The fall of Peking and the flight of the imperial court to Jehol two years later, following close upon the resurgence of Taiping power, transformed alarm to panic. When news of the fall of Peking reached the Korean capital, government leaders were seized with fear. Some warned that, should residence in Manchuria, the Ch'ing imperial homeland, become untenable in the face of the advancing barbarians, the fleeing Ch'ing emperor might seek refuge on Korean soil. This would inevitably bring, it was feared, Chinese interference in Korean affairs and might even invite Western attacks on Korea.[5]

Without waiting for the return of the regular tributary embassy, which had left for Peking the previous fall, the Korean government dispatched a special embassy to Jehol in January 1861. Ostensibly, the embassy's mission was to inquire after the well-being of the Hsien-feng emperor. But its more important mission was to obtain the latest, firsthand information on the situation in China. In April the regular embassy returned home, with the report that although the fighting had ceased the imperial court was still in Jehol. Shortly afterward, the special embassy returned with the news of China's final capitulation to the "barbarians."[6] Restoration of the peace in north China and the subsequent return of the court to Peking eased the panic that had swept the Korean court and officialdom. But the sense of crisis engendered by the shocking spectacle of China suffering the ultimate humiliation at the hands of the Western "barbarians" remained with the Koreans. The threat of Western military invasion, hitherto a remote possibility, now loomed large.

In Korea, meanwhile, growing social unrest and smolder-

5. Yi Sŏn-gŭn, *Han'guksa ch'oegŭnse p'yŏn*, 140–144.
6. CWS, *Ch'ŏljong sillok* (the veritable record of Ch'ŏljong), 12.9b, 13.1b, 13.4a, 13.6a.

ing popular discontent, caused by decades of misgovernment, exploded in spontaneous peasant uprisings in the early 1860s. An uprising by several thousand peasants in Chinju, Kyŏngsang Province, in late March 1862 touched off waves of similar disturbances throughout the southern provinces. During the next two years, peasant riots or uprisings, often led by impoverished local *yangban* or disgruntled ex-officials, broke out in scores of districts. A total of more than 100,000 persons took part.[7]

At this time, December 1863, when the kingdom was facing mounting disorder and unrest at home and growing pressures from abroad, Ch'ŏljong died without leaving an hier. Of the three surviving dowagers in the royal family, Queen Dowager Cho (the widow of Ikchong, Sunjo's crown prince who died before ascending the throne) was the eldest and senior in status. As such she was empowered by tradition to name a successor to the vacant throne. A daughter of the P'ung'yang Chos, the chief rival of the Andong Kims, she was determined to strengthen the influence of her own male relatives at the court and in the government. She therefore chose one who had absolutely no ties with the Andong Kims as the new king: Kojong, the second son of Prince Hŭngsŏn (Yi Ha-ŭng), an impoverished second cousin of the late king. Moreover, she declared the new king to be the adoptive son of Ikchong, her late husband, not of Ch'ŏljong, the late king.

Kojong was only twelve *sui* of age; Queen Dowager Cho assumed the regency and invited Hŭngsŏn to assist her. Hŭngsŏn was given the title of Taewŏn'gun (Prince of the Great Court), an honor traditionally accorded the unenthroned father of a Yi king. Although Queen Dowager Cho retained the regency until March 1866, she was not personally interested in the day-to-day exercise of power. Until the end of 1873, it was the Taewŏn'gun who exercised authority as de facto ruler of the kingdom.[8]

7. Yi Sang-baek, *Han'guksa kŭnse hugi*, 357–364.

8. On the Taewŏn'gun's rule, see James B. Palais, *Politics and Policy in Traditional Korea;* Ching Young Choe, *The Rule of the Taewŏn'gun, 1864–1873.* See also Han Woo-keun, *The History of Korea*, 361–370; Yi Sang-baek, *Han'guksa kŭnse hugi,* 373–396; Yi Sŏn-gŭn, *Han'guksa ch'oegŭnse,* 151–223.

This hitherto inconsequential figure became one of the strongest personalities in the history of the Yi monarchy. Born in 1821, fourth son of Prince Namyŏn, an obscure member of the royal clan, the Taewŏn'gun had been barred from political office by law and had spent half his lifetime in poverty and forced idleness. Scorned by the powerful *yangban,* he had witnessed the steady erosion of royal power under the consort clans' domination of the court and the bureaucracy, and he believed this was the principal cause of the country's social and economic maladies. A strong-willed prince, proud of his royal heritage, the Taewŏn'gun dreamed of dynastic revival through the restoration of royal authority to what it had been in earlier days.[9] But he had discreetly concealed his ability, ambitions, and resentment from the watchful Andong Kims. Upon gaining power as de facto regent for his young son, however, the Taewŏn'gun immediately set out to fulfill his lifelong dream.

Like most of his contemporaries, the Taewŏn'gun was ignorant of the outside world. Nevertheless he had a real appreciation of the fundamental nature of the Western threat to the traditional way of life in Korea. He was convinced that both China and Japan unwittingly had invited calamity when they first allowed the Western "barbarians" to establish a foothold on their soil. He was determined to maintain Korea's seclusion in order to insulate the kingdom from Western influence. Underestimating Western military strength, the Taewŏn'gun believed that Korea had sufficient military capability to hold out indefinitely against the Western powers.[10]

While the fear of an Anglo-French invasion proved to be groundless, the threat of Russian expansion in the north became a real concern in the early 1860s. Russian colonization of the Maritime Provinces proceeded, and the Korean government grew fearful of encroachment upon its northeastern frontier. After 1863 in particular, Korea became increasingly concerned over the flight of peasants across the

9. Choe, *Rule of the Taewŏn'gun,* 32–33.
10. Palais, *Traditional Korea,* 252.

border into Russian territory. Fearing collusion between these "renegade" Koreans and the Russians, the government tightened border security and ordered frontier officials not to let foreigners enter the country. During 1864–1865, however, dozens of Russians came to the border town of Kyŏnghŭng to demand trade. The alarmed Korean officials refused to talk with the Russians, and they arrested and executed Koreans who allegedly had aided the intruders.[11] The Seoul government repeatedly appealed to the Chinese authorities to check Russian activities along Korea's northern border. When the Ch'ing Board of Rites asked the Tsungli Yamen to take up the matter with the Russians, the latter refused, saying that it was a Korean responsibility. But the Koreans preferred to have China deal with this troublesome issue, and they continued to refer the matter to Peking.[12]

In 1865, several prominent Korean Catholics allegedly approached the Taewŏn'gun with a proposal for an alliance with France and Britain as a means of warding off the Russian threat. The Catholics were emboldened by the freedom that they had been enjoying since the 1850s, by their belief that French influence was on the rise in China, and by what they perceived as a friendly attitude toward the Catholics on the part of the Taewŏn'gun. They assured him, it is said, that certain French priests would act as intermediaries in negotiations with France, and they asked for the official ban on Christianity to be lifted in return for their proffered service.[13]

The Taewŏn'gun's initial reaction is not known. But it is alleged that in early 1864 Bishop Simon-Francois Berneux, who was in charge of the underground Korean diocese, was contacted by a high-ranking Korean official acting as the Taewŏn'gun's emissary. The official told Berneux that if he, Berneux, could prevail upon the Russians to refrain from

11. Choe, *Rule of the Taewŏn'gun*, 84–85.
12. Wright, "Ch'ing Diplomacy," 373–374.
13. Yu Hong-nyŏl, *Kojong ch'iha ŭi Sŏhak sunan ŭi yŏn'gu* (A study of Christian ordeals under the rule of King Kojong), 169–172; Yi Sang-baek, *Han'guksa kŭnse hugi*, 385–388.

encroaching upon Korean territory, the Taewŏn'gun would lift the ban on Christianity. Berneux replied that he was anxious to be of service to Korea but he was in no position to influence the Russians. Having turned down the proposal, Berneux reported the incident to French Minister Berthemy in China and asked for the dispatch of a French warship, apparently for the protection of the missionaries and Korean converts from possible reprisal by the Taewŏn'gun. The request was denied. In a report to Paris, Berthemy explained that the Korean government was tacitly tolerating Christianity, and a French expedition, if not successful, would needlessly provoke Korean hostility.[14]

If the above account is true, then it is not difficult to understand why the Korean Catholic leaders were unable to follow their words with action. Months went by without word from them; this apparently angered the Taewŏn'gun, a proud and powerful man. In February 1866 suddenly he ordered the arrest of all foreign priests and native converts in the country, touching off waves of bloody persecution in which thousands of Catholics were to perish during the next several years.[15]

It is difficult to determine precisely what the reasons were behind the Taewŏn'gun's sudden move: his motives may be sought in his ideological and political position, in Korea's circumstances of the time, and in contemporary events in China. Despite his reputedly friendly attitude toward some individual Catholics, the Taewŏn'gun's Confucian training and outlook were definitely incompatible with Christianity. Even though his pragmatism is well known, as de facto ruler determined to restore the authority of a decaying Confucian monarchy, he could not tolerate Christianity's challenge

    14. Ch'oe Sŏg-u, "Pyŏng'in yang'yo," 111.
    15. Choe, *Rule of the Taewŏn'gun,* 98; Yi Sang-baek, *Han'guksa kŭnse hugi,* 389–392. Many writers, relying chiefly on missionary sources, estimate that 8,000 to 10,000 converts were executed, but these figures seem exaggerated. In the capital region, where there was probably the largest concentration of Christians, a total of 407 persons were arrested, including 107 women, during the period 1866–1878; of the 300 men arrested, only 131 were found guilty (Catholic) and executed. See Yamaguchi, *Chōsen Seikyō shi,* 189–200.

to ideological orthodoxy. For nearly a century Catholicism had been the object of official fear and suspicion as a heretical faith and as an agent of an aggressive foreign power. The court and the bureaucracy were solidly anti-West and anti-Christian. Queen Dowager Cho, in particular, was uncompromisingly anti-Catholic; she inherited her family's strong antipathy toward Christianity, and—as de jure regent—she was the only person in the kingdom with the authority to deprive the Taewŏn'gun of his power.[16]

Irrespective of his personal view or the official position of the government, so long as there was a Russian threat to the country, the Taewŏn'gun could not lightly antagonize France, a power which had joined forces with Britain only a few years before to humiliate China. By the end of 1865, however, the Russian threat seemed to have receded. The Taewŏn'gun still would have hesitated to move had he anticipated unfavorable Chinese reaction to precipitate anti-Christian action on his part. While there was no encouragement for such action from China at this time, the news of alleged anti-Christian persecution in China, brought back by members of the tributary embassies, may have been a factor in the Taewŏn'gun's decision against the Catholics.[17]

By the end of March 1866, nine of the twelve French missionaries in the country and some forty native converts had been arrested. The missionaries refused to leave the country, and they were executed along with the native converts. In spite of the Taewŏn'gun's sweeping orders, the government's drive against the Catholics was relatively limited in scope during its initial phase.[18] Of the three surviving missionaries, Father Felix-Clair Ridel succeeded in fleeing the country and reported the whole affair to the French officials in China. Upon receiving the report, Henri de Bellonet, French chargé d'affaires in Peking, decided, without authorization from Paris, to send a punitive expedition to

16. Yi Sŏn-gŭn, *Han'guksa ch'oegŭnse,* 237–238.
17. *Ibid.,* 238; W. J. Kang, "Early Korean Contact with Christianity and Korean Response," in Yung-hwan Jo, ed., *Korea's Response to the West,* 46.
18. Choe, *Rule of the Taewŏn'gun,* 96.

Korea. On July 13, Bellonet sent a note to Prince Kung at the Tsungli Yamen to inform the prince of his decision inasmuch as Korea was a "country sending tribute" (*na-kung-chih pang*) to China. Predicting easy French victory, Bellonet declared that, in view of China's past disclaimer of responsibility for Korea and its refusal to apply the Treaties of Tientsin to Korea, China could not intervene in a war between France and Korea.[19]

Neither refuting Bellonet's contention directly nor agreeing to assume responsibility for the Korean action, Prince Kung tried to soothe Bellonet with an offer of mediation. In his reply, dated July 16, the prince observed that Korea had always acted with propriety and that he did not know what had led Korea to execute the missionaries and converts. Since war between France and Korea would affect the lives of both people, he felt compelled to mediate. "If indeed Korea killed missionaries and converts," he said, "it seems that it would be best first to inquire into the reasons behind its action and that there is no need for a hasty resort to arms."[20]

Meanwhile, the Chinese authorities decided to warn the Korean government of the intentions of the French. Accordingly, the Board of Rites sent a note to Korea, which reached Seoul on August 17. The Korean government immediately replied to the Board. While admitting to the executions, it stated that the missionaries had deserved their fate since they had illegally entered Korea and had engaged in the dissemination of a proscribed faith. Stating that it would not resent the execution of its own nationals by another country for similar offenses, the Korean government termed the French protest incomprehensible. Professing its ignorance in diplomatic matters, it asked for Chinese guidance and protection.[21]

19. *Ibid.*, 97–98; *Ch'ou-pan i-wu shih-mo: T'ung-chih ch'ao* (The complete account of the management of barbarian affairs: the T'ung-chih reign) (hereafter cited as IWSM-TC), 42.54a–b.

20. IWSM-TC, 42.54b–55a.

21. *Ibid.*, 44.12b–14a; *Ilsŏngnok: Kojong p'yŏn* (The record of daily reflection: Kojong reign) (hereafter cited as ISN-KJ), 3/7/8; *Kojong Sunjong sillok: Kojong sillok* (The veritable record of Kojong and Sunjong: the veritable record of Kojong) (hereafter cited as KJS), 3.37a–b.

Thus the Chinese warning failed to moderate Korean intransigence toward the French. On the contrary, it had disastrous consequences for the surviving Korean Catholics. The authorities concluded that the French were able to learn of the execution of the missionaries because the native converts maintained secret communication with them. This revived the old suspicion that the Roman Catholic church was an agent of the French government and that the native converts were not only heretics, but traitors serving a hostile foreign power. On the same day the reply was sent off to Peking, the king approved the State Council's recommendation that provincial and local officials and military commanders execute anyone trying to contact foreign ships or engaging in suspicious conduct along the coast.[22] When the *Sherman* incident occurred, less than two weeks later, fear of collusion between foreigners and native Christians caused the government to step up the drive against the Catholics and to tighten border and coastal security. On September 11 a royal edict was issued, reiterating the "evils" of Christianity.[23]

Rear Admiral Pierre-Gustave Roze, commander of the French fleet in the Far East, in consultation with Bellonet, undertook a ten-day reconnaissance of the Korean west coast in late September. In early October Roze announced a French blockade of the Han River estuary. On October 11 he left China, without authorization from Paris, with seven ships and 600 men on a "punitive" expedition to Korea. Three days later the French troops landed on Kanghwa Island, and they captured its principal city with little resistance from the defenders. On October 19 Roze received a letter, bristling with angry admonitions for the "unprovoked" invasion and warning of an impending Korean counteroffensive, from the commander of the Korean forces in the area. Roze countered with a letter of his own, demanding the punishment of the officials responsible for the "murders" of the missionaries and the dispatch of a plenipotentiary to his headquarters for the negotiation of a

22. ISN-KJ, 3/7/30.
23. *Ibid.*, 3/8/3.

treaty. Reminding the Koreans of what had happened to China when it had committed similar outrages against missionaries a few years before, he warned them of the dire consequences that would follow should they refuse his demands.[24]

The Koreans angrily rejected Roze's demands. Branding them "arrogant" and "threatening to China," they reported the matter to the Ch'ing Board of Rites.[25] Under the Taewŏn'gun's direction, forces totaling 20,000 men were deployed on Kanghwa Island and in coastal and inland areas leading to the capital within a few weeks. On November 9, when a French detachment of 160 men tried to seize a mountain fort at the southern end of Kanghwa Island, it was ambushed and routed. Realizing the inadequacy of his strength in the face of determined Korean resistance and the approach of winter, Roze decided to call off the expedition. After more burning and looting, he withdrew from Korea, on November 18.[26] His withdrawal gave the Koreans the illusion of victory. They reported to the Ch'ing Board of Rites that Korea—though small in size and weak in military power—had defended itself from the "barbarians" by virtue of the unity of its people and their adherence to rules of propriety" *(li).*[27]

The Korean authorities were convinced that the French invasion came as a result of treasonous collaboration by the native Catholics with the French. On November 21 government agencies and offices throughout the kingdom were ordered to hunt down the "heretics" relentlessly. Anyone catching more than twenty "heretics" was promised an appointment as an officer of the border guard in a good district.[28] Regarding the "victory" over the French as a vindication of its exclusionist policy, the government tightened its restrictions even further. Not only was intercourse with

24. KJS, 3.6lb-62a; TNS, vol. 1, 67–68.
25. ISN-KJ, 3/9/12.
26. On the French expedition, see Choe, *Rule of the Taewŏn'gun,* 91–108; Yi Sŏn-gŭn, *Han'guksa ch'oegŭnse,* 246–274.
27. For the Korean report, see IWSM-TC, 47.1a-3a.
28. ISN-KJ, 3/10/15; KJS, 3.79b.

Westerners forbidden, but Western goods, some of which had found their way into Korea via China or Japan, were strictly banned.[29]

While pursuing these measures vigorously at home, the Korean government left the burden of diplomacy with the French in the hands of the Chinese authorities. Professing ignorance in diplomacy, Korea appealed to China for further guidance in the future so that it "might live in eternal peace and reverently fulfill its tributary duties."[30] The Chinese authorities, while trying to protect Korea by diplomacy, steadfastly refused to intervene in Korea directly. Throughout the affair, the Tsungli Yamen insisted that China was neither responsible for the Korean action, nor could it force Korea to accept the French demands. When the Yamen recommended that the Board of Rites inform the Korean government of the advisability of negotiating should the French return, the Board refused to take such action.[31]

AMERICA'S "LITTLE WAR" WITH KOREA, 1871

Despite its exclusionism, Korea treated foreign sailors and fishermen in distress with kindness. Except for the Japanese, who were handed over to the Tsushima officials at Pusan, such aliens were delivered to the Chinese authorities in Manchuria for repatriation to their homelands. In June 1866 when an American merchantman, the *Surprise,* was wrecked off the coast of P'yŏng'an Province, its crew was rescued, treated kindly, and handed over to the Chinese authorities. Two months later, however, an incident occurred which seemed to depart sharply from this humane tradition.

In early August 1866—when the Tsungli Yamen was engaged in diplomatic exchanges with the French over the

29. ISN-KJ, 3/7/30; KJS, 3.44b.
30. See n. 27.
31. IWSM-TC, 46.13b–14a, 47.8b–10a; Wright, "Ch'ing Diplomacy," 379.

execution of the French missionaries in Korea—a heavily
armed American merchantman, the *General Sherman*, left
north China for Korea with a crew of Americans, English
Chinese, and Malays. Also aboard was an Anglican missionary named Robert Thomas. In mid-August the ship
reached the coast of P'yŏng'an Province and sailed up the
Taedong River, in defiance of the local officials who repeatedly tried to turn it back. The Koreans pleaded that
foreign commerce and proselytism were banned in Korea
by the laws of the Ch'ing imperial court, and that Korea was
not free to change the laws. Ignoring the plea, the *Sherman*
continued and reached the provincial capital of P'yŏng'yang
on August 27. Late that afternoon, when the *Sherman*'s crew
forcibly detained a Korean investigating officer, hostile
crowds gathered on the shore. Frightened, the crew fired
into the crowds and burned some small Korean junks anchored nearby. This angered Pak Kyu-su, governor of the
province. Ordinarily a man of mild temper and tolerant
disposition, Pak ordered the *Sherman* destroyed. When the
ship was caught in a receding tide and ran aground a few
days later, the Koreans set it afire and killed its twenty-
four-man crew in the ensuing battle. The Koreans suffered
thirteen casualties.[32]

The fate of the *Sherman* remained a mystery for years.
Because of the presence of Father Thomas aboard the ship,
the Korean authorities believed that they had destroyed a
British vessel, and they so reported to China. Korea's
humane treatment of shipwrecked American sailors in the
past caused American officials to discount the rumor that
the *Sherman* had been destroyed and its crew killed.[33]
S. Wells Williams, secretary of the American legation in Peking, made an inquiry into the matter at the Tsungli Yamen
on October 23, 1866. Recalling the mistreatment the crew
of the *Surprise* had suffered at the hands of the Chinese
officials in Manchuria, Williams specifically requested the
Yamen to instruct officials at Mukden not to mistreat the

32. ISN-KJ, 3/7/27; KJS, 3.39a–41a; IWSM-TC, 45.3a–4b.
33. KJS, 3.87b; IWSM-TC, 45.3a–4b.

Sherman's crew, if and when they were delivered by the Koreans. The Yamen agreed.

Meanwhile, careful examination of the Korean report on the destruction of a "British" vessel at P'yŏng'yang led the Yamen to suspect that the vessel in question might have been the *Sherman*. In view of the British concern, the Yamen feared that Korea might be involved in a dispute with Britain and the United States, in addition to France. Therefore Prince Kung and other Yamen ministers decided to bring the matter to the attention of the throne. In a memorial received on October 24, they pointed out that, should Korea become involved in hostilities with these three powers, it would face demands for trade and proselytism, and it would also face the possibility of indemnity, the consequences of which could be highly detrimental. The ministers requested that the Board of Rites be ordered to advise the Korean government to act with circumspection and to avoid trouble with these powers. So ordered, the Board sent such a communication, which reached Seoul in early December.[34]

Fresh from what they considered to be a great victory over the French, the Taewŏn'gun and his advisors were in no mood to heed the Chinese advice. In its reply to the Board dated December 11, the Korean government reminded the Chinese authorities that they were already in possession of a detailed report on the destruction of a "British" ship at P'yŏng'yang, assuring them that absolutely no Americans had been involved. Williams's inquiry, it said, was probably based on an erroneous report of the destruction of the "British" ship. As for questions of trade, proselytism, and indemnity, it declared, "the temper and feelings of the people of our country are such that they will never accept them, no matter how many years they may suffer from the Western barbarians." The reply ended with the customary expressions of gratitude for Chinese concern and a request for continued guidance and protection.[35]

34. IWSM-TC, 45.10b–13b; ISN-KJ, 3/11/5.
35. IWSM-TC, 47.3a–5a.

Discouraged by the responses of the Chinese authorities, American officials began to explore other avenues. In contrast to the Chinese reluctance to intervene in Korea, Japan was eager to help. Disregarding Korean objections, the bakufu decided unilaterally early in 1867 to send a mission to Korea to mediate between Korea and the two Western powers. The mission was aborted by the fall of the bakufu, but the Americans remained hopeful of Japanese assistance. In January 1868, when the bakufu had ceased to exist, Secretary of State William H. Seward stated that "the United States may be able to avail themselves of the good offices of the proposed Japanese legation."[36]

American officials initiated a direct investigation, too. Upon receiving reports of the disappearance of the *Sherman* and the failure of the French expedition to Korea, Seward proposed a joint expedition to Korea to "obtain satisfaction for the murders of the French and Americans." The French government had little inclination to cooperate with the United States, which had just forced France out of Mexico. Moreover, embarrassed by the failure of Roze's unauthorized action, it announced that the expedition had been a great success and that there was no need for another. The American proposal was thus turned down.[37] Thereafter, Seward abandoned the idea of military action against Korea. A strong believer in the expansion of American influence in East Asia, he was, however, determined to assert American power in Korea at some future time.

Meanwhile, in an effort to ascertain the *Sherman*'s fate, the American officials in China dispatched the warship *Wachusett*, under Commander Robert W. Shufeldt, to Korea in January 1867, and another warship, the *Shenandoah*, under Commander John C. Febiger, in April 1868. Neither mission was successful.[38] A third mission planned for the summer of 1868, to be led by George F. Seward, Secretary

36. Tyler Dennett, *Americans in Eastern Asia*, 434.
37. *Ibid.*, 419.
38. On the Shufeldt and Febiger missions, see Charles O. Paullin, *Diplomatic Negotiations of American Naval Officers*, 284–286.

Seward's nephew who served as American consul-general at Shanghai, was cancelled when it was learned that any mission to Korea was unlikely to succeed unless backed by force.[39]

Anti-Western xenophobia in Korea, intensified by the French invasion and the *Sherman* incident, was exacerbated by the freebooting activities of Ernest J. Oppert, a Shanghai-based Prussian merchant. Oppert hatched a bizarre scheme: to steal the bones of the Taewŏn'gun's father from his tomb and use them to blackmail the Korean government into accepting trade with the West and Christianity. In May 1868 Oppert set out aboard a chartered vessel with a crew of some one hundred Chinese and Filipinos. Upon arriving at the site of the tomb, Oppert's party found the structure too large and too solid for them to destroy. They abandoned their plan when Korean troops arrived on the scene, and they sailed north to Yŏngjong Island in the Inch'ŏn Bay. Oppert told the startled local officials that he had desecrated the tomb of the royal ancestor in retaliation for the "murders" of the missionaries, and he demanded that Korea be opened to Western trade and Christianity. He and his party were driven off by the outraged officials.[40] Though somewhat comical in retrospect, the incident violated deeply the moral and religious sensibilities of the rigidly Confucian nineteenth-century Koreans. Undoubtedly it complicated the already-difficult American efforts to solve the mystery of the *Sherman*.

Meanwhile, having abandoned hope of rescuing the *Sherman*'s crew alive, American officials began planning an expedition to seek a shipwreck convention or treaty with Korea. Although Seward left office in 1869, with the change of administration in Washington in early 1869, his successor, Hamilton Fish, went ahead with the plan. Formal decision in favor of an expedition was reached in early 1870.

39. Dennett, *Americans in Eastern Asia*, 419–420; Choe, *Rule of the Taewŏn'gun*, 121.
40. Choe, *Rule of the Taewŏn'gun*, 112–114; Wright, "Ch'ing Diplomacy," 371; TNS, vol. 1, 76–80.

Rear Admiral John Rodgers, commander of the American
fleet in the Far East, wished to lead it. The assignment,
however, went to Frederick F. Low, newly appointed American minister to China. The selection of Low over Rodgers
was influenced by the belief that "political relations between
China and Korea are such as to make it desirable to first
obtain the goodwill and possibly the good offices of the
Chinese government."[41]

Following his arrival in Peking in May 1870, Low began
to collect information on this "semi-barbaric and hostile"
country. With regard to Korea's status relative to China,
Low reached the conclusion that Korea was substantially
an "independent state." In a dispatch to Washington dated
July 16, 1870, he stated: "To be sure, it sends tribute to
China annually, but from the best information I am able to
obtain, the tribute is sent rather as a quid pro quo for the
privilege of trading with the Chinese than as government
tribute. . . . China claims or exercises no control in any way
over Korea."[42]

To convince the Koreans of his peaceful intentions, Low
wished to inform them in advance of his coming. On February 11, 1871, he informed the Tsungli Yamen of his mission to Korea and requested its good offices. The Yamen,
however, refused his request, saying that Korean affairs
were under the jurisdiction of the Board of Rites.
Moreover, the Yamen tried to dissuade Low from going
forward with his plans. When Low repeated his request a
few days later, the Yamen turned it down again. On March
7 Low informed the Yamen that he had been appointed
American envoy to Korea and that he was going to that
country with Admiral Rodgers. The Yamen replied that, although Korea was a tributary state of China, it was "wholly
autonomous in government, religion, prohibitions, and laws
and China never interfered in its affairs."[43]

41. For details on the American expedition, see Choe, *Rule of the Taewŏn'gun*,
109–133; Albert Castel and Andrew C. Nahm, "Our Little War with the Heathen,"
American Heritage 19.3 (April 1968), 19–23, 72–75.
42. Choe, *Rule of the Taewŏn'gun*, 123.
43. *Ibid.*, 124.

Impressed by Low's determination, this time the Yamen complied with his request. In a memorial requesting that the Board of Rites be ordered to forward Low's letter to Korea, the Yamen explained its change of heart: "We have done everything possible to prevent the Americans from sending warships to Korea, but they have to the end refused to listen. In view of America's firm determination, whether or not its warships go to Korea does not depend at all upon whether or not this letter is forwarded. If we do not forward the letter, Korea, not knowing why the Americans are coming, would probably take a wrong course of action." The throne approved the Yamen's request. Accordingly, on March 12 the Board of Rites forwarded Low's letter to Korea with a covering letter of its own, which emphasized that Korea was "free to make whatever decision it deemed appropriate."[44] At the same time, unhappy with the intermediary role which it had been forced to play, the Board memorialized the throne that it would not forward letters to Korea in the future, for to do so would undermine China's imperial dignity. The throne approved.[45]

Low's letter reached Seoul on April 10. In it he stated that he was proceeding to Korea in order to ascertain the *Sherman*'s fate and to make necessary arrangements for the protection of the American merchants and sailors who might encounter distress in Korean waters. He did not want the Korean authorities to be alarmed by his arrival with warships and expressed the hope that, since he was coming in peace and friendship, he would be received in peace and friendship. Finally, Low said that he would arrive in Korea within the next three months and requested that the king appoint an envoy to negotiate with him.[46]

The Korean government was disturbed by Low's letter. The Taewŏn'gun, however, was confident that Korea could repel an American invasion as it had repelled the French invasion. The country's defenses had been improved under

44. IWSM-TC, 80.12a–13b.
45. *Ibid.*, 80.19b–20b.
46. See the Chinese text of Low's letter *ibid.*, 80.14a–15a.

his leadership during the past five years. He therefore decided to reject the American request. Moreover, he believed that the Korean government should not communicate its decision to Low directly, for it would set an undesirable precedent. Accordingly, a note was sent to the Ch'ing Board of Rites asking the Chinese authorities to give the Americans the message. It stated that, inasmuch as Korea had always treated shipwrecked aliens well and Korea was a small country with little surplus produce to trade with any country, there was no need for a shipwreck convention or a commercial treaty between Korea and the United States. As for the *Sherman,* the ship had brought destruction upon itself by its pirating activities. The note asked the Board to submit all facts concerning the matter to the throne so that the latter might instruct the American minister to "overcome his doubts and dispel his worries."[47] Meanwhile, the Taewŏn'gun ordered a strengthening of coastal defenses throughout the kingdom in preparation for a possible armed confrontation with the Americans.

Low and Rodgers left Shanghai on May 9 with five ships and 1,200 men. Their primary mission was, as has been stated, to secure a shipwreck convention from the Korean government. If the opportunity seemed favorable, they were told, they might seek commercial advantages for Americans. They were instructed that, should any cause arise for hostilities, they should refer to Washington for a decision for war or peace.[48] After a stopover at Nagasaki, the American squadron reached the waters near Kanghwa Island in late May. It was contacted by the local officials, who seemed friendly. Low, however, was unable to get in touch with an official of sufficient rank to commence substantive negotiations.

On June 1 a surveying party from the squadron, believing it had tacit approval from the Korean authorities, entered the estuary of the Han River, an area off limits to unauthorized ships, and was fired upon by Korean shore

47. *Ibid.,* 81.8b–12a; ISN-KJ, 8/2/21; KJS, 8.12b–13b.
48. Choe, *Rule of the Taewŏn'gun,* 122.

batteries. The Americans returned the fire and destroyed the shore guns. At this time Low's intention was to withdraw from Korea, after establishing diplomatic contact with the Korean government, and to return later for a reply to his demands. Since the initial reception had not been hostile, he and Rodgers were surprised by the sudden Korean attack. But thinking that it might have been caused by a misunderstanding on the part of the local commanders, they spent the next few days hoping that the Korean government would come forward with an apology and commence negotiations.[49]

Upon receiving the report on the incident, the Tae-wŏn'gun immediately ordered Chŏng Ki-wŏn, prefect of Kanghwa and commander of the forces on the island, to send a stern note to the Americans. He also took steps to reinforce the forces guarding Kanghwa and adjacent areas. Chŏng's note reached Low on June 6. Denouncing the American intrusion into a restricted inland waterway, it declared that non-intercourse with foreign countries was Korea's ancestral law, which had Chinese imperial sanction. Moreover, matters that the American envoy wished to negotiate were fundamentally non-negotiable, and there was no reason why he should meet with Korean officials. In case the Americans were unfamiliar with the Korean position, Chŏng attached a copy of the earlier Korean note to the Ch'ing Board of Rites asking the Chinese authorities to reject the American request.[50] Low did not see the note prior to his departure from China.

If Low did not know the Korean intentions earlier, there was little doubt now as to what they were. In the face of clear demonstrations of Korean intransigence, he and Rodgers faced a difficult choice: further military action or withdrawal. They considered the possible effect of a hasty withdrawal not only upon Korea, but upon China as well. In a report to Fish, Low stated: "If the squadron retires now, the effect upon the minds of the Koreans, and, I fear, upon the

49. Castel and Nahm, "Our Little War," 72; TNS, vol. 1, 92–93.
50. KJS, 8.26b–27a.

Chinese, will be injurious, if not disastrous, to our future prospects in both countries. Korea will rest firmly in the belief that she is powerful enough to repel any of the Western states singly, or even all of them combined; and this opinion will be likely to react upon China, and strengthen the influence of those who insist that it is practicable to drive out by force all the foreigners. I cannot advise the admiral to abandon the field without further attempts at redress for the wrongs and insults which our flag suffered." Low and Rodgers thus decided upon a retaliatory use of force, which they believed would improve the prospects for negotiation.[51] Considering it beneath his dignity to communicate with Chŏng directly, Low ordered his secretary, Edward Drew, to reply to Chŏng. Drew warned Chŏng that if the Korean government failed to indicate its willingness to negotiate within the next three or four days, the American envoy would take whatever action he deemed necessary.[52]

After waiting for a few more days in the vain hope that the Korean government would reconsider its position, Rodgers ordered his men into action on June 10, and during the next few days the Americans bombarded the city of Kanghwa and destroyed several forts on the island, killing or wounding some one hundred Koreans and capturing a few. Undaunted by the overwhelming superiority of American firepower, the Koreans "fought with desperation," Low reported later, "rarely equaled and never excelled by any people. Nearly all the soldiers at the main forts were killed at their posts." In a major engagement on June 11, the Koreans offered stiff resistance, inflicting more than a dozen casualties upon the Americans.[53]

The American attacks stiffened rather than softened the attitude of the Korean government. Outraged by the American action, Kojong declared that it was utterly inconceivable for Korea "to make peace with the likes of dogs and

51. Castel and Nahm, "Our Little War," 72; Choe, *Rule of the Taewŏn'gun,* 130–131.
52. For the Korean (Chinese) text of Drew's letter, see KJS, 8.27a.
53. Castel and Nahm, "Our Little War," 72–74; Choe, *Rule of the Taewŏn'gun,* 131–132; TNS, vol. 1, 93–95.

sheep!" The Taewŏn'gun ordered anti-foreign stelae erected in the major cities throughout the country, with a slogan reading: "The Western barbarians have invaded our country. Either we fight or make peace. Advocating peace is treason!"[54]

In the face of determined Korean resistance, Low and Rodgers realized that they had neither the authority nor the means to pursue further military action. Moreover, there was little hope that such action would "bring the king to any proper terms." Therefore the Americans decided to end military operations and to adopt a conciliatory approach. For three weeks Low exchanged letters with the local officials, imploring them to convey America's goodwill and peaceful intentions to the Korean court. In one of his letters Low stated that, if the officials refused his request, it would become necessary for him to transmit it through a "different channel." When this was reported to Seoul, Kojong declared that, although the Americans seemed to refer to China by the words "different channel," there was no reason why China should communicate to Korea regarding the matter, and even if China did, Korea could not and would not obey.[55] Convinced that there was no longer any prospect for fruitful negotiation, Low and Rodgers left with their forces for China on July 3.

Despite the overwhelming superiority of American arms, which had resulted in heavy Korean losses, the withdrawal of the American forces once again convinced the Koreans that they had defeated the Westerners. Reporting the "victory" to the Ch'ing Board of Rites, the Korean government stated proudly that, although Korea was "a small country deficient in wealth and military power, its reputation and culture can stand by themselves." Attributing this to Chinese imperial guidance and protection, it asked the Board to memorialize the throne for an edict instructing the American envoy to lay aside worries about shipwrecked Ameri-

54. KJS, 8.28b–29a.
55. For the Korean (Chinese) text of Low's letter, see IWSM-TC, 83.12a–b; for Kojong's remarks, see ISN-KJ, 8/5/15.

cans, to abandon plans to negotiate on other matters, and
not to make any more trouble.[56] On October 2, 1871, Prince
Kung sent, at imperial command, a note to Low to inform
him of the Korean position. It is Korea's established law,
said the prince, to protect all aliens in distress and not to
engage in foreign commerce; China never interfered with
the administration of that law. China and the United States
were friends, he added, and Korea, being a tributary of
China, believed that the best way for the United States to
promote friendship with Korea was to treat Korea as China
did.[57]

America's "Little War with the Heathen", as the expedition was called by a New York newspaper, ended without
achieving any of its stated objectives. Instead of convincing
the Koreans of Western strength or of the advantage of intercourse with America, it resulted, as Low feared, in rein-
forcing the Korean belief that the Western powers were all
piratical in behavior, and that Korea could repel them if it
remained united, stout of heart, and upright in morality.
Korea's centuries-old wall of seclusion remained solid.

CHINESE AND KOREAN REACTIONS

Emphasizing the "adaptability of Ch'ing diplomacy" in contrast to Korea's "absolutely rigid policy" during the 1860s,
Mary C. Wright wrote, "By 1867 the Tsungli Yamen knew
that the traditional Sino-Korean relationship could no
longer be maintained, that the tributary tie was a logical impossibility in the modern world."[58] In light of what we have
seen, there is little need for further proof of the rigidity of
the Korean stand against the Western world during the
1860s. It will be useful, however, for us to examine the
historical circumstances and background that bred such
rigidity.

Centuries of rigid and effective isolation, save for limited
intercourse with China and Japan, left Yi Korea hopelessly

56. KJS, 8.32b–34a; IWSM-TC, 83.4a–8a.
57. IWSM-TC, 83.29b–30a.
58. Wright, "Ch'ing Diplomacy," 369.

ignorant of the outside world. During the late 1860s and
early 1870s, when both China and Japan possessed considerable knowledge about the Western world, Korea's knowledge of that world was still limited to what could be
gleaned from a handful of Chinese works written immediately after the Opium War. During the American invasion of Kanghwa Island, Chief State Councilor Kim
Pyŏng-hak, a sophisticated scholar, told Kojong that the
United States was merely a sundry collection of settlements.
Kim's authority was Wei Yüan's *Hai-kuo t'u-chih.* Kim also
told the young monarch that the Americans were little different from pirates and that their comings and goings,
though swift and unpredictable, should not cause undue
alarm.[59] Despite the amply demonstrated superiority of
Western arms, few Koreans in this period, including the
Taewŏn'gun, had the necessary knowledge or information
to appreciate correctly the strength of the Western powers.[60] As Low observed in a report to the State Department,
the American naval action, "which would have produced a
profound impression upon any other government," had "no
or little effect" upon the Korean government.[61]

Rigid conformity to Neo-Confucianism, reinforced by ignorance about the outside world, had bred in Korea, as it
had in China and Japan, a militant form of cultural
chauvinism, which in turn intensified Korea's traditional
exclusionism. The tendency was more pronounced in Korea
because Korean isolation had been far more rigid and effective than that of either China or Japan. The relative lack of
sustained Western interest in Korea made it possible for the
peninsular kingdom to maintain its traditional isolation in
this period. But most Koreans believed that their superior
"moral virtue" enabled them to withstand Western pressure.
Moreover, the belief that Korea alone was standing up
against the Western powers at a time when China was
crumbling under Western attacks and Japan was succumb-

59. ISN-KJ, 8/4/20.
60. Ch'oe Ch'ang-gyu, *Han'gug'in ŭi chŏngch'i isik* (The political consciousness
of the Koreans), 16–17.
61. Choe, *Rule of the Taewŏn'gun,* 133.

ing to Western cultural enticement apparently gave the
Koreans a sense of national pride and, perhaps, a sense of
mission. Most Korean scholar-officials and literati believed
that, with China and Japan already "contaminated" by the
"evil" influence of the Western barbarians, it was essential
for Korea to remain free of that influence and uphold Eastern (Chinese) tradition if civilization was to be saved.[62]

At the outset of the French invasion of Kanghwa Island,
the Taewŏn'gun addressed a letter to the State Council, in
which he stated: "Ever since China made peace with the
Western barbarians, their rampant desires have become
doubly unfathomable. They have perpetrated outrages
everywhere; everyone has suffered their evils. That our
country alone has been spared is due to the grace of Sage
Kija (Ch'i-tzu in Chinese) in Heaven. At this juncture, the
only thing we understand is propriety and the dictates of
duty; the only thing on which we rely is the will of the mul-
titude standing firm in the face of enemies."[63] Though his
writing was perhaps rhetorical, the fact that the Taewŏn'gun
was a highly pragmatic man rather than an idealist lends
conviction to his statement. Yi Hang-no, the country's leading scholar and chief advocate of *wijŏng ch'ŏksa,* who was
called out of retirement to serve as royal mentor during the
French invasion, declared in a memorial to the king that,
although war with the invader "would preserve inherited culture in the country, peace with the invader would reduce
mankind to the state of the beast."[64] During the American
invasion, Kojong exclaimed rhetorically: "How can a country which has upheld propriety and justice for thousands of
years make peace with the likes of dogs and sheep?" Third
State Councilor Hong Sun-mok responded: "Every corner
of the world today has been contaminated by a dark and
evil spirit; only our country remains clean. This is because
we have guarded our land with propriety and justice!"[65] On
another occasion, Kojong observed with obvious pride:

62. Ch'oe Ch'ang-gyu, *chŏngch'i isik,* 42–44; Kang Chae-ŏn (Kyō Zai-gen), *Kindai Chōsen no shisō* (Modern Korean thought), 44–45.

63. KJS, 3.62a–b.

64. *Ibid.,* 3.62b–63b; ISN-KJ, 3/9/12.

65. ISN-KJ, 8/4/25.

"Our eastern land still upholds the Way of the Master. If we ever make peace with the bandits, it will be the end of the Master's Way!"[66] Kojong was so convinced of the moral rectitude of Korea's position that he declared supreme duty dictated that it disobey, even if China commanded it to grant the American demand for intercourse.[67]

If the French invasion left the Koreans with the belief that they could repel any Western invasion, the American expedition reinforced that belief. Similarly, if the French action hardened the anti-Christian feelings of the Korean literati into an anti-Western xenophobia in the late 1860s, the American action transformed that xenophobia into a militant cultural chauvinism, which rejected everything Western in the name of *wijŏng ch'ŏksa* in the 1870s. A major characteristic of this chauvinistic doctrine, whose proponents regarded themselves as true inheritors and preservers of Eastern (Chinese) culture, was its strong Ming loyalism tinged with anti-Manchu sentiment. One of Yi Hang-no's official acts upon his appointment as assistant royal secretary during the French invasion was to memorialize the king for the restoration of the Mandongmyo, which had been abolished earlier by the Taewŏn'gun with Queen Dowager Cho's approval. Extolling the harmonious suzerain-vassal relations between Ming China and Yi Korea, Yi declared that there was nothing in Korea, however insignificant, that had not been graced by the imperial virtue of the Wan-li emperor, the Ming ruler who had defended Korea from the Hideyoshi invasions. Observing that "the whole world has gone barbarian today," Yi implored the king to order the immediate restoration of the defunct shrine "so that our countrymen will understand the significance of repelling the barbarians and the Western pirates will have fear in their hearts."[68]

As the Korean authorities grew confident of their ability to cope with the Western military threat and became convinced of the moral rectitude of their position, they were in-

66. *Ibid.*, 8/5/7.
67. See n. 55.
68. ISN-KJ, 3/10/7; KJS, 3.77b.

creasingly critical of China's policy of cooperation with the Western powers. Identifying that policy with the Manchus rather than the Han Chinese, they singled out Prince Kung for criticism and attack. At a royal lecture during the American invasion, Kojong wondered how the Western "barbarians" had been able to make peace with China so easily. Minister of War Kang No, who had recently visited Peking as a tributary envoy, responded that they had been able to do so because of Prince Kung's help. Kang further stated that it was Prince Kung who had forced the Board of Rites to forward the letter from the American (Low) to Korea even though the Board had repeatedly refused to do so. The king asked Kang if Wan Ch'ing-li, president of the Board, was a Han Chinese; Kang replied that he was, adding that, although both Han Chinese and Manchu officials at the Ch'ing court treated Koreans cordially, only Han Chinese would socialize with Korean envoys. The king asked again if it was known in China that the Korean court maintained a secret shrine to the Ming emperors; Kang replied that every Chinese knew of it, including the Manchus.[69]

More serious charges were leveled at Prince Kung by others. Chief State Councilor Kim Pyŏng-hak, the highest official of the government, told Kojong that the prince aided the Westerners because they had bribed him. Supporting the allegation that Prince Kung had forced a reluctant Board of Rites to forward the American note to Korea, Kim lamented that the effect of the prince's "contamination" by heresies "has spread as far as our country." A royal lecturer went so far as to liken the prince to Ch'in Kuai, the twelfth-century Chinese official whose advocacy of peace with the barbarian state of Chin allegedly led to the fall of the Sung.[70]

Taking a dim view of China's accommodation of the Western powers in this period, the majority of Korean officials viewed Prince Kung and his associates who were in

69. ISN-KJ, 8/4/17.
70. *Ibid.*, 8/4/20.

charge of Ch'ing foreign policy with moral reprobation and suspicion, no doubt influenced by their anti-Manchu sentiment. They had little inclination to follow China's lead in establishing relations with Western countries. In fact, they considered it their supreme moral duty not to follow the Chinese lead in this matter. This in no way implied that they were disloyal to China. Whatever their private feelings about the Manchus and whatever their domestic policy or position, the king, the Taewŏn'gun, and all Korean officials were submissive and fundamentally loyal to China, the Middle Kingdom. Neither they nor the Chinese authorities saw a conflict between Korean political independence and its ceremonial submission to China.

Guarding its political independence and freedom jealously, the Korean government nevertheless tried to shift responsibility for dealing with the troublesome Westerners to China. Whenever approached or confronted by foreigners seeking trade or proselytism, the Koreans referred them to the Chinese authorities by invoking the alleged Chinese prohibition against a tributary state having unauthorized relations with foreign countries. Pleading ignorance in the art of diplomacy and emphasizing its "total dependence" on China, the Korean government appealed to China for guidance, while in fact it was determined to pursue an independent course.

The Taewŏn'gun's conduct of tributary relations with China under this policy was classic in style and execution. He professed an undying devotion to China without any intention of following the Chinese lead in establishing relations with Western countries. Convinced that Korea could ward off the Western threat by itself if it remained united under his leadership, the Taewŏn'gun pursued the goal of preserving Korean isolation. Although his headstrong stand against the Western world was myopic and foolhardy, he provided superb leadership in organizing defenses against the French and American intruders. But it was not, as we have seen, the strength of his personality or leadership alone that sustained the morale of the officials and fighting

men. While many of the Taewŏn'gun's domestic policies and
programs were controversial and aroused strong opposition
among the *yangban* literati, his relentless persecution of
Christians and his uncompromising stand under Western
pressures enjoyed their wholehearted support. His resolve
was no doubt strengthened by the belief that China's cooperation or accommodation with the Western powers was not
only morally wrong but represented Prince Kung's personal
diplomacy of collaboration, something the Chinese people
heartily detested. This belief gained wide currency in Korea
after the apparent collapse of the "cooperative policy" in
China, which led to increasing difficulties with the Western
powers and culminated in the Tientsin Massacre in 1870.
In light of the prevailing conditions and popular sentiment in China in this period, such a belief was not wholly
unwarranted.

In comparison with Korea's rigid and unrealistic stand
against the Western world, few can deny the adaptability of
Ch'ing diplomacy in this period. The question remains,
however, to what degree was it adaptable? Did the Tsungli
Yamen really consider the Sino-Korean tributary tie a "logical impossibility" in the modern world? Was it prepared to
modify traditional Sino-Korean relations? Was the Yamen
really inviting Korea to get out of the Ch'ing tribute system,
as Wright stated, or was it urging Korea to accept treaty
relations with Western countries as a temporary measure of
expediency?[71] In short, did Ch'ing diplomatic adaptability
represent a reluctant but genuine change of heart or a temporary accommodation with reality?

In the late 1860s, the Ch'ing government emerged victorious from the great mid-century rebellions at home, but
it was still faced with enormous difficulties and problems in
postwar reconstruction and in its relations with Western
powers. It was at this difficult time, when its energies and
resources were still taxed to the limit, that China found
Korea—traditionally the eastern shield of the empire— fac-

---

71. Wright, "Ch'ing Diplomacy," 369.

ing growing pressure from both the Western powers and Japan, all seeking open and regular intercourse. Yet, living in a dream world created by its own centuries-old isolation, Korea refused adamantly to accommodate these powers. As Wright observed, this put China in a difficult, if not impossible, position: "On the one hand, it was physically impossible for China to defend Korea's extreme stand against all the world at a time when China's own energies were bent on the domestic reconstruction, which dictated the avoidance of any international entanglement. On the other hand, it was morally impossible for China either to renounce its suzerainty over Korea or to force Korea to abandon the Confucian tradition which China itself had not yet abandoned."[72] In these circumstances, neither innovation nor activism could be expected of China in the conduct of its relations with Korea. Chinese policy toward Korea in this period therefore remained as traditional as it was practical.

First of all, despite the diplomatic innovations inaugurated under the treaty system, leaders of the Ch'ing government did not anticipate or contemplate any fundamental change in China's relations with traditional tributary states such as Korea and Vietnam.[73] The treaty system itself was regarded by many Chinese officials as a temporary expedient to be discarded as soon as China regained sufficient strength to reassert its imperial authority. It is highly unlikely that the equal sovereignty of all states—the basic concept underlying the treaty system—was genuinely or fully accepted by its chief supporters in China, such as Prince Kung and Wen-hsiang. As far as China was concerned, the treaty system was to apply to its relations with Western countries while the tribute system was to continue to govern its relations with non-Western countries. Under this dualistic concept, China did continue to conduct its relations with East Asian countries, such as Korea and Vietnam, under the

72. *Ibid.*, 369.
73. Both Tseng Kuo-fan and Li Hung-chang defended the 1871 treaty with Japan, an East Asian state, partly on the ground that Japan, unlike Korea or Vietnam, had not been a Chinese tributary since the Yüan period. For details, see Chapter IV, Section 3.

traditional tribute system after the treaty system had been fully inaugurated.

Korea, the model tributary state, was clearly differentiated from any Western country by the Ch'ing authorities. Despite frequent and almost inevitable involvement in Korean affairs, the Tsungli Yamen did not seek authority to manage Korean affairs or to communicate with Korea directly. Relations with Korea were handled by the Board of Rites, as before. Rather than viewing the traditional Sino-Korean, suzerain-vassal relationship as "a logical impossibility" in the modern world, leaders of the Ch'ing government considered the relationship to be compatible with China's relations with Western countries under the treaty system.[74] The Tsungli Yamen hoped that Korea would accept some form of accommodation with the Western powers, if only to avoid immediate military catastrophe, but it never explicitly advised Korea to do so. Even if it had, for China to urge Korea to negotiate a treaty with France or the United States certainly would not mean that China wanted Korea to leave the Ch'ing tribute system or the Chinese orbit. It should be remembered that Korea had been free to maintain relations with any country so long as such relations did not conflict or interfere with its tributary obligations toward China. Korea's frequent invocation of the alleged Chinese law forbidding it to have relations with other countries was, in fact, no more than an excuse for refusing Western demands and was not based on a Chinese statute.

This basic Ch'ing policy of maintaining nominal suzerainty over Korea was consistent with tradition in Ch'ing-Korean relations. As in the past, in this period China persistently disclaimed any responsibility for Korean action and refused to interfere in its affairs. It would have been an act of folly, as has been noted, for China to assume responsibility beyond its own borders at this time, when it was faced with enormous problems at home. More fundamentally, it would have been against tradition for China to have acted

74. T. F. Tsiang, "Sino-Japanese Diplomatic Relations, 1870–1894," *Chinese Social and Political Science Review* 17.1 (April 1933), 55.

otherwise. China exercised ceremonial authority and moral leadership over Korea; it did not exercise political domination or control. Korea acknowledged Chinese titular superiority and acted with respect and Confucian decorum toward China, but Korea did not necessarily follow every Chinese example or wish. In fact, one of the basic conditions that insured harmonious relations between the two countries during the Ch'ing period—a period marked by persistent anti-Manchu sentiment in Korea—was China's non-interference in Korean affairs. Not once since the mid-seventeenth century did the Ch'ing government interfere in Korea politically. Its refusal to do so at this time was entirely within tradition. It indicated neither China's lack of authority in nor its abandonment of responsibility for Korea, as interpreted by most contemporary Western observers.[75]

Finally, apart from the ideological and institutional traditions in Ch'ing-Korean relations, there was a very important practical reason why China chose, despite its growing concern for Korea's security, not to intervene actively in the peninsula at this time. On the basis of their experience with Western intentions in China, Prince Kung and his associates were convinced that the French and Americans were interested only in trade and proselytism in Korea, not in territorial aggrandizement. While these men did not much care about either Western trade or Christianity, they knew that neither trade nor Christian proselytism would immediately endanger Korea's national survival. An obscure but highly revealing incident illustrates this view of the Tsungli Yamen and its Korean policy.

In early 1867, newspapers in Shanghai and Hong Kong carried statements attributed to a Japanese visitor named Hachinohe Junshuku concerning Japanese plans and intentions toward Korea. In the *Chung-wai hsin-wen* (*Chinese and Foreign News*) of Hong Kong, January 18, 1867, Hachinohe boasted that Japan had made great strides in the introduc-

75. The views expressed by Bellonet and Low in their exchanges with the Tsungli Yamen with regard to Korea were representative of the Westerners' interpretation of Sino-Korean relations in this period.

tion of Western arms and technology and that it had more than eighty modern warships. He stated that the bakufu was planning a military expedition to Korea, in order to "punish its king for his failure to send the quinterrenial tribute that he was required to send to the shogun." Hachinohe made other statements containing distorted accounts of the historical relations between Japan and Korea, including the assertion that the ancient Korean kingdoms had been tributaries of Japan. Newspaper clippings containing these statements were forwarded to the Tsungli Yamen by local officials.

Prince Kung, Wen-hsiang, and other Yamen ministers, already troubled by the French-Korean armed clash over the missionary issue and the American inquiries concerning the *General Sherman,* were disturbed by the report of a possible Japanese expedition to Korea. On March 20, 1867, they jointly addressed a secret memorial to the throne to express their concern. Beginning with a brief reference to Japan's historical "depredations" against China and its "conceited" self-image, the memorialists stated that they had watched Japan's "wars" with Britain and France because Japan was so close to China that "its victory or defeat would alike affect China greatly." Although Japan has met military defeat in recent years, they continued, it "has greatly exerted itself and become strong." Noting Japan's progress in arms expansion and modernization, the memorialists said that "Japan's ambitions are not small" and that "it is now seeking a quarrel with Korea." While Britain and France might quarrel with Korea, they observed, these countries would seek only trade and proselytism in Korea, not territorial aggrandizement. On the other hand, "should Korea ever be occupied by Japan," China's troubles would become "far more serious, and trade and proselytism in Korea would become merely secondary issues." Warning that Japanese military action against Korea would have consequences for China far graver than any that might arise from French military action, the memorialists recommended that the Board of Rites be ordered to send a confidential inquiry to

Korea.[76] So ordered by the throne, the Board sent a note with a Korean tributary embassy, which returned to Seoul on April 10 and presented the Chinese note to the Korean court.

Startled by the Chinese note, the Korean government immediately sent a reply to the Board, pointing out errors in the Hachinohe statements. It assured China that Korea had long maintained peaceful relations with Japan and that it had always faithfully reported to China any untoward incident between itself and Japan. It asked the Board to convey to the emperor Korea's eternal gratitude for his concern and protection.[77] At the same time, offended by Hachinohe's allegation that the Korean king was required to send quinterrenial tribute to the shogun, the Korean government sent a stern note of inquiry to Tsushima. Stressing the inviolability of the treaty and mutual trust, which had been the foundation of peaceful relations between the two countries for more than two centuries, the Korean government demanded full and satisfactory explanations for Hachinohe's statements.[78]

The bakufu knew nothing of Hachinohe's statements. Nor had it any plans for sending a military expedition to Korea, although it was planning to send a diplomatic mission to that country. When they received the Korean note from Tsushima in mid-June, the bakufu immediately directed Tsushima to reply to Korea and to deny Hachinohe's allegations. Tsushima sent such a reply to Korea in late October. Branding Hachinohe's statements completely false and groundless, Tsushima stated that the bakufu had no hostile plans or intentions toward Korea. The recent acquisition of ships and guns was solely for Japan's self-strengthening and own protection. Tsushima also reaffirmed the bakufu's friendship and goodwill toward

76. For excerpts from the newspaper articles and Prince Kung's secret memorial, see IWSM-TC, 47.20a–23b.
77. KJS, 4.15b–16a; IWSM-TC, 48.25b–27a.
78. KJS, 4.16a. See also TNS, vol. 1, 124–126.

Korea. Along with the reply, Tsushima sent a separate note informing the Korean government of the decision of the bakufu to send a diplomatic mission to Korea to mediate Korea's disputes with France and the United States.[79] The decision had been made unilaterally by the bakufu in disregard of an earlier Korean refusal to receive such a mission.

The Hachinohe affair was dismissed by the bakufu in a rather cavalier fashion, but not by the Korean government. Despite the bakufu's denial and reassurances, Hachinohe's language uncomfortably reminded the Korean officials of the Hideyoshi invasions three centuries earlier, stirring up fear of an imminent Japanese invasion in some quarters. Although the bakufu categorically disavowed any aggressive plans or intentions toward Korea, the fact of its unilateral decision to send an unwanted mission deepened Korean suspicion. The bakufu's apparent eagerness to "help" France and the United States made it doubly suspect in the eyes of Korean authorities. A second Korean note to Tsushima, delivered early in 1868, clearly indicated this reaction. Beginning with a blunt reminder of its earlier rejection of the bakufu's offer of mediation, the Korean government declared that inasmuch as Korea had strengthened its coastal defenses, leaving nothing for its neighbors to worry about, there was no need for the bakufu to concern itself with a distant foreign problem. The note reminded the bakufu of the existence of the "unalterable law" between the two countries that all business between them should be conducted through Tsushima.[80]

Involving China, Japan, and Korea, the Hachinohe affair illustrates the prevailing views and attitudes of these countries toward one another during this period. Although Hachinohe was a man without any official connection with the bakufu, reputedly he was a scholar. His views concerning Korea were typical, if not representative, of his contemporaries in Japan. His knowledge of the historical

79. TNS, vol. 1, 112, 127–128. For Tsushima's note, see ISN-KJ, 4/10/1; KJS, 4.44b–45a.
80. TNS, vol. 1, 119–120.

Japanese-Korean relations was inaccurate. But he was no exception in this regard; most Japanese of his time believed, as he did, that ancient Korea had been a tributary of Japan. Many even considered, as he did, that the Korean relations with Tokugawa Japan were essentially tributary in nature. The presumption of Japanese titular superiority over Korea inherent in this misconception was to become one of the basic assumptions underlying Japan's "restorationist" diplomacy toward Korea following the Meiji Restoration. Hachinohe's allegation that the bakufu was planning an expedition to Korea was without foundation in fact, but the call for the subjugation or conquest of Korea was voiced by many in bakumatsu Japan. It was to attract more persistent, and even fanatical, advocates in the early Meiji period.

For Korea the Hachinohe affair was an alarming reminder of its precarious position in a world dominated by two powerful neighbors and now increasingly threatened by predatory Western powers. The Korean government's response to the Chinese inquiry about the Hachinohe statements betrayed its concern not to give China cause to question its loyalty at a time when Korea might need Chinese protection from rising external threats. The affair stirred up the long-dormant Korean distrust of Japan and sowed the seed of suspicion about Japanese-Western collaboration against Korea in the minds of the Korean authorities. Taking a dim view of Japan's "friendly" dealings with the Western "barbarians," the Taewŏn'gun and other Korean leaders redoubled their determination not to have any more business with Japan than was absolutely necessary.

Finally, the episode shows clearly the perception by the Chinese authorities of the nature of the Western threat to Korea and their awareness of a potential Japanese threat to the peninsular kingdom. Despite the possibility of further French retaliation and of American military action against Korea, Prince Kung and his associates did not consider either France or the United States to be a real threat to Korea. This accounted for, at least in part, the Chinese refusal to intervene in Korea directly or actively. On the other hand, even in this early period, when few considered Japan a major power, Japan was regarded as a threat to Korea and hence to China, a threat potentially more dangerous than any Western power.

Following the collapse of the Western powers' cooperative policy in China, the late 1860s and early 1870s were marked by increasing Sino-Western discord. In addition, leaders of the Ch'ing government, such as Li Hung-chang, saw a growing threat from Russia and Japan. In the circumstances, it is highly unlikely that the Ch'ing government, even if it were not doctrinaire about China's traditional position in the world, would entertain the idea of abandoning Chinese suzerainty over Korea, an area considered vital to the security of the Ch'ing state. Although in practice China had limited the exercise of its suzerainty over Korea to ceremonial matters, its authority under the tribute system was absolute in theory. In a period of China's military weakness, its authority as the suzerain was the best and perhaps the only available means by which China could keep the peninsula under its control and to prevent it from falling under foreign domination.

CHAPTER III

Nascent Japanese Expansionism

Hideyoshi's invasions of Korea during the 1590s were the first explosive manifestation of Japan's urge for continental expansion. Having failed in that bold attempt, Japan turned its attention to the task of reestablishing domestic order and stability after a century of incessant warfare and destruction at home and abroad. In the early seventeenth century, when most of the Japanese people were weary of devastating civil wars and exhausting military adventures abroad, the founders of the Tokugawa shogunate bent their energies and resources to the consolidation of their rule at home. Although the bakufu took steps, within a few years of its establishment, to restore formal relations with Korea, it was motivated primarily by domestic political considerations. It apparently desired formal ties with China, but made no overt efforts to establish such ties. Meanwhile, growing antipathy for Christianity, which the bakufu considered a threat to socio-political order at home, and perhaps also desire to monopolize a flourishing European-Southeast Asian trade, led the bakufu in 1639 to proscribe Japanese contact with the outside world save a limited and rigidly regulated trade with the Chinese and Dutch at Nagasaki. Relations with Korea were not affected by this policy of seclusion; they were left largely in the hands of Tsushima.

Internal stability and external peace were the two principal conditions that ensured success of the Tokugawa seclusion policy. However, these conditions had ceased to exist by the early nineteenth century. Increasing social and

economic difficulties began to undermine the Tokugawa
feudal order from within, while Western expansionism
began to threaten Japan's security and independence from
without. Internal and external threats combined to engen-
der a growing sense of national crisis, which in turn stimulated, among other things, a revival of Japanese interest in
continental East Asia. By the mid-nineteenth century, increasing numbers of influential men in and out of government councils began to view continental East Asia in terms
of Japan's security and survival in a world threatened by an
aggressive West. Their hopes and fears about the future of
Japan and their views and attitudes toward continental
neighbors, such as China and Korea, anticipating those of
the early Meiji leaders in many ways, took the form of a
nascent expansionism, which was to grow during the next
decade into a major challenge to the traditional world order
and Chinese supremacy in East Asia.

RESURGENCE OF JAPAN'S CONTINENTAL INTEREST

The reawakening and growth of Japan's active interest in
continental East Asia, dormant since the end of the sixteenth century, coincided with the rise of Western expansionism in East Asia. In fact it was stimulated to a large degree by fear of Western aggression and expansion, and
therefore it paralleled closely rise of the Western threat to
Japan. It was a gradual, but steadily accelerating, process
that went through three major phases. The first phase occurred during the period between the late eighteenth century, when Japan became aware of Russian expansion on its
northern frontiers, and the mid-1850s, when Japan was
opened by Perry's black ships. The second phase continued
less than a decade thereafter, until the early 1860s, during
which time the great *jōi-kaikoku* ("expel the barbarians—
open the country") controversies rocked Japan. The third
phase took place in the mid-1860s, years when the bakufu
fought for survival until its fall in 1868. Each phase re-

flected major events and changes in Japan's internal and external circumstances.

During the first phase, interest in continental East Asia was confined to a small number of scholars, particularly those of Dutch studies, whose knowledge of the West gave them an understanding of the nature and gravity of the threat posed by the Western powers to Japan and East Asia. The first Japanese who tried to rekindle his countrymen's interest in the Asian continent was Hayashi Shihei, an early specialist in Dutch studies. Hayashi's interest in China and Korea was aroused by his concern over Russia's eastward expansion, which by the late eighteenth century seemed to threaten Japan's northern frontiers.[1] In 1781 he wrote a geographical survey of Korea, Liu-ch'iu (Ryūkyū), and Ezo (Hokkaidō and adjacent islands), entitled *An Illustrated Survey of Three Countries (Sankoku zusetsu tsūran)*. Hayashi pointed out that the Korean peninsula held a position strategically vital to the security of Japan from Western (Russian) encroachment.[2] In 1791 he completed his major work, *Military Talks for a Maritime Country (Kaikoku heidan)*, in which he warned that, either on its own or under Western instigation, Manchu China could turn into an aggressive military power that might seriously threaten the security and independence of Japan.[3]

Hayashi's interest in China and Korea was defensive rather than expansionist in nature, concerned chiefly with the strategic problem of how to defend Japan from Russian aggression. On the basis of a rational appraisal of Japan's circumstances in the world at that time, he warned his countrymen against what he considered their unwarranted complacency and indifference toward China and Korea and urged them to study these countries for their strategic importance in the defense of Japan from Western aggression. Although he did not explicitly call for aggressive or expan-

---

1. On Hayashi's views, see Donald Keene, *The Japanese Discovery of Europe, 1720–1830*, 39–46.

2. Hatada Takashi, *Nihonjin no Chōsenkan* (Japanese views on Korea), 16.

3. Keene, *Japanese Discovery of Europe*, 41–42.

sionist action against these countries, the possibility of such action, at least in Korea, was not wholly absent from Hayashi's thought. In *Military Talks for a Maritime Country,* he stated that he had made a geographical study of Korea and two neighboring areas, partly to meet the possible needs of military operations in these areas.[4]

The fear of Russian expansion and encroachment worried other Japanese intellectuals. Honda Toshiaki, a remarkable thinker trained in Dutch studies, called for the Japanese colonization of Sakhalin, the Kuriles, and Kamchatka, as well as Ezo, to counter Russian expansion in these areas.[5] But it was Satō Nobuhiro, a scholar of encyclopedic interests and a student of the West, who turned expansionist attention to the continent. In 1808, Satō wrote that, while Russia was a strong country, China was potentially far more powerful and Japan should cultivate friendly relations and expand trade with China even if it must humble itself in the process.[6] Subsequently, Satō came under the influence of the Shinto religion and became chauvinistic and visionary. In a treatise written in 1823, entitled *A Confidential Plan for World Unification (Udai kondō hisaku),* he asserted that Japan was the first land created at the beginning of the earth and that, as such, it was destined to rule the whole world. He proposed the taking of Manchuria, to be followed by the conquest of China, as the way for Japan to begin the fulfillment of this mission.[7] After the Opium War, which apparently had a sobering effect upon Satō's visionary expansionism, he more or less returned to his earlier position. In a treatise written in 1849, he hoped for a resurgence of Ch'ing power, which he said was essential for restoring China's tarnished image and for ensuring the secu-

4. Hayashi Shihei, *Hayashi shihei zenshū* (Complete works of Hayashi Shihei), vol. 1, 388.

5. Keene, *Japanese Discovery of Europe,* 115–122.

6. Mukai Toshio, "Bukumatsu ni okeru Shina keiryakuron no hatten to sono seishitsu" (The rise of the proposal for the subjugation of China in the bakumatsu period and its nature), pt. 1, *Shirin* 25.4 (October 1940), 20.

7. Ryusaku Tsunoda, et al., eds., *Sources of Japanese Tradition,* vol. 2, 70–73; Hilary Conroy, "Government versus 'Patriot': The Background of Japan's Asiatic Expansion," *Pacific Historical Review* 20.1 (February 1951), 38.

rity of Japan and other Eastern countries in the face of rising barbarian (Western) rampage.[8]

Satō's proposal for the conquest of China and Korea marked him as the first advocate of Japanese continental expansion whose ideas were to be elaborated and utilized by Japan's twentieth-century expansionists.[9] Despite his chauvinism, however, Satō retained some of the traditional respect that most of the Tokugawa scholars held for China. When confronted by a growing threat from the West, Hayashi, Satō, and their contemporaries seem to have turned to China, not for expansion or conquest but for mutual cooperation against the West.

Perry's black ships brought home to many Japanese the gravity of the Western threat facing their country and deepened their sense of national crisis. This stimulated a corresponding rise in Japan's renewed interest in continental East Asia, ushering in the second phase of its development and growth. Two important changes marked this phase. One was largely quantitative: after Perry, interest in the continent was no longer confined to a small circle of scholars or armchair strategists removed from governmental policy-making or merely engaged in speculation. It came to be shared by many others and centered among men of political action. The second was a qualitative change of the interest itself: in the past it had been largely defensive in nature, concerned chiefly with the strategic importance of continental East Asia in the defense of Japan from Western aggression; now it took the form of an aggressive call for continental expansion by Japan. There were three major groups among these early proponents of Japan's continental expansion, which represented the diverse political forces and interests in the country: restorationists, advocating overthrow of the shogunate and the restoration of imperial rule in Japan; conservatives, supporting the bakufu and endeavoring to preserve the status quo; and reformists, seeking change and innovation in the existing Tokugawa order.

8. Mukai, "Shina keiryakuron," pt. 1, 21–22.
9. *Ibid.*, pt. 1, 20; Conroy, "Japan's Asiatic Expansion," 38.

A leading figure among the restorationists was Yoshida Shōin, the famous loyalist ideologue of Chōshū. Yoshida argued that losses Japan might suffer as a result of open intercourse and trade with Western countries should be made up by Japanese seizure of adjacent countries, such as Korea and Manchuria. With regard to Korea in particular, Yoshida said, "Korea must be admonished and ordered to send tribute to the Japanese court, as it did in ancient times."[10] As the initial step toward the "resubjugation" of the peninsula, he proposed the colonization of Ullŭng (Dagelet) Island off southeast Korea by his domain, Chōshū.[11] Yoshida's views were shared by other radical loyalists. Maki Yasuomi (Izumi) called for the seizure of Korea, Manchuria, and adjacent areas in order to "restore Japan's imperial authority to what it had been before the Heijō [Nara] period." Hirano Kuniomi wrote in the early 1860s that Japan "must reconquer Korea and restore the prefecture of Mimana" on the peninsula as the first step toward global hegemony.[12]

Restorationists such as Yoshida were inspired by both the Mito school of Neo-Confucianism, which preached "reverence for the emperor and the expulsion of the barbarians" (*sonnō jōi*), and the school of national learning (*kokugaku*), which asserted the divine origin and superiority of the Japanese race. In a period of growing internal and external crisis, Yoshida and fellow loyalists called for return to ancient Japanese tradition—a mythical golden age, which existed in remote antiquity and during which Japan, under the personal rule of the divine emperor, held sway not only over its homeland but also beyond the seas. Politically, Yoshida represented the loyalist samurai throughout Japan, whose cause was championed chiefly by Chōshū in this period. Their call for continental expansion was a corollary to their call for the restoration of imperial rule at home in Japan.

10. Yoshida Shōin, *Yoshida Shōin zenshū* (Complete works of Yoshida Shōin), vol. 1, 122, 350–351; Yoshi S. Kuno, *Japanese Expansion on the Asian Continent*, vol. 2, 354–355.
11. Yoshida, *Shōin zenshū*, vol. 6, 11, 50; Kikuda Sadao, *Sei-Kan ron no shinsō to sono eikyō* (The truth about the sei-Kan controversy and its effect), 18–19.
12. Mukai, "Shina keiryakuron," pt. 1, 24.

An important figure among the conservative proponents of continental expansion was Yamada Hōkoku, a noted Confucian scholar-administrator from Bitchū. In the late 1850s Yamada advocated military expeditions to Korea, Manchuria, and Taiwan, to be undertaken by leading domains such as Satsuma and Chōshū under overall bakufu supervision. In 1861, upon hearing the news of the resurgence of the Taipings in China and the Anglo-French seizure of Peking the previous autumn, Yamada recommended a three-pronged invasion of China and Korea before a new conqueror appeared in China. The northern and southern armies of the proposed expeditionary forces, said Yamada, would take Korea and Taiwan, while the central army would invade the Chinese mainland from Shantung. The entire expedition would be organized with troops contributed by various domains, with the bakufu supplying only military inspectors; one-third of all territory seized by them should be surrendered to the bakufu.[13] The following year, when the bakufu began to view the rising power of Satsuma in national politics with alarm, Yamada proposed that the bakufu deal with this potentially dangerous situation by ordering Satsuma to send expeditions to Taiwan and other southern islands.[14] Mori Sukenobu, a traditional military science instructor of Zeze, a small *fudai* (hereditary) fief in Ōmi, wrote in the early 1860s that the bakufu should undertake an invasion of China as a "strategy of averting internal crisis by an overseas campaign" *(kōgai naikyū no jutsu)*. Since Japan was not strong enough to launch such an operation independently, Mori made the remarkable suggestion that the bakufu secure British support for the project under false pretense of surrender to the British, against whom it should turn as soon as it became strong enough![15]

The ideological background of these men was predominantly Confucian. They represented the small or medium domains and fiefs ruled by the *fudai* daimyo, who had tradi-

13. Yamada Hōkoku, *Yamada Hōkoku zenshū* (Complete works of Yamada Hōkoku), vol. 3, 222–223.
14. *Ibid.*, 223–224.
15. Mukai, "Shina keiryakuron," pt. 2, *Shirin* 26.1 (June 1941), 106.

tionally manned the top echelons of the bakufu bureaucracy. While not unaware of the danger of Western
encroachment facing Japan, these men were concerned
immediately with the survival of the bakufu and the preservation of the status quo. Willing to accept accommodation
with Western countries as a matter of expediency, not of
conviction, they wished to utilize whatever advantages ac-
crued from such accommodation to strengthen the bakufu
against its domestic foes. Their call for continental expansion, invariably to be undertaken by potential rivals or
enemies of the bakufu, represented the position of conservatives with a vested interest in the Tokugawa system who
tended to seek adventures abroad as a means of averting or
coping with internal threats.

Hashimoto Sanai, a brilliant student of the West and
political activist from Echizen, was a representative figure
among the reformist advocates of continental expansion. In
1857 Hashimoto wrote to a friend that it was unlikely that
Japan could survive as an independent country in the modern world unless it strengthened itself by annexing Korea,
parts of Manchuria and maritime Siberia, and even parts of
the North American and Indian continents. Since Japan was
too weak to challenge the Western powers militarily, it
would be impossible to achieve such objectives unless it allied itself with one of the two leading powers, Britain and
Russia. Predicting an eventual Anglo-Russian confrontation in East Asia, Hashimoto argued that Japan ally itself
with Russia because the latter was a close neighbor and
"more trustworthy" than Britain.[16]

Hashimoto was neither a radical loyalist seeking overthrow of the bakufu and the restoration of imperial rule
nor a conservative defending the status quo. Intellectually,
he was a product of late Tokugawa Western studies (*yōgaku*),

16. Hashimoto Sanai, *Hashimoto Keigaku zenshū* (Complete works of Hashimoto
Sanai), vol. 1, 552–554; Conroy, "Japan's Asiatic Expansion," 33–34; George M.
Wilson, "The Bakumatsu Intellectual in Action: Hashimoto Sanai in the Political
Crisis of 1858," in Albert M. Craig and Donald H. Shively, eds., *Personality in
Japanese History*, 245–246.

convinced that Japan must modernize and strengthen itself
by adopting Western science and technology. Politically, he
championed the cause of enlightened bakufu officials and
"reforming lords," who sought to restructure the bakufu as
a more representative and efficient national coalition in
which the shogun would share power with the leading
daimyo in the country.[17] Hashimoto and like-minded reformists supported the opening of the country because they
realized that exclusionism was not only dangerous and impossible but an absurd and unwise policy in a changing
world. Their call for continental expansion, visionary as it
may have seemed at that time, was not inspired by a dream
of restoring Japan's "ancient glory" or by a narrow desire
for the preservation of the bakufu. It stemmed from the
belief that continental expansion was essential for the enhancement of Japan's national strength and necessary for its
survival in a world dominated by predatory powers. Theirs
was an incipient form of the doctrine of "a rich country and
a strong army" (*fukoku kyōhei*), which was to become Japan's
supreme goal during the Meiji period.

With the possible exception of Yamada, none of these
men was directly responsible for or involved in the formulation of bakufu policy. Nor was any of their proposals or
ideas immediately incorporated into an official policy.
Nonetheless their views were of historical significance. They
were influential figures, widely known and respected not
only within their own domains or circles but throughout
the country. Yoshida was one of the most influential men in
the restoration movement during its early stage. Although
he was executed by the bakufu at age twenty-nine, during
the Ansei Purge of 1859, he left a lasting imprint in the
minds of his famous disciples of Chōshū: Kusaka Genzui,
Takasugi Shinsaku, Katsura Kogorō (Kido Takayoshi), Itō
Hirobumi, Yamagata Aritomo, and Inoue Kaoru. While
Kusaka and Takasugi died on the eve of imperial restoration, the others all became top leaders in the new regime

17. For Hashimoto's career and thought, see Wilson, "The Bakumatsu Intellectual," 234–263.

and members of the oligarchy that was to guide Meiji Japan.[18]

Hashimoto was no anti-bakufu radical. But because of his reformist activities he, too, became a victim of the Ansei Purge, at the early age of twenty-five. Despite his youth, Hashimoto was effective and influential during his meteoric career as a political agent of his lord, Matsudaira Yoshinaga, ruler of Echizen. A collateral Tokugawa relative and leading daimyo, Yoshinaga was a major figure representing the reformist group in bakumatsu politics and served as the shogun's supreme political advisor during 1862–1863.[19] After his death, Hashimoto's influence continued through the activities of important personalities from Echizen, including Yoshinaga. Moreover, one may say that, except for his choice of Russia as Japan's future ally, in spirit and rationale it was Hashimoto's version of continental expansionism that was pursued by the Japanese government during the Meiji period.

In terms of immediate impact upon bakufu policymakers, Yamada occupied an important position. Although less well known in history than Yoshida or Hashimoto, Yamada had direct access to the bakufu leadership as a trusted retainer and mentor of his lord, Itakura Katsukiyo, daimyo of Bitchū. From the late 1850s until the fall of the bakufu in 1868, Itakura continually held top posts in the bakufu administration—including the highest post of senior councilor (*rōjū*) twice, from April 1862 through September 1864 and from April 1865 through February 1868. Yamada served as Itakura's personal aide and confidential adviser throughout these years.[20] In 1861, when Itakura was the bakufu superintendent for temple and shrine affairs, he proposed expeditions to China and Korea precisely along the line suggested by Yamada, in order to "transform

    18. For Yoshida's political thought and his role in the restoration movement, see Albert M. Craig, *Chōshū in the Meiji Restoration*, 156–164; H. D. Harootunian, *Toward Restoration*, 184–245.
    19. For Matsudaira Yoshinaga's political role in this period, see W. G. Beasley, *The Meiji Restoration*, 129–139; Wilson, "The Bakumatsu Intellectual," 234–263.
    20. For Yamada's career, see Yamada, *Yamada Hōkoku zenshū*, vol. 1, 1–136.

internal dissension into external conquest."[21] As will be shown, Itakura was subsequently involved in projects concerning Korea.

The principal historical significance of the late 1850s and the early 1860s in the rise of Japanese interest in continental Asia lies in the fact that the major schools of continental expansionism emerged and crystalized during this period. Of particular interest is the fact that, despite their varying intellectual and ideological backgrounds and their opposing political positions at home, these early proponents of Japanese continental expansion held identical or similar views and attitudes toward the outside world. Although they differed from one another in their fundamental attitude toward the West, they all recognized the superiority of its power and accepted accommodation, if not cooperation, with the West. While they retained some traditional deference toward China and even desired some form of Sino-Japanese cooperation in meeting the Western threat, China generally suffered a marked decline in their estimation. In their thinking, areas such as Korea, Manchuria, and Taiwan became either immediate or potential objects of Japanese expansion.

It is important to note that, except for the reformists, the fear of Western aggression, urgent though it was, was not the only, or even the principal, factor that inspired expansionist sentiment among the Japanese in this period. The interest in China and Korea on the part of the restorationists and the conservatives, whose views were still largely parochial, should be termed a form of foreign adventurism in a time of domestic uncertainty, rather than a well-articulated expansionism. It stemmed, as we have seen, from the desire to use military action against China or Korea, usually to be undertaken at the expense of their domestic rivals, chiefly to safeguard or advance their particular political interests at home. However, fear of Western aggression was definitely the principal factor with the re-

21. Ienaga Saburō, et al., eds., *Kindai Nihon no sōten* (Controversies in modern Japan), vol. 1, 205.

formists. With a better comprehension of the Western world, they apparently believed that an undertaking abroad would provide an opportunity to achieve national unity at home in the face of the Western threat. Beyond that, they believed that expansion in the neighboring Asian continent was essential if Japan was to acquire the wealth and strength necessary to survive in the hazardous new international environment dominated by the Western powers. These twin causes of expansionism—fear of Western aggression and domestic political considerations—were to continue to influence Japanese policy toward China and Korea during the decades ahead.

THE BAKUMATSU *SEI-KAN RON*

The early 1860s were a turbulent time in Japan, as elsewhere in East Asia. The period began ominously with the assassination of Ii Naosuke, in March 1860, in retaliation for the Ansei Purge of the previous year. One of the most powerful of the *fudai* daimyo, Ii had been named great councilor (*tairō*), the highest post in the bakufu administration and filled only in times of national emergency, to guide the country through the stormy opposition to the opening of ports to the treaty powers. Determined to shore up the sagging authority of the bakufu and to maintain the traditional *fudai* control of the bakufu bureaucracy, Ii ruthlessly imprisoned, executed, or punished critics of bakufu policy—including radical loyalists, who opposed the opening of the country, and reformists, who supported Hitotsubashi Yoshinobu as shogunal heir against the bakufu's choice of the younger Tokugawa Yoshitomi. Following Ii's assassination, anti-bakufu and anti-foreign agitation grew in intensity in Japan, leading to further violence and finally to armed clashes with the treaty powers. These and other events at home and abroad, including the Anglo-French invasion of north China, combined to deepen the sense of crisis that contributed to the transition from the second to the third phase in the rise of Japanese interest in the continent.

Important changes marked the third phase, which began in 1863. One was the fact that China and Korea were no longer objects of abstract thought or idle speculation by men without official responsibility. They became subjects of serious policy debate by men in responsible positions in the bakufu and the domains. Measures were proposed and, in some cases, concrete decisions were made with regard to Korea. Most remarkable were the efforts of the bakufu to establish direct contact with the Korean government; this represented a major departure from the traditional conduct of Korean relations through Tsushima. Although the term *"sei-Kan ron"* usually refers to the celebrated Korean controversy within the Meiji government in 1873, it is used here to signify arguments advanced and measures proposed in Japan with regard to Korea in this period, representing in many respects similar views and motives to those behind the *sei-Kan* debate of 1873.

The news of the Anglo-French capture of Peking prompted Yamada and Itakura to propose continental expeditions in 1861, including an invasion of Korea. In the same year another incident created an even more direct and sustained concern with Korea in Japan. On March 13, 1861, the *Possadonick*, a Russian warship commanded by Captain Birileff, reached Tsushima without warning. Birileff told the local officials that his ship was in need of repair and requested permission to anchor. Granting the request reluctantly, the Tsushima authorities immediately reported the matter to the bakufu. Meanwhile the Russians built permanent shore facilities and several more Russian ships visited the island. Moreover, the Russians demanded permanent lease of the land for a naval base. In response to Tsushima's repeated appeals for aid and instructions, the bakufu dispatched Oguri Tadamasa, superintendent of foreign affairs (*gaikoku bugyō*), to the island to investigate the incident and to effect the withdrawal of the Russians. Oguri and his party reached

Tsushima on June 14; they spent the next two weeks consulting with local officials and negotiating with the Russians, all to no avail.[22]

While the matter dragged on, the British—who had for some time been thinking of leasing the island themselves — stepped in. On August 14 and 15, the British minister to Edo, Sir Rutherford Alcock, accompanied by Rear Admiral Sir James Hope, commander-in-chief of the East Indies and China Station, conferred with bakufu Senior Councilor Andō Nobumasa and formally offered British assistance in ejecting the Russians from Tsushima.[23] Fearing that a formal Japanese request for or acceptance of British assistance might invite Russian protest, Andō simply "acquiesced" to the British offer.[24] Two British men-of-war went to Tsushima in late August. The commanders of the British ships conferred and exchanged gifts with Tsushima officials. Impressed by this demonstration of Anglo-Japanese solidarity, the Russians abandoned their plan and withdrew from the island in September.

The *Possadonick* incident caused panic in Tsushima and alarmed the bakufu. It starkly reminded them of their inability to fend off any serious Western naval challenge. Although the immediate threat receded, the fact that Japan had to rely on the British in ejecting the Russians was hardly reassuring. The danger remained that Tsushima might be seized by either Russia or Britain, almost at will. The situation was even more alarming to the Tsushima authorities for their domain was faced with serious economic difficulties at this time. The trade with Korea, the island's principal industry, had declined steadily since the early nineteenth century, causing corresponding deterioration in the island's economy. Since the opening of Japan, increasing foreign trade at nearby Nagasaki reduced the importance of

22. For details concerning the *Possadonick* incident, see Hino Seizaburō, *Bakumatsu ni okeru Tsushima to Ei-Ro* (Tsushima, Britain, and Russia in the bakumatsu period).

23. Grace Fox, *Britain and Japan, 1858–1883*, 219–232.

24. Kokubu Taneyuki, ed., *Gyosui jitsuroku* (Correspondence between Lord Itakura of Bitchū and his retainers), vol. 1, 99–100.

the Korean trade to the rest of Japan and caused further economic dislocation in Tsushima. It was therefore impossible for Tsushima to develop a significant defense capability against Western naval intrusion, which would have been beyond its meager resources even under the best of circumstances.

Opinion within the Tsushima government was sharply divided as to how to meet this dual crisis. Sasu Iori, leader of the *han* government and its resident representative in Edo, had long maintained that, since Tsushima's problems such as defense against Western naval intrusion were clearly of national magnitude and beyond its independent capacity to solve, the island should be taken over by the bakufu; its daimyo, Lord Sō, should be compensated with the grant of another fief. Prompted by the *Possadonick* incident, Sasu renewed his proposal. In September 1861 he submitted, in the name of his daimyo, a petition to the bakufu requesting that the bakufu take over Tsushima and that the Sō family and their retainers be transferred to another fief of equivalent size in Kyūshū. Although the petition was denied, it found many supporters among bakufu officials who believed that Tsushima, like Ezo, should be placed under direct bakufu administration and that a treaty port should be established on the island—a lesser evil than its possible seizure by a Western power.[25]

Sasu's proposal as well as his other controversial activities, including a plot that resulted in the deposing of Yoshisato, the young heir-designate of Lord Sō, aroused strong opposition within Tsushima. The opposition was led by Ōshima Tomonojō, a high-ranking *han* official and Tsushima's leading loyalist. Accusing Sasu and his men of scuttling the island that had been the home of their ancestors for six centuries, Ōshima argued that the island should and could be defended with the help of the bakufu and the powerful domains, such as Chōshū. Its economic health, he argued, could be restored through the expansion of Korean trade

25. Hino, *Tsushima to Ei-Ro*, 91–92, 198–200.

and the opening of trade with China. To achieve these
goals, Ōshima and his supporters had to wrest control of
the *han* government from Sasu and his men. For support in
their internal power struggle within Tsushima, Ōshima and
his followers turned to Chōshū, Tsushima's powerful next-
door neighbor, whose ruling house was related by marriage
to the house of Sō.[26]

With its geographical proximity to Korea, Chōshū had a
long history of relations with Korea. Direct intercourse had
ceased in the eighteenth century, but interest in the peninsula had survived in the domain and it began to rise again
in the mid-nineteenth century. It was Yoshida Shōin's idea
that Chōshū should play the leading role in Japanese expansion onto the Korean peninsula and beyond, as evidenced in his call for the colonization of Ullŭng Island. In
1858—when he was in prison in Chōshū under bakufu orders for his attempt to stow away with the Perry mission to
America—Yoshida wrote twice to his disciple, Kido
Takayoshi (known as Katsura Kogorō at this time), in Edo,
asking him to seek bakufu authorization for Chōshū to undertake the project. Working with his friend, Ōmura Masujirō (known as Murata Zōroku at this time), Kido succeeded
in winning support for the project from key Chōshū and
bakufu officials. But it was not until August 1860—some
nine months after Yoshida's execution—that Kido was able
to approach the bakufu for formal approval. In a petition
addressed to bakufu Senior Councilor Kuze Hirochika,
Kido asserted that Ullung Island belonged to Japan rather
than Korea and that its immediate exploration and development by Japan was essential to prevent it from "falling
into the hands of some Western power, which would pose a
serious threat not only to Chōshū but to all of Japan."[27] Although Kido was unable to obtain bakufu approval and the
project was shelved indefinitely, his interest in Korea remained undiminished.

26. Ōe Shinobu, *Kido Takayoshi* (Kido Takayoshi), 106–107; Kido Takayoshi,
Kido Takayoshi ibunshū (Miscellaneous letters of Kido Takayoshi), 9–10.
27. Kikuda, *Sei-Kan ron no shinsō*, 19.

Ōshima and his followers found in Kido, a fellow loyalist and a leading figure in the restoration movement in Chō-shū, a sympathetic supporter of their cause. During the *Possadonick* incident, concerned over the fate of Tsushima, Kido petitioned the Chōshū authorities to send arms and provisions to the island. In response to the appeal from Ōshima and his men for help, in 1862 Kido secured for them the influential support of his lord, Mōri Takachika, who in turn was instrumental in obtaining the bakufu's decisive intervention in favor of Ōshima and his party in Tsushima's internal power struggle. In early 1863 the bakufu ordered the retirement of Sō Yoshikazu as daimyo of Tsushima and the investiture of his son, Yoshisato, as the island's new ruler. Sasu was forced to commit suicide, and his men were ousted from the Tsushima government.[28] In the process Kido and Ōshima became lifelong friends. The two were to work closely together in the formulation of Japanese policy toward Korea in the years ahead.

Having installed themselves in power in Tsushima, Ōshima and his men set out to achieve their next goals: strengthening Tsushima's defenses against the Western threat and solving its economic problems. Again they worked closely with Kido. Kido and Ōshima may have preferred to have the bakufu take over the entire burden of the island's defense. Short of that, they wanted large-scale military and financial aid from the bakufu in building up Tsushima's virtually non-existent defenses. The expansion of the Korean trade, envisioned by Ōshima as a solution to Tsushima's economic problems, would require the negotiation of a new trade agreement with Korea. But this was plainly beyond Tsushima's ability as a semi-tributary and suppliant of Korea, especially at a time when isolationist Korea showed no inclination to change its existing relations with Japan. Here, too, Tsushima would need strong support from the bakufu or some powerful domains. It is not clear precisely what kind of action Kido and Ōshima contemplated toward

28. *Shōgiku Kido kō den* (A biography of Kido Takayoshi), vol. 1, 162–176.

Korea at this time. At any rate, in early 1863 they launched an active campaign to win bakufu approval and support for their plans.[29]

One of the first men they approached was Yamada Hōkoku, personal aide of Senior Councilor Itakura. As we have seen, Yamada repeatedly recommended Japanese invasion of Korea. His advice to Kido and Ōshima was entirely consistent with his earlier proposals: Tsushima should undertake an expedition to Korea with the help of Satsuma and Chōshū. So anxious was Yamada to convince Kido and Ōshima that he reportedly drew up detailed plans for an invasion of Korea.[30] Encouraged by this enthusiastic response from a man close to the top bakufu leadership and acting at least in part on his advice, Ōshima submitted on behalf of his daimyo a petition to the bakufu for an expedition to Korea. Ōshima argued that, if the bakufu, in the name of its long-standing friendship toward Korea, "helped" Korea before the latter was invaded by the Western barbarians, "Korea would surely be submissive. If Korea did not become submissive, then, even if the bakufu used its military might, there would be no criticism against it, as there had been against Hideyoshi."[31]

Kido and Ōshima also contacted Katsu Yasuyoshi, brevet superintendent of the bakufu navy. Born the son of a *hatamoto* (bannerman) of modest rank and an outstanding student of the West, at this time Katsu was Japan's leading naval authority. One of the ablest bakufu officials, it was by sheer intelligence and ability that Katsu had risen to top positions within the bakufu administration, positions which until then had been reserved for men of nobler birth. In 1860 he visited the United States as first officer of the bakufu warship *Kanrin-maru*, which escorted the first Japanese embassy to Washington. In the 1860s Katsu was probably the man in Japan best informed about the West. Loyal to the bakufu, he was an enlightened official, sym-

29. Kikuda, *Sei-Kan ron no shinsō*, 22.
30. Yamada, *Yamada Hōkoku zenshū*, vol. 1, 79.
31. *Ibid.*, vol. 3, 233–241.

pathetic toward reformers such as the late Hashimoto Sanai and his lord, Matsudaira Yoshinaga. Katsu was convinced that Japan could not survive as an independent nation unless it modernized and strengthened itself by adopting Western science and technology. Specifically, he believed that the key to Japan's national survival lay in the expansion of its naval power.[32]

Katsu had been deeply disturbed by the *Possadonick* incident. He feared not only the seizure of Tsushima by Britain or Russia, but the possibility that Korea might be seized by one or more Western powers, which would seriously threaten the security and independence of Japan. He shared with other officials, such as Senior Councilor Itakura, the suspicion that both Britain and Russia wanted Tsushima as a base for future operations against Korea. His concern was heightened by the fact that the Russians intimated that they were planning an expedition to Korea during their occupation of Tsushima. Before departing from Tsushima, the Russians requested Korean-speaking interpreters from the Tsushima authorities.[33] On October 8, 1862, three days after his appointment as brevet naval superintendent, at a high-level conference attended by top bakufu leaders including Matsudaira Yoshinaga, then supreme political adviser to the shogun, Katsu expounded his views on the question of naval expansion. Since both Britain and Russia coveted Tsushima as a naval base, he said, the bakufu should take over the island and establish a trade port there, in order to forestall its seizure by either of these powers. This, he explained, would lead not only to the opening of relations with Korea and China but would contribute to the strengthening of Japan's naval power.[34] In his new position Katsu immediately proposed the expansion of the bakufu naval training facilities and the construction of a new naval base on Tsushima. He also recommended that

32. Katsu Yasuyoshi, *Katsu Kaishū zenshū* (Complete works of Katsu Kaishū), vol. 18, 3–4.

33. Katsu Yasuyoshi, *Kaikoku kigen* (Origins of the opening of the country), vol. 2, 100.

34. See n. 32.

Japan establish naval bases in Korea and China at some future date.[35]

On June 13, 1863, Kido and Ōshima called on Katsu to seek the latter's support for their plans. Katsu needed no persuasion. Instead, he expounded his own views with regard to Tsushima and Korea. Asian countries, Katsu told his visitors, could not resist the Europeans because their plans and actions were on a small scale, and none of them had long-range plans. Unless Japan took the lead and sent ships to these countries "to persuade their rulers to form an alliance, expand their navies, help one another, and pursue learning together, these countries would not be able to escape European domination." Katsu's own plans were to work for a naval alliance with Korea and then to extend it to include China. Kido and Ōshima expressed their wholehearted agreement.[36]

Three days later, on June 16, Katsu submitted his proposal to the bakufu councilors, including Itakura Katsukiyo, for immediate consideration. Although the initial response was favorable, opposition subsequently developed, blocking early approval of Katsu's proposal.[37] Meanwhile, Katsu lobbied actively for Tsushima's appeal for military and economic aid. Apparently as a result of the efforts by Katsu, Yamada, and others, the bakufu announced on July 19 that it would grant 30,000 *koku* of rice in economic aid to Tsushima every year. It also promised a loan of warships at some future date. The grant was made ostensibly in support of Tsushima's preparations for a Korean expedition. The following day Senior Councilor Itakura issued an order directing Katsu to "proceed to Tsushima as soon as preparations can be completed, in order to investigate and report in detail the conditions in Korea."[38]

Other official business constantly demanded Katsu's time and attention, preventing him from making the proposed

35. Katsu, *Kaishū zenshū*, vol. 11, 316.
36. *Ibid.*, vol. 18, 50.
37. *Ibid.*, 51, 58–59.
38. *Ibid.*, 68–69.

trip to Tsushima. But he remained in close contact with Kido and Ōshima, who apparently kept pressing him for action. Katsu used every opportunity to promote his project, and once he apparently obtained authorization to lead a mission to Korea. In June 1864 he was promoted to the full superintendency of the navy. However, his project suffered a major setback in late July when Senior Councilor Itakura, its principal backer, resigned from office. The outbreak of war between the bakufu and Chōshū in late August virtually killed the project, although Ōshima apparently remained in contact with Katsu. The final blow came at the end of that year when Katsu was relieved of his post on the charge that the Kōbe naval training center under his supervision was sheltering anti-bakufu radicals, such as Sakamoto Ryōma of Tosa.[39] Faced with mounting military and financial problems of its own, the bakufu was unable to deliver in full its promised military and economic aid to Tsushima. In May 1865 Katsu ruefully recorded his frustration and disappointment in his diary: "It was my plan to develop relations first with Korea and then with Peking. I recommended this three or four years ago. Last year I was ordered to go to Korea but was unable to do so because of the change of senior councilors."[40] Katsu apparently was referring to Itakura's resignation.

Thus the Korean enterprise which Katsu and his collaborators set out to undertake never fully developed, and it is difficult to determine precisely what their intentions were with regard to Korea. However, certain inferences as to their motives may be made. Of those directly involved in or actively supporting the plan, Kido and Ōshima obviously represented the restorationist position. Both men regarded the eventual conquest or subjugation of Korea as a corollary to the restoration of imperial rule that they sought at home. It was imperative, in their view, to forestall the seizure of Korea by a Western power until Japan itself was able to establish influence in or control over the peninsula. Beyond

39. Yamaji Aizan, *Katsu Kaishū* (Katsu Kaishū), 171–172.
40. Katsu, *Kaishū zenshū*, vol. 18, 256.

this, each man acted in the immediate interest of his *han*. In the proposed expedition, which he apparently visualized as one in which Chōshū would play the leading role, Kido saw an opportunity to enhance his domain's influence and prestige in the anti-Western exclusionist movement at home and thereby to strengthen its position in the domestic power struggle against the bakufu.[41] The project may have been doubly tempting because it could be undertaken with large-scale logistic support from the bakufu and other domains. For Ōshima's Tsushima, facing the threat of Western intrusion from without and economic collapse from within, only an undertaking of national magnitude, such as an invasion of Korea, could provide solutions to its many problems and ensure its economic survival.

Itakura and Yamada represented conservative bakufu officials striving to preserve the status quo. Whatever undertaking they contemplated with regard to Korea was one that would mobilize the resources of Satsuma or Chōshū, not those of the bakufu. Such an undertaking would deflate the rampant exclusionist agitation, which was creating difficulties in the bakufu's relations with the treaty powers. More importantly, it would reduce or eliminate a grave internal threat facing the bakufu by diverting the attention and energies of its two most powerful potential enemies at home. Even if not successful, a Korean expedition would exhaust Chōshū and Satsuma militarily and materially and reduce or destroy their ability to challenge the bakufu at home.[42]

Katsu was motivated largely by his broad, reformist concern for the future of Japan. No available evidence suggests that he subscribed to the chauvinistic views of the restorationists concerning Japanese-Korean relations. As a loyal bakufu official, undoubtedly he would have welcomed a move that might weaken domestic political opposition to the bakufu. As an informed student of the West, he cer-

41. Ōe, *Kido Takayoshi*, 107.
42. Mukai, "Shina keiryakuron," pt. 2, 106–107.

tainly would have welcomed any measure that might deflate xenophobic agitation against the opening of Japan to the Western countries. But the most important objective that he sought through his proposed Korean enterprise seems to have been the expansion of the bakufu navy, which he obviously regarded as the most important shield protecting Japan from external threats. While Katsu freely used terms such as *"sei-Kan"* (conquer Korea) in reference to his Korean plans, it appears that what he meant was a mission to seek an alliance with Korea, not "conquest" or "subjugation." But at the same time, he definitely envisioned Japan as the leader or senior partner in such an alliance, which eventually would include China. However enlightened his motives and intentions, Katsu's plans, if implemented, would have most likely resulted in expansionistic activities toward Korea and China.

Though never fully defined or developed, the Katsu project was highly significant in several respects. It showed that Japan's growing interest in the Asian continent had gone beyond the stage of abstract speculation or idle discussion by men not involved in governmental decision-making. It reached a point where it produced a concrete proposal for action with regard to Korea that was seriously debated by the top bakufu leadership. Moreover, certain preliminary steps for implementing that decision apparently were taken. This was the first instance in the evolution of Japanese policy toward China and Korea in modern times in which action was authorized or taken by the central authorities. Another significant aspect was that the project combined the diverse and opposing interests of different schools of continental expansionism in Japan in this period. The restorationists, the conservatives, and the reformists were bedfellows here, each with a different dream.

Interrupted by the civil war between the bakufu and Chōshū, this incipient partnership in continental expansion crumbled, but the conditions under which it was conceived remained essentially unchanged. Once the war was brought to conclusion, the bakufu would make another and more serious attempt to use Korea to strengthen its weakened position at home.

ABORTED BAKUFU INTERVENTION IN KOREA

Throughout the years 1864–1866 Japan continued to seethe with internal and external turmoil. The *sonnō-jōi* movement gained momentum and intensity after the late 1850s and climaxed in the summer of 1864. In August 1864 Chōshū, the leader of the movement, staged a putsch in Kyoto in an attempt to regain influence at the imperial court, where moderate elements prevailed. The attempt was roundly defeated by the bakufu with the support of the leading domains, including Satsuma, which had learned a lesson in the folly of exclusionism from its own defeat in a short war with Britain the previous year. Chōshū suffered another sobering setback the following month, when it was attacked by a fleet of British, French, American, and Dutch ships in retaliation for the Chōshū attacks on allied shipping the year before.

Anxious to regain some of its lost authority and prestige by "chastising" Chōshū in its moment of weakness, the bakufu launched a punitive expedition against the recalcitrant domain in the fall of 1864. Although the expedition brought the bakufu limited success, it resulted in the establishment of a revolutionary leadership in Chōshū; the leadership rejected the terms of the settlement with the bakufu, including surrender of some Chōshū territory. Meanwhile the bakufu's high-handed attempt to reestablish semi-feudal control over Japan antagonized other leading domains. A crucial result of this was the secret pact of mutual support between Chōshū and Satsuma, signed in March 1866. The alliance of the two most powerful *tozama* (outside) domains, which had been at odds with each other in national politics in the past, virtually sealed the fate of the bakufu. Despite this altered situation, the bakufu launched a new expedition against Chōshū the same month. The outcome was a military disaster for the bakufu. In this predicament, the bakufu found young Shogun Iemochi's untimely death in August 1866 a blessing in disguise. In the name of the national emergency created by the shogunal death, the bakufu obtained a special edict ordering an immediate cessation of hostilities from the imperial court. Armed with the edict, Katsu, now restored to official grace for his talent, negotiated an unconditional cease-fire with Chōshū, narrowly averting, at least for the time being, further catastrophe for the bakufu.[43]

Meanwhile, 1866 saw Korea embroiled in domestic turmoil and foreign entanglement. The execution that year of nine French Roman Catholic missionaries by the Korean authorities led to the retaliatory French invasion of Kanghwa Island in October. The *General Sherman* incident in August 1866 developed into a protracted dispute with the United States, and possibly with Britain as well. From foreign sources in Japan, the bakufu authorities learned of the French expedition and the *Sherman* incident. In the wake of the failure of the French expedition and of the unsuccessful American efforts to ascertain the *Sherman*'s fate, rumors were rife in China and Japan: a new expedition would be undertaken by France and the United States the following spring, and Britain might join in such a venture.[44]

In the midst of all this, following Iemochi's death, the shogunate remained vacant for four months. Although Hitotsubashi Yoshinobu, the erstwhile shogunal candidate of the reformists, immediately succeeded Iemochi as the head of the house of Tokugawa, at first he refused to accept the post of shogun. Not until January 1867 did Yoshinobu accept formal investiture as the new shogun.

Within weeks of his investiture, Yoshinobu made a decision with regard to Korea that had no precedent in the history of Japanese-Korean relations since the founding of the bakufu: to send a high-level bakufu mission to Korea. Os-

43. On the bakufu expeditions to Chōshū, see Craig, *Chōshū in the Meiji Restoration*, 236–250.
44. TNS, vol. 1, 104–106.

tensibly the purpose of the proposed mission was to be mediation of Korea's disputes with France and the United States. Yoshinobu announced the decision personally at a meeting with French Minister Leon Roches at Ōsaka on March 12. Roches raised no objection. The following day, however, when the bakufu senior councilors called on him for further consultation, it became apparent that Roches had had second thoughts. Referring to Korea's tributary ties with China, Roches said that the French minister in Peking was holding talks with the Chinese authorities on the Korean question. Should China decide to intervene in the matter, the French dispute with Korea would properly become a matter that should be settled between the Chinese authorities and the French minister in Peking. In such an event, he added, Japanese mediation would be of little value.[45]

Despite Roches' discouraging reaction, the bakufu decided to proceed with its plans. On March 15, it appointed Superintendent of Foreign Affairs Hirayama Takatada to head the proposed mission to Korea. A month later, Koga Kin'ichirō, an inspector, was named Hirayama's deputy; nine junior officials were assigned to the mission.[46] At this point, the bakufu authorities received from Tsushima the Korean government note containing an account of the French invasion of Kanghwa Island the previous October. While warning Japan against similar Western armed intrusion, the Korean government made no request for aid or mediation.[47] Still refusing to be discouraged, the bakufu senior councilors wrote a letter to Robert B. Van Valkenburg, American minister to Japan, informing him of the bakufu's decision to mediate between Korea and the United States. Conveying the shogun's deep distress over the news of the "outrages" committed by Korea, Japan's neighbor, against citizens of the United States, Japan's friend, they

45. *Ibid.*, 107–108.
46. *Ibid.*, 109–111; Choe, *Rule of the Taewŏn'gun*, 139–142.
47. For the text of the Korean note, see ISN-KJ, 3/10/15; KJS, 3.80a–81b; TNS, vol. 1, 114.

told the American minister: "Should Korea, by Japanese influence, abandon its mistaken ways and sue for peace, it is hoped that the United States would bury its grudges and establish friendly relations with Korea." The American minister responded favorably, but it was not until the end of that year that the bakufu received a formal note from American Secretary of State Seward accepting its offer.[48]

Upon receiving his appointment, Hirayama announced his intention to go not only to Pusan, but to the Korean capital, if necessary, in order to accomplish his mission. Expressing the view that, unless the bakufu demonstrated its might as well as its goodwill, it might not be able to achieve its objectives in Korea, Hirayama requested a number of warships and two battalions of troops to escort his party. He also requested the preparation of suitable lodging facilities at both Hyōgo and Edo for Korean envoys who might arrive, should his mission prove successful. Except for the troop escort, all his requests were granted.[49]

Meanwhile, under bakufu instructions, in August, Tsushima sent a note to the Korean government to inform it of the bakufu decision. The note, addressed to the Korean vice minister of rites from Lord Sō, stated that, out of his sincere desire to see Korea remain at peace, the shogun was sending envoys to explain the "prevailing state of affairs in the world."[50] Preparations for the mission proceeded smoothly, but its departure was delayed by Hirayama's involvement in other official business.

The Korean officials at Pusan at first refused to receive Sō's note on the ground that there was no precedent for a bakufu mission to Korea, but they relented and forwarded the note to Seoul. In September they informed the Tsushima authorities that the Korean government was grateful for the bakufu's goodwill; nevertheless it would not be able to receive the proposed Hirayama mission because it was preoccupied with "urgent domestic problems arising

48. Tyler Dennett, *Americans in Eastern Asia,* 433–434; TNS, vol. 1, 108–109.
49. TNS, vol. 1, 110–111.
50. *Ibid.,* 112; ISN-KJ, 4/10/1; KJS, 4.44b–45a.

from famine, epidemics, and Western invasion." The message was immediately forwarded to Senior Councilor Itakura. Although this put the bakufu authorities in an awkward position, it did not deter them. They announced that, "in view of the official understanding already reached with the United States government on the matter, the project cannot be cancelled merely because of a note from the Korean government." Hirayama, however, modified his earlier plans. He decided that, should the Korean officials at Pusan refuse to receive him, instead of forcing his way to Seoul, he would withdraw to Tsushima and take appropriate measures to insulate the island from any hostilities that might break out on the Korean peninsula. The departure of his mission was set for late November or early December.[51]

On November 9, however, Yoshinobu suddenly surrendered his political and administrative authority as shogun to the emperor; the latter accepted his resignation the following day. The imperial court was not able to take over the reins of government immediately, and the emperor ordered Yoshinobu to carry out all his duties as before, for the time being. It looked as if Hirayama's mission might be cancelled. But Ōshima Tomonojō memorialized the imperial court, on behalf of Tsushima, against the cancellation of the mission; he argued that, since Korea had been notified, the mission should not be cancelled merely for reasons of domestic political change. Yoshinobu memorialized the emperor for permission to proceed with the project, and he obtained imperial sanction on November 29.[52] Accordingly, Hirayama and his party left Edo on December 20 and reached Ōsaka on December 26. The following day Hirayama went to Kyoto to see Yoshinobu for further instructions. At this point civil war broke out between the former bakufu and the restorationist forces, preventing the mission from departing for Korea. In the midst of the military and political upheavals that ensued, the ill-fated mission was forgotten.

51. TNS, vol. 1, 115.
52. NGB, vol. 1, 67–69, 104–105.

The bakufu's aborted mission to Korea amounted to nothing more than an interesting episode in history. However, the great length to which the bakufu went to carry out its decision, in the face of discouragement and setbacks at a time of mounting internal crisis, suggests that there were compelling reasons behind the decision other than professed goodwill toward Korea. From their experience with the Western powers, the bakufu authorities were aware that, for their efforts to succeed, there had to be a minimum degree of accommodation by Korea with France and the United States. In concrete terms, this would have meant at least partial opening of the country to Western trade, not merely settlement of the immediate disputes. There was little likelihood at this time that Korea would make such accommodations. Why, then, did the bakufu authorities try so persistently to undertake an unprecedented diplomatic mission with little prospect of success?

Certainly, there was in Japan at this time fear that Korea might be seized by some Western power. This was particularly true of the domains close to Korea, such as Chōshū and Tsushima, whose security would be threatened immediately by the Western seizure or control of Korea. Russian intimation of its intentions toward Korea during the *Possadonick* incident was a reminder of this potential danger. The French expedition, though not successful, threatened to turn potential into reality. This was succinctly stated by Ōshima in his memorial on behalf of the Hirayama mission. He said: "In view of the fact that Korea is a country that either stands or falls with us, our imperial country cannot stand idly by when Korea is faced with mortal danger as it is today. Should these three powers [France, the United States, and Britain] jointly send an expedition to Korea, Korea would fall within weeks and the whole country would be seized by the barbarians. It is difficult to measure how dangerous this could be to our divine land."[53]

From the bakufu's standpoint, the Korean situation, seri-

53. *Ibid.*, 69–71.

ous as it was, presented only a remote danger, not an immediate threat. The situation at home was far graver. The disastrous outcome of the second Chōshū expedition revealed the bakufu's appalling weakness and did irreparable damage to its authority and prestige. Gone was its military power, which had commanded ready submission and obedience from all the daimyo in the land for more than two centuries. Britain, the leading treaty power, remained officially neutral in Japan's domestic power struggle, but its neutrality was colored increasingly by sympathy for the anti-bakufu forces led by Satsuma and Chōshū. France, on the other hand, was actively supporting the bakufu, while the United States remained friendly. It was at this critical moment, when the bakufu was at the nadir of its authority at home and prestige abroad, that Yoshinobu became the shogun in January 1867.

Born the son of the famous Tokugawa Nariaki, lord of Mito, in 1837, Yoshinobu was a man of superior intelligence. The youthful shogun gained considerable political experience as guardian for his predecessor, Iemochi. Apparently he had few illusions about the bakufu's chances of survival and accepted his lofty position with utmost reluctance. Having done so, however, Yoshinobu was determined to do everything in his power to strengthen the bakufu and to restore its authority. His decision to send an unprecedented mission to Korea, taken within weeks of his accession, undoubtedly was part of his overall program to strengthen the bakufu against its foes in Japan's deepening domestic power struggle. It seems that the responsibilities of the shogunate transformed, at least in part, a man who had been a defender of the reformists into a champion of conservative bakufu leadership. In his unprecedented diplomatic undertaking toward Korea, Yoshinobu was assisted by such men as Senior Councilor Itakura.

Successful diplomatic intervention in Korea would enhance the new shogun's authority and prestige at home and abroad. It would increase French and American goodwill and support for the bakufu. Growing British skepticism may have discouraged the bakufu from offering its good offices to Britain, despite the possibility that the latter might be involved in a dispute with Korea. But bakufu diplomatic success in Korea might change the British attitude and shift its support to the bakufu, which would go a long way toward strengthening its position at home. An aggressive diplomatic venture in Korea at this time seemed almost certain to win approval and support from all internal elements, friends and foes of the bakufu alike. If the venture led to a dispute with Korea—a distinct possibility in view of Korea's militant exclusionism—the bakufu could mobilize the resources of Satsuma, Chōshū, and other leading domains in the name of national unity to face an external crisis and thereby divert the ambitions and energies of these domains to adventures abroad. This was the principal reason the bakufu authorities refused to abandon the project, in spite of the deepening political crisis at home and even after Korea turned down the offer of mediation. With the fall of the bakufu, however, this situation ceased to exist. The project was briefly resurrected by Tsushima's efforts, but the island domain alone was not powerful or influential enough to ensure its execution, even had domestic upheaval not intervened.

Unlike the Katsu project, in which the interests of the restorationist, conservative, and reformist groups merged, if only temporarily, the Hirayama mission represented the political interests of the conservative bakufu leadership almost solely. In undertaking the project, Yoshinobu and his advisers had no apparent hostile or expansionistic designs toward Korea. They were motivated by the same political considerations for survival of the bakufu that inspired the conservative advocates of continental expansion. However, their project, if carried out, could have resulted in actions hostile to Korea. It can be said, therefore, that the Hirayama mission was in part a manifestation of the conservative version of late Tokugawa continental expansionism.

The Katsu project and the Hirayama mission, though aborted, confirm that all the major political forces in bakumatsu Japan, irrespective of their political interests and positions at home, shared the belief that Korea would have to be brought under Japanese influence or control if Japan were to be made safe from Western aggression. Even more interestingly, they confirm that opposing political forces in Japan in this period—and subsequent periods—tended to regard Korea as a frontier that could provide a solution to their problems or needs in Japan's domestic power struggle. To obtain this "Korean panacea" for Japan's domestic problems, most Japanese leaders were inclined to resort to unilateral action toward Korea in complete disregard of Korean interests or wishes. Criticism or opposition came chiefly from those who opposed such action, not in principle, but because of timing and, even more likely, because it might adversely affect their own domestic political interests. This propensity continued to characterize Japanese policy toward Korea in the decades ahead.

Finally, brief comments are in order on the international significance of the Hirayama mission. The aborted bakufu mission was the first instance in which a Japanese government indicated eagerness or willingness to identify itself with the Western powers rather than its Asian neighbors— an attitude that was to become a pattern of Japanese behavior in international relations in subsequent periods. Of equal interest were the positions taken by Britain, France, and the United States with regard to the mission. Absence of formal communication between the bakufu and Britain on the matter seems to suggest that Britain took a skeptical or negative view of this particular bakufu enterprise and, in general, of Japanese pretentions with regard to Korea at this time. Although France actively supported the bakufu in Japan's domestic power struggle, it was not enthusiastic or even receptive to the latter's offer of its good offices in Korea. France recognized, as did Britain, Chinese suzerainty over Korea and preferred to rely on China rather

than Japan for settlement of its dispute with Korea. The
United States, on the other hand, readily accepted the
Japanese offer of mediation. It preferred to rely on Japan,
rather than on China. The United States apparently had
little faith in the Chinese claim of suzerainty over Korea and
was ready to dismiss it as irrelevant or unacceptable in modern international relations. This clearly forecast the attitudes of these countries concerning Sino-Japanese rivalry
in Korea in the coming decades.

CHAPTER IV

Restoration Diplomacy: Japanese Policy Toward China and Korea, 1868–1871

The Meiji Restoration of 1868 ended seven centuries of military government and restored imperial rule in Japan. Since the shogun had exercised political and military control at home and full power in foreign affairs during the Tokugawa period, restoration of imperial rule necessitated adjustment in Japan's relations with foreign countries. Accordingly, on February 3, 1868, the imperial court proclaimed that henceforth the emperor would personally conduct the nation's external as well as internal affairs. Five days later the court announced that treaties with foreign countries signed by the bakufu in the shogun's name would be honored, subject to revision of unsatisfactory clauses. The same day it notified the representatives of the treaty powers that a new office had been created to handle external relations.[1] Thus, three months after the shogun surrendered his powers, the imperial court formally took over management of the nation's foreign affairs.

Sole exception to this was the management of relations with Korea, the only country with which Tokugawa Japan had maintained formal relations. Preoccupied with more pressing domestic and foreign problems, the new regime decided to continue, for the time being, Tsushima's tradi-

1. NGB, vol. 1, 227–228, 229–236.

tional role as intermediary in the conduct of relations with Korea. Under this anomalous arrangement, the readjustment of relations with Korea proved difficult and time consuming, creating a diplomatic interregnum between the two countries that was to last eight years. It was during this period that the new imperial government of Japan evolved its policies toward China and Korea step by step, amid momentous changes and dramatic events at home and abroad.

In terms of the evolution of Japanese policy toward China and Korea, the interregnum consisted of three phases. The first phase began with the restoration of imperial rule in early 1868 and lasted through the end of 1871, the year in which Japan signed its first modern treaty with China. The second phase occurred during 1872–1873, when the tumultuous *sei-Kan* controversy rocked the fledgling Meiji government and split asunder its top leadership. Thereafter the third phase commenced with the launching of the Taiwan expedition in the spring of 1874, and it ended with the signing of the Treaty of Kanghwa with Korea in February 1876.

During the first phase, the new Japanese government tried to readjust existing relations with Korea and to establish formal ties with China, in conformity with the spirit and principles of imperial restoration in Japan.

THE CLAIM OF TITULAR SUPERIORITY OVER KOREA

In the wake of the bakufu's fall in 1868, for a time there was no group in Japan save Tsushima which had an active or immediate interest in Korea. The new imperial government, a loose coalition of princes, court nobles, leading daimyo, and their samurai agents, had more the pretension than the substance of power and was far from functioning as an effective national government. In addition to military campaigns to eliminate the armed resistance of pro-Tokugawa forces in the country, it faced the formidable task of creating a new political structure and governing machinery. Having come to power chiefly with the support of the chauvinistic exclusionist forces, it faced the crucial external problem of winning the confidence of the Western treaty powers. In these circumstances, the new regime had neither necessary resources nor compelling reason to take a diplomatic initiative toward Korea or China.

The situation, however, was different for Tsushima. The restoration of imperial rule was no instant blessing for the island. It brought no relief from Tsushima's long-standing economic difficulties, nor did it reduce the danger of Western military intrusion threatening the remote offshore island. On the contrary, the political and military upheavals attending the fall of the bakufu and the restoration of imperial rule caused confusion and uncertainty for the insular domain. Need and desire for an expanded trade with Korea to solve its economic difficulties remained as urgent as ever. Immediately after the Restoration, therefore, Tsushima decided to appeal to the new regime for the dispatch of a diplomatic mission to Korea, one similar to the aborted Hirayama mission. Fortunately, it had influential friends in the new government.[2]

Ōshima Tomonojō, leader of the Tsushima *han* government, was a loyalist of some prominence, and he had many friends in the restoration movement who were taking up important positions in the new regime. Foremost among them was Kido Takayoshi of Chōshū. The Restoration brought power and prestige to men of Chōshū. As their acknowledged leader, Kido became one of the most powerful figures in the new regime. In late February 1868 he was appointed junior councilor and put in charge of foreign affairs.[3] Enough has been said of Kido's long and active interest in Korea. Because of the war between the bakufu and Chōshū, he was not involved in the Hirayama mission. Had the circumstances been different, it is almost certain that he would have supported it actively. With the Restoration, Kido

2. TNS, vol. 1, 135–137.
3. *Shōgiku Kido kō den,* vol. 1, 904.

became the new regime's foremost advocate of an active Korean policy.

Anxious to retain its traditional rights and privileges with respect to Korea under the new regime, Tsushima decided to seek an imperial commission for its daimyo, Lord Sō, to enable him to continue his hereditary role as intermediary between Japan and Korea. In March 1868 Ōshima went to Kyoto to seek Kido's help in securing such a commission from the court.[4] As a result of the help, the court on April 15 confirmed Sō's traditional role in the conduct of Japanese-Korean relations. At the same time, it ordered Sō to "discontinue outmoded practices which might blemish Japan's national polity" in conducting relations with Korea.[5]

Upon receiving his new commission, on May 27 Sō submitted a memorial to the court, outlining a policy that he thought the new regime should pursue toward Korea. He began with a brief account of the history of Japanese-Korean relations. Subsequent to the termination of the three Han [Korean] kingdoms' "tributary ties" to the Japanese imperial court, said Sō, relations with Korea during the middle ages had been conducted by military regimes on the basis of equality between the two countries. Consequently, many errors were made, which tended to undermine Japan's imperial polity and authority. During the Tokugawa period, official relations between the bakufu and Korea were largely ceremonial, and substantive relations between the two countries were only those between Korea and Tsushima. Since the Korea-Tsushima relations were essentially "private" in nature, Sō asserted, they could not serve as a permanent model for future Japanese-Korean relations. In an accompanying memorandum, Sō set forth specific measures for "reforming" the existing relations with Korea. These included (1) takeover of the Korean trade by the national government, in order to eliminate the disadvantages of the existing arrangement, under which economically weak Tsushima was left to deal with Korea alone; (2)

4. Kido Takayoshi, *Kido Takayoshi ibunshū*, 42–44.
5. NGB, vol. 1, 573–574; TNS, vol. 1, 136.

termination of Tsushima's "humiliating" semi-tributary ties
with Korea, which the island had been forced to maintain
because of its economic dependence on Korea; (3) establishment of new regulations and procedures governing the
conduct of relations with Korea consistent with the spirit of
the imperial restoration in Japan; and (4) punitive action
against Korea in case Korea was unresponsive to the proposed changes. Sō emphasized that while the Korean question might not be as urgent as the colonization of Ezo,
Japan could not remain indifferent toward the peninsula,
which was "virtually the same as Japanese territory," when it
was involved in disputes with Western powers. If the imperial court took the initiative and pursued a proper policy
that combined "benevolence and might," Korea could become an "outer base" (*gaifu*) in a few years.[6]

There is little doubt that Ōshima was the principal author
of the memorial. Most likely he prepared it in Kyoto after
Sō's arrival there in late April. It is certain that Ōshima consulted closely with Kido in drafting it. In addition to their
frequent earlier meetings, Ōshima called on Kido on May
26—the day before the memorial was formally submitted to
the court—to discuss its contents.[7] A few days later, Kido
urged approval of Sō's recommendations in a letter to Sanjō
Sanetomi and Iwakura Tomomi, two court nobles holding
the highest positions in the newly created Council of State
(*Dajōkan*).[8]

Understandably, Tsushima was interested chiefly in advancing its own concerns. The proposal for national
takeover of the Korean trade, for example, represented not
so much an act of deference to imperial authority as a move
to have the imperial government assume a large amount of
debts that Tsushima owed Korea as the result of a chronic
trade deficit. Although its language was couched in the
rhetoric of imperial restoration, Tsushima, like other *han*,

6. NGB, vol. 1, 657–666; TNS, vol. 1, 137–143.
7. Kido, *Kido Takayoshi ibunshū*, 44.
8. For Kido's letter to Sanjō and Iwakura, see NGB, vol. 3, 205–208; *Kido Takayoshi monjo* (Kido Takayoshi papers), vol. 3, 72–75.

had no inclination to surrender its feudal prerogatives and traditional rights, especially those related to the management of Korean affairs. As is evident from Sō's recommendations, what was sought was to elevate Tsushima's own status and to strengthen its position in dealing with Korea by taking advantage of the imperial restoration in Japan. Sō's memorial embodied Tsushima's self-interest and the restorationist approach of the new Japanese regime toward Korea, which had been anticipated in the restorationist version of bakumatsu continental expansionism.

Kido, Ōshima, and other erstwhile loyalists now installed in the seat of power took the position that as a consequence of the restoration of imperial rule at home, relations with Korea should no longer be conducted on the basis of the equality of the two countries; they should be "restored" to their "proper" form, which the loyalists believed existed in ancient times when Korea had been a "tributary" of Japan. Kido revealed this fundamentalist view when he accused Korea of "insolence" toward Japan in a conversation with Iwakura in early January 1869. Since Korea had not yet been informed of the imperial restoration in Japan, by "insolence" Kido could have meant only what he considered Korea's "past neglect of its tributary duties" to the Japanese imperial court.[9] In Sō's memorial, Kido and Ōshima set forth the basic ideological framework within which the new Japanese regime would conduct its "restoration" diplomacy toward Korea in its early years.

Despite Tsushima's repeated requests for instructions, the new Foreign Office did not take action with regard to Korea for months. In late June 1868 it directed Tsushima henceforth to refer all matters pertaining to Korea to its branch office in Osaka. Accordingly, during the first week of July, Ōshima went to Osaka to confer with officials of that office on the proposed readjustment of the relations with Korea.

9. It was in February 1869, about one month after Kido had talked of "Korean insolence," that Korea was officially informed by Tsushima of the imperial restoration in Japan. On Kido's talk with Iwakura, see Kido Takayoshi, *Kido Takayoshi nikki* (Diary of Kido Takayoshi), vol. 1, 159–161.

The conferees agreed, among other things, that in official communications to Korea, Tsushima should stop using the seal given it by the Korean court, for that had been a "questionable practice incompatible with the Japanese national polity." They further agreed that in future state messages, which would be sent in the emperor's name, the king of Korea should be assigned a "somewhat inferior" status, which would be "consistent with his vassalage to the Ch'ing court." Finally, Ōshima requested that Sō's court rank and title be raised so that his authority would be enhanced in Korean eyes.

Crux of their discussions was the issue of economic aid to Tsushima. Ōshima warned that should Tsushima stop the use of the Korean seals, Korea would certainly retaliate by refusing to receive any more envoys and trading ships from Tsushima and that this would endanger its economic life. The first step toward implementation of the proposed diplomatic reform, Ōshima emphasized, was to provide Tsushima with sufficient aid to guarantee its economic survival without supply of provisions from Korea. Ōshima asked for large loans from the imperial government to pay Tsushima's outstanding debts to Korea. Although the Foreign Office officials understood Tsushima's position and needs, such aid was plainly beyond the new regime's ability. For the time being all that they could do was to assure Ōshima that Tsushima's request would be given sympathetic consideration.[10] Despite brave language, the imperial government could not effectively launch "restoration" diplomacy toward Korea until it had consolidated its power at home. For all its fervent loyalist protestations, Tsushima's zeal for "reforming" relations with Korea stemmed chiefly from its own economic interests.

In August, as requested by Ōshima, the court raised Sō's rank and gave him a new title. It then ordered him to send a formal notification of the imperial restoration in Japan to Korea.[11] Sō left Kyoto in September and returned to

10. TNS, vol. 1, 143–146.
11. NGB, vol. 1, 931–932.

Tsushima in early October. He immediately proceeded to make preparations for sending a special envoy to Korea to announce Japan's imperial restoration. Realizing that the steps which he was taking would lead to the termination of Tsushima's centuries-old, semi-tributary ties with Korea, Sō issued a special proclamation on November 21. He warned his people that his efforts to "right an ancient wrong" and to "uphold the Japanese national polity" might bring Korean retaliation that could jeopardize the economic life of the *han*. He assured them, however, that the imperial court would not be indifferent to Tsushima's plight in such an eventuality. Finally, Sō exhorted them to stand loyally by him, no matter what difficulties or hardships might befall them.[12]

On January 31, 1869, Higuchi Tesshirō, Tsushima's special envoy, arrived at Pusan with Sō's letters to the Korean vice minister of rites and the prefect of Tongnae, announcing the abolition of the bakufu and the restoration of imperial rule in Japan. The letters, virtually identical in content, began with a brief reference to Japan's unbroken imperial line that "had ruled the country for more than 2,000 years." During the middle ages, the letters continued, management of military and diplomatic affairs was entrusted to the shogun. Since the establishment of the Tokugawa bakufu, a peace of more than a dozen generations inevitably led to the spread of corruption. Upon ascending the throne, His Majesty the reigning emperor decided to tighten official discipline and to conduct the affairs of state personally. "It is His Majesty's sincere wish," the letters concluded, "to further Japan's traditional friendship with your country and to see to it that this friendship lasts ten thousand generations." Sō signed the letters with his new court rank and title and stamped them with a new seal of office given him by the Japanese court, instead of the traditional Korean seal which he had been required to use in his communications to Korea.[13]

12. TNS, vol. 1, 152–153.
13. *Ibid.*, 153–156; NGB, vol. 4, 223–225.

On February 2 Higuchi met with An Tong-jun, Korean language officer in charge of Japanese affairs at Pusan. He asked An to forward Sō's letters to the prefect of Tongnae for transmission to Seoul. Forewarned of Higuchi's mission by an advance messenger, An instantly rejected his request. He pointed out that it was outrageous for Tsushima to use such terms as "emperor" (*kōjō* in Japanese; *hwangsang* in Korean) and "imperial edict" (*choku* in Japanese; *ch'ik* in Korean) in reference to the Japanese ruler, because they could be used only for the Chinese emperor in a diplomatic document. Characterizing Tsushima's unilateral decision to discard the Korean seal as "appalling," An declared Sō's letters unacceptable and demanded Higuchi's immediate departure from Pusan.[14]

Informed of Korea's adamant position, Ōshima personally went to Pusan in late March with the hope of breaking the impasse in the negotiations. He pleaded with An for sympathy for the Tsushima envoy's predicament. But An would not budge. In response to Ōshima's entreaties, however, An promised a more definitive reply after making inquiries with his superiors at Tongnae. On April 10 An delivered his promised reply in writing. Setting forth the reasons why Sō's letters were unacceptable, he emphasized the inviolability of the existing relations and arrangements between Japan and Korea. He said that Korea was outraged by Tsushima's characterization of its relations with Korea as "private." As for Tsushima's unilateral discarding of the Korean seal, An reminded the Tsushima officials that the seal had been originally given to Lord Sō as a special favor at Sō's own request. Then he asked: "Now, suddenly, you want to discard it. Is this really an act promoting neighborly relations?"[15]

Despite his low position, An spoke with authority. Though humble in birth, he had gained, by intelligence and ability, the trust of the Taewŏn'gun. An's immediate

14. TNS, vol. 1, 156.
15. *Ibid.,* 157–160.

superior was Chŏng Hyŏn-dŏk, another Taewŏn'gun confidant and prefect of Tongnae at this time. While exercising supervisory authority over the management of Japanese affairs from his prefectoral seat at nearby Tongnae, Chŏng seldom participated in negotiations with the Japanese. Kim Se-ho, governor of Kyŏngsang Province and Chŏng's superior, was also a confidant of the Taewŏn'gun. Although technically responsible for whatever took place at Pusan and Tongnae, both of which were within his administrative jurisdiction, Kim remained at his provincial headquarters in Taegu and was far removed from the scene. His role in the management of Japanese affairs was nominal.[16]

These men, closely identified with the Taewŏn'gun politically, shared his strong exclusionist views and his well known distrust of the Japanese. A measure of the Taewŏn'gun's confidence in these men and of the importance he attached to their posts is seen in the fact that all of them were kept in their posts far beyond the normal tenure of office, until his own fall from power at the end of 1873. Apparently he did not wish to leave the conduct of relations with Japan in less-experienced or less-reliable hands. An played the most direct and crucial role in implementing the Taewŏn'gun's policy toward Japan. There is a strange paucity of material on the negotiations with Japan in the Korean government archives for the period 1868–1871. As has been suggested by some historians, this seems to indicate that An probably communicated directly and confidentially with the Taewŏn'gun instead of receiving his instructions and reporting his activities through the regular official channels.[17] At any rate, there is little doubt that An represented the views and attitude of the Taewŏn'gun closely and faithfully.

An believed that Tsushima, which he thought should mediate between Japan and Korea if and when the former

16. *Ibid.*, 181–182; Yi Sŏn-gŭn, *Han'guksa ch'oegŭnse p'yŏn*, 363–365; Ching Young Choe, *The Rule of the Taewŏn'gun, 1864–1873*, 148.

17. Neither ISN-KJ nor KJS contains much useful information concerning the Japanese-Korean negotiations during 1868–1871.

tried to create difficulties, actually was urging the new
Japanese regime to change the existing relations between
the two countries. Therefore Korea should not grant
Tsushima's request, but instead should cut off trade with
Tsushima and wait for its capitulation. An also doubted the
truth of the report that the Japanese imperial court had
taken over the conduct of relations with Korea from the
bakufu. Most importantly, An saw in Tsushima's unprecedented insistence on the use of the terms "emperor" and
"imperial edict" a scheme to reduce Korea to the status of a
Japanese tributary.[18]

Unable to make headway in the negotiations, Ōshima returned to Tsushima late in April. He proceeded to Kyoto
and met with Kido, on June 15, to report on his trip to
Korea. He told Kido that the dispute with Korea could be
settled only by direct talks with the Korean authorities in
Seoul.[19] The following month he repeated this opinion in a
lengthy report to the Foreign Office. He said that, although
Korea knew it would not be in its interest to lose the peace
with Japan, it wished to avoid direct relations with the
Japanese imperial government because it feared that
acknowledgment of Japanese imperial authority would not
only reduce Korea to a Japanese tributary, but would offend
the Ch'ing court. Since Korea obviously was engaged in de-
laying tactics without intention of reaching an accord,
Ōshima said, the only way to settle the issue quickly was "to
go to the Korean capital for direct talks with the king." Emphasizing that Japan's strategy to manipulate or control
Korea must combine benevolence with might and tolerance
with sternness, Ōshima declared that Japan must pursue a
just but firm course, "even if it might result in a temporary
breach of the peace." He concluded his report by reminding
the Foreign Office of Tsushima's indispensable experience
and expertise in handling the "complex" Korean problem.[20]
There is little doubt that Ōshima's views were fully en-
dorsed by Kido.

18. For An's views as recorded by Tsushima officials, see NGB, vol. 4, 237–239.
19. *Shōgiku Kido kō den*, vol. 2, 1284–1285.
20. NGB, vol. 4, 217–223.

The impasse at Pusan continued through 1869 and into 1870. Tsushima's failure to accomplish its diplomatic assignment in Korea inevitably drew criticism. In a desperate effort to redeem himself and his *han,* Ōshima conceived a new formula to meet the Korean objections. He decided to eliminate terms objectionable to Korea from Tsushima's communications and to stamp communications with the traditional Korean seal. The issue of the seal was to be settled after relations between the two countries had been readjusted. To implement his scheme, Ōshima chose Urase Yutaka, an able Tsushima interpreter respected by the Koreans at Pusan.[21]

Urase arrived at Pusan early in June 1870, and he held his first meeting with An on June 11. He told An that Korean refusal to receive Tsushima's notification of the Japanese imperial restoration had put Tsushima in a difficult position, and that there were men clamoring for "punitive" action against Korea within the new Japanese regime. He assured An, however, that Ōshima and his friends were doing their best to restrain such extremists. Expressing his sympathy, An said that he would do whatever he could to help Tsushima. Encouraged by An's friendly response, Urase proceeded to explain Ōshima's new formula. Tsushima would substitute the word "court" (*chōtei* in Japanese; *chojŏng* in Korean) for the word "emperor" and use the Korean seal in its message. In the future, Japan and Korea would communicate with each other in the name of their respective governments, without mentioning their rulers. Expressing agreement, An promised Urase a formal reply by July 11, after making the necessary inquiries to the authorities in Seoul.[22] Unknown to either man, this sensible scheme had been foredoomed by an incident that had occurred earlier in June.

Late in May 1870, Maximilian von Brandt, German chargé d'affaires in Japan, after a tour of southwestern Japan, decided to take a side trip to Korea. At Nagasaki he engaged the services of a Korean-speaking interpreter named

21. TNS, vol. 1, 231–232.
22. *Ibid.,* 233–234; NGB, vol. 6, 151–153.

Nakano. A native of Tsushima, Nakano had served previously as an interpreter in Pusan. On June 1 Brandt arrived at Pusan harbor aboard the German warship *Hertha*. With him were several Japanese, including a Foreign Office official and Nakano. Arrival of the *Hertha*, first Western warship to visit Pusan, caused consternation and alarm among the local officials. Their alarm turned into anger when they learned of the presence of Japanese, particularly Nakano, aboard the German vessel. Viewing this as evidence of Japanese collaboration with the Westerners in a deliberate attempt to breach Korean seclusion, the Pusan officials lodged a protest with the Tsushima officials at Japan House. They demanded that all Japanese be removed from the *Hertha* and that the ship leave Pusan immediately. Realizing that his visit had caused unexpected complications for the Japanese, Brandt left Pusan the following day without protest.[23]

Despite Brandt's prompt and peaceful departure, however, the alarm and the suspicion of Japanese-Western collusion aroused by his visit remained with the Koreans. Upon receiving the report of the incident, the Taewŏn'gun promptly ordered a strong protest sent to Tsushima. Accordingly, on June 11 the Ministry of Rites dispatched a stern note. At the same time, it reported the incident to the Ch'ing Board of Rites, saying that there was reason to believe that "the Japanese were conspiring with the Western barbarians" against Korea.[24] On July 11 An informed Urase that Tsushima's new proposal had been turned down by the government because "the Japanese at Pusan had conspired with the Western barbarians."[25] Trivial though it may seem in retrospect, the Brandt incident excited Korea's fear of the West and its distrust of Japan in a period of heightened xenophobia following the French invasion and other Western activities along the Korean coast. It destroyed

23. ISN-KJ, 7/5/11–12.
24. *Ibid.*, 7/5/12; *Ch'ing-chi Chung-Jih-Han kuan-hsi shih-liao* (Historical materials on Sino-Japanese-Korean relations during the late Ch'ing period) (hereafter cited as CJHK), vol. 2, 126.
25. ISN-KJ, 7/8/25; NGB, vol. 6, 156–157.

whatever chances there might have been of a Japanese-Korean accord and virtually ended Tsushima's effectiveness in conducting Japan's new diplomacy with Korea.

For two and a half years after the Meiji Restoration in Japan, the relations between Japan and Korea changed little from what they had been during the Tokugawa period. On the Japanese side, this was due partly to the new regime's inability to centralize political and administrative authority over internal and external affairs. It was also due in part to Tsushima's unwillingness to relinquish its "feudal" prerogatives, particularly those in the area of trade and diplomacy with Korea. In addition to Korea's traditional reluctance to change or broaden its relations with Japan, this attitude on the part of Tsushima undoubtedly contributed to Korean refusal to enter into direct relations with the Meiji government. So long as Tsushima was anxious to continue its role as intermediary between the two countries, there was little reason for Korea to accept any basic or extensive change in existing relations. This was all the more true because, while renouncing its semi-tributary obligations toward Korea unilaterally, Tsushima tried to retain its traditional privileges, which were contingent precisely upon faithful fulfillment of these obligations. But there were two more important reasons behind the Korean stand. One was its growing suspicion of Japanese collaboration with the Western powers against Korea. The other, and more fundamental, reason was the Japanese claim of titular superiority over Korea. While leaders of the new Japanese regime considered it a corollary to the restoration of imperial rule in Japan, such a claim had no historical or legal validity and was regarded as insulting and unacceptable by the Koreans.

KOREA: A "PANACEA" IN JAPANESE POLITICS

With the imperial restoration, Kido emerged as the chief architect of the new regime's Korean policy. He was concerned with Tsushima's economic plight and shared its desire for expanded Korean trade. No doubt he also shared the general fear that Korea might be seized by a Western power, which would pose a serious threat to Japanese security. But in the early days of the Restoration, Kido had no plan for action with regard to Korea other than the general restorationist position that Japan must "reestablish" its imperial authority in Korea. When he wrote to Sanjō and Iwakura in June 1868 to urge their approval of the new Korean policy recommended by Sō, he stated broadly and expansively that Japan "must annex" Korea. Short of this, he added, it must at least "reestablish its ancient prefecture of Mimana" on the peninsula.[26] However, as men in power before him had conceived plans for action against Korea primarily as a means of achieving their political goals at home, Kido developed ideas for action against Korea mainly as a means of solving the new regime's inability to establish effective national control at home. For him, as for others, Korea was a readily available panacea for Japan's domestic problems.[27]

The pacification campaigns by the imperial forces brought quick results. Except for Hokkaidō, organized armed resistance to the new regime in the country ceased by the end of 1868. Rapid submission of the *han*, however, came largely as a result of their apathy and indecision, not as an upsurge of loyalism. While former bakufu territories and those *han* that had fought for the Tokugawa cause were placed under the direct control of the imperial government, others remained intact and retained their semi-feudal autonomy. If anything, the removal of central control exercised by the bakufu gave these *han* greater freedom, sometimes making them "behave like numerous small bakufu." Without any army of its own other than the sundry forces placed at its service temporarily by loyalist domains such as Satsuma and Chōshū, the new imperial government had no effective means of exacting compliance with its wishes. Meanwhile, its policy of open intercourse with foreign countries, representing an almost complete reversal of the stand

26. *Kido Takayoshi monjo*, vol. 3, 72–75.
27. See Kido's recommendations in NGB, vol. 3, 205–208.

taken by most of Japan's new leaders prior to the Restoration, aroused opposition among the court conservatives and diehard exclusionists while it caused bewilderment and confusion among the populace. Within the ruling coalition, dominance by Satsuma and Chōshū caused resentment on the part of lesser partners such as Tosa and Hizen. Kido believed that a war with Korea would be the best way to bring about national unity in a nation divided by ideological dissension, feudal separatism, and resultant regional jealousy and rivalry. With a strong, independent imperial army, to be fashioned in the course of a victorious campaign against Korea, he thought, the new regime could make its political authority and control at home effective and impose its will upon the still largely intact feudal components in the country.[28]

In his conversation with Iwakura in January 1869, Kido recommended the immediate dispatch of a mission to admonish Korea for its insolence toward Japan. Calling the subjugation of Korea one of the most important tasks facing Japan, Kido argued that if Korea refused to submit to Japan, Japan should "denounce Korea's guilt, attack its land, and thereby enhance greatly the authority and prestige of our divine land." He assured Iwakura that a victorious expedition to Korea "would instantly change Japan's outmoded customs, set its objectives abroad, promote its industry and technology, and eliminate jealousy and recrimination among its people."[29] On February 11 Kido discussed his proposal with his friend, Ōmura Masujirō, who was now a top War Office official. In a letter to Ōmura dated March 12, Kido reiterated his views. Upon the completion of the pacification campaign in Hokkaidō, he suggested, the imperial government should raise an army of its own and use it to "open the port of Pusan." While material benefits from such a venture might not be sufficient to cover its cost, it would be the best way, he asserted, for Japan to "set its fun-

28. *Kido Takayoshi monjo,* vol. 3, 232, 239–241, 251; Kido, *Kido Takayoshi nikki,* vol. 1, 159, 186, 193.
29. Kido, *Kido Takayoshi nikki,* vol. 1, 159.

damental national direction, to turn the eyes of its people abroad, to develop its military and naval technology and skills step by step, and thereby to lay a foundation for great national expansion in the future." He said that the subjugation of Korea was more important than the colonization of Hokkaidō, because the former was a task that would "strengthen and uphold the national polity of our imperial country."[30] The following day Kido sent a virtually identical letter to Sanjō and Iwakura, asking for their approval of his proposal. He requested an appointment for himself as imperial envoy to Korea.[31] On March 29 Kido visited Ōmura at the War Office to discuss plans for using the troops made available recently by the completion of the pacification of northeastern Honshū for the proposed Korean venture.[32]

No doubt Kido's views were reinforced by the report, which he received from Ōshima upon the latter's return from Korea in June 1869. During the following months, he talked or wrote to Sanjō, Iwakura, Itō Hirobumi, and other top government leaders on numerous occasions to solicit their support for his proposal. To reassure those unwilling to commit themselves to a foreign military venture at a time when the domestic situation was precarious, he repeatedly stated that his *sei-Kan* plan did not entail outright or immediate military conquest of Korea, but rather its subjugation by "persuasion."[33] On November 17, 1869, Kido noted with frustration in his diary that the government "does not understand the fundamental significance of *sei-Kan*."[34]

Kido's energetic campaign finally paid off, at least partially. On January 5, 1870, the Dajōkan tentatively approved his proposal and appointed him as imperial envoy to China and Korea.[35] This put him virtually in charge of the government's policy toward the two countries. His departure

30. *Shōgiku Kido kō den,* vol. 2, 1279; *Kido Takayoshi monjo,* vol. 3, 228–234.
31. *Kido Takayoshi monjo,* vol. 3, 237–243.
32. Kido, *Kido Takayoshi nikki,* vol. 1, 193.
33. See Kido's letter to Sanjō and Iwakura in *Kido Takayoshi monjo,* vol. 3, 239–241 and his letter to Itō *ibid.,* 412–415.
34. Kido, *Kido Takayoshi nikki,* vol. 1, 280.
35. NGB, vol. 5, 433–434.

was set tentatively for sometime in the coming spring. Meanwhile, the idea of sending an expedition to Korea was gaining support within the Foreign Ministry (renamed in a governmental reorganization in July 1869) under its minister, Sawa Nobuyoshi, a court noble with close ties with Chōshū.[36]

Although the imperial government of necessity had recognized Tsushima's traditional role in the conduct of Korean affairs, as the government developed its own administrative machinery the demand inevitably arose that the management of all foreign relations, including those with Korea, be unified under central authority. Tsushima's inability to perform its role effectively reinforced this demand. Following the surrender of *han* registers (*hanseki hōkan*) in July 1869—whereby Sō lost his feudal status as hereditary ruler of Tsushima and theoretically his intermediary role between Japan and Korea—the management of Korean affairs was transferred to the Foreign Ministry in October. However, partly because of Tsushima's protest, but mainly because of the Ministry's inability to take on additional responsibilities immediately, Tsushima was allowed to continue its traditional role under the Ministry's general supervision.[37]

On October 25, 1869, the Foreign Ministry submitted a detailed memorandum to the Dajōkan, in which it spelled out its official position with regard to Korea for the first time. It rejected both the Korean contention that Japanese-Korean relations must continue to be conducted through the medium of Tsushima as before and Tsushima's desire to retain its intermediary role in the conduct of Korean affairs. Other than this, however, there was little in the memorandum that indicated any significant departure in the attitude of the Foreign Ministry from the traditional East Asian concept of interstate relations. It was a reaffirmation of the restorationist view of Japanese-Korean rela-

36. Sawa was one of the seven loyalist court nobles who fled to Chōshū after the Chōshū coup in Kyoto in September 1863 had failed.
37. TNS, vol. 1, 186–187.

tions mixed with fear of Western aggression. Since Korea
"had been subjugated by the imperial court" in ancient
times, said the Ministry, it was desirable for Japan to "preserve Korea permanently even if it were not made a tributary of the imperial court." Declaring that Japan was "the
only country capable of saving Korea" from the predatory
Western powers, the Ministry warned that, if Korea were
allowed to "be gobbled up by Russia or some other power, it
would become a permanent threat to our imperial country."
The Ministry wished to send an imperial envoy to Korea;
inasmuch as Korea probably would not receive an envoy if
he went with messages only, the Ministry recommended that
he be escorted by warships and troops to break "Korean
arrogance" and to facilitate agreement between the two
countries.[38]

As the initial step, the Ministry decided to send officials to
Tsushima and Pusan to study conditions at both places. In
December 1869 Sada Hakubō, a former loyalist samurai
from Saga, was appointed to head this fact-finding mission.
Moriyama Shigeru and Saitō Sakae, two junior officials who
were to become the Ministry's leading "Korea specialists" in
the years ahead, were ordered to accompany Sada. Their
instructions were to ascertain the precise nature of Tsushima's relations with Korea and to study Korea's military and
naval strength, its internal administration, and, particularly,
its relations with China.[39] Leaving Tokyo on January 7,
1870, Sada and his party arrived in Tsushima on February
7. After spending three weeks on the island, they departed
for Korea on March 12 and reached Pusan on March 23.
Posing as Tsushima officials, they spent about twenty days at
Japan House.[40]

Upon their return to Tokyo, the three submitted a joint
report to the Foreign Ministry, along with their individual
recommendations. In the joint report, they stated that, although Korea acknowledged vassalage and remained out-

38. NGB, vol. 4, 854–858.
39. *Ibid.*, vol. 5, 457–458.
40. TNS, vol. 1, 227.

wardly loyal to the Ch'ing, it revered the memory of the
Ming and resented the Manchus. In internal and external
affairs Korea exercised full autonomy. While Korea would
refer troublesome matters to Peking for help, it had never
reported matters concerning relations with Japan to Peking.
The joint report added that the Koreans were so crafty that
they took advantage of their ties with Peking when dealing
with Japan and took advantage of their relations with Japan
when dealing with Peking.[41]

In their individual recommendations, all three advocated
the subjugation of Korea by force, if necessary. In fanatical,
loyalist rhetoric, Sada called for "conquest" to "punish"
Korea for its "crime" against the Japanese imperial court.
He proposed the dispatch of an imperial envoy with a force
of thirty battalions, which, if Korea refused to submit,
"would overrun the country and capture its king within fifty
days." He urged early action because "France will not let
Korea survive long, Russia is watching its moves, and the
United States has its own designs" on Korea. Calling Korea
a gold mine, Sada argued that its conquest would enrich
Japan and strengthen its army. Pointing out the potential
danger of keeping discontented fighting men idle in Japan,
he recommended their employment in a Korean campaign.
Moriyama and Saitō also recommended an expedition if
Korea refused to submit to Japanese demands. Voicing the
same fear of civil war in Japan as did Sada, Moriyama argued, too, that a Korean expedition would be a good way to
divert the energies and ambitions of the discontented soldiery at home. He proposed that Japan sell the island of
Sakhalin and use the funds earmarked for its colonization
to finance a Korean campaign. Saitō thought such a campaign could be financed through governmental economy
and austerity.[42]

Although Sada's proposal was rejected by the Japanese
authorities as "impractical," he voiced an emotional urge felt
by many restorationists in the government. While a military

41. NGB, vol. 6, 131–138.
42. *Ibid.*, 138–143.

expedition to Korea was justified on the ground of Korea's alleged "insolence" toward Japan, perhaps they found it appealing as a substitute for *jōi*, the expulsion of the Western "barbarians." A war with Korea might relieve the emotional strain and moral dilemma of those who, having overthrown the bakufu with the pledge of expelling the Westerners, found themselves incapable of honoring that pledge. At any rate, there were many in the Foreign Ministry at this time who rejected Sada's drastic proposal but supported some sort of military action as the best way to settle the Korean question.[43]

Late in May, on the basis of the report of the Sada mission, the Foreign Ministry submitted an important memorandum to the Dajōkan, outlining three alternative plans that might be used to deal with Korea. The first plan called for a temporary break in relations with Korea, including those between Korea and Tsushima. While this had the merit of terminating Tsushima's "improper" relations with Korea, the Ministry pointed out it might leave Japan standing by hopelessly while Korea was seized by Russia. It "might undo everything that successive emperors, Hideyoshi, and the Tokugawas have done for a millennium." But until Japan gained sufficient strength, this would be preferable to a policy of indecision.

The second plan called for the dispatch of a mission headed by Kido, as had been recommended earlier and tentatively approved. The mission would notify Korea of the imperial restoration in Japan and negotiate a new treaty with the Korean government. It would be escorted by two warships and an unspecified number of troops. If Korea refused to submit to Kido's demands, Japan would immediately resort to arms.

The third plan was to send an envoy to China, instead of Korea. The envoy would first negotiate a treaty with China and then proceed to the Korean capital. Since Korea was a tributary of China, once Japan established itself as an equal

43. Kemuriyama Sentarō, *Sei-Kan ron jissō* (The truth about the *sei-Kan* controversy), 149.

of China, Korea would have no cause for complaint even if
treated as an inferior by Japan. With a treaty between China
and Japan, if hostilities broke out between Japan and
Korea, China would not be able to aid Korea readily—as it
had during the Hideyoshi invasions. Although there was no
urgent reason for Japan to seek a treaty with China at this
time, said the Ministry, such a treaty would be a good diplomatic step to take to bring about Korean submission to
Japan. The Ministry asked the Dajōkan to approve one of
the three alternative plans without delay, for further delay
might bring more "national humiliation" to Japan.[44]

The Foreign Ministry preferred the second plan, which
was identical with its recommendations of the previous October and similar to another proposal made by Miyamoto
Okazu, one of its officials in charge of Korean affairs, toward the end of 1869. In a lengthy memorandum entitled
"A Treatise on Korea" (*Chōsen ron*), Miyamoto rejected the
restorationist position, based on the view that Korea had
been a tributary of ancient Japan, as invalid in the modern
world. Instead he proposed a Japanese overlordship in
Korea that combined the traditional East Asian concept of
suzerainty with certain features of modern colonial rule. Although Japan had nothing to gain materially by maintaining
relations with Korea, said Miyamoto, if left alone, Korea
would be seized by Russia, and this would pose a serious
threat to Japan. Aiding Korea was therefore in Japan's interest. Since Japan was not strong enough to "annex"
Korea, he went on, the next best thing was to persuade
Korea to join in a "fraternal union" with Japan. Miyamoto
thought that this could be accomplished by sending an imperial envoy to Korea with one or two warships and some
troops. The envoy would convince the Koreans of the
Japanese emperor's sincere concern for Korea and explain
the "unreliability" of China as Korea's defender. Since it
would be "improper" as well as costly for Korea as a semi-
independent state to maintain treaties with foreign coun-

44. NGB, vol. 6, 144–145.

tries, Korea should accept Japan's existing treaties with Western powers and let Japan handle its foreign relations. Under such an arrangement, Miyamoto added, "it would be necessary for Korea to accept the Japanese calendar, reign title, criminal code, currency, and military system."[45]

Needless to say, Kido was for the second plan. Subsequent to his appointment as envoy to China and Korea in January 1870, Kido spent six months at home in Chōshū, mustering up active support for the tottering imperial government. While there, he contacted Ōshima, who had been keeping himself abreast of the situation at Pusan, in order to obtain the latter's aid in preparing for his proposed mission to Korea.[46] Upon returning to Tokyo at the end of June, Kido immediately resumed his campaign for the Korean project with active support from the Foreign Ministry. In July he "reluctantly" accepted promotion to an imperial councilorship, when told that without elevation in rank he would not qualify as an imperial envoy. He told his friend and protégé, Itō Hirobumi, that he remained in the government solely because he wished to head the proposed mission to Korea.[47]

Although Kido had been appointed as envoy to China as well as Korea, there is no evidence that he seriously considered a journey to China. Upon hearing the news of the Tientsin Massacre, he openly voiced skepticism about the wisdom of sending a mission to China at such a time. On July 22 he discussed the Korean question with Vice Foreign Minister Terashima Munenori and Assistant Foreign Minister Yanagiwara Sakimitsu. The following day he submitted a memorial to the court to petition for an immediate expedition to Korea, without sending a mission to China. Kido accused Korea of "resisting the superior country [Japan], without understanding the principles of free intercourse and trade among all nations." Though a tributary of China, he said, Korea's relations with China in recent years had been limited to the use of the Chinese calendar. If Japan dealt with Korea in justice, China would not be able to in-

45. *Ibid.*, vol. 4, 858–865.
46. *Shōgiku Kido kō den*, vol. 2, 1287–1289.
47. *Kido Takayoshi monjo*, vol. 4, 64–65.

tervene. Since "the Korean question has now reached a point of no return," Kido argued, Japan "must prepare its armies, ships, and weapons, for it might become necessary to take decisive action if Korea persisted in its refusal to accept universal principles." Although Kido used terms such as "justice" (*kōgi*) and "universal principles" (*kōri*), which had a ring similar to those of international law, to him Japan remained a "superior country" (*jōkoku*) vis-à-vis Korea.[48]

The following day, July 24, Kido called on Sanjō to seek the latter's approval of his proposal. He then visited Ōkubo Toshimichi, a fellow councilor, for support. But in Ōkubo, Kido found an implacable opponent of his proposal. Together with his friend, Saigō Takamori, Ōkubo had led his domain, Satsuma, in the restoration movement. Following the Restoration, he became the pivotal figure in organizing the new regime.[49] As leaders of the Chōshū and Satsuma factions respectively in the ruling coalition, Kido and Ōkubo were archrivals—the two politically most powerful men in the government at this time. Although the two men worked together to strengthen the imperial government, their approaches were as different as their personalities.[50] Imaginative, straightforward, emotional, and often impatient, Kido envisioned a victorious campaign in Korea as a quick way to create an independent imperial army with which the new regime could impose unity upon a divided nation. Steadfast, rational, shrewd, and always calm, Ōkubo believed that the government should proceed step by step to consolidate its power, avoiding unnecessary risks. He was unalterably opposed to any foreign venture before the new regime consolidated its power and achieved internal stability.[51]

The confrontation between the two powerful men ended

48. TNS, vol. 1, 302–304.
49. For studies on the career of Ōkubo Toshimichi, see Iwata Masakazu, *Ōkubo Toshimichi: The Bismarck of Japan;* Sidney Devere Brown, "Ōkubo Toshimichi: His Political and Economic Policies in Early Meiji Japan," *Journal of Asian Studies* 21.2 (February 1962), 183–197.
50. For the contrasting personalities of Ōkubo and Kido, see Albert M. Craig, "Kido Kōin and Ōkubo Toshimichi," in Albert M. Craig and Donald H. Shively, eds., *Personality in Japanese History,* 264–308.
51. Kido, *Kido Takayoshi nikki,* vol. 1, 368–370; *Ōkubo Toshimichi monjo* (Ōkubo Toshimichi papers), vol. 3, 477.

with Ōkubo's victory. While Kido had the Foreign Ministry on his side, Ōkubo prevailed in the Dajōkan, where apparently he was supported by Iwakura, the tougher-minded of its two top ministers. On July 27 the Dajōkan announced that it would send a fact-finding mission to China, instead of Korea. The mission was to be headed by Yanagiwara Sakimitsu, a young court-noble-turned-diplomat.[52] Not happy with the decision, Yanagiwara visited Kido the following day to discuss the Korean question.[53] Apparently as a result of the discussions, the Foreign Ministry on July 30 repeated its earlier recommendations regarding Korea. In view of the well-known designs of the Western powers on the peninsula, said the Ministry, the government should immediately send a mission to Korea—while China and the Western powers were in dispute over the Tientsin Massacre and related problems. The Dajōkan, however, deferred decision on the matter, saying that there were other matters to consider.[54]

Although the Dajōkan's decision was final, one last effort was made on behalf of the Kido proposal. In a memorandum written before his departure for China in late August, Yanagiwara made an impassioned plea for the immediate dispatch of a mission to Korea; the plea revealed his expansionist views, which were based on his concept of imperial restoration and his fear of Western aggression. He asserted that the subjugation of Korea was fundamental to Japan's security and would be the foundation for its future expansion abroad. He argued that France, Russia, and the United States coveted Korea, and that Russia, in particular, would surely try to achieve its aggressive ambitions in East Asia by taking advantage of Europe's preoccupation with the Franco-Prussian War. "This is no time," he declared, "for our imperial country to vacillate!"[55]

Following defeat of his proposal, Kido's interest in Korea

52. NGB, vol. 6, 195.
53. *Kido Takayoshi monjo*, vol. 1, 370.
54. NGB, vol. 6, 147–148.
55. *Ibid.*, 149–150.

cooled, but this did not put an end to the controversy generated by an idea as deeply rooted in Japanese political consciousness as *sei-Kan*. Two minor but dramatic episodes indicated the intensity and persistence of feelings aroused by the controversy. On August 22, shortly after the defeat of the Kido proposal, Yokoyama Shōtarō, a young Satsuma samurai, committed *seppuku* as the ultimate act of remonstrance against *sei-Kan*. In two letters clutched to his bosom, Yokoyama criticized those advocating *sei-Kan* for doing so out of their frustration over Japan's internal disunity and dissension. An unjust war with Korea, even if victorious, he wrote, would never escape the censure of history. He argued that if Japan were strong and prosperous, Korea would not dare be disrespectful toward Japan. Warning that Korea, having fought the Western intruders in recent years, might not be as weak as it had been at the time of the Hideyoshi invasions, Yokoyama emphasized that it was no time for Japan to denounce Korea's guilt, but the time to bring about public tranquility at home.[56]

There was an equally startling manifestation of pro-*sei-Kan* sentiment. In May 1871 Maruyama Sakura, assistant foreign minister, was arrested and imprisoned. A fanatical loyalist, Maruyama had grown dissatisfied with the government's cautious approach in the negotiations with Korea and proposed bolder measures to Foreign Minister Sawa. Finding the minister unresponsive, he began secretly raising funds and volunteers for a private army for an invasion of Korea. His scheme was foiled when it was discovered by unsympathetic officials. Although the plot had no official connection or backing, Maruyama's key position as an official in charge of Korean affairs at the Foreign Ministry made it as shocking as it was incredible.[57]

The first concerted drive by top Japanese government leaders for an expedition to Korea after the Meiji Restoration was thus unsuccessful. It was motivated, as a similar

56. TNS, vol. 1, 307–308; Hilary Conroy, *The Japanese Seizure of Korea, 1868–1910*, 29–30.
57. Conroy, *Japanese Seizure of Korea*, 30.

attempt would be later, by a variety of internal and external considerations. The fundamental factor was the ideology of imperial restoration in Japan. In the eyes of the loyalists now occupying top positions in the regime, Korean refusal to submit to the restored political authority of the Japanese imperial court was "insolent," and the use of force by Japan for the "subjugation" of Korea was therefore justified. Their views were reinforced by immediate and practical considerations. In the face of what they perceived as a growing Western threat to Japan and Korea, most Japanese believed that they must gain control of the Korean peninsula in order to secure the national survival of their own country. Contemporary events and developments abroad, such as the Sino-Western discord in the wake of the Tientsin Massacre and the Franco-Prussian War in Europe, were regarded as providing opportunities to be seized upon by Japan to gain its objectives in Korea. But the most important factor was Japan's internal condition, the continued weakness of the new imperial government, jealousy among the largely still intact *han,* and the danger of revolt by a discontented soldiery. A victorious campaign in Korea would be a panacea that would provide solutions to these problems and bring about national unity.

THE QUEST FOR EQUALITY WITH CHINA: THE SINO-JAPANESE TREATY OF 1871

The old Sino-Japanese trade, which had been growing steadily since the early 1860s, increased more rapidly after the Meiji Restoration. Chinese merchants visited not only Nagasaki but other open ports in Japan, while Japanese merchants began to visit China in increasing numbers. Yet neither country took steps to establish formal ties with the other. In view of this growing trade, and especially in view of the fact that both China and Japan were entering into treaty relations with more Western countries in this period, their diplomatic indifference toward each other indicated, at least in part, that neither country saw any reason to change the traditional relations or to make them conform to Western diplomatic practice based on international law.

The idea of sending a diplomatic mission to China was first discussed by Japanese officials shortly after Kido's tentative appointment as envoy to China and Korea in January 1870. In response to an inquiry from Grand Councilor Iwakura, the Foreign Ministry submitted detailed memoranda to the Dajōkan in February 1870 on the procedures that might be followed in establishing initial diplomatic contact with the Chinese government. In one memorandum, Miyamoto Okazu estimated that it would cost 50,000 to 60,000 *ryō* to send a full mission led by an imperial envoy. Pointing out that the Ministry's total annual budget was approximately 100,000 *ryō*, Miyamoto argued that there was no urgent reason for Japan to establish formal relations with China, except perhaps for trade, which was flourishing between the two countries despite the absence of a treaty. Instead he urged early action to settle what he termed the two most urgent diplomatic problems facing Japan: the dispute with Russia over Sakhalin and the readjustment of relations with Korea.[58] Few Japanese at this time, either in or out of the government, called for formal ties with China.

On the other hand, many Japanese were calling for an early settlement of the Korean question. In view of the intransigence of the Korean government under the Taewŏn'gun, however, direct confrontation, as proposed by Kido and his supporters, would almost surely result in armed conflict with Korea—and possibly with China as well. The decision to send Yanagiwara to China, instead of sending Kido to Korea, was therefore made by Iwakura and Ōkubo as a prudent alternative that would enable Japan to achieve its objectives in Korea without risking war. A treaty with China would not only endow Japan with titular equality with that country, but would establish Japan's titular superiority over Korea.[59]

The question of how to establish diplomatic contact with

58. NGB, vol. 6, 180–183.
59. *Ibid.*, 144–145.

the Chinese government was carefully studied. Some argued that Japan should secure the good offices of Britain or
some other Western power before approaching the Chinese
authorities. On August 19, several days before Yanagiwara's
departure for China, British Minister to Japan Harry S.
Parkes warned Foreign Minister Sawa that it would be difficult for Japan to approach China directly without Western
help.[60] Others, however, doubted the trustworthiness of any
Western power as intermediary, since "the Western countries do not welcome a treaty between our imperial country
and China." The Foreign Ministry decided on a direct approach, because China and Japan had long historical ties
and close cultural affinity with each other.[61]

The kind of treaty Japan should seek from China was
considered carefully. Conservatives representing the old
school of Chinese learning (*kangaku*) preferred a broadly
worded document without specific or detailed provisions; in
their view such provisions were "unnecessary," even "undesirable," between China and Japan, "two fraternal countries" sharing a common cultural heritage. Foreign Ministry
officials wanted a precisely worded treaty based on Western
international law, preferably one similar to China's existing
treaties with Western countries. Articulating this position,
Miyamoto stated that, in negotiating a treaty with China,
Japan must exercise special care "not to blemish" its national polity.[62] The Japanese were determined to establish
their country's titular equality with China, for anything less
than that would "blemish" Japan's restored imperial polity.
This was essential since Japan had decided to seek a treaty
with China mainly to establish Japan's titular superiority
over Korea.

Accompanied by four junior officials, Yanagiwara left for
China on August 25. His principal mission was to sound out
the Chinese government's willingness to enter into treaty relations with Japan. Not being a formal envoy, Yanagiwara

60. *Ibid.*, 205–206.
61. *Ibid.*, 186–187.
62. *Ibid.*, 180–181.

was not authorized to negotiate a treaty.[63] After a week-long visit in Shanghai, where he conferred with local officials on the treatment of Japanese residents, Yanagiwara and his party reached Tientsin on September 28. On October 1 he called on Ch'eng-lin, acting commissioner of trade for the three northern ports opened by treaty, to announce the purpose of his visit. He told Ch'eng-lin that he wished to proceed to Peking immediately, in order to present a formal note from his government to the Tsungli Yamen and to commence talks with Yamen officials. Ch'eng-lin told him that a representative of a country without treaty relations with China must obtain advance consent of the Yamen before entering Peking. Offering to transmit the Japanese note to the Yamen, he told Yanagiwara to wait in Tientsin for the Yamen's reply.[64]

The following day Yanagiwara called on Tseng Kuo-fan, governor-general designate of Liang-Kiang, and Li Hung-chang, new governor-general of Chihli, to pay his respects to China's two leading statesmen and seek their assistance. Although Li subsequently was to take over foreign affairs at Tientsin, it was not until the following November that he was given additional duties as imperial commissioner of trade, replacing Ch'eng-lin. Li found Yanagiwara humble and courteous in manner and speech. Reporting their meeting in a letter to the Yamen the next day, Li said that Yanagiwara had told him that Japan, forced by Britain, France, and the United States to trade with them, was not happy because it had been "taken advantage of" (*ch'i-fu*) by these powers; but it could not resist them alone and wished to cooperate with China. Noting Japan's energetic efforts in the pursuit of Western arms and technology, Li argued that China should ally itself with Japan and should not let Japan become a base of Western aggression against China. Should trade with Japan be approved by the throne, he proposed

63. *Ibid.*, 197–199.
64. IWSM-TC, 77.24a–25b; NGB, vol. 6, 220–223; Tabohashi Kiyoshi, "Nisshi shinkankei no seiritsu" (The establishment of new Sino-Japanese relations), pt. 1, *Shigaku zasshi* 44.2 (February 1933), 168–169.

China station its officials in Japan in order to control
Chinese merchants and to maintain close liaison with the
Japanese. Thus Japan would not turn against China in
the event of conflict between China and Western powers.
However, Li advised the Yamen that a treaty with Japan
should not be modeled on China's treaties with Western
countries.[65]

On October 5 Ch'eng-lin informed Yanagiwara of the
Yamen's ruling: although Japan was a close neighbor with
historical ties to China, there was no treaty between the two
countries; the Japanese representative would not be permitted to come to Peking. Yanagiwara should discuss the proposed treaty with Ch'eng-lin at Tientsin. Though not happy,
Yanagiwara accepted the ruling. At the request of Ch'eng-
lin, he prepared a draft treaty and presented it to him on
October 10.[66]

Consisting of sixteen articles, Yanagiwara's draft contained many provisions copied from China's existing treaties
with Western countries. It also contained unique features
designed specifically to establish Japan's titular equality with
China. One article stated that the two countries would station plenipotentiaries in each other's capital, that such
plenipotentiaries would communicate with the highest officials of the host country "on the basis of the equality of the
two countries," and that they would enjoy the same
privileges as those enjoyed by the representatives of the
Western treaty powers. Another article stipulated that consular representatives of the two countries would communicate with local officials of the area where they were
stationed, on the basis of equality. Other provisions guaranteed that the two countries would extend to each other the
same diplomatic, consular, and commercial privileges as
were extended to the Western treaty powers, including con-

65. Li Hung-chang, *Li Wen-chung-kung ch'üan-shu* (Complete works of Li
Hung-chang) (hereafter cited as LWCK), *I-shu han-kao* (hereafter cited as *Tsungli
Yamen Letters*), 1.3b–4a; Tabohashi, "Nisshi shinkankei," pt. 1, 170.
66. Tabohashi, "Nisshi shinkankei," pt. 1, 169; IWSM-TC, 77.34b–36b.

sular jurisdiction and most-favored-nation treatment.[67] In the past Western powers had exacted from China more extensive concessions than they had from Japan; if adopted, therefore, Yanagiwara's draft would actually result in an "unequal" treaty, favorable to Japan. As Parkes remarked during his earlier conversation with Sawa, Japan was trying to reap the fruit of a decade's labor by the Western powers in one day.

Even before receiving Yanagiwara's draft, the Tsungli Yamen had decided to reject the Japanese request for a treaty. Although the Yamen realized the difficulty of denying Japan the same treatment as that accorded Western countries, it did not wish to sign a treaty that could create future complications. In fact, it was unwilling to grant Japan the same status as that of Western powers. Believing that Japan was interested chiefly in trade, the Yamen decided simply to allow the existing trade between the two countries to go on. Accordingly, on October 13 it sent its reply to the Japanese government note to Yanagiwara. China and Japan trusted each other completely, the Yamen said blandly, and there was no need for a formal treaty between the two countries.[68]

This unexpected setback angered Yanagiwara. On October 21, the day after he received the Yamen's reply, Yanagiwara called on Tseng, Li, and Ch'eng-lin for assistance. He told them that, in the absence of a formal treaty in the past, China and Japan had been forced to conduct their relations with each other through Western representatives, thereby subjecting themselves to Western deception and insult. Prior to his departure from Tokyo, he said, the Western representatives warned that, if Japan approached China directly without Western mediation, China would reject its request. Should his mission fail, Yanagiwara warned, the

67. For the text of Yanagiwara's draft treaty, see Fujimura Michio, "Meiji shonen ni okeru Ajia seisaku no shūsei to Chūgoku" (The revision of Asian policy and China during the early Meiji years), *Nagoya daigaku bungakubu kenkyū ronshū* 53 (March 1968), 10–12.

68. IWSM-TC, 77.37a–b; NGB, vol. 6, 238–239.

Westerners would heap ridicule upon Japan and the influence of those advocating an anti-Chinese alliance with the West would rise in Japan.[69]

This must have reminded Tseng and Li of their own fear of Japanese-Western collaboration against China. Tseng promised that he would take up the matter with the Tsungli Yamen during his forthcoming visit to Peking.[70] Li and Ch'eng-lin immediately wrote to the Yamen again, urging reconsideration of the matter. Li, who had no illusion that Japan could be treated as a tributary, argued that it was not right for China to deny a treaty to a close neighbor such as Japan when it had treaties with many Western countries. Moreover, should Japan approach China with the good offices of Britain or France, China would have no choice but to accede to a Japanese request. Not only would this hurt Chinese prestige, it might turn Japan into an enemy. Since a treaty with Japan was inevitable, he argued, it would be best if China told Japan precisely when it would be signed. The Yamen acted on Li's advice and reversed its position.[71] Obtaining the throne's approval, it sent a second note to Yanagiwara, informing the Japanese government that China would receive a Japanese mission the following spring for the purpose of negotiating a treaty between the two countries.[72] His mission accomplished, Yanagiwara left Tientsin on November 11.

Although the treaty system had been established a decade earlier with the signing of the Peking Conventions, it had not been applied to China's relations with an East Asian country that had traditionally acknowledged Chinese suzerainty or titular superiority. While China rapidly gained knowledge of international law and diplomacy during the 1860s and 1870s, this duality of Ch'ing foreign policy remained unchanged. Moreover, the Japanese request for a treaty came at a time when conservative opposition to the

69. For Yanagiwara's reaction, see his note to Ch'eng-lin, dated October 20, 1870, in NGB, vol. 6, 243–244.
    70. *Ibid.*, 237.
    71. IWSM-TC, 78.23a–24b.
    72. *Ibid.*, 78.24b–25a; NGB, vol. 6, 239–240.

treaty system was heightened by the collapse of "cooperative policy," as a result of Britain's refusal to ratify the Alcock Convention and in the wake of the Tientsin Massacre. The Yamen's decision to sign a treaty with Japan was not to go unchallenged.

In a memorial reaching the court on December 18, 1870, Ying-han, ultraconservative governor of Anhwei, strongly urged rejection of the Japanese request. Unlike Western countries, such as Britain or France, said Ying-han, Japan was a tributary of China and therefore should not be treated in the same manner. Recalling Japanese piracy during the Ming period, he questioned Japan's motives in seeking a treaty from China at a time when China was in the midst of a foreign crisis. Should the Japanese request be granted, he warned, it would set a bad example and other tributaries would follow with similar requests.[73]

In the face of strong conservative opposition, Prince Kung and other Yamen ministers decided to seek support from Tseng and Li, the two most influential governors-general and leading proponents of the proposed Japanese treaty. Accordingly, the matter was referred to the two men by imperial command.[74] In a memorial reaching the court on January 22, 1871, Li refuted Ying-han's views by arguing that Japan had ceased to be a tributary of China in the early Yüan period and therefore could not be treated in the same manner as Korea, Liu-ch'iu, or Vietnam. As for Japanese piracy, Li said originally it had started as a result of the Ming prohibition of trade. Should China reject the Japanese request now, he warned, Japan would surely align itself with Western powers—an eventuality highly detrimental to Ch'ing interests. After noting Japan's progress in the adoption of Western arms and technology, Li emphasized that Japan would become useful to China if handled properly, but if turned away, it would become an enemy. Unlike distant Western countries visited by few Chinese, Japan was a

73. For passages concerning the Japanese treaty in Ying-han's memorial, see IWSM-TC, 79.7b–8b.
74. *Ibid.*, 79.14a–b.

neighbor and perpetual source of trouble. He repeated his earlier proposal that China should station its diplomatic and consular representatives in Japan after signing the proposed treaty.[75] In a separate letter to the Tsungli Yamen, Li was specific: qualified Chinese merchants familiar with the Japanese trade might be selected as such representatives; 20,000 to 30,000 taels might be appropriated from Kiangsu and Chekiang each year to maintain representatives in Japan.[76] Apparently fearing that the Yamen might reverse its position again, Li wrote to Tseng a few days later, imploring his senior colleague to take charge of the matter.[77]

Tseng presented virtually identical views in a memorial reaching the court on March 9. If China rejected the Japanese request, said Tseng, other countries might conclude that they could not get anything from China except by force. Recalling the disastrous Mongol invasions of Japan, Tseng argued that, unlike Korea or Vietnam, Japan had never feared China and always considered itself equal to China. It was therefore natural for Japan to follow the Western example and to seek a treaty with China. Tseng stated that there would be nothing improper if China granted Japan the same privileges as those granted to the Western treaty powers, provided that they were not explicitly spelled out in a treaty. In particular, Tseng emphasized that Japan should not be granted most-favored-nation treatment.[78]

The support of the proposed treaty by Tseng and Li did not mean that they had repudiated the tribute system. Both men justified their position, at least in part, on the technical ground that Japan was not a Chinese tributary. By implication they made it clear that bona fide tributaries such as Korea and Vietnam did not qualify for a treaty with China. Accepting their arguments, the court ordered Li, who had

75. *Ibid.,* 79.46b–48b.
76. LWCK, *Tsungli Yamen Letters,* 1.10a–12a.
77. LWCK, *P'eng-liao han-kao* (hereafter cited as *Letters*), 10.30b–31a.
78. IWSM-TC, 80.9b–11b.

been appointed imperial commissioner of trade for the northern ports the previous November, to make preparations, in consultation with Tseng, for the negotiation of a treaty upon the arrival of a Japanese delegation.[79]

In undertaking his assignment, Li enlisted the services of the two specialists in foreign affairs whom he had earlier recommended to the Tsungli Yamen: Ying Pao-shih, former customs taotai at Shanghai and currently judicial commissioner of Kiangsu; and Ch'en Ch'in, customs taotai at Tientsin.[80] Li and his aides dismissed Yanagiwara's draft as unacceptable and proceeded to produce a new draft. While willing to grant Japan most of the privileges granted to the Western treaty powers, Li was determined not to make any concession that might prove harmful to China. Moreover, he wished to make the proposed treaty a tool for preventing Japan from allying itself with Western powers against China. This was evident in the draft which Li and his aides produced. Consisting of eighteen articles, the draft contained provisions guaranteeing non-aggression against each other's territory and mutual assistance in the event of a conflict between either of the contracting parties and a third power. However, it did not contain a most-favored-nation clause. On the whole, the draft reflected a spirit of strict reciprocity and guaranteed equal treatment, if not equal status, between China and Japan. On July 9 the court appointed Li as the chief Chinese negotiator and Ying and Ch'en as his deputies to meet with the Japanese.

In Tokyo, the Japanese government was making its own preparations for the forthcoming treaty negotiations with China. When Yanagiwara returned home from China the previous December, his mission was hailed as a great success. However, since he had acted without authority when he presented a draft treaty to the Chinese government, the Foreign Ministry decided to discard the draft and to produce a new one. For this task, the Ministry secured the ser-

79. *Ibid.*, 80.11b–12a.
80. LWCK, *Tsungli Yamen Letters,* 1.12b.

vices of Tsuda Masamichi, a Ministry of Justice official and leading specialist in international law.[81]

Officials chiefly responsible for Chinese and Korean affairs at the Foreign Ministry at this time—such as Sawa, Yanagiwara, and Miyamoto—were either court nobles or former loyalist samurai with limited knowledge of the West, who initially had gained their positions because of family background or political connections. Tsuda, however, represented a new breed of Western-trained specialists which was beginning to fill key positions in the government on the strength of professional or technical expertise. A former instructor in the now-defunct bakufu Office for the Investigation of Barbarian Books (*Bansho Shirabedokoro*), Tsuda studied international law in Holland from 1862 through 1865. In preparing the draft treaty, Tsuda worked with Kanda Takahira, another specialist in international law and also a former instructor in the Bansho Shirabedokoro. In addition to their bureaucratic careers, both men subsequently were active as members of the Meirokusha, a society of leading early Meiji intellectuals organized for the propagation of Western thought in Japan. Both Tsuda and Kanda viewed Japan's future relations with China and Korea, not in terms of the traditional East Asian system of interstate relations, but in terms of Western international law. Emulation of the West was their motto in foreign as well as in domestic affairs.

The draft treaty prepared by Tsuda and his colleagues—and approved by the Dajōkan—was modeled closely on China's existing treaty with Prussia. Signed in 1861 and ratified in 1863, this was the treaty whereby Prussia, a relative latecomer on the Chinese scene, gained from China, by virtue of the most-favored-nation clause, all the privileges gained previously by Britain, France, and other Western countries. It represented the sum total of unilateral concessions exacted from China by Western powers since

81. Fujimura, "Ajia seisaku no shūsei," 16.

the Opium War. While the Sino-Prussian treaty had no provisions concerning the treatment of Chinese in Prussia, the Tsuda draft had provisions for the mutual exercise of consular jurisdiction by the contracting parties. However, while Japanese consular jurisdiction in China was defined precisely and specifically, Chinese consular jurisdiction in Japan was defined only vaguely. In short, the Tsuda draft represented a typical "unequal" treaty; it was even less favorable to China than the Yanagiwara draft.[82] In their zeal for emulating the West, Tsuda and his colleagues apparently felt that Japan should gain not only titular equality with China but the same privileges in China as had been exacted by the Western treaty powers, often by the force of arms. The Tsuda draft furnishes evidence of Meiji Japan's efforts to "part with Asia" (*datsu-A*) in international life.

The Japanese delegation, led by Finance Minister Date Munenari and including Yanagiwara and Tsuda, left Yokohama aboard an American steamship on July 5, 1871. Anxious to impress the Chinese, the Foreign Ministry originally requested a warship to transport the delegation, but none was available. The delegation arrived at Tientsin on July 24. On August 1 it formally presented the Tsuda draft to the Chinese. The Chinese delegation put forward its own draft the following day. This took the Japanese by surprise, for in the past China had never produced a draft in treaty negotiations with foreign representatives.[83] The Chinese delegation declared the Tsuda draft unacceptable, characterizing it as a sundry collection of excerpts from China's existing treaties with Western countries. Unlike the one-sided intercourse between China and the Western countries, said the Chinese, trade and travel between China and Japan would be bilateral. A treaty between the two countries must therefore spell out mutual obligations and guarantee reciprocal benefits. The Chinese further stated that, in preparing their draft, they had paid close attention to the Yanagiwara

82. *Ibid.,* 16–21.
83. *Ibid.,* 21; Tabohashi, "Nisshi shinkankei," pt. 1, 180–181.

draft. Therefore, they declared, negotiations must be conducted on the basis of the Chinese draft.[84]

The Japanese delegation found the Chinese draft unsatisfactory because it would deny Japan many of the privileges enjoyed in China by the Western treaty powers. Although Yanagiwara had told Li during his previous visit that the desire to cooperate with China against Western countries was Japan's principal motive in seeking a treaty with China, the Japanese delegation now objected to the mutual good-offices clause in the Chinese draft. Confiding that prior to the Japanese delegation's departure for China, some Western representatives in Tokyo had asked Minister Date if his mission was to conclude a treaty of alliance with China, Yanagiwara argued that such a clause would arouse Western suspicion. He also argued that China should treat Japan no better and no worse than it treated Western countries.[85]

Determined to avoid protracted arguments, Li instructed his deputies to reply in strong terms. Accordingly, Ying and Ch'en told Yanagiwara that if Japan wished to avoid Western suspicion, the best thing would be not to sign any treaty at all. They pointed out that the mutual good-offices clause was not a Chinese invention, but was taken from China's treaty with the United States. Reminding Yanagiwara it was Japan, not China, that was seeking a treaty, Ying and Ch'en further stated: "When you sent your draft to us last year, we found several clauses unsatisfactory, but the rest of it was acceptable. Now your side has come forward with an entirely different draft and wants to discard the earlier one. Your conduct amounts to a breach of faith even before signing a treaty!"[86] Realizing that there would be no treaty unless they accepted the Chinese position, the Japanese delegation gave in. Having thus seized the initiative, Li went on to dominate the negotiations. In a letter to Tseng on August 19, Li confidently predicted the signing of a treaty on Chinese terms within a month, adding that although the

84. IWSM-TC, 82.1a–2a; NGB, vol. 7.1, 241–242.
85. IWSM-TC, 82.2b–4b; NGB, vol. 7.1, 240–241.
86. IWSM-TC, 82.2b–6a; NGB, vol. 7.1, 241–242.

Japanese were clever and crafty, they were no match for the "savage and untamable" Westerners.[87] After some hard bargaining, the delegations signed, as Li predicted, a treaty of friendship and accompanying trade regulations between the two countries on September 13, 1871.

The eighteen-article Sino-Japanese Treaty of Amity began with a preamble which, without reference to the rulers of the two countries, stated that "Great Ch'ing" and "Great Japan" were signing a treaty to further their traditional friendship. This was, of course, a device to sidestep the issue of titular precedence between the two rulers. Anxious to establish their sovereign's titular equality with the Chinese emperor, the Japanese delegation had argued that the preamble should refer to both the Chinese and Japanese emperors, the former by the traditional Chinese term *"huang-ti"* (*kōtei* in Japanese) and the latter by the traditional Japanese term *"tennō"* (*t'ien-huang* in Chinese). This was rejected by the Chinese, who apparently found the term *"tennō"* (heavenly emperor) for the Japanese ruler preposterous. When the Japanese declared that in future messages to the Chinese emperor, the Japanese ruler would refer to himself as *"tennō,"* Li retorted that while the Japanese ruler might call himself by whatever term he chose, no one but the Chinese emperor had authority to decide whether or not such messages should be answered or how the Japanese ruler should be addressed if his messages were to be answered.[88]

Article I of the treaty contained a pledge of non-aggression against each other's "states and territories" (*pang-t'u* in Chinese; *fōdo* in Japanese). Without so specifying, Li inserted the phrase chiefly to protect Korea from future Japanese aggression. Unaware of Li's intentions, the Japanese delegation readily accepted it, assuming that it did not apply to tributary states.[89] Despite Japanese objections, the mutual good-offices clause was retained; it was Li's de-

87. LWCK, *Letters*, 11.11a.
88. LWCK, *Tsungli Yamen Letters*, 1.22b.
89. On Li's intentions, see IWSM-TC, 82.31b. For the Japanese interpretation of the article, see NGB, vol. 7.1, 223.

vice for preventing a possible Japanese-Western alliance against China. Article III gave both countries consular jurisdiction over their own nationals at open ports in each other's territory. China, however, firmly rejected the persistent Japanese demand for most-favored-nation treatment. It also denied Japan the right to trade in China's interior, which the latter sought as a substitute for most-favored-nation treatment. A unique feature of the treaty was the prohibition of sword-carrying by Japanese in China. On the whole, the treaty guaranteed reciprocity and equality between the two countries.[90]

The signing of the treaty was an event of great significance in the history of international relations in East Asia. It was the first modern treaty ever signed between two East Asian countries on the basis of Western international law. It was a treaty based on the equality of the contracting parties—a principle which China and Japan had not considered applicable to their relations with one another in the past. The treaty was a revolutionary departure from traditional practice in East Asian diplomacy, a major step toward the ultimate incorporation of East Asia into the Western system of international relations.

The treaty damaged—perhaps far more than Li and his associates cared to admit—China's efforts to preserve the traditional world order and Chinese supremacy in East Asia. Even if it was not a fundamental challenge to the basic concept underlying the traditional order, it was certainly an effective challenge to Chinese supremacy in that order. Despite their argument that the treaty was acceptable because Japan was not a Chinese tributary, as Korea or Vietnam, it is doubtful that Tseng and Li really regarded China and Japan as belonging in the same category as Western countries.[91] Whatever logic or power of persuasion the argument had, it was negated by the undeniable fact that Japan was a

90. For the text of the treaty and regulations, see IWSM-TC, 82.33a–46b; NGB, vol. 7.1, 203–221.

91. The Ch'ing government recorded the Date mission as a "tributary embassy." See John K. Fairbank, "The Early Treaty System in the Chinese World Order," in John K. Fairbank, ed., *The Chinese World Order*, 266.

bona fide member of the East Asian world that had in the past acknowledged, tacitly or otherwise, Chinese titular superiority and cultural leadership. This is all the more true because Japan's initial objective in seeking a treaty with China was to establish its titular equality with China, which it hoped to translate into titular superiority over Korea.

On the other hand, the treaty may be regarded as an important victory for Tseng, Li, and other proponents of pragmatic diplomacy such as Prince Kung and Wen-hsiang at a time when conservative reaction and widespread anti-foreign sentiment were making China's accommodation with reality in the modern international world difficult. It was the most equitable treaty signed by China with a foreign country up to that point, after a long series of humiliating, unequal treaties, which it had been forced to accept out of weakness, ignorance, or both. The initiative maintained by the Chinese delegation throughout the negotiations attested to China's self-confidence and newly gained knowledge of modern international diplomacy. The treaty was an example of China's skillful use of international law for the protection of its national interests. It also demonstrated China's desire to alter the system of unequal treaties. Perhaps it should be regarded as a continuation of the effort at treaty revision first made in the negotiations with Alcock in 1868.

With his negotiation of the Japanese treaty, Li emerged as a principal architect of Ch'ing policy toward Japan and Korea, a role he was to continue for the next quarter century. With a clear perception of the potential threat to China and Korea posed by Meiji Japan, he maneuvered to turn the treaty into a tool to forestall Japanese-Western collaboration against China and Japanese aggression against Korea. In light of his strong interest in Korea and of the debate that attended the decision of the Ch'ing government to sign the treaty, it is not likely that Li was unaware of the moral dilemma and practical difficulties which the treaty might create for Korea in its relations with Japan. Probably Li simply could not avoid these problems because he regarded the treaty as essential in order to prevent a Japanese alliance with Western powers against China. He had to choose between two undesirable alternatives. Were it not for his fear of Japanese-Western collaboration against China, he might not have supported a treaty with Japan at this time.

For Japan the treaty was an unqualified success of historic significance. It was the first "equal" treaty signed by Japan in modern times. More significantly, the treaty formally established Japan's titular equality with China for the first time in the history of Sino-Japanese relations. The Meiji government achieved one of the major goals of the "restoration" diplomacy it had launched toward East Asian countries following the imperial restoration. Yet, even as this goal was being attained, the traditional East Asian concept of interstate relations, which formed the ideological basis of that diplomacy, was being discarded by a new Western-oriented leadership emerging within the Japanese government. Therefore the treaty was extremely unpopular among those Japanese leaders and officials who, in their eagerness to emulate the West, ignored its eminently equitable nature and its revolutionary significance.[92] This most important achievement of "restoration" diplomacy also marked its end.

Despite the modern character of the treaty, the circumstances leading to its signature and some of its contents clearly show that neither China nor Japan had at this time fully abandoned their traditional attitudes and ideas concerning their relations with each other and with other East Asian countries. The terminological dispute over the titles of the rulers of the two countries seems to indicate that while willing to treat Japan the same way it treated Western countries, China was unwilling to grant Japan the same formal status, let alone titular equality with China. Though possessing considerable knowledge of international law, neither country seems to have understood fully at this time the absolute nature of the sovereignty of the individual state

92. Fujimura, "Ajia seisaku no shūsei," 22–23; Tabohashi, "Nisshi shinkankei," pt. 2, *Shigaku zasshi* 44.3 (March 1933), 314–315.

under Western international law, for the two countries readily granted each other consular jurisdiction—a concession which no Western state would have granted to a foreign power. Traditional ideas persisted most firmly, however, in the attitudes of China and Japan toward Korea, whose ultimate control was the principal reason behind the decision to sign a treaty with each other at this time. Scholars have pointed out that China's determination to maintain its suzerainty over Korea and the latter's acceptance of traditional Chinese authority were contrary to the modern concept of international relations. But what has been generally overlooked is the fact that in this period Japan also retained the traditional East Asian concept of hierarchical interstate relations when dealing with Korea. Japan's desire to establish titular superiority over Korea by gaining equality with China was, after all, its principal reason, at least initially, for seeking a treaty with China.

CHAPTER V

Aspiration for "Western" Identity and Expansionism: Japan's New East Asia Policy, 1872–1875

Abolition of the domains and creation of the prefectures in August 1871 marked the final step in dismantling Japan's feudal political structure, which had begun with the abolition of the bakufu. The last institutional legacies of feudal separatism in government were eliminated. A series of governmental reorganizations carried out before and after this important step paved the way for other far-reaching reforms during the following years: the disestablishment of the samurai class, the introduction of compulsory education, national conscription, and a new land tax system. These and related measures laid the foundation for the integrated, centralized state that emerged during the following decade.

Sweeping measures of reform and modernization within Japan were closely paralleled by the inauguration of an activist foreign policy abroad. With regard to the West, the new policy manifested itself in the first major diplomatic undertaking of Meiji Japan: the dispatch of the Iwakura embassy to the United States and Europe. In East Asia, it was manifested in a series of moves affecting China and Korea, including: (1) termination of Tsushima's intermediary role in the conduct of Japanese-Korean relations; (2) Japan's claim of exclusive jurisdiction over Liu-ch'iu; (3)

an unsuccessful attempt to revise the newly signed Sino-Japanese treaty; and (4) Foreign Minister Soejima's mission to China.

Together, these events and activities represented the Meiji government's first drive for diplomatic reform, a concerted effort to change the arrangement of foreign relations it had inherited from the bakufu. Specifically, it decided to gain equality with Western powers for Japan through revision of the unequal treaties. In East Asia, Japan was no longer content with titular equality with China, but would seek diplomatic and commercial parity with the Western treaty powers in China. Moreover, it would reject the Chinese claim of suzerainty over Liu-ch'iu. With regard to Korea, rather than titular superiority it had attempted to establish under the "restoration" diplomacy, Japan wished to gain the same privileged status vis-à-vis Korea as that enjoyed by the Western treaty powers in China and Japan. Japan's drive for diplomatic reform signified its conversion to the Western concept of international relations and its conscious decision to emulate predatory Western practices in international diplomacy.

THE QUEST FOR EQUALITY
WITH THE WEST, 1872–1873

In the immediate post-Restoration period, the imperial government was preoccupied with the task of establishing its authority at home. This goal was largely attained when the prefectural system placed the country under direct central control, and it enabled leaders of the new regime to turn their attention to the nation's problems abroad, where revision of the unequal treaties with Western countries presented a formidable task. The treaties which the bakufu had signed with the Western powers were due for revision in 1872. Early in 1871 the Foreign Ministry notified the treaty powers of its intention to seek treaty revision the following year.[1] In a move heralding the advent of this activist foreign

1. NGB, vol. 7.1, 57–63.

policy, Grand Councilor Iwakura, the second highest official
of the government, was appointed foreign minister in August 1871 in the government reorganization that accompanied the abolition of the domains. Iwakura's willingness
to accept this technical demotion was an indication of the
extraordinary determination with which he and the government approached the task of treaty revision.

The following October, Sanjō, now elevated to the highest post of the chancellorship, addressed a long letter to
Iwakura on the subject of diplomatic reform. All nations,
large and small, said Sanjō, are equal in status, and treaties
between them must be based on this equality guaranteed by
international law. Exceptions may be made, however, if
backward customs or archaic institutions of some countries
make the uniform application of international law impractical. Since the imperial restoration, Sanjō went on, Japan has
centralized political authority, modernized its laws and institutions, liberalized its authoritarian rule, and broadened
civil rights, thereby laying the foundation for equality with
the Western countries. Now, therefore, Japan should regain
its full authority as an independent state by revising its unequal treaties with Western powers. However, in view of the
fact that Japan introduced these reforms only recently and
that there are still more to be undertaken, the government
should postpone the work of treaty revision for two to three
years. In the meantime, it should send a large diplomatic
mission to Western countries to present Japan's views and to
study advanced institutions of these countries.[2]

Sanjō's letter is a document of major import in the history
of modern Japanese foreign policy, for it sets forth the early
Meiji government's position on the issue of treaty revision
and the basic principles that were to guide its policy toward
China and Korea. First, by fully accepting the Western international system based on the equal sovereignty of all
states, it rejected the traditional East Asian concept of
hierarchical relations among states and peoples and thereby

2. For the text of Sanjō's letter to Iwakura, see *ibid.*, 67–73; Tada Kōmon, ed.,
Iwakura kō jikki (The authentic records of Prince Iwakura), vol. 2, 926–938.

repudiated the traditional East Asian world order founded upon that concept. Second, it accepted the Western argument that unequal treaties were justified and necessary when there were substantial differences in the level of cultural enlightenment between the contracting parties. Third, having accepted these premises, Sanjō proceeded to declare that while late Tokugawa Japan with its feudal social and political institutions had not qualified for equality with the West, Meiji Japan was on the threshold of achieving complete equality with the West as a result of the reforms carried out since the restoration of imperial rule.

Sanjō's proposal resulted in the appointment of the Iwakura embassy in November. Iwakura was relieved from his Foreign Ministry post, elevated to the post of minister of the right, and concurrently appointed ambassador extraordinary and plenipotentiary to the United States and Europe. Councilor Kido Takayoshi and Finance Minister Ōkubo Toshimichi, the two most powerful figures in the government, were among four deputy ambassadors who were to accompany Iwakura. On December 21, 1871, the Iwakura embassy left Japan for an extended tour of the United States and Europe. Its chief mission was to sound out the governments of the Western treaty powers on the feasibility of treaty revision.[3]

If Sanjō's letter represented a basic repudiation by the Meiji government of its initial "restoration diplomacy" toward China and Korea, the dispatch of the prestigious Iwakura embassy signaled the shift of Japan's main interest and attention in foreign affairs from East Asia to the West. While not unimportant in themselves, Japan's relations with China and Korea would be subordinated to or even determined by its relations with the West. Moreover, while Japan's principal diplomatic goal in China in the past had been to gain titular equality with China, it would now seek legal parity with the Western treaty powers in China. Regarding itself as sufficiently "advanced," Japan considered

3. NGB, vol. 7.1, 75–77, 96–99.

itself deserving of the same privileges in China and, in the future, Korea, as enjoyed by Western powers. It was with these assumptions that new Foreign Minister Soejima Taneomi, handpicked by Iwakura as his successor to implement the new foreign policy, embarked upon the task of redefining Japan's relations with China and Korea.[4] We may note here that, contrary to the hopes of Li Hung-chang and other like-minded Chinese leaders, there was little in the views and attitudes of their counterparts in Japan at this time that suggested the possibility of Sino-Japanese cooperation against the Western powers.[5]

Before proceeding to deal with Soejima's foreign policy, we should examine briefly what transpired between Japan and Korea since the Ōshima-Urase compromise formula had been frustrated by the Brandt incident in June 1870. Although the Japanese government's decision the following month to send the Yanagiwara mission to China meant that the main stage of Japanese diplomacy concerning Korea had shifted to China, desultory negotiations continued at Pusan. Following his return from Pusan, Urase went to Tokyo in September to report to the Foreign Ministry on his talks with An Tong-jun. After hearing Urase's report, Foreign Minister Sawa concluded that Korea still might be willing to establish direct relations with the new Japanese regime without Tsushima acting as intermediary, if it did not involve the exchange of state messages between the rulers of the two countries. Neither Urase nor the Foreign Ministry fully appreciated the gravity with which the Korean authorities viewed the Brandt incident or the depth of their suspicion and fear of Japanese-Western collaboration against Korea. This led to the dispatch of another mission, led by Yoshioka Kōki, a Foreign Ministry official known for his moderate views, to Korea. Since the mission was to be an

4. Tei Nagayasu, "Soejima taishi teki-Shin gairyaku" (A general account of Ambassador Soejima's mission to China), in *Meiji bunka zenshū* (Collected works on Meiji culture), vol. 11, 63.

5. On Li Hung-chang's hope for Sino-Japanese cooperation against the West, see his memorial in IWSM-TC, 79.46b–48b.

informal one, Yoshioka was not given the formal status of an envoy.[6]

Leaving Tokyo in late October, Yoshioka and his party reached Pusan via Tsushima in late December. Yoshioka carried two official letters, one of which was addressed to the Korean minister of rites from Foreign Minister Sawa. To sidestep the issue of titular precedence between the rulers of the two countries, Sawa avoided direct references to the Japanese emperor or court in his letter. He simply expressed Japan's sincere desire for renewing the traditional friendship between the two countries, which were "mutually dependent on each other for survival" in a world where distance had been rendered unimportant by technological progress in navigation and weaponry. In order to contrive the "proper circumstances" in which the letters might be presented, Yoshioka was instructed to have Tsushima officials suggest confidentially to the Koreans that they, the Koreans, should appeal for direct relations between the "governments" of the two countries on the basis of equality. The letters were to be presented after such an appeal had been made.[7]

Upon his arrival at Pusan, Yoshioka sent his interpreters to An Tong-jun to request a meeting. An, however, turned down the request on the ground that Yoshioka was not a Tsushima official.[8] Despite his repeated efforts, it was not until May 17, 1871, nearly half a year later, that Yoshioka was able to meet with An, and then only "informally." Yoshioka took pains to explain the significance of the imperial restoration in Japan and the subsequent takeover by the Foreign Ministry of the management of Korean affairs. He mentioned Japan's recent, successful negotiations for a treaty with China. Unimpressed, An merely repeated that the new Japanese regime, like the bakufu before, should conduct its business with Korea through Tsushima. Yoshi-

6. NGB, vol. 6, 158; TNS, vol. 1, 239–241, 244–245.
7. NGB, vol. 6, 161–163; TNS, vol. 1, 242–243.
8. NGB, vol. 6, 267–268.

oka realized that Tsushima's semi-tributary relations with Korea, which the island still maintained, were a serious obstacle to the establishment of new relations between the two countries. In a report to Tokyo, he therefore recommended the immediate and complete termination of Tsushima's intermediary role between the two countries, emphasizing the futility of trying to "extend Japanese imperial authority to Korea" while Tsushima continued sending envoys to and receiving largess from Korea in the traditional manner.[9]

Around this time the Tokyo government learned of American plans to send an expedition to Korea. Anticipating an armed clash between Korea and the United States, it decided to avail itself of whatever opportunity such a clash might present for Japan to advance its own cause in Korea. In early May 1871 Sawa sent confidential instructions to Yoshioka at Pusan, stating that although Korea was a close neighbor, Japan was under no obligation to help Korea, whereas as an ally Japan had an obligation to help the United States. Should hostilities break out, said Sawa, Japan should step aside and let the United States pursue its course of action in Korea without interference. Should Korea appeal to Japan for help, Japan should first make Korea prove its friendship toward Japan and then mediate between the two countries to bring about a just settlement. Finally, Sawa warned Yoshioka to act with utmost caution so as to keep good faith with the Americans and to avoid Korean suspicion.[10] One might add that the Korean suspicion of Japanese collaboration with Western powers was not entirely unfounded.

With the abolition of the domains in August 1871, Tsushima ceased to exist as a *han*. This automatically ended the island's centuries-old role as intermediary between Japan and Korea. The management of Korean affairs was finally taken over by the Foreign Ministry. But preoccupied as it was with preparations for the Iwakura embassy, the

9. *Ibid.*, 284–285.
10. *Ibid.*, vol. 7.1, 276–278.

Ministry was not immediately able to take any action with regard to Korea. It was not until after Soejima's assumption of office as foreign minister in mid-December that the Korean question received high-level official attention.[11]

Soejima's appointment reflected the change taking place in the top leadership in the government after the abolition of the domains, as men of ordinary samurai background began to eclipse imperial princes, court nobles, and former daimyo in power and influence. While his two predecessors, Sawa and Iwakura, were both court nobles who had little knowledge about the West prior to the Meiji Restoration, Soejima acquired considerable knowledge of the West before the Restoration. The son of a Confucian scholar of Hizen, Soejima was an accomplished scholar and in his twenties served as an instructor at the official Confucian academy of his *han*. Subsequently, he studied English at Nagasaki and became a keen student of the West. His first contact with Western international law was through *Wan-kuo kung-fa,* W. A. P. Martin's Chinese translation of Henry Wheaton's *Elements of International Law.* Following the Meiji Restoration, Soejima served in the new regime as junior councilor and then as councilor, and he was actively involved in foreign affairs, particularly in the negotiations with Russia over Sakhalin. Through all this he developed highly nationalistic views on foreign policy. He believed that Japan must not only consolidate its claims on such peripheral areas as Sakhalin, the Bonins, and Liu-ch'iu, but extend its control to Korea and Taiwan. Soejima's educational background and intellectual outlook were precisely in accord with the spirit of the diplomatic reform he was to pursue in regard to China and Korea, strongly oriented toward the West while retaining some roots in East Asian tradition.[12] His vigorous assertion of Japan's national rights,

11. TNS, vol. 1, 262–263.
12. On Soejima's life and career, see Maruyama Kanji, *Soejima Taneomi haku* (Count Soejima Taneomi); Wayne C. McWilliams, "Soejima Taneomi: Statesman of Early Meiji Japan, 1868–1874" (Ph.D. dissert., University of Kansas, 1973).

which earned the label of "national rights diplomacy" (*kok-ken gaikō*), reflected the growing self-confidence of the Meiji government, which had succeeded in establishing effective control at home.[13]

Following the abolition of the domains, Sō Shigemasa (formerly Yoshisato), formerly daimyo and then governor of Tsushima, was appointed assistant foreign minister in a move to ensure smooth transition in the management of Korean affairs. Sō was to go to Korea to explain the termination of his hereditary role in the conduct of relations with Korea as a result of the abolition of the domains.[14] Apparently anxious to make as complete a break with the past as possible, however, Soejima rescinded the decision. Instead, on January 16, 1872, he appointed Sagara Masaki, a former Tsushima official, to undertake the mission. Although Sagara was to go to Korea as Foreign Ministry official, as a concession to tradition he was permitted to act as Sō's personal representative.[15] In view of Korea's past intransigence, Soejima was not optimistic about the success of Sagara's mission. He therefore approved a contingency plan to be put into effect in case the mission failed. Under this plan, Yoshioka, who was still at Pusan, was given full discretionary power to choose whatever course of action he deemed appropriate for all Japanese at Pusan, including the withdrawal of all personnel save a caretaker crew at Japan House. Soejima was thus prepared for a complete break in the negotiations.[16]

Sagara and his party arrived at Pusan on February 22 aboard a steamship, the *Manju-maru*. Sagara carried two let-

13. For views on Soejima's foreign policy, see Haraguchi Kiyoshi, *Nihon kindai kokka no keisei* (The formation of the modern Japanese state), 154–158; Wayne C. McWilliams, "East Meets West: The Soejima Mission to China, 1873," *Monumenta Nipponica* 30.3 (Autumn 1975), 237–275; Marlene J. Mayo, "The Korean Crisis of 1873 and Early Meiji Foreign Policy," *Journal of Asian Studies* 31.4 (August 1972), 803–805.

14. NGB, vol. 7.1, 314–317.

15. *Ibid.*, 339–341.

16. *Ibid.*, 344–345. Although the text of Soejima's instructions to Yoshioka is missing, Yoshioka mentioned a possible withdrawal of Japanese personnel from Korea in his acknowledgment of the instructions. See *ibid.*, vol. 8, 304–305.

ters from Sō, one of which was addressed to the Korean vice minister of rites. Sō explained his new role in the management of Korean affairs at the Foreign Ministry. He reiterated Japan's desire to renew its friendship with Korea and expressed the hope that the Korean authorities would receive Yoshioka and other Foreign Ministry officials.[17]

Not surprisingly, the use of a steamship by Sagara and his party in traveling to Korea became an issue, for at this time the Koreans associated steamships exclusively with Westerners. They considered the Japanese use of such a craft not only a violation of the old treaty which specified the type of ship that Tsushima could send, but further evidence of Japanese-Western collaboration against Korea. The Korean authorities demanded the immediate departure of the *Manju-maru* with all those whom it had brought from Japan. The ship left Pusan two days later, taking back Higuchi, the rejected Tsushima envoy who had spent more than three years in vain at Pusan.[18] For months thereafter, despite repeated Japanese requests, the Koreans would neither accept Sō's letters nor arrange a meeting between Sagara and the prefect of Tongnae. Mention of Japan's new treaty with China brought no favorable Korean reaction. Finally, Yoshioka was forced to conclude that the best course of action under the circumstances was a temporary withdrawal of all Japanese from Pusan except for a caretaker crew at Japan House. On May 9 he sent a request to Tokyo for approval of his intended action.[19]

Though outwardly adamant, the Taewŏn'gun and his advisers viewed the situation at Pusan with concern. They ordered An Tong-jun, the veteran negotiator at Pusan who was in Seoul mourning his father's death, to return to his post.[20] Reaching Tongnae on June 28, An met with Sagara at Japan House two days later, but he refused to meet with Yoshioka or any other Foreign Ministry official. Sagara

17. *Ibid.*, vol. 7.1, 336–339.
18. *Ibid.*, vol. 8, 305–307.
19. *Ibid.*, 313–314.
20. ISN-KJ, 9/4/2; KJS, 9.15a–b.

briefed An on what had transpired at Pusan during his absence and asked An about the Seoul government's decision regarding Sō's letters. An replied that an important decision such as whether or not to receive Sō's letters, which represented a departure from established practice, could be reached only through public debate throughout the country and that he was in no position to predict how long such a process would take. This dashed the last lingering hope which Yoshioka and Sagara had of reaching some kind of accord or understanding. They decided to cut off the negotiations and return home.[21]

Before departing from Korea, Sagara and other Tsushima officials staged a final act of protest with Yoshioka's approval. At midnight on July 1, 1872, some fifty Tsushima men, led by Sagara, marched out of the Japanese compound at Pusan and headed for Tongnae in a desperate attempt to see its prefect. Blocked at numerous points and hampered by inclement weather, it took Sagara and his men six days to make a journey of no more than a dozen miles. Their protest was as futile as it was dramatic. Although they spent several days at Tongnae, they were unable to see the prefect. Nor did they receive satisfactory word from anyone else. On July 11 they gave up and returned to Pusan. On July 20 Yoshioka, Sagara, and others departed from Pusan, after sending a lengthy letter of protest to the Koreans.[22]

Formal termination of Tsushima's centuries-old role between Japan and Korea came three months later when Assistant Foreign Minister Hanabusa Yoshimoto went to Pusan to take over Japan House. Accompanied by four Foreign Ministry officials, three army officers, one naval officer, and two platoons of infantry soldiers, Hanabusa arrived at Pusan on October 16 aboard the warship *Kasuga*. Acting with dispatch, he took over Japan House from the Tsushima officials the following day and renamed it the Japanese Mission. While most of its former Tsushima personnel, numbering some two hundred persons, were ordered to return

21. NGB, vol. 8, 330.
22. *Ibid*. 330–334. For a Korean account of the incident, see ISN-KJ, 9/6/7–8.

home, a few were given new assignments as Foreign Ministry employees. Hanabusa next turned to the question of settling Tsushima's outstanding debts to Korea. The Korean officials, however, refused to meet with him on the ground that he was not a Tsushima official. Realizing that his continued presence at Pusan would further complicate an already difficult situation, Hanabusa departed from Pusan with his party on October 25, leaving behind some eighty Japanese, most of whom were Tsushima merchants. Supply of provisions for the Japanese, which the Koreans had suspended during Hanabusa's stay, was resumed upon his departure. Whatever formal relations that had existed between Japan and Korea since the Meiji Restoration ceased; the diplomatic interregnum between the two countries became a fact.[23]

Termination of Tsushima's intermediary role was the first significant step toward the modernization of relations with Korea under Japan's diplomatic reform program. In the past the Meiji government had not taken this essential step, partly because of its inability to assume full responsibility for the management of Korean affairs and partly because of Tsushima's unwillingness to relinquish its traditional role. Another, more fundamental, reason was the largely traditional views and attitudes toward Korea held by the leaders of the Restoration government. Seeing the establishment of Japan's titular superiority as the primary diplomatic objective vis-à-vis Korea, they did not object to Tsushima's continued role in the conduct of relations with Korea, as long as that role did not interfere with the attainment of titular superiority or compromise the "restored" imperial dignity of Japan. After the failure of the Sagara mission— Tsushima's last attempt to retain influence, if not an active role, in Japanese-Korean diplomacy—the Meiji government realized that Tsushima's retention of any role whatever was not only impracticable but incompatible with the new form of relations Japan wished to establish with Korea.

23. For Hanabusa's report on his mission, see NGB, vol. 8, 355–357.

The decisive manner in which the Japanese government took over Japan House from Tsushima against Korean objections indicated its determination to alter relations with Korea and its growing strength and self-confidence. Internally, with the abolition of the domains, the government was now able to impose its will upon Tsushima. Moreover, it was ready to assume Tsushima's outstanding Korean debts—a responsibility that in the past had made it reluctant to take over the conduct of Korean affairs from Tsushima. Externally, the expectation that Japan would gain equality with Western powers through the success of the Iwakura embassy made Japan confident in the conduct of its East Asian diplomacy. Its diplomatic morale and self-confidence in Korea was boosted even more by the signing of the Sino-Japanese treaty in 1871. And the fact that Hanabusa went to Korea on a warship with a military escort to perform a relatively minor diplomatic mission indicated the Meiji government's eagerness to emulate Western gunboat diplomacy—its readiness to flex growing military muscles in order to achieve its diplomatic objectives.

The Japanese decision to seek diplomatic and commercial parity with the Western treaty powers in China led to an attempt to revise the treaty with China even before its ratification. As we have seen, the Western treaty powers were uneasy over the treaty between China and Japan. Throughout the summer and early fall of 1871 rumors were rife in diplomatic circles in China and Japan concerning the Sino-Japanese negotiations at Tientsin and the resultant treaty, signed in September. Some speculated that the two countries had signed a mutual defense pact against Western powers.[24]

When the mutual good-offices clause of the treaty became known, the British, American, and French representatives in Tokyo complained to the Japanese government, urging it either to delete the clause or not to ratify the treaty. Alarmed by these adverse reactions, Sanjō and Iwakura

24. *Ibid.*, 238, 245; Tabohashi Kiyoshi, "Nisshi shinkankei no seiritsu," pt. 1, *Shigaku zasshi* 44.2 (February 1933), 186.

promised to follow the advice.[25] The Japanese government itself considered the treaty unsatisfactory: the Iwakura embassy was expected to negotiate the removal of extraterritorial provisions from Japan's existing treaties with Western powers, and the government did not wish to include similar provisions in the new treaty. It was particularly unhappy because the treaty denied Japan most-favored-nation treatment in China. Upon their return home, Date and his aides faced a storm of criticism from the government, which had discarded its earlier objective of seeking titular equality with China in favor of seeking diplomatic and commercial parity with the Western treaty powers in China. On December 1 the Left Secretariat of the Dajōkan declared formally that the Date mission had exceeded its authority. It recommended sending a new mission to China to seek changes in the treaty, and, should China refuse the Japanese demand, discarding the whole treaty.[26] Before leaving for the United States, Iwakura asked his successor, Soejima, to obtain Chinese consent to postpone the ratification of the treaty until his return. Accordingly, in the spring of 1872, the Japanese government sent Yanagiwara to China again to seek the recommended changes in the treaty.[27]

Yanagiwara arrived in Tientsin on May 4, accompanied by two aides. He had been instructed to seek: (1) deletion of the mutual good-offices clause; (2) elimination of Chinese consular jurisdiction in Japan; and (3) removal of the ban on sword-carrying by Japanese in China. He was also to seek most-favored-nation treatment for Japan and the same trade privileges in China as those enjoyed by the Western treaty powers.[28]

25. Grace Fox, *Britain and Japan, 1858–1883,* 277–278. On Western criticism and Japanese reactions, see NGB, vol. 7.1, 171–172, 238, 251–252; vol. 8, 246–249, 251–252.

26. Fujimura Michio, "Meiji shonen ni okeru Ajia seisaku no shūsei to Chūgoku," *Nagoya daigaku bungakubu kenkyū ronshū* 53 (March 1968), 34. For Date's rebuttal, see NGB, vol. 7.1, 258–260.

27. Tabohashi, "Nisshi shinkankei," pt. 2, *Shigaku zasshi* 44.3 (March 1933), 314–315.

28. NGB, vol. 8, 242–243, 245–246.

Li Hung-chang considered the Japanese attempt to revise a signed treaty prior to its ratification "crafty and offensive." It reinforced his fear that Japan, intent upon emulating the West in arms and technology, would become a source of serious trouble to China.[29] When Yanagiwara presented the Japanese demands on May 15, Li angrily rejected them, branding the Japanese action a breach of faith and an insult to China and himself. He lectured the Japanese envoy on how reprehensible it was for one country to break faith with another in international diplomacy. Yanagiwara tried desperately to explain that Japan was seeking the changes in the treaty solely because it wished to bring the treaty with China in line with the expected revision of its treaties with Western countries. Relenting a little, Li suggested that the Japanese envoy discuss his proposal with Ch'en Ch'in and Sun Shih-ta, the latter a Kiangsu taotai who had escorted the Date mission to Peking the previous year.[30]

After protracted discussions, China agreed to remove the ban on sword-carrying in China, as a concession to Japanese national tradition, and in the future to negotiate changes in provisions dealing with tariffs and consular jurisdiction if Japan succeeded in negotiating such changes in its treaties with Western countries. Li was adamant, however, in his refusal to delete the mutual good-offices clause and to grant Japan most-favored-nation treatment. He cut off Yanagiwara's arguments by stating bluntly that since Japan was an independent state, there was no reason why any Western power should dictate to it concerning its relations with China. He assured Yanagiwara, however, that invocation of the good-offices clause would not entail material or military assistance by either signatory power.[31]

Yanagiwara returned to Tokyo on August 11. It was understood that ratification of the treaty would take place after the return of the Iwakura embassy from Europe. The

29. LWCK, *Letters*, 11.13b–14a.
30. LWCK, *Tsungli Yamen Letters*, 1.30a; IWSM-TC, 86.42b; NGB, vol. 8, 265–267.
31. For Chinese and Japanese accounts of the negotiations, see IWSM-TC, 86.42a–53a; NGB, vol. 8, 280–298.

changes which Yanagiwara had negotiated were to be put into effect through an exchange of notes following ratification of the treaty.[32]

CHAUVINISM AND REACTION: THE *SEI-KAN RON* OF 1873

Japan's conversion to the Western concept of international relations constituted a fundamental ideological and institutional challenge to the traditional world order still functioning in intra-regional relations within East Asia. At the same time, Japan's growing strength, incipient expansionism, and increasing desire to emulate predatory Western diplomacy posed a serious threat to China's historical supremacy in East Asia.

During his first year as foreign minister, Soejima's policy toward China and Korea was not a shining success. Japan's newly gained equality with China failed to make a significant impression upon the Koreans, and it did not produce hoped-for Korean humility toward Japan. Although Soejima terminated Tsushima's intermediary role in the conduct of Korean affairs, the change resulted in a rupture of official communication between the two countries. While willing to sign a treaty with Japan, China dismissed with disdain Japan's request for the same privileges the Western treaty powers enjoyed. The most sobering disappointment for Japan was the "failure" of the Iwakura embassy. By late 1872 it became clear that the Western treaty powers had no intention of granting Japan's request for treaty revision. The setbacks abroad apparently gave those unhappy with the domestic reforms instituted under the leadership of Iwakura, Ōkubo, and Kido an opportunity to agitate for *sei-Kan*—the perennial "panacea" for Japan's domestic problems—as a means of attaining their political objectives. Their agitation resulted in a government decision in mid-1873 that, if implemented, would almost certainly have

32. IWSM-TC, 86.44b; NGB, vol. 8, 267.

brought on an armed confrontation with Korea, and possibly with China.

This major policy reversal was made possible by the absence from the country of members of the Iwakura embassy. Although Chancellor Sanjō stayed home, the caretaker government was dominated by Councilor Saigō Takamori. Saigō was the hero of the conservative samurai and the leader of the Satsuma militarists, who were growing increasingly dissatisfied with the new reforms that deprived them of their traditional social and political privileges. Saigō was accorded the foremost place among the leaders of ordinary samurai origin within the new regime, but he was a simple warrior whose vision did not widen with time. His intellectual outlook remained narrow, provincial, and essentially feudal. His conception of post-Restoration Japan was of a semi-feudal state where the samurai would retain their hereditary role as the warrior-administrator ruling class.[33] Dissatisfied with the reform and modernization programs instituted by his more progressive colleagues, Saigō resigned from the imperial government and returned to Kagoshima in early 1870.

At the entreaties of Ōkubo and Kido, who needed the benefit of his enormous popularity in the country to undertake difficult and unpopular reforms, Saigō rejoined the government in 1871 and worked for the abolition of the domains and the creation of the prefectural system. However, fear that Saigō and his "reactionary" followers might undo some of the reforms during their absence led members of the Iwakura embassy to seek a pledge from the caretaker government that no major change would be introduced in foreign or domestic policy until they returned from abroad.[34]

In foreign affairs Saigō entertained a chauvinistic dream of expansion abroad to enhance Japan's national glory. He regarded Korea and Taiwan as immediate objects of

33. See Saigō's reform proposal submitted to Iwakura in 1871 in *Ōkuma bunsho* (Ōkuma papers), vol. 1, 3–7.
34. NGB, vol. 7.1, 102–103.

Japanese expansion. In the fall of 1872, Saigō's attention was drawn to Taiwan by news of the murders the previous December of shipwrecked Liu-ch'iuans by the aborigines of southern Taiwan. Liu-ch'iu had long been a fief (*fuyō*) of Satsuma, and most Japanese officials regarded Liu-ch'iuans as Japanese subjects. Saigō proposed a military expedition to Taiwan to avenge the murdered Liu-ch'iuans, but his proposal was opposed by Acting Finance Minister Inoue Kaoru, who feared that it might upset the precarious financial position of the government. Councilor Ōkuma Shigenobu also urged caution, saying that such an undertaking could not be seriously considered before Liu-ch'iu's relations with China were clarified.[35]

The archipelagic kingdom of Liu-ch'iu, lying between southern Kyūshū and Taiwan, for centuries had been a Chinese tributary while it was under Satsuma control. After abolition of the domains, the Japanese government took the position that Liu-ch'iu's feudatory obligations to Satsuma had been automatically transferred to the imperial court. In July 1872 Inoue Kaoru recommended that Liu-ch'iu be absorbed gradually into the Japanese administrative system. However, the Left Secretariat of the Dajōkan studied the recommendation, and it rendered a legal opinion calling for the preservation of the status quo for the island kingdom: Since China exercised nominal suzerainty over Liu-ch'iu while Japan actually controlled it, it would be pointless for Japan to risk war with China over an empty claim. It would be better, if Liu-ch'iu were retained as a separate kingdom with its ruler required to obtain investiture from the Japanese court.[36]

Soejima, a champion of Japanese expansion in East Asia, took exception to this view. Moreover, while Inoue called for peaceful absorption of Liu-ch'iu, Soejima was willing to use force, if necessary. Supporting Saigō's proposal for an expedition to Taiwan, Soejima took steps to consolidate the Japanese claim to Liu-ch'iu and establish a legal basis for the

35. Hilary Conroy, *The Japanese Seizure of Korea, 1868–1910*, 36–37.
36. *Meiji bunka shiryō sōsho* (Meiji cultural material series), vol. 4, 8–9.

proposed expedition. In October 1872 Liu-ch'iuan envoys were escorted to Tokyo and presented with an imperial edict declaring their homeland an imperial domain (*han*) of Japan and their king a "vassal king" (*han'ō*) of the Japanese court. In November the Japanese government notified the treaty powers that it was assuming diplomatic responsibility for Liu-ch'iu.[37] All this was done unilaterally, without consultation with the Chinese or the Liu-ch'iuan authorities.[38]

Soejima's enthusiasm for the proposed expedition to Taiwan, inspired by his own vision of Japanese expansion, was reinforced by advice and encouragement that he received from two American diplomats: American Minister to Japan Charles E. De Long and former American Consul at Amoy Charles W. LeGendre. LeGendre had considerable experience in dealing with the tribes of southern Taiwan. In the fall of 1872, when he stopped in Tokyo, en route home for reassignment, De Long introduced LeGendre to Soejima, who was eager for information about Taiwan. Impressed by LeGendre's knowledge of Taiwan, Soejima offered him an advisership in the Foreign Ministry; LeGendre accepted, apparently with the blessing of the State Department.[39]

De Long and LeGendre discussed the question of redress for the murdered Liu-ch'iuans and the annexation of Taiwan by Japan with Soejima in a series of talks in late October. Maintaining that China had neither claimed nor exercised jurisdiction over the aborigines of southern Taiwan, LeGendre asserted that their land would be the

37. NGB, vol. 8, 373–385; Sophia Su-fei Yen, *Taiwan in China's Foreign Relations, 1836–1874,* 158–159.

38. On the Sino-Japanese dispute over Liu-ch'iu, see Pak-Wah (Edwin) Leung, "China's Quasi-war with Japan: The Dispute over the Ryūkyū (Liu-ch'iu) Islands, 1871–1881" (Ph.D. dissert., University of California, Santa Barbara, 1978); Hyman Kublin, "The Attitude of China during the Liu-ch'iu Controversy, 1871–1881," *Pacific Historical Review* 18.2 (May 1949), 213–231; Liang Chia-pin, "Liu-ch'iu wang-kuo Chung-Jih cheng-ch'ih k'ao-shih" (A factual study of the Sino-Japanese dispute over the demise of the Liu-ch'iuan kingdom), *Ta-lu tsa-chih* 48.5 (May 1974). 193–218; 48.6 (June 1974), 263–290.

39. NGB, vol. 10, 4–16; Yen, *Taiwan in China's Foreign Relations,* 159–170; Payson J. Treat, *Diplomatic Relations between the United States and Japan,* vol. 1, 474–483.

possession of whatever country effectively occupied it, and he urged Japan to seize it. He advised, should the Sino-Western dispute over the issue of an imperial audience reach an impasse, Japan to seize an opportune moment to take Taiwan by diplomacy or force. Two thousand men, he said, could easily subdue the aborigines, and once entrenched, the occupying force could not be easily dislodged.[40] Apparently working closely with De Long, LeGendre submitted five memoranda on Korea and Taiwan to the Japanese Foreign Ministry between November 1872 and February 1873. He assured Soejima that the United States would not oppose such action by a friendly power, such as Japan. Moreover, involved as they were in mutual rivalries in East Asia, the European powers would acquiesce; each would rather see Taiwan in the hands of Japan than those of its rivals. LeGendre emphasized Korea's strategic importance and urged Japan to seize it before Russia or another power did so.[41] Apparently this reassured Soejima, who believed that Japan would have to resort to arms sooner or later in order to settle its dispute with Korea.

Heightened interest in Taiwan and Korea as well as dim prospects for treaty revision with the Western powers persuaded Soejima to reverse the earlier decision not to ratify the treaty with China until after the Iwakura embassy's return home. He wished to use the exchange of ratifications of the treaty as a pretext for leading a mission to China to clarify the Chinese position on Taiwan and Korea and to take the necessary steps to forestall Chinese intervention against Japanese action in both areas.[42] His self-confidence

40. NGB, vol. 10, 8–15; Marlene J. Mayo, "The Korean Crisis of 1873 and Early Meiji Foreign Policy," *Journal of Asian Studies* 31.4 (August 1972), 801–802.

41. For English summaries of LeGendre's memoranda, see Yen, *Taiwan in China's Foreign Relations*, 176–180. For Japanese translations of LeGendre's memoranda nos. 1, 2, 3, and 5, see *Ōkuma bunsho*, vol. 1, 17–47; for the gist of his memorandum no. 4, see Fujimura Michio, "Meiji shoki ni okeru Nisshin kōshō no ichidammen" (An aspect of Sino-Japanese relations in the early Meiji period), *Nagoya daigaku bungakubu kenkyū ronshū* 47 (March 1967), 1–2.

42. Tei, "teki-Shin gairyaku," 75; Maruyama, *Soejima Taneomi*, 221–222; Mayo, "Meiji Foreign Policy," 805–807; McWilliams, "The Soejima Mission," 242.

bolstered by American encouragement, Soejima memorialized the court for an appointment as imperial envoy
to China, stating unabashedly that he, Soejima, was
"probably the only person capable of preventing foreigners
coveting Taiwan from interfering in Japan's imperial undertaking and of persuading the Chinese to cede willingly the
aboriginal land" to Japan. On February 28, 1873, he was
appointed ambassador extraordinary and plenipotentiary to
China.[43]

Soejima and his party, which included LeGendre, left
Yokohama on March 13, aboard two Japanese warships.
The gratitude of the Chinese government to Soejima for his
action the previous year in rescuing Chinese laborers from
the *Maria Luz,* a Peruvian ship engaged in coolie trade, assured him of a cordial reception. Apparently as a diplomatic
ruse to conceal Japan's intentions, the letter of credence
which Soejima carried authorized him only to exchange
ratifications of the treaty and to congratulate the Chinese
emperor on his recent marriage and assumption of personal
rule. It contained no reference whatever to Korea or
Taiwan.[44] Soejima broke his journey at Kagoshima for a
brief consultation with Saigō, who was home on leave, and
he arrived at Tientsin on April 20.

On April 30 Li Hung-chang and Soejima formally exchanged ratifications of the treaty between their two countries, which had been signed the year before. The text of the
ratified treaty was the same as that which had been originally signed. Soejima asked for no change in the text; he
stated that, should the Iwakura embassy succeed in revising
Japan's treaties with Western countries, Japan would seek
corresponding changes from China.[45] Li and Soejima had a
cordial talk the following day on a number of subjects. Li
was not lulled by Soejima's feigned indifference toward
Korea, and he asked about Japan's intentions toward that
country. Soejima replied that Japan was having difficulties

43. For Soejima's memorial, see Maruyama, *Soejima Taneomi,* 205–206.
44. For Soejima's letter of credence, see NGB, vol. 8, 300–301.
45. *Ibid.,* vol. 9, 138–139; LWCK, *Tsungli Yamen Letters,* 1.43b.

in readjusting its relations with Korea, but it was seeking only friendship and had no intention of taking aggressive or military action against Korea. Li said that if Japan oppressed Korea, other countries would not think well of Japan. Moreover, he added, this would be a violation of the treaty just ratified. While indicating his agreement, Soejima did not pursue the matter. Li expected that Soejima would bring up the matter of the murder of the Liu-ch'iuan sailors by the Taiwan aborigines, but he did not.[46]

Soejima left Tientsin on May 5, and he reached Peking two days later, at a time when the resident Western ministers were pressing for an audience with the T'ung-chih emperor, who had recently assumed personal rule. Earlier Li had urged the Yamen to grant Soejima's request for an imperial audience, even if Soejima refused to perform the kowtow.[47] Upon his arrival, Soejima requested an audience with the Chinese emperor to present the message of the Japanese emperor. Soejima refused to perform the kowtow, arguing that he represented the ruler of a country that was a "friend," not a tributary, of China. After some seven weeks of argument and maneuvering, Soejima was victorious: on June 29 he was received by the T'ung-chih emperor in a separate audience, ahead of the Western ministers, who were received afterward in a group. This signal honor was accorded the Japanese ambassador in respect for his superior rank. Soejima did not perform the kowtow to the Chinese emperor, but he followed the standard Western practice of three bows.[48] By this tradition-shattering feat of diplomacy, he transformed Japan's newly gained equality with China into an established fact and completed the process of modernizing Sino-Japanese relations in accordance with Western international law.

Although Soejima spent most of his time in Peking wrangling over the issue of an imperial audience, Korea

46. LWCK, *Tsungli Yamen Letters,* 1.45a–46a; McWilliams, "The Soejima Mission," 250–251.

47. LWCK, *Tsungli Yamen Letters,* 1.45b.

48. For detailed accounts of Soejima's diplomatic maneuvers in Peking, see McWilliams, "The Soejima Mission," 251–262. See also NGB, vol. 9, 160–186.

and Taiwan were uppermost in his mind. While confiding this to Western representatives in Peking, he himself never discussed Korea or Taiwan with the Chinese officials. When the Tsungli Yamen delayed its decision on his request for an imperial audience, Soejima threatened to leave Peking and return home. Then he sent his aide, Yanagiwara, to the Yamen to make informal inquiries about Korea and Taiwan. In an interview with two Yamen ministers, Mao Ch'ang-hsi and Tung Hsun, on June 21, Yanagiwara inquired about Chinese relations with Korea and Taiwan. With regard to Korea, the Yamen ministers reaffirmed the Chinese position: although Korea was a tributary of China, it was autonomous in its internal administration and external affairs, and China never interfered in Korean affairs—even in matters of war or peace. As for Taiwan, the ministers stated that Taiwan was a Chinese territory, but some of its aborigines were beyond Chinese administrative control. When Yanagiwara said that the Japanese government intended to send an expedition to Taiwan in the future to punish the aborigines for murdering the Liu-ch'iuan sailors, the Yamen ministers declared that Liu-ch'iu was a Chinese tributary and that the Chinese authorities had already taken full measures for relief of the families of the murdered sailors. Although no agreement or understanding was reached between Yanagiwara and the Yamen ministers, Soejima decided that he had obtained a Chinese guarantee of non-intervention in future Japanese action in Korea and Taiwan.[49]

Li was in mourning for the death of his brother when Soejima returned to Tientsin from Peking, but he decided to receive the Japanese envoy. The two had another long talk on July 8. Li told Soejima of his own efforts to strengthen China, including the establishment of arsenals, modern military and naval training, and, particularly, the establishment of the China Merchants' Company. Expressing the fear that Britain might cut off its exports of coal to

49. NGB, vol. 9, 160–161, 171–179; Yen, *Taiwan in China's Foreign Relations,* 186–189; McWilliams, "The Soejima Mission," 263–266.

China, Li asked for Soejima's help in purchasing Japanese coal for his steamship company. Showing interest in Japan's efforts for the revision of the treaties with Western countries, Li remarked that "we wish to make use of your country's diplomacy as a guide" in similar efforts in the future.[50] But it was Li's apprehension about Japanese ambitions toward Korea that made him lay aside his ritual obligations of mourning in order to have another opportunity to impress upon the Japanese envoy China's concern for Korea. He recalled that even Hideyoshi, with his military genius, had failed to conquer Korea. Calling the Koreans "the descendants of the sages and Korea a land of propriety and righteousness," Li said that Korea "was created by Heaven and should therefore not be brought to an end." Noting that the Koreans were still deeply resentful of the Hideyoshi invasions, Li emphasized that if Japan used force against Korea, there could be no friendship between the two countries. Soejima expressed his agreement, but, again, failed to pursue the subject further.[51] The Japanese envoy and his party left Tientsin for home the following day.

With the termination of Tsushima's intermediary role between Japan and Korea, Japanese presence at Pusan lost its legal basis and authorized trade ceased between the two countries. In practice, however, an illegal trade flourished at Pusan with the open encouragement of the Tokyo government and acquiescence and connivance by local Korean officials and their underlings, who obviously profited from it. By the spring of 1873, the situation reached the point where leading commercial houses in Tokyo sent their agents to Pusan to participate in the illegal trade. When this came to the attention of Prefect of Tongnae Chŏng Hyŏn-dŏk, he reacted strongly. In late May he issued a directive to the Korean operatives at Pusan, ordering them to tighten up their vigilance against "smuggling." Observing that the Japanese felt no sense of shame even though they were under foreign (Western) domination, Chŏng declared that

50. NGB, vol. 9, 192–194; McWilliams, "The Soejima Mission," 194.
51. LWCK, *Tsungli Yamen Letters*, 1.48b–49b.

inasmuch as the Japanese had changed their dress and customs they could no longer be considered Japanese and therefore should not be permitted to trade at Pusan. Denouncing the recent Japanese activities at Pusan as "lawless," Chŏng reminded them that only Tsushima Japanese were allowed to trade at Pusan and that anyone wishing to trade in Korea must abide by Korean laws.[52]

Chŏng's language was blunt and undiplomatic; his words were addressed to his subordinates, not to the Japanese.[53] His action was entirely legitimate and completely justified—directed chiefly against the influx into Pusan of non-Tsushima Japanese merchants in open disregard of the long-standing Korean trade restrictions, at a time when there was no treaty or trade agreement between the two countries. The directive did not affect Tsushima merchants. In fact, there is reason to believe that it was issued as a result of complaints from the Tsushima merchants, who were no longer able to maintain their traditional monopoly of the Korean trade as more and more merchants from other parts of Japan arrived on the scene with encouragement from Tokyo.[54] Contrary to the allegations made by Japanese officials, Chŏng's directive notwithstanding, there was no threat of violence or eviction against the Japanese at Pusan at this time—or any other time—even though their presence no longer had a legal basis.

When Chŏng's directive was reported to Tokyo, it was seized upon eagerly by the conservatives and chauvinists within the government, who were unhappy with the government's cautious Korean policy, as a pretext to renew their demand for *sei-Kan*. The leaders were two imperial councilors: Saigō and Itagaki, especially the former. In the face of their clamor for "punitive" action against Korea, Chancellor Sanjō directed that a proposal be submitted to the Dajōkan, recommending the dispatch of warships and

52. NGB, vol. 9, 282–283; TNS, vol. 1, 293–296.

53. On the basis of its crude wording and of the mysterious circumstances in which it appeared, a Korean historian questions the authenticity of Chŏng's directive. See Yi Sŏn-gŭn, *Han'guksa ch'oegŭnse p'yŏn*, 334.

54. Inoue Kiyoshi, *Nihon no gunkokushugi* (Japanese militarism), vol. 2, 90–91.

troops to Pusan for the protection of Japanese residents. It also recommended the dispatch of an envoy to open negotiations with the Korean government. At this point, Saigō came forward with the proposal that the government should send him to Korea for talks with the Korean authorities before sending ships and troops. The Dajōkan tentatively approved Saigō's proposal, final decision being deferred until after Soejima's return from China.[55]

In late July Soejima returned to Tokyo in triumph. He claimed that he had obtained a guarantee from China that it would not intervene in Korea even if Japan sent troops to that country. Moreover, he said that Eugene Butzow, Russian chargé d'affaires, had assured him that Russia had no intention of intervening in a Japanese-Korean conflict. He demanded that, as foreign minister, he be sent to Korea to initiate negotiations.[56] Lest Soejima get the assignment, Saigō wrote a letter to Itagaki on July 29 to seek the latter's support for his own appointment. While he could not be as splendid an envoy as Soejima, said Saigō, he could at least manage to get killed by the Koreans.[57] On August 3 he addressed a letter to Sanjō, imploring the chancellor to send him to Korea. He also appealed personally to Soejima to let him have the assignment. In a meeting with Sanjō on August 16, Saigō made another impassioned appeal for his appointment. At a full-dress meeting of the councilors the following day, Saigō's proposal was formally adopted and he was designated envoy to Korea. The decision was given imperial sanction the next day on the condition that Saigō's appointment be formalized after the Iwakura embassy's return from Europe.[58]

Why was Saigō so eager for a diplomatic mission for which he was admittedly not well qualified and for which

55. Tada, ed., *Iwakura kō jikki,* vol. 3, 46–50.

56. Maruyama, *Soejima Taneomi,* 226; Conroy, *Japanese Seizure of Korea,* 41–42.

57. Saigō Takamori, *Dai Saigō zenshū* (Complete works of Saigō Takamori), vol. 2, 736–737.

58. Conroy, *Japanese Seizure of Korea,* 42–43; Iwata Masakazu, *Ōkubo Toshimichi: The Bismarck of Japan,* 165–166.

there was little hope of success? It is clear that he wanted war, not a peaceful settlement, with Korea. In his August 3 letter to Sanjō, Saigō said that "surely it was not to seek friendship, but to pursue other objectives that the government embarked on its Korean enterprise after the Restoration." In a letter to Itagaki on August 14, Saigō was even more explicit: "If we fail to seize this chance to bring us into war," he wrote, "it would be difficult to find another." Repeating his belief that the Koreans would kill a Japanese envoy, he wrote again to Itagaki three days later: "This will bring home to the entire nation the necessity of punishing their [Korean] crime. This is the situation which we must bring to pass if our plan is to succeed!"[59] Clearly, Saigō's intention was to create an incident in which the Koreans would be provoked or tricked into attacking or killing him so that Japan might have a *casus belli.* He simply could not afford to have a seasoned diplomat like Soejima settle the dispute by diplomacy and thereby frustrate his war plans.

Why did Saigō want war with Korea? As suggested by many historians, Saigō's chauvinism was certainly a factor. Like other restorationists, Saigō, who was to be revered by Japan's ultra-nationalists, apparently believed that the restoration of imperial rule in Japan should be followed by the extension of Japanese imperial authority to Korea. Korea's refusal to submit to that authority was regarded by men like him as an act of insolence deserving "chastisement." Some historians suggest that Saigō's drastic proposal served as an outlet for his resentment of the impelling power of the reformers, such as Ōkubo Toshimichi, and also against the incessant personal attacks on him by Shimazu Hisamitsu, the disgruntled, reactionary father of his former Satsuma lord.[60] Others believe that Saigō was a "man of sincerity, indulgently responsive to the dissatisfaction of the disestablished samurai, who wanted to expiate his failure in Korea with death." Then "his beloved samurai would have a final

59. For Saigō's letter to Sanjō, see Saigō, *Dai Saigō zenshū,* vol. 2, 742–743.
60. Masumi Junnosuke, *Nihon seitō shiron* (A historical survey of political parties in Japan), vol. 1, 139–144; Iwata, *Ōkubo Toshimichi,* 165.

moment of glory before a new world of modernization closed on them, a new world which Saigō could not face."[61]

These psycho-historical explanations seem plausible and valid. But some of them are more convincing when applied to his motives for rebelling against the government four years later in 1877. The years 1872–1873, during which Saigō fought for *sei-Kan,* were not for him a period of bitter disappointment and frustration that might drive some men to extreme action. On the contrary, in the absence of rivals such as Ōkubo and Kido, Saigō was unquestionably the most powerful figure in the government. He was at the peak of his career, wielding enormous political and military power as the nation's senior imperial councilor and highest-ranking general. In part it was Saigō's extraordinary power and prestige, particularly his control of the imperial army dominated by his Satsuma followers, that made the mild-mannered Sanjō go along reluctantly with the *sei-Kan* proposal.[62]

To state a complicated story simply, Saigō, like other proponents of continental expansion before him, sought war with Korea chiefly as a means of attaining his conservative political goals at home: the creation of a semi-feudal state in which the samurai, reestablished as an integrated ruling elite with the Satsuma samurai as its core and placed under direct imperial control, would retain their hereditary administrative and military functions.[63] Perhaps it was with this long-range goal in mind that Saigō, despite his basic differences with Ōkubo and Kido, rejoined the imperial government in the summer of 1871 and lent his prestige to the government in carrying out the abolition of the domains. Perhaps with the same goal in mind, he remained in the caretaker government in spite of the humiliating restrictions imposed by the Iwakura embassy. He probably believed that during their absence he could consolidate his

61. Conroy, *Japanese Seizure of Korea,* 34.
62. Tada, ed., *Iwakura kō jikki,* vol. 3, 54; Inoue, *gunkokushugi,* vol. 2, 119.
63. Inoue, *gunkokushugi,* vol. 2, 118–119; Tamamuro Taijō, *Saigō Takamori* (Saigō Takamori), 132–134.

position to a point where it would enable him to achieve his ultimate goal.[64]

In the summer of 1872, he escorted the young Meiji emperor on a 44-day tour of southwestern Japan, which was intended to soothe the disgruntled daimyo of the region. The imperial entourage stayed eleven days in Saigō's hometown of Kagoshima, a signal honor for Satsuma and a personal triumph for Saigō. Following the emperor's return to Tokyo, Saigō was given, in addition to his imperial councilorship, the highest rank in the army, field marshal, and placed in command of the Imperial Life Guard. Having assumed enormous power, both civil and military, he may have felt justifiably that he was moving closer to the fulfillment of his goal.[65] Late that year, however, Saigō made a fateful "error" by agreeing reluctantly, probably in an ambiguous state of mind, to Yamagata Aritomo's proposal for national conscription, which was contrary to his own idea of an elite, hereditary military establishment.

Following the introduction of conscription in early 1873, strong protest from the disestablished samurai throughout the country, particularly from his own followers in Satsuma, made Saigō realize his "mistake." It seems that, upon hearing the reports of "intolerable Korean arrogance and insolence," he conceived of an expedition to Korea as the means of redeeming his mistake.[66] Being a man of heart rather than reason, he would have readily laid down his own life to create a *casus belli*, but he must have wished to lead his followers in a Korean campaign as he had led them in the campaign against the pro-Tokugawa forces five years before.

A victory over Korea, he seems to have calculated, would not only vindicate his concept of an elite samurai army by demonstrating the valor and fighting abilities of the renowned Satsuma warriors but would endow him and his fol-

64. Inoue Kiyoshi, *Nihon gendaishi* (History of modern Japan), vol. 1, 362–363; Iwata, *Ōkubo Toshimichi*, 154.
65. Tamamuro, *Saigō Takamori*, 126–127.
66. Ōkuma Shigenobu expressed this view of Saigo's motive behind his *sei-Kan* proposal. See Masumi, *Nihon seitō shiron*, vol. 1, 143–144.

lowers with power and prestige to enable them to carry out their political program at home. Anticipating opposition from members of the Iwakura embassy, Saigō was anxious to have his proposal approved by the emperor before its return. He was nearly delirious with joy when given imperial sanction.[67]

Iwakura and his embassy returned to Japan in September 1873. Both Ōkubo and Kido had returned earlier, but for various reasons neither had participated in the government deliberations on Korea or raised objections to Saigō's proposal. However, Iwakura immediately plunged into the affair and fashioned a powerful coalition to block what he considered a disastrous course of action. The dramatic showdown that ensued the following month between the proponents and opponents of *sei-Kan* split the top leadership of the government down the middle. Standing with Saigō for *sei-Kan* were four imperial councilors: Itagaki Taisuke and Gotō Shōjirō of Tosa, and Soejima Taneomi and Etō Shimpei of Hizen. Arrayed against them were Minister of the Right Iwakura and the four remaining imperial councilors: Kido Takayoshi of Chōshū, Ōkubo Toshimichi of Satsuma, and Ōkuma Shigenobu and Ōki Takatō of Hizen. Caught between his earlier commitment to Saigō and his basic agreement with Iwakura, the hapless Sanjō found himself in a quandary and desperately sought a compromise.[68]

Although Ōkubo joined the anti-*sei-Kan* coalition reluctantly—undoubtedly because of his friendship with Saigō and his personal ties with Satsuma—his pivotal position in the government and the force of his personality led to his emergence as the chief antagonist of Saigō, his lifelong friend and fellow clansman. With cold and precise logic, Ōkubo articulated his opposition to foreign entanglement before the internal reforms were consolidated; a position no doubt reinforced by his recent tour of the West.

67. See Saigō's letter to Itagaki, in Saigō, *Dai Saigō zenshū,* vol. 2, 758.
68. On the October showdown, see Nobutaka Ike, "The Triumph of the Peace Party in Japan in 1873," *Far Eastern Quarterly* 2.3 (May 1943), 286–295.

In a memorandum to Sanjō in early October, he cited seven reasons for his opposition to war with Korea at this time: (1) war might lead to civil disturbances, in view of widespread popular resentment against the recent reforms entailing the loss of property and privilege for many; (2) war might cause fiscal bankruptcy; (3) war would force the abandonment of domestic programs for educational, industrial, and military modernization; (4) war would increase Japan's trade deficit and cause general impoverishment of the nation; (5) war would make Korea and Japan easy prey for Russia, which was waiting for an opportunity to fish in troubled waters in East Asia; (6) war would reduce Japan's ability to service its foreign debts and thereby invite interference in its internal affairs by Britain, its chief creditor; and (7) war might hamper Japan's efforts toward treaty revision with the Western powers.[69]

Despite Ōkubo's cogent arguments, a decision in favor of Saigō's adventurous proposal appeared certain. But events took a dramatic turn at the last minute: the exhausted Chancellor Sanjō collapsed in the early morning on October 18. With Sanjō incapacitated, Iwakura, as acting chancellor, moved swiftly and decisively against Saigō's group. Rejecting their demand that the earlier decision to send Saigō to Korea be put into execution without delay, Iwakura obtained an imperial edict rescinding the decision on October 24. Saigō, Itagaki, Gotō, Soejima, and Etō immediately tendered their resignations, and these were promptly accepted. Thus ended the greatest political crisis in Japan since the Meiji Restoration.[70]

In concluding our account of one of the great policy disputes in the history of modern Japan, we may make a few observations regarding its significance in the evolution of Japanese policy toward China and Korea in the early Meiji period.

First, despite the shrill cries of "Korean insult" raised by the proponents of *sei-Kan*, there was no justifiable ground

69. Tsunoda Ryusaku, et al., eds., *Sources of Japanese Tradition*, vol. 2, 151–155; Conroy, *Japanese Seizure of Korea*, 47–49; Iwata, *Ōkubo Toshimichi*, 168–169.
70. Tada, ed., *Iwakura kō jikki*, vol. 3, 80–84.

for "retaliatory" action against Korea by Japan at this time. Saigō's decision to go to Korea was actuated by his desire to create a pretext for such action. This was pointed out by Ōkubo, when he said: "Some argue that the arrogance of Korea toward our country is intolerable. But as far as I can see, the reasons for sending an envoy extraordinary seem to be to look for a positive excuse for war by having him treated arrogantly and discourteously."[71] It is reasonable, therefore, to conclude that the alleged Korean arrogance or provocation was not a cause of the upsurge of *sei-Kan* sentiment within the Japanese government at this time. Moreover, contrary to most accounts of the event, outside the limited official circles, in this period there was almost no public outcry in Japan for war with Korea.[72]

Second, unlike earlier and later debates on Korea, during the October debate the proponents of *sei-Kan* made no effort to justify their position with the argument that danger of the Western seizure of Korea compelled preemptive action by Japan. Instead, they contended that the proposed action toward Korea would not invite Chinese or Russian intervention. At any rate, fear of Western encroachment upon Korea was not a factor that contributed significantly to the rise of *sei-Kan* sentiment in the Japanese government at this time.

Third, both the proponents and opponents of *sei-Kan* were motivated primarily by their desire to advance their political causes at home. Saigō and his samurai followers saw a victorious war with Korea as an opportunity for partial restoration of the traditional order and its value system of martial virtue, which they believed were being discarded unwisely by the Western-oriented reformers. Iwakura, Ōkubo, Kido, and others feared that protracted and costly conflict with Korea would halt reform and modernization programs at home, and that, once victorious in Korea, Saigō and his followers would use their enhanced power and prestige to undo major domestic reforms, such as national conscription. The *sei-Kan* debate was a dispute over the basic

71. Tsunoda, et al., eds., *Japanese Tradition*, vol. 2, 155.
72. Inoue Kiyoshi, *Meiji ishin* (The Meiji restoration), 332–333.

direction in which the new Japanese state should move. To
its proponents, *sei-Kan* was not an end, but a means to attain
political goals at home.[73]

The primacy of domestic political considerations is best
seen in Kido's reversal of his earlier pro-*sei-Kan* position.
Although his global tour must have deeply influenced
Kido's thinking, it was the altered political and military position of the imperial government, not any change in the
international situation, that was responsible for his conversion. During 1868–1871, Kido advocated *sei-Kan* in the belief that it would provide an excellent opportunity for the
new regime to develop an independent military capability
with which it could impose unity upon a divided country.
With the foundation for national integration and unity
firmly laid by the abolition of the domains, the establishment of the prefectural system, and, especially, by the creation of a conscript army, he regarded an expedition to
Korea as a threat to efforts to consolidate these reforms at
home.[74] In a sense, Kido was entirely consistent in his position. While Itagaki, Gotō, and Etō advocated *sei-Kan* for a
variety of reasons different from those of Saigō and his followers, they, too, were motivated by their factional domestic
political interests.[75]

All this does not mean that these men were not interested
in *sei-Kan* per se. On the contrary, desire for continental expansion, for which the control of Korea constituted the first
step, was shared universally by the early Meiji leaders. Even
an articulate and determined opponent of *sei-Kan* such as
Ōkubo did not oppose it in principle. The difference between Ōkubo and his opponents was disagreement over timing and feasibility. In his memorandum to Sanjō, Ōkubo
qualified his opposition by repeatedly stating that he was
against "a hasty commencement of war" with Korea.[76] He

73. *Ibid.*, 333–334; Tamamuro, *Saigō Takamori*, 134.
74. *Kido Takayoshi monjo*, vol. 8, 129–134; Mayo, "Meiji Foreign Policy," 813.
75. For the views of Itagaki and Etō on Korea, see Inoue, *Nihon no gunkoku-shugi*, vol. 2, 121–129; Haraguchi, *Nihon kindai kokka*, 163–165; Mayo, "Meiji Foreign Policy," 812–813.
76. Tsunoda, et al., eds., *Japanese Tradition*, vol. 2, 151–154; Iwata, *Ōkubo Toshimichi*, 170.

and his associates did not hesitate to take expansionist action against China and Korea subsequently, when they thought that the conditions at home and abroad favored such action and that it would serve their own cause.

Thus our analysis suggests that the *sei-Kan* controversy was a dramatic manifestation, not a cause, of a profound and irreconcilable schism that had existed within the ruling coalition in Japan since the Meiji Restoration. It further confirms the view that Korea represented a frontier for expansion and the desire for its conquest or subjugation became strong and even overpowering in the Japanese national consciousness in times of internal disunity or instability, especially among those who regarded it as a means of maintaining or attaining power at home. Finally, regardless of whether the *sei-Kan ron* was a manifestation of a domestic political schism or of Japanese expansionism, the potential consequences for Korea would be the same: it portended a vigorous, if not aggressive, policy toward Korea, thereby posing a threat not only to Korea itself but to China's traditional influence in the peninsula.

EXPANSIONISM AND TERRITORIAL CONSOLIDATION

In the new administration formed in the wake of the departure of Saigō and his supporters, predictably Ōkubo emerged as the dominant figure. Kido remained in the government, but he was prevented from playing an active role by both his temperament and poor health. After Kido's resignation in May 1874, as a result of his disagreement with the government's Taiwan policy, there was no one in the administration to rival or challenge Ōkubo's power. In addition to his imperial councilorship, concurrently Ōkubo held the newly created post of home affairs minister, with vast jurisdiction over domestic affairs. Political stature and force of personality led Ōkubo to play the role of a prime minister, exercising far-reaching authority over foreign and domestic policy. The administration under his leadership between November 1873 and the time of his assassination in May 1878 is referred to by historians as the "Ōkubo regime."

Ōkubo took a keen interest in foreign affairs and he actively participated in them, ushering in the third phase in the evolution of Japanese policy in East Asia in the early Meiji period. As foreign minister Ōkubo installed Terashima Munenori, a fellow Satsuma clansman who had just returned from England, where he had served as Japanese minister to the Court of St. James. Son of a low-ranking samurai, Terashima studied Western (Dutch) medicine in his youth. During the Anglo-Satsuma war in 1863, when negotiations broke down, Terashima was taken to England by the British. He spent three years studying there. Following his return from England, he served as instructor at the Kaiseijo, the bakufu school for Western studies, and again visited Europe with a bakufu mission. After the Meiji Restoration, Terashima was appointed junior councilor and served successively as governor of Kanagawa and vice foreign minister until he was appointed minister to England.[77] Terashima's educational background and professional career presented a marked contrast to those of his predecessors, including two court nobles with little Western education and a Confucian scholar with a veneer of Western knowledge. His elevation to a ministerial position was symbolic of the rise of men with similar backgrounds to positions of authority and leadership in the Meiji government. Japan's "parting with Asia" in foreign policy became a reality under Ōkubo's leadership.

The policy which Ōkubo and Terashima pursued toward China and Korea may best be characterized as pragmatic. Although both Soejima and Ōkubo accepted the principles of Western international law as the fundamental rules governing Japan's foreign relations, there were significant differences in the basic attitudes of the two. For all his interest in the West, Soejima's knowledge of the Western world was secondhand. He was a Confucian scholar who retained

77. *Nihon rekishi daijiten* (Great dictionary of Japanese history), vol. 7, 93.

some of the respect and admiration for Chinese culture traditionally held by scholars of Chinese learning in Japan. His acceptance of the Western concept of international relations was perhaps not as complete as it seemed. Such was definitely not the case with Ōkubo, a man of practical bent who had no significant training in Confucian scholarship, hence no particular awe of China or its culture.[78] Moreover, Ōkubo's extended tour of the United States and Europe with the Iwakura embassy evidently convinced him of the superiority and strength of Western culture. This was true of Terashima, too; his education and training were as Western as was possible in late Tokugawa and early Meiji Japan. Acceptance of the Western international system by Ōkubo and Terashima was wholehearted and complete.

Despite all this, the difference between Soejima's "reform" diplomacy and Ōkubo's pragmatic diplomacy was chiefly one of the degree of each man's pragmatism, realism, and flexibility. In foreign relations and in domestic affairs, Ōkubo was a supreme realist with few ideological dogmas or *idées fixes* concerning Japan's relations with its neighbors. In fact, his realism bordered on cynicism. Explaining his opposition to *sei-Kan*, Ōkubo said: "Every action, whether progressive or conservative, must be taken in response to an occasion, and if it develops unfavorably should be abandoned. This may entail shame, but it is to be endured; justice may be with us, but we are not to choose that course."[79] By the same token, moral or ideological considerations alone would not deter Ōkubo from a promising or profitable venture at home or abroad.

Ōkubo's assessment of Western intentions in East Asia at this time differed sharply from those of Soejima and LeGendre. Convinced that armed conflict between Japan and China, or Korea, would bring Western intervention, he opposed any such venture without the assurance of Western

78. Sidney Devere Brown, "Ōkubo Toshimichi: His Political and Economic Policies in Early Meiji Japan," *Journal of Asian Studies* 21.2 (February 1962), 189–191; Iwata, *Ōkubo Toshimichi,* 154–159.

79. Tsunoda, et al., eds., *Japanese Tradition,* vol. 2, 151.

support or, at least, non-intervention.[80] He was eager to emulate and to cooperate with the Western powers in China, as evidenced by his readiness to offer the use of Japanese ports to the French for military or naval action against China at the time of the Tientsin Massacre.[81]

During the early 1870s, Japan faced major foreign policy problems in three East Asian areas: Sakhalin, Korea, and Taiwan. The Ōkubo government's decision with regard to each of them reflected the spirit of pragmatic diplomacy. Japan had solid historical and legal claims against the growing Russian penetration of Sakhalin, but Czarist Russia was a strong power which Japan was not as yet ready to tackle militarily. Hence the use of force was firmly ruled out; settlement of the jurisdictional dispute with Russia had to be reached by negotiation.[82] Japanese military action in Korea would not only encounter determined Korean resistance but might invite Russian and Chinese intervention. Here, too, the risk was great and the prospect of success was not good; Japan continued its diplomatic approach, without ruling out use of force in the future. A Japanese expedition in Taiwan would encounter little effective resistance from the aborigines and might even win Western support against likely Chinese protest. Therefore Ōkubo and his colleagues decided on an expedition in Taiwan even though they had just driven Saigō and his supporters out of the government for demanding a similar undertaking against Korea.[83]

The proposal for an expedition to Taiwan, originally made by Saigō, had been relegated to the background during the *sei-Kan* dispute. Apart from its feasibility and prospect of success, other important considerations caused Ōkubo and Iwakura to revive it. An expedition, if successful, would enhance Japanese prestige abroad and might

80. *Ibid.*, 153–154.
81. See Ōkubo's memorandum to Iwakura in *Ōkubo Toshimichi monjo*, vol. 3, 480–482.
82. Iwakura returned from his European tour, convinced that Japan should not quarrel with Russia. See Ian Nish, *Japanese Foreign Policy, 1869–1942*, 23.
83. For the decision on policy priorities, see *Iwakura Tomomi kankei monjo* (Papers related to Iwakura Tomomi), vol. 7, 464–466.

bring the aboriginal land under Japanese control. Even if not successful, an expedition would strengthen Japan's claim of exclusive jurisdiction over Liu-ch'iu. More importantly, it would be a diversionary enterprise to pacify the restive samurai, particularly Saigō's followers in Satsuma, who might rise in revolt against the government.[84] An attempt on Iwakura's life by disgruntled *sei-Kan* advocates and the outbreak of a rebellion by *sei-Kan* fanatics, led by former Councilor Etō Shimpei in Saga in January 1874, rendered the project more urgent.

In January the Dajōkan ordered Ōkubo and Ōkuma to study the Taiwan question and recommend a solution. Early in February the two councilors submitted their report, which had been prepared with LeGendre's help. They recommended a punitive expedition to chastise the aborigines, justifying the action partly on the ground that China did not exercise effective jurisdiction over the aborigines. The proposal was approved by the Dajōkan on February 6.[85] In view of De Long's encouragement and LeGendre's active involvement in the project, Ōkubo and his colleagues had reason to believe that they had tacit American support.

An expeditionary force of 3,000 men was quickly organized; it included a contingent of three hundred Satsuma samurai. In early April, Lieutenant General Saigō Tsugumichi, the 28-year-old younger brother of Saigō Takamori, was named commander-in-chief—obviously a move calculated to appease the elder Saigō, who was brooding vengefully over his defeat of the previous October. LeGendre was appointed chief adviser to the expedition. Two more Americans, U.S. Navy Lieutenant Commander Douglas Cassel and former U.S. Army Lieutenant James R. Wassen, were appointed as Saigō's staff officers. American and British ships were engaged to transport men and

84. Conroy, *Japanese Seizure of Korea*, 53–54; Haraguchi, *Nihon kindai kokka*, 173.

85. NGB, vol. 10, 1–3; Tada, ed., *Iwakura kō jikki*, vol. 3, 127–130. For Iwakura's comments on the Ōkubo-Ōkuma proposal, see *Ōkubo Toshimichi monjo*, vol. 5, 343–348.

supplies to Taiwan.[86] At this point, the project was nearly halted by the unexpected disapproval of Britain and the United States.

Harry Parkes, British minister in Tokyo, on the basis of his observations and inquiries, concluded that Japan's intentions toward Taiwan were not merely to chastise the aborigines but in fact to seize their land, perhaps the whole island. Parkes was convinced that such Japanese action would result in war with China, and this would hurt British trade in East Asia. In common with most Western traders in the area, he apparently believed that Japanese-occupied Taiwan would be less favorable to Western trade than Chinese-controlled Taiwan. On April 13 Parkes addressed a note to Foreign Minister Terashima, informing him of the decision of the British government not to permit its subjects or ships to participate in the expedition without advance clearance from the Chinese authorities.[87] Meanwhile, De Long was replaced as American minister in Tokyo by John A. Bingham, "a man of cautious temperament who gave meticulous attention to his duties." Bingham disapproved of the participation of United States personnel and ships in the expedition. On April 18 he, too, addressed a note to Terashima to protest the employment by the Japanese government of any American citizens or ships in an enterprise hostile to China.[88]

Ōkubo and his colleagues had refused earlier to be deterred from their chosen course, even in the face of protest from as powerful a figure as Kido, who insisted that the government give priority to internal consolidation and development.[89] But the British and American disapproval alarmed Ōkubo and his colleagues. In particular, they were surprised by a sudden reversal of the American position. Ōkubo immediately rushed orders to General Saigō at Nagasaki, where the expeditionary force was assembled for

86. Conroy, *Japanese Seizure of Korea,* 54–55; Yen, *Taiwan in China's Foreign Relations,* 203–205.
87. NGB, vol. 10, 30–32, 37.
88. *Ibid.,* 38–40, 45–46.
89. Kido, *Kido Takayoshi nikki,* vol. 3, 13; *Kido Takayoshi monjo,* vol. 8, 147–155.

embarkation, to halt proceedings until further notice. This
infuriated Saigō, and, ignoring orders, Saigō dispatched
one troopship on April 27 and four more on May 2. Cassel
and Wassen sailed with the ships. Ōkubo, who had just
returned to Tokyo from Kyūshū after directing the campaign for the suppression of the Saga Rebellion, rushed
back to discuss the matter with Saigō. Arriving at Nagasaki
on May 3, Ōkubo found that the major portion of the expeditionary force had departed for Taiwan. A defiant Saigō
told him that if the expedition were called off at this late
hour, he, Saigō, could not be responsible for the conduct of
his men.[90]

Realizing the difficulty, and perhaps even danger, of restraining soldiers bent on adventure and glory, Ōkubo
permitted the expedition to proceed. With Saigō and
Ōkuma, who was at Nagasaki to supervise the enterprise as
chief commissioner for Taiwan affairs, Ōkubo worked out
a formula to meet the American and British objections. The
following day the three released a statement announcing
removal of the three Americans from the expedition. Saigō
was to limit operations to the punishment of the aborigines
and await the outcome of diplomatic negotiations with
China. After his return to Tokyo, Ōkubo told his colleagues
that the affair at Nagasaki was most unfortunate and that
he would personally undertake to negotiate a settlement if it
led to serious difficulties with China and embarrassed relations with other countries.[91] Approving Ōkubo's action, the
Dajōkan on May 19 formally announced the dispatch of
troops to Taiwan. At the same time it ordered Yanagiwara,
appointed earlier as envoy to China, to leave for China immediately to explain the purpose of the expedition.[92]

The Japanese expedition quickly accomplished its announced objectives in Taiwan. Reaching the island on

90. Tada, ed., *Iwakura kō jikki*, vol. 3, 149–152; Iwata, *Ōkubo Toshimichi*, 198;
Yen, *Taiwan in China's Foreign Relations*, 207–208.

91. Tada, ed., *Iwakura kō jikki*, vol. 3, 149–152; NGB, vol. 10, 61–62; Iwata,
Ōkubo Toshimichi, 200; *Ōkubo Toshimichi monjo*, vol. 5, 504.

92. NGB, vol. 10, 90. For Yanagiwara's departure, see Tada, ed., *Iwakura kō
jikki*, vol. 3, 171–173.

May 22, Saigō, as he had promised, sent the Americans back and conducted a limited campaign, without venturing into the territory under the control of the Chinese officials. By the end of June all the hostile tribes of southern Taiwan had surrendered to the Japanese. Holding the occupied territory, Saigō awaited the outcome of Yanagiwara's mission to China.[93]

The Tsungli Yamen first learned of the Japanese plan to send an expedition to Taiwan from British Minister Wade in Peking in mid-April. Since there were conflicting reports on the matter, the Yamen was not convinced of the accuracy of Wade's information.[94] Even Li Hung-chang, who was aware of Japan's ambitions, discounted it at first. Influenced perhaps by his overriding concern for Korea's security, Li observed that if Japan wanted war it would be likely to take action against Korea.[95] The Yamen's initial response was to instruct the officials in the coastal provinces to gather more information on the matter.[96]

On May 11 the Yamen received a report of the arrival of a Japanese troopship at Amoy, en route to Taiwan, and it immediately sent a note of protest to the Japanese Foreign Ministry. Declaring Chinese jurisdiction over Taiwan aboriginal land, it demanded to know why the Japanese government had failed to consult China in advance concerning the expedition against the aborigines.[97] Acting on Li's recommendations, the Yamen memorialized the throne to place Shen Pao-chen, director of the Foochow Navy Yard, in charge of Taiwan defense. The throne approved Shen's appointment as imperial commissioner for Taiwan affairs the same day. On May 21 P'an Wei, financial commissioner of Fukien, was appointed Shen's deputy.[98] About this time Yanagiwara arrived in Shanghai.

93. For Saigō's first report from Taiwan, see NGB, vol. 10, 107–109. For a brief account of the Japanese operations, see Fox, *Britain and Japan*, 292–297.
94. IWSM-TC, 93.26b–28b; Yen, *Taiwan in China's Foreign Relations*, 212–213.
95. LWCK, *Tsungli Yamen Letters*, 2.20a–b.
96. T. F. Tsiang, "Sino-Japanese Diplomatic Relations, 1870–1894," *Chinese Social and Political Science Review* 17.1 (April 1933), 18.
97. IWSM-TC, 93.29b–30b; NGB, vol. 10, 72–77.
98. LWCK, *Tsungli Yamen Letters*, 11.23b–25b; IWSM-TC, 93.28a–29b.

Negotiations were conducted between P'an Wei and Yanagiwara in Shanghai and then between P'an and Saigō in Taiwan in June and July. The talks were inconclusive, however, partly because Yanagiwara did not have authority to sign an agreement. His mission may have been simply to maintain a dialogue with the Chinese authorities in order to give Saigō time to finish his military task.[99]

When Saigō's first report from Taiwan reached Tokyo, in late June, Ōkubo was elated by the initial success of the expedition. He took a belligerent stand, and this led to an official decision on July 9 to risk war with China, if necessary, in order to justify the expedition and achieve its objectives. The army and navy ministers were ordered to draw up war plans.[100] On July 15 the government instructed Yanagiwara to inform the Chinese that: (1) the land occupied by the expedition was unclaimed territory under international law; (2) the purpose of the expedition was to subdue and civilize the aborigines, not territorial aggrandizement; and (3) if China feared the presence of Japan on Taiwan, Japan was ready to turn over the occupied territory to China in return for adequate compensation and guaranteed safety of navigation in Taiwanese waters. In separate instructions, Yanagiwara was informed that he would not be held responsible if faithful execution of his orders resulted in a breach of peace between the two countries.[101]

Despite Ōkubo's confident and uncompromising posture, it is doubtful that he was willing to risk war with China. There were several factors which must have given him pause. One was his knowledge of Japan's military capabilities. During July and August, War Minister Yamagata warned Ōkubo repeatedly of the weak condition of the military and discouraged large-scale troop movement abroad, pointing out the danger at a time when the domestic situation was

99. On P'an's negotiations with Yanagiwara and Saigō, see Yen, *Taiwan in China's Foreign Relations,* 222–226.

100. Hsü Shih-chiai (Kyo Sei-kai), "Taiwan jiken, 1871–1874" (The Taiwan incident, 1871–1874), *Kokusai seiji* 28 (April 1964), 46. For the orders to the service ministers, see NGB, vol. 10, 150–151; Tada, ed., *Iwakura kō jikki,* vol. 3, 178–179.

101. NGB, vol. 10, 155–157; Tada, ed., *Iwakura kō jikki,* vol. 3, 177–182.

unstable. All but two Satsuma men among the army's seven top generals opposed war with China at this time.[102] Another factor was the difficulties which the expedition encountered after its initial success. With the advent of summer, malaria and other diseases began to decimate the troops; illnesses claimed some 530 lives, as compared with twelve combat fatalities. The deaths necessitated successive reinforcements and caused unforeseen logistic problems and soaring expenditures.[103] A short, easy campaign threatened to become a nightmare. In addition, there were important external factors: the Chinese military build-up in Taiwan, which was progressing steadily under Shen's able leadership, and the unfavorable reactions of Western powers, which might lead to their intervention in the event of an armed conflict between China and Japan. All these influenced Ōkubo's decision to go to China to negotiate a settlement, as he had promised earlier.

By adroit maneuvering, including a threat of resignation, Ōkubo succeeded in obtaining his commission as ambassador extraordinary and plenipotentiary to China on August 1. He received broad discretionary power for implementing the instructions previously given to Yanagiwara. While the objective of his mission was preservation of the peace with China, Ōkubo was empowered to opt for war if he deemed it unavoidable. He was authorized to negotiate and sign a treaty with Chinese representatives. Accompanied by LeGendre and his French legal adviser, Gustave Boissonade, Ōkubo and his party left Tokyo on August 6.[104] Although he refused to reveal his intentions before his departure, it is unlikely that he would have undertaken the mission unless he had decided to seek a peaceful settlement.

In Peking, an impasse had developed in the talks between the Tsungli Yamen and Yanagiwara, which had begun following the latter's arrival there on July 31. The Yamen maintained that China had jurisdiction over aboriginal land in

102. *Ōkuma bunsho*, vol. 1, 75–77; Hsü, "Taiwan jiken," 47.
103. Inoue, *gunkokushugi*, vol. 2, 159; Hsü, "Taiwan jiken," 51.
104. NGB, vol. 10, 171–172.

Taiwan and that it was China's responsibility, not Japan's, to punish the aborigines for murdering the Liu-ch'iuans, subjects of a Chinese tributary. Accusing Japan of violating the 1871 treaty by failing to consult China in advance on the matter, the Yamen demanded immediate withdrawal of the Japanese expedition from Taiwan. Yanagiwara countered that he had informed the Yamen of Japanese intentions during his visit to Peking with Foreign Minister Soejima the previous year. He argued that since the aboriginal land had never been under effective Chinese administrative control, under international law Japan had the right to subdue the aborigines and assimilate them into Japanese culture.[105] At this point Ōkubo and his party arrived in Peking, on September 10.

Ōkubo made little headway in his initial discussions with the Yamen, but he scored a strategic success by confining the discussions to the question of Chinese jurisdiction over the aboriginal land and avoiding discussion of the jurisdictional dispute over Liu-ch'iu. Putting the Yamen on the defensive, he demanded evidence of Chinese jurisdiction over the aboriginal land. Then he rejected as insufficient the information supplied by the Yamen. When the Yamen ministers refused further discussion on the ground that the Japanese action constituted an unwarranted interference in Chinese internal affairs, Ōkubo threatened, on October 5, to leave Peking unless the Chinese were willing to settle the dispute. Professing a sincere desire for peace, Ōkubo asked the Yamen to come forward with a mutually satisfactory solution within five days. The Yamen objected to the time limit. Nevertheless it acknowledged Ōkubo's desire for peace and proposed another meeting to discuss measures that would satisfy both sides.[106]

Meanwhile, Ōkubo intimated to British Minister Wade and French Minister de Geofroy in Peking that although Japan wanted no territory its honor must be upheld; it must

105. For Yanagiwara's talks with the Tsungli Yamen, see Yen, *Taiwan in China's Foreign Relations*, 236–242.

106. *Ibid.*, 252–264; Iwata, *Ōkubo Toshimichi*, 211–219.

be compensated for its human losses and material outlays. When informed of this, Grand Councilor Wen-hsiang told the Western envoys that China would not hold the case against Japan, would deal with the aborigines itself, and would compensate those Japanese who had suffered at the hands of the aborigines if Japan withdrew from Taiwan. He insisted, however, that the compensation would not be an indemnity to the Japanese government, but relief money for the families of the murdered Liu-ch'iuans. Moreover, it would be paid only after the Japanese troops had withdrawn from Taiwan. When Ōkubo set the amount at three million dollars and demanded a written guarantee for payment, the Yamen rejected both demands. On October 23 Ōkubo threatened again to leave Peking, declaring that Japan had no alternative but to proceed with its original plan to annex the aboriginal land under its occupation.[107]

Wade intervened. Working behind the scenes, he secured some Chinese concessions. On October 25 he informed Ōkubo that China would pay 500,000 taels—100,000 taels for the families of the murdered Liu-ch'iuans and 400,000 for the facilities the Japanese would leave behind in Taiwan. Ōkubo accepted the offer with the conditions that China acknowledge the justness of the Japanese action, expurgate all references to the case from the diplomatic documents exchanged between the two countries, promise to refrain forever from reopening the case, and pay the compensation prior to the withdrawal of the expedition. Wade persuaded him to agree to payment of half the amount in advance and the remainder upon the completion of the withdrawal, and he obtained Chinese consent to the arrangement the following day. Formal agreements were signed by the two countries on October 31; Wade countersigned the contract guaranteeing payment of the compensation by China.[108]

The following day Ōkubo left for Taiwan, where he in-

107. Fox, *Britain and Japan*, 306.
108. The texts of the agreements are in IWSM-TC, 98.16a–17b; NGB, vol. 10, 316–318. For an English translation of the same, see Yen, *Taiwan in China's Foreign Relations*, 281–284.

formed Saigō of the settlement and directed arrangements
for the withdrawal of the expedition. Ōkubo returned to
Tokyo to a hero's welcome on November 7. Saigō and his
forces returned to Japan in December.

The expedition was hailed as a great success in Japan. In
fact, it was a costly adventure. It began in anticipation of
Western diplomatic acquiescence, if not support, but it received unfavorable, generally critical reaction. It failed to
demolish Chinese sovereignty over Taiwan aboriginal land
or to obtain compensation commensurate to the cost of the
campaign. It accomplished little of military importance at
the cost of over 500 lives, and it seriously strained the army's resources and logistic capabilities. It was a financial
disaster. The expedition cost more than ¥3,610,000, against
an original estimate of ¥500,000. In addition, the Japanese
government was compelled to spend ¥4,000,000 to purchase ships to transport troops, when the British and American governments refused to permit their ships to be
employed in the expedition. The expedition was the chief
cause of a record budgetary deficit of ¥9,000,000 for the
Japanese government in 1874.[109] Were it not for Wade's
timely intervention and his pressuring of China toward a
compromise settlement, which apparently saved Japan from
a prolonged military and diplomatic stalemate with China,
the whole venture could have proved disastrous to the
Ōkubo regime.

Nevertheless, the expedition accomplished some important objectives. First, by demonstrating Japan's growing
military capabilities, the expedition enhanced Japan's prestige in the eyes of the Western powers. This was an important factor in the British and French decisions to withdraw
their garrisons from Yokohama in early 1875.[110] Second, it
resulted in China's tacit, indirect recognition—brought on
largely by diplomatic ineptness—of Japanese suzerainty
over Liu-ch'iu, which paved the way for its subsequent annexation by Japan. The archipelagic kingdom was the first

109. Inoue, *gunkokushugi*, vol. 2, 159.
110. Iwata, *Ōkubo Toshimichi*, 220.

of China's tributary states to be alienated from the tribute system and the traditional East Asian world order that the system symbolized. Third, by demonstrating Japan's military prowess and diplomatic skill, the expedition served as an indirect but clear warning to Korea, the important tributary which Japan was bent upon weaning away from China. In all, the expedition constituted a serious challenge to China's traditional supremacy in East Asia.

Chinese response to the expedition, both diplomatic and military, was tardy and ineffective. The reason for this was China's lack of preparedness. Its self-strengthening programs for military modernization and diplomatic innovation had been initiated more than a decade earlier by such officials as Prince Kung and Wen-hsiang in Peking and Tseng Kuo-fan, Tso Tsung-t'ang, and Li Hung-chang in the provinces. Under the rule of Empress Dowager Tz'u-hsi, they had not received full political support or the funds necessary to ensure their success. On the contrary, they had been disparaged and attacked by conservative officials, whose activities were encouraged overtly or covertly by Tz'u-hsi. Despite the efforts of pragmatic officials, the programs therefore had failed to develop sufficient modern military capabilities for China to meet the rising threat of Japanese expansionism. Moreover, beginning with the Tientsin Massacre in 1870, China faced one foreign or domestic crisis after another, all of which taxed its strength. In particular, preoccupied with the task of recovering Sinkiang from its Muslim rebels and Russian occupiers, the Ch'ing government year after year devoted most of its available financial and military resources to Tso Tsung-t'ang's campaigns for the pacification of the region. This denied adequate funds for the maritime defenses, which Li Hung-chang and his associates were struggling to develop to meet the growing Japanese threat.[111]

China suffered from internal and external diplomatic disadvantages during the 1870s, a period marked by

---

111. For the effect of Ch'ing court politics on the self-strengthening programs, see Ting-yee Kuo and Kwang-Ching Liu, "Self-strengthening: the Pursuit of Western Technology," in *Cambridge History of China*, vol. 10, 491–542.

Sino-Western discord. China no longer enjoyed the same degree of Western goodwill and cooperation it had during the 1860s, the period of the Western Cooperative Policy. Internally, this was also the period when the influence of the Tsungli Yamen, particularly that of Prince Kung, declined further. During 1874—the year of the Taiwan crisis—the prince was publicly disgraced for the second time since 1865.[112] This could not but have adversely affected the effectiveness of the Yamen in the conduct of the crucial negotiations with the Japanese. And there was inadequate diplomatic and military intelligence. Li Hung-chang's proposal for stationing Chinese officials in Japan after the signing of the Sino-Japanese treaty was ignored by the Ch'ing government. Consequently, during the Taiwan crisis, the Yamen was forced to operate without information concerning Japan's intentions, plans, and capabilities. Had the Yamen been aware of the political weakness and financial predicament of the Ōkubo regime, despite Wade's mediation it might not have accepted a compromise settlement.

Apparently better informed than the Yamen as to Japan's military capabilities, Li Hung-chang repeatedly advised the Yamen to maintain a firm stand against the Japanese. He discounted newspaper reports alleging that Japan was readying large forces for an invasion of the Chinese mainland in the event of a breakdown in the negotiations in Peking. He obviously agreed when his friend, Shen Pao-chen, wrote that Ōkubo's personal journey to China was an indication of Japan's internal weakness and that Japan, not China, wanted an early settlement.[113] When Ōkubo threatened to leave Peking if his demands were not met, Li told the Yamen that Ōkubo was bluffing by imitating the tactics used by Soejima the previous year.[114] Although Li urged a speedy military buildup in Taiwan, he wished to avoid open hostilities with Japan at this time,[115] for he knew of China's appalling lack of military preparedness. Moreover, probably

112. S. M. Meng, *The Tsungli Yamen: Its Organization and Functions,* 51.
113. LWCK, *Tsungli Yamen Letters,* 2.45a–b.
114. *Ibid.,* 2.52a.
115. *Ibid.,* 2.41a; Immanuel C. Y. Hsü, *China's Entrance into the family of nations,* 173.

he believed that Korea, not Taiwan, was the real object of Japanese ambitions at this time, and he considered Korea more important than Taiwan to the security of the Ch'ing state.

The Taiwan expedition was Japan's first venture in predatory expansionism in East Asia in modern times. As we have seen, Taiwan had long been an object of deep-rooted Japanese expansionism, which tended to become difficult to restrain in times of domestic unrest or instability. Having gone as far as they had, if Japan had enjoyed a margin of military superiority over China at this time, the Ōkubo government would not have sought a peaceful settlement with China. It might have insisted on terms unacceptable to China, thereby precipitating open hostilities between the two countries. Or it might have simply refused to withdraw from Taiwan, retaining the occupied territory indefinitely.[116] Ōkubo apparently realized the predatory, or at least excessive, nature of the Japanese action. Otherwise, he would not have made the contradictory demands that China acknowledge the justness of the Japanese action and expurgate all references to it from diplomatic documents after its settlement.

On the other hand, Ōkubo and his colleagues were almost forced into undertaking this bold venture as a diversionary enterprise—not so much for the aggrandizement of Japanese interests abroad as for the consolidation of their position at home. Had the domestic situation been more stable and had they been able to estimate the cost and predict the Western reactions more accurately, probably they would not have undertaken the project—at least at this time. Japan's claim of exclusive jurisdiction over Liu-ch'iu, in defense of which the expedition was ostensibly undertaken, was an expansionist act in that it was asserted in complete disregard of the views of the Liu-ch'iuan people and their authorities, let alone those of the Chinese. Yet in view of Japan's long, actual control of the archipelagic kingdom, it

116. Iwata, *Ōkubo Toshimichi*, 207.

is understandable that Ōkubo and his associates acted in the honest belief that its absorption into Japan was an act of territorial integration, not of territorial aggrandizement.[117] Whatever justification was behind the action, it indicated that the Meiji government under Ōkubo's leadership rejected the viability, if not validity, of the traditional modus vivendi whereby Liu-ch'iu for centuries had a separate political identity under the Chinese tribute system while remaining under actual Japanese control. This venture constituted the first concrete Japanese challenge to the sinocentric traditional world order in East Asia.

117. Marius B. Jansen, "Modernization and Foreign Policy in Meiji Japan," in Robert E. Ward, ed., *Political Development in Japan,* 164–166.

CHAPTER VI

The Japanese-Korean Rapprochement and New Treaty, 1874–1876

During the fall of 1873, when Japan was in the grip of political crisis over the Korean question, an equally momentous political upheaval was approaching its climax in Korea. The crisis in Japan ended with the defeat of the *sei-Kan* advocates led by Saigō Takamori; the Korean upheaval ended with the retirement of the Taewŏn'gun, de facto ruler and implacable foe of Japan and the West for a decade. The contemporary events removed from power in each country those most likely to precipitate war between them. These and subsequent occurrences in and around Japan and Korea formed the backdrop against which the two countries moved gradually toward a rapprochement to end the diplomatic interregnum, which had begun with the restoration of imperial rule in Japan in 1868.

The rapprochement that was achieved by the Treaty of Kanghwa in 1876 was not a restoration of traditional Japanese-Korean relations; it laid the foundation for a new form of relations between the two countries based on the Western concept of international relations. The Meiji government achieved in Korea one of the major goals it had set for itself under its diplomatic reform program, launched in late 1871: diplomatic and commercial parity with Western powers in dealing with other East Asian countries. Moreover, in pursuing this goal in Korea, the Japanese government emulated predatory Western diplomatic tactics, or gunboat diplomacy.

THE TAEWŎN'GUN'S FALL
AND CHANGE IN KOREAN POLICY

When he was catapulted from relative obscurity to a position of authority and power as de facto regent for his son, King Kojong, at the beginning of 1864, the Taewŏn'gun faced the formidable task of strengthening Korea against foreign invasion and the Yi dynasty against internal rebellion. Although he was not formally appointed regent and his authority was never clearly defined, he "ruled" the kingdom for the next ten years with authority and power normally exercised by an enthroned monarch.

While maintaining a rigid policy of exclusion toward the West and an uncompromising stand against Japan, the Taewŏn'gun introduced a wide range of domestic reforms with the aim of revitalizing the decaying Yi dynasty. He put an end to the "rule of the consort clans" by ousting the Andong Kims from their position of dominance at court and in the government, and he instituted measures designed to strengthen the enfeebled royal institution. He relaxed the centuries-old ban on participation in state administration by members of the royal family, rehabilitated many princes and royal kinsmen condemned for "treason" in past political purges, and restored extinct branches of the royal line by means of posthumous adoption, often going back several generations. Further he sought to enhance royal dignity and prestige with a program of palace construction, the best example of which is the rebuilding of the Kyŏngbok Palace, which had lain in ruin since the Hideyoshi invasions of the 1590s.[1]

1. For the Taewŏn'gun's efforts to strengthen the royal institution, see James B. Palais, *Politics and Policy in Traditional Korea*, 36–42; Ching Young Choe, *The Rule of the Taewŏn'gun, 1864–1873*, 64–69.

The Taewŏn'gun also introduced reforms in state administration to eliminate bureaucratic inefficiency and corruption and to strengthen central control. Reforms included the abolition of tax privileges traditionally enjoyed by the *yangban* class, revision of the grain loan system for relief of the peasantry, closure of all but forty-seven of the country's some 600 private Confucian academies, issuance of a large, inflationary denomination of copper coin, called the 100-cash, and the importation of Ch'ing cash for circulation in the country.

Despite their wide range and seemingly broad scope, the Taewŏn'gun's reforms were conservative in character, designed to preserve the existing socio-political order with minor modifications. While none of the reforms was aimed at seriously weakening the position of the *yangban* class as the ruling elite of the kingdom, most of the reforms affected the *yangban's* vested interests and privileges adversely. For this reason, most of its members, particularly the literati—who included non-official scholars and former officials residing in their native district—regarded the Taewŏn'gun's reforms as violations of fundamental Confucian precepts of government and as a massive assault on their own traditional role in society and government, sanctioned by those precepts.[2]

The consequent rift between the Taewŏn'gun and the literati came to the fore during the French invasion in 1866, when Yi Hang-no, voicing growing "literati" discontent, criticized the Taewŏn'gun's domestic policy while supporting his stand against the French. In memorials to the king, Yi urged suspension of the Kyŏngbok Palace project and called for the immediate restoration of the Mandongmyo, abolished earlier by the Taewŏn'gun, as the true way to "revere China and expel the barbarians" (*chonhwa yang'i*).[3] The rift widened in 1868, when Ch'oe Ik-hyŏn, one of Yi's disci-

2. On the Taewŏn'gun's domestic reforms, see Palais, *Traditional Korea*, 23–175; Choe, *Rule of the Taewŏn'gun*, 32–90; Yi Sŏn-gŭn, *Han'guksa ch'oegŭnse p'yŏn*, 151–224.

3. Palais, *Traditional Korea*, 178–179. For Yi's memorials, see ISN-KJ, 3/9/12, 3/10/4; KJS, 3.62b–63b, 3.74a–76b.

ples, attacked the Taewŏn'gun's domestic programs in a memorial to the throne. Ch'oe called for the suspension of the Kyŏngbok Palace project, the termination of the special levies instituted to finance it, and abolition of the 100-cash. Although Kojong praised Ch'oe for his "true loyalty" and tried to promote him to a higher post, the king was too young—only sixteen *sui* old—to challenge his father's leadership.[4] The situation was to change drastically in a few years as Kojong grew conscious of his own authority as ruler and his queen began developing her ambition for power.

A sixteen-*sui*-old orphan when she married Kojong in 1866, Queen Min was a distant cousin of the Taewŏn'gun's wife, of the Yŏhung Min lineage. Her lonely circumstances as the sole offspring of her parents, both of whom had died during her childhood, allegedly led the Taewŏn'gun to choose her as his son's queen. The Taewŏn'gun reputedly believed that, with her family background, it would be neither likely nor easy for the young queen and her relatives to establish a position of dominance at court, as the Andong Kims and the P'ung'yang Chos had before.[5] In a few short years, however, this innocent girl was to mature into a woman of exceptional intelligence and ambition and become the most formidable of all the enemies of the Taewŏn'gun.

The queen's relations with the Taewŏn'gun soured when the latter began lavishing his affection on Prince Wanhwa, his first royal grandson, born to Kojong and one of his concubines in 1868. Since both the Taewŏn'gun and Kojong regarded the boy as a potential candidate for the throne, he became a threat to the future position of the queen and her relatives. The queen's resentment of the Taewŏn'gun turned into personal animosity when her son died only three days after birth in 1871, allegedly after the Taewŏn'gun had administered ginseng as a palliative. Precisely what role Queen Min and her relatives played in the

4. Palais, *Traditional Korea*, 182–183. For Cho'e's memorial, see ISN-KJ, 5/10/10; KJS, 5.46a–b.
5. Yi Sŏn-gŭn, *Han'guksa ch'oegŭnse*, 343–344.

Taewŏn'gun's eventual retirement in 1873 remains a mystery.[6] But there is little doubt that they welcomed, if they did not actively plot, his ouster from power.

In November 1873, Ch'oe Ik-hyŏn, out of office since his unsuccessful attack on the Taewŏn'gun in 1868, was suddenly appointed royal secretary. It is not known whether the appointment was initiated by Kojong or engineered by the queen and her relatives. At any rate, clearly it was a move calculated to rally the disgruntled literati against the Taewŏn'gun. The following month, in two sharply worded memorials to the king, Ch'oe mounted the boldest and most scathing attack yet made on the Taewŏn'gun. In fanatical Confucian and anti-Manchu rhetoric, Ch'oe denounced the abolition of the Mandongmyo as an evil deed violating the suzerain-vassal relationship between China and Korea. Closure of private academies was condemned as destructive of the proper Confucian teacher-student relationship. The restoration of the extinct branches of the royal line, said Ch'oe, distorted the father-son relationship, while the rehabilitation of the condemned royal kinsmen and purge victims blurred the distinction between loyalty and treason. The importation of Ch'ing cash—which Ch'oe pointedly called the "northern barbarian cash" (*hojŏn*)—was denounced as a measure disrupting the separation of civilized society from barbarity. Finally, Ch'oe bluntly asked Kojong to honor the Taewŏn'gun as his father, but not to let him interfere in the affairs of state.[7]

Kojong, now a youth of 23 *sui*, praised Ch'oe's loyalty and promoted him to vice minister of revenue. When top officials of the government protested, Kojong dismissed all but the three highest: Royal House Administration Director Hong Sun-mok, Second State Councilor Kang No, and

6. Palais, *Traditional Korea*, 45–46. The prevalent view among Korean and Japanese historians is that Queen Min and her relatives engineered the Taewŏn'gun's ouster from power. See Yi Sŏn-gŭn, *Han'guksa ch'oegŭnse*, 345–358; TNS, vol. 1, 28–29.

7. For more detailed accounts of the events, see Palais, *Traditional Korea*, 183–192; Yi Sŏn-gŭn, *Han'guksa ch'oegŭnse*, 345–350. For Ch'oe's memorials, see ISN-KJ, 10/10/25, 10/11/3; KJS, 10.24a–b, 10.31a–35a.

Third State Councilor Han Kye-wŏn. The language of Ch'oe's memorials, however, was so blunt that Kojong was compelled to dismiss him from office. In order to spare him harsher punishment, the king hastily exiled Ch'oe to Cheju Island, where he remained in safety until the storm raised by his action subsided. Kojong announced that henceforth he would conduct all the affairs of state personally. When Hong, Kang, and Han pressed for the reopening of Ch'oe's case, the king relieved them of their posts.[8] On January 2, 1874, Kojong appointed Yi Yu-wŏn—his former tutor and former second state councilor reputedly not well regarded by the Taewŏn'gun—as chief state councilor. On January 19 Pak Kyu-su, the reform-minded former governor of P'yŏng'an Province who was on friendly terms with the Taewŏn'gun, was appointed third state councilor.[9]

While all this was going on, the Taewŏn'gun apparently did what he could to retain power. But when he realized all was in vain, he retired to a mountain villa outside the capital. His fall from power was as sudden and swift as his rise a decade earlier. The animosity, fear, and ambitions of Queen Min and her relatives, as well as the dissatisfaction of the literati, undoubtedly contributed to the circumstances which forced him out of power. But as James Palais points out, it was the king's attitude, rather than the power struggle at court or factional rivalry, that was crucial and decisive. The Taewŏn'gun's position as father of the reigning monarch gave his rule a moral, if not legal, basis during Kojong's minority. But once the king reached adulthood and declared his independence, the Taewŏn'gun did not have legitimate claim to authority.[10] Even those officials who remonstrated with Kojong did so in protest against what they considered his too lenient treatment of Ch'oe Ik-hyŏn, whose accusations were directed as much against them as against the Taewŏn'gun. No one protested Kojong's assumption of personal rule.

8. Palais, *Traditional Korea*, 195–198.
9. Yi Sŏn-gŭn, *Han'guksa ch'oegŭnse*, 353–354.
10. Palais, *Traditional Korea*, 176, 199.

While the Taewŏn'gun remained a potent political force, even in retirement, his withdrawal from politics made possible a readjustment of Korean policy toward Japan as well as a revision of domestic policy. As we have seen, there was no disagreement between the Taewŏn'gun and the literati over foreign policy. Nor was there any basic difference among the Taewŏn'gun, Kojong, and his new ministers over the fundamental concept, ideology, and goal of foreign policy. Kojong and his ministers had no intention of opening the country to the West. Nor did they intend to broaden or substantially change Korea's traditional relations with Japan. The difference between them and the Taewŏn'gun concerned the assessment of Korea's internal and external circumstances at the time and the method of policy execution, not goals. While the Taewŏn'gun believed that Korea had sufficient military capabilities to hold out against the Western powers, Kojong and his ministers had a realistic appreciation of Western strength and Korean weakness. In particular, the ministers were more concerned about China's inability to expel the Western barbarians.[11]

The Taewŏn'gun viewed Japan's adoption of Western arms, technology, and institutions with deep suspicion and antipathy. He regarded Japan's discarding of tradition and its "collaboration" with the West as a threat to the traditional order in East Asia. Therefore he rejected compromise or accommodation with Japan on any issue, however minor or trivial. While they shared the Taewŏn'gun's distrust of the Japanese and his fear of Japanese-Western collaboration against Korea, Kojong and his ministers nevertheless considered it unwise for Korea to antagonize Japan needlessly. They believed that Japan could be mollified and peace could be maintained if Korea simply changed its attitude from hostility to friendship, without compromising on substantive issues. On the basis of this naive assumption, Kojong's government adopted a policy of reconciliation with Japan early in 1874. They did not show an understanding

11. *Ibid.*, 253. Members of the Korean embassies returning from China during this period were always asked by Kojong about Westerners in China.

of the modern concept of international relations or an awareness of Japan's growing interest in Korea.[12]

First step toward the implementation of the new policy was the appointment of a secret censor in February 1874 to inquire into the conduct of relations with Japan at Pusan under the Taewŏn'gun's rule. This was accompanied by a change of officials responsible for the management of Japanese affairs. Prefect of Tongnae Chŏng Hyŏn-dŏk and Governor of Kyŏngsang Province Kim Se-ho—both Taewŏn'gun confidants—were replaced by Pak Che-gwan and Yu Ch'i-sŏn, respectively. On the basis of their separate investigations, the secret censor and Prefect Pak reported to Seoul that An Tong-jun, during his long tenure as language officer at Pusan, had willfully obstructed communication between Japan and Korea and caused a breakdown in the relations between the two countries. They also charged that Chŏng and Kim had been negligent of their duties as An's supervisor.[13] While the Seoul government was pondering how to punish these men, on August 4 Kojong received an urgent note from the Ch'ing Board of Rites; the note heightened Korean fear of Japanese invasion, aroused earlier by the news of violent *sei-Kan* agitation and disturbances in Japan.

Informing the king of the Japanese invasion of Taiwan, the Board explained that this was a diversionary act of the Japanese government to siphon off samurai discontent over defeat of the *sei-Kan* proposal the previous fall. The Board also forwarded a copy of a Tsungli Yamen memorial, which reported the rumor that, upon the withdrawal of its expedition from Taiwan, Japan might use 5,000 troops allegedly at Nagasaki for an invasion of Korea, and that France and the United States, still harboring grudges against Korea, might join Japan in such an undertaking. The information was supplied to the Yamen by Shen Pao-chen, imperial commis-

12. For a detailed analysis of the Taewŏn'gun's foreign policy and of Kojong's initial policy toward Japan, see James B. Palais, "Korea on the Eve of the Kanghwa Treaty, 1873–1876" (Ph.D. dissertation, Harvard University, 1968), 490–605.
13. ISN-KJ, 10/12/30, 11/1/3; KJS, 10.59b; Palais, *Traditional Korea,* 255.

sioner for Taiwan affairs, along with the recommendation
of his French adviser, Prosper Giquel, that if China could
persuade Korea to enter into treaty relations with France
and the United States, it might deter Japan from attacking
Korea.[14]

Alarmed but incredulous, the Korean authorities believed
that this was a plot by France and the United States to obtain a treaty from Korea. France was identified with the
Roman Catholic church and viewed with deep hostility by
the Korean authorities. Moreover, Kojong's government did
not intend to change the traditional policy of seclusion. In
his reply to Peking, on August 9, Kojong reiterated the
reasons why Korea could not trade with the West, which he
said had already been explained to the Americans. As for
Japan, Kojong believed that Japan would "not dare disobey
the Heavenly Court" now that it had been granted a treaty
by China. He asked the Board to appeal to the emperor on
his behalf to instruct the French and American ministers
and Japanese officials in China not to create trouble for
Korea needlessly.[15]

Five days later, on August 14, Chief State Councilor Yi
Yu-wŏn told Kojong that by following An's words blindly,
the government (the Taewŏn'gun) had needlessly invited a
rupture of the relations with Japan, which had been peaceful for three centuries. Accusing An of embezzlement and
other wrongdoings, Yi recommended that An be put to
death and an investigating officer be dispatched to
Tsushima to ascertain the extent of the damage caused by
An's activities. Third State Councilor Pak Kyu-su argued
that official communications from Japan should not be rejected merely because they deviated in wording from established practice. He took the opportunity to emphasize the
urgent need for military preparedness against growing external dangers. On the basis of these recommendations, An
Tong-jun was arrested and remanded to Seoul for investiga-

14. Palais, *Traditional Korea*, 253. For the Tsungli Yamen memorial, see
IWSM-TC, 94.37a–b. For Korean reactions, see ISN-KJ, 11/6/25; KJS, 11.56a–b.
15. IWSM-TC, 97.15b–17b.

tion and trial, Chŏng was exiled, and Kim was dismissed from office.[16] When further evidence of malfeasance was brought forward against these men by the secret censor in January 1875, Chŏng and Kim were barred permanently from holding office; An was executed the following April.[17] The punishment of these men, particularly the execution of An, marked the end of the Taewŏn'gun's Japan policy.

During the early months of 1874, the Japanese government, preoccupied with the suppression of the Saga Rebellion and preparations for the projected Taiwan expedition, relegated the Korean question to the background. The resultant passivity in Japanese policy toward Korea was evident in a decision taken in April 1874, which was almost as traditional and conciliatory as the changed Korean policy toward Japan. On the basis of recommendations made by Moriyama Shigeru, the Foreign Ministry resurrected an earlier plan to send Sō Shigemasa to Korea to undertake another effort to restore ruptured relations with that country. To allay Korean suspicion, the former Tsushima daimyo was to travel to Korea the "old-fashioned" way, by traditional Japanese-style ship instead of steamship, and accompanied by former Tsushima samurai with experience in Korean affairs. Apparently it was assumed that even after a restoration of relations Korean affairs would continue to be handled by Sō and his former retainers for some time.[18] Though a temporary expedient, the decision amounted to a reversion to the traditional method of conducting relations between the two countries through the medium of Tsushima.

Shortly thereafter, however, the Foreign Ministry learned of the fall of the Taewŏn'gun. Eager to take advantage of the political change in Korea, on May 15 the Ministry ordered Moriyama to go to Pusan to study the situation firsthand. Moriyama was to find out whether or not it would be advisable for Sō to visit Korea at this time. Main-

16. ISN-KJ, 11/6/29, 11/7/3; KJS, 11.59a–60a, 11.61a–b.
17. ISN-KJ, 11/12/13; KJS, 11.97a–98a.
18. TNS, vol. 1, 336–337.

taining a cautious posture, the Ministry instructed Moriyama to travel to Korea by Japanese-style boat and to refrain from doing anything that might arouse Korea's suspicion or offend its sensibilities.[19]

Reaching Pusan in mid-June, Moriyama was pleasantly surprised by the change in Korean official attitude he found. Although he had no authority to conduct negotiations with Korean officials, encouraged by their uncustomary eagerness to learn his views, Moriyama began informal communications with them. He indicated that the Japanese government would agree to restore relations through an exchange of notes between its Foreign Ministry and the Korean Ministry of Rites, instead of formal state messages between the rulers of the two countries.[20]

Meanwhile, the Chinese warning of a possible Japanese invasion made Kojong and his officials even more anxious to reestablish communication with Japan. On August 16—a week after the Seoul government sent off its reply to Peking—an unidentified Korean official, reputedly an aide to the prefect of Tongnae, visited the Japanese mission at Pusan for a confidential talk with Moriyama. The latter took the opportunity to explain the Japanese government's position. He also mentioned Japan's recent "great victory" in Taiwan, which "astonished" the visitor. The visitor told Moriyama that he was convinced that the Japanese government's friendly intentions toward Korea had been distorted by a handful of interpreters at Pusan and that he would do everything in his power to speed up reconciliation between the two countries. Reporting the meeting to Tokyo, Moriyama declared confidently that Japan could achieve its objectives in Korea with a "little show of force." He recommended that Sō should visit Korea on the earliest possible date.[21]

On September 4 Hyŏn Sŏg-un, the language officer who had replaced An Tong-jun, paid an official visit to the

19. *Ibid.*, 338–340; NGB, vol. 10, 360–361.
20. TNS, vol. 1, 340–344.
21. NGB, vol. 10, 369–371. On Moriyama's talk with the Korean visitor, see *ibid.*, 378–383.

Japanese mission, the first such visit by a Korean official. In their talks that day, Hyŏn and Moriyama worked out alternative formulas, any one of which might be used to restore relations between the two countries: (1) for Korea to accept Sō's notes, brought over by the Sagara mission in 1872; (2) for the Japanese foreign minister to write a new letter to the Korean minister of rites, which would be presented to the prefect of Tongnae by a Japanese envoy; or (3) for Korea to send an envoy to Japan to discuss other possible alternatives. Growing confident of his own ability to handle negotiations, Moriyama asked Tokyo to postpone Sō's trip to Korea.[22]

There was an even more important indication of Korean eagerness to reach an accord with Japan. On September 24 Moriyama received a confidential letter from Cho Yŏng-ha, commander of the Royal Guard. Queen Dowager Cho's nephew, Cho was legally Kojong's cousin. Expressing regrets over the breakdown of relations between the two countries, for which he blamed Korean interpreters at Pusan, Cho conveyed the Korean court's sincere desire for an early restoration of relations with Japan. Cho apparently wrote the letter under confidential orders from Kojong, who was willing to bypass the regular government agencies in order to establish a direct line of communication with the Japanese, presumably because of strong anti-Japanese sentiment prevailing at court and in the government. Moriyama replied to Cho rather perfunctorily, merely asking for assistance in obtaining speedy approval of one of the three alternative formulas agreed upon earlier between himself and Hyŏn.[23] It is inconceivable that Moriyama did not know the identity of his correspondent or did not realize the importance of his letter. His "casual" reply may have been a diplomatic ruse to conceal his own delight at the favorable turn of events.

A few days later, Moriyama was informed by Hyŏn that the Seoul government had opted for the second of the al-

22. See Hyŏn's report to Seoul in ISN-KJ, 11/8/9 and Moriyama's report to Tokyo in NGB, vol. 10, 396–400.
23. NGB, vol. 10, 409–410.

ternatives. Hyŏn expressed the hope that in his official note
the Japanese foreign minister would avoid direct references
to the Japanese ruler by terms unacceptable to Korea. On
October 2 Moriyama received an official confirmation of
the Seoul government's decision from the prefect of
Tongnae. In turn he notified the prefect that the Japanese
government would dispatch an envoy to Pusan with the
foreign minister's note within five months.[24] On October 6
Moriyama departed from Pusan for home, convinced that it
was no longer necessary for Japan to compromise in order
to reach accord with Korea.

JAPANESE RESPONSE: SHIFT TO GUNBOAT DIPLOMACY

Moriyama returned to Tokyo in late October. The Japanese government ratified the agreement which he had
negotiated at Pusan. Upon his recommendation it cancelled
Sō's postponed trip to Korea altogether. On December 29 it
appointed Moriyama as commissioner to lead a new mission
to Korea.[25] It soon became clear that the cancellation of the
Sō mission and the appointment of Moriyama marked a
shift from passivity and compromise to aggressiveness and
intransigence in Japanese policy toward Korea. Several factors contributed to this shift.

First, there were the change in Korean attitude and the
Japanese interpretation of that change. Although Moriyama
had recommended compromise with Korea, he regarded
Korea's uncustomary eagerness to accommodate Japan as a
sign of weakness. Former loyalist samurai and a firm believer in "restoration diplomacy" toward Korea, Moriyama
had always supported *sei-Kan*.[26] Now he was convinced that
intimidation or the use of force was the best way to deal
with Korea. Second, there was Japan's growing self-
confidence, freshly bolstered by the success of its Taiwan

24. *Ibid.*, 411–415.
25. *Ibid.*, vol. 11, 45.
26. *Nihon rekishi daijiten*, vol. 9, 292.

venture. Immediately after the withdrawal of the expedition from Taiwan, LeGendre urged the Foreign Ministry that, without losing the momentum of victory in Taiwan, Japan should proceed to open Korea. Ōkubo's self-confidence must have been bolstered by his recent diplomatic success in China. With the Taiwan question successfully settled, he was now ready to tackle the Korean question. Finally, there was the prospect of an early settlement of the Sakhalin dispute with Russia, which seemed to have encouraged bolder Japanese action toward Korea. Since the settlement of the Korean question was linked closely with the settlement of the Sakhalin issue in the calculations of the Japanese leaders in this period, we should review briefly the history of the Russo-Japanese jurisdictional dispute over Sakhalin.

The treaty between Japan and Russia signed in 1855 left the status of the island of Sakhalin undefined, permitting its joint settlement by Japanese and Russians.[27] As colonization of the island proceeded, this inevitably led to clashes between Japanese and Russian settlers. After the Meiji Restoration, the Japanese government tried to clarify the island's status, alternately offering to partition it, purchase the Russian claim, or sell Japan's claim to Russia. Rejecting these proposals, Russia insisted that it must have the entire island as a penal colony and offered some islands in the Kurile archipelago in exchange for the surrender of the Japanese claim on Sakhalin. While foreign minister during 1872–1873, Soejima held a series of talks with Russian Chargé d'Affaires Butzow in Tokyo on the Sakhalin question. Soejima offered to give up the Japanese claim on Sakhalin in return for certain "equivalent concessions" from Russia.[28]

Soejima's offer, uncharacteristic of his nationalistic foreign policy, was closely related to Japanese policy toward Korea. The Russian concessions he sought in return reportedly included a guarantee of free passage for Japanese

27. Gaimushō, comp., *Nichi-Ro kōshō shi* (A history of Japanese-Russian relations), 57–58; John J. Stephan, *Sakhalin: A History,* 53.
28. For an account of the Russo-Japanese dispute over Sakhalin, see Stephan, *Sakhalin,* 42–64.

troops through Russian territory and a pledge of neutrality in the event of war between Japan and Korea.[29] Before agreement was reached, however, the talks were suspended by Soejima's departure for China in the spring of 1873. They were never resumed because of the political crisis over the *sei-Kan* debate and the consequent resignation of Soejima from the government. Meanwhile, Russian violence against Japanese settlers on Sakhalin became so frequent that in September 1873 Kuroda Kiyotaka, deputy director of the Office of Colonization, proposed the dispatch of troops to the island for the protection of Japanese settlers.[30]

During the October 1873 *sei-Kan* debate, one of the principal arguments advanced by Ōkubo and Iwakura against war with Korea was, as we have seen, that the Russian threat in the north was so serious that it must be dealt with first.[31] Following their victory, the two men discussed the Sakhalin situation on several occasions during late 1873 and early 1874. Rejecting the Kuroda proposal, they decided to reopen negotiations with Russia along the line followed by Soejima: to give up the Japanese claim on Sakhalin in exchange for the Kuriles and a Russian pledge of nonintervention in future Japanese action in a "neighboring country." Regarding such a guarantee as a prerequisite for the implementation of their Korean strategy, Sanjō, Iwakura, and Ōkubo agreed that the government should not address itself to the Korean question before it settled the Sakhalin question. Only after the Sakhalin issue was settled, said Ōkubo, should Japan send a mission to Korea with several warships. He believed that such a mission would not succeed unless Japan was prepared to use military force.[32]

The task of negotiating a Sakhalin settlement with the Russians was entrusted to Enomoto Takeaki, former bakufu naval commissioner. Commissioned vice admiral in the new

29. Gaimushō, comp., *Nichi-Ro kōshō*, 124–128. For Soejima's proposal for Russian neutrality in the event of war between Japan and Korea, see Maruyama Kanji, *Soejima Taneomi haku*, 177; NGB, vol. 10, 445.

30. *Ōkubo Toshimichi monjo*, vol. 5, 223–224.

31. Tsunoda Ryusaku, et al., eds., *Sources of Japanese Tradition*, vol. 2, 153.

32. *Iwakura Tomomi kankei monjo*, vol. 7, 464–465.

imperial navy and appointed minister extraordinary and plenipotentiary to Russia in January 1874, Enomoto left Tokyo in March and arrived at the Russian capital in June. Although his formal instructions contained no reference to Korea, there is little doubt that during the negotiations with the Russians, Korea was constantly on Enomoto's mind. In a report to Foreign Minister Terashima dated November 22, 1874, Enomoto expressed his belief that Russia would not intervene in a conflict between Japan and Korea. However, it might protest, he said, if Japan permanently occupied an area opposite Tsushima, for that would seal off the Russian outlet from Vladivostok. Enomoto therefore suggested that "even if we had no plans at this time to conquer Korea, we should still enter into some kind of secret agreement with Russia" along the line discussed earlier between Soejima and Butzow. Apparently urging early action in Korea, Enomoto added that the Russian garrisons in the Maritime Provinces were purely for defensive purposes and inadequate for war against any foreign country.[33] Although Enomoto was not to reach an agreement with Russia on Sakhalin until March 1875, early that year the Japanese government had reason to believe that there would be no serious Russian intervention in its future action in Korea.

Before his departure for Korea in February 1875, Moriyama met with British Minister Parkes in Tokyo, apparently in a bid for British support for Japan's new Korean policy, support which would provide an additional insurance against Russian intervention. Comparing his mission to that of Perry to Japan two decades earlier, Moriyama told Parkes that he was hoping to meet with high-ranking Korean officials and return home with a Korean envoy. If these expectations were not realized, he said, it would be difficult for Japan to open Korea by peaceful means.[34] The Moriyama mission thus signaled Japan's tactical shift to gunboat diplomacy toward Korea. Moreover, confidential

33. NGB, vol. 10, 446–447.
34. Hirose Yasuko, "Kōka-tō jiken no shūhen" (Circumstances surrounding the Kanghwa Island incident), *Kokusai seiji* 37 (1967), 27–28.

instructions to Moriyama from Chancellor Sanjō showed
that despite its pragmatism, the Ōkubo government retained some of the "restoration diplomacy" mentality as well
as the traditional East Asian concept of interstate relations.

Sanjō instructed Moriyama to find out whether Korea
claimed independence from China and wished to establish
relations with Japan on the basis of the titular equality of
the rulers of the two countries, or whether it acknowledged
Chinese suzerainty and wished to follow Chinese directions.
In either case, Moriyama was to report the matter to Tokyo
and await further instructions. Regardless of whether Korea
claimed independence or acknowledged vassalage to China,
if the Koreans were willing to establish new relations with
Japan through an exchange of notes between "their king
and the Japanese chancellor" or between their minister of
rites and the Japanese foreign minister on the basis of
"equality," Moriyama was to agree to the Korean request
without further instruction from Tokyo.[35]

Moriyama arrived at Pusan on February 24 aboard a
steamship with two official notes from the Foreign Ministry.
The principal note from Foreign Minister Terashima to the
Korean minister of rites was short. Terashima stated that he
was sending Moriyama and his deputy, Hirotsu Hironobu,
to Korea by imperial command, in order to convey Japan's
sincere desire to further the traditional friendship between
the two countries. The accompanying note was addressed to
the Korean vice minister of rites from Sō in the latter's
capacity as assistant foreign minister. Sō explained that the
restoration of imperial rule and subsequent political
changes in Japan had terminated his own hereditary role in
the management of Korean affairs. Korea's refusal to receive his communications during the past several years, he
went on, not only made it impossible for him to carry out
imperial commands abroad, but aroused strong popular
indignation in Japan. The Japanese court was pleased,
however, to learn that the Korean government, having discovered that a few of its officials had willfully obstructed

35. NGB, vol. 11, 53.

communication between the two countries, was taking steps
to correct the matter. Sō concluded his note with an expression of fervent hope for the success of Moriyama's mission.
Along with his note, Sō returned his official seal from the
Korean court, which he had been required to use in communications to Korea.[36]

Instead of classical Chinese—the traditional language
used in diplomatic communications in East Asia—
Terashima and Sō wrote their notes in mixed Sino-Japanese
script. Moreover, they used the terms "emperor" and "imperial edict" in reference to the Japanese ruler, terms which
the Koreans had consistently objected to and which
Terashima's predecessor, Sawa, and Sō himself had refrained from using in 1872. Deliberate reversion to an earlier practice, along with the use of a steamship, reflected the
aggressive and uncompromising stand taken by the Ōkubo
government in the flush of its success in Taiwan. Wording
of the Japanese notes was reported to Seoul in mid-March,
and it aroused strong opposition from top government officials.[37] No one, however, protested the Japanese use of a
steamship.

Although Kojong's government was anxious to bring
about an early reconciliation with Japan, it was not prepared to accept a significant alteration in the traditional
form of relations. Only one high official, Pak Kyu-su, argued that friendship with Japan must be secured, even
through compromise on substantive issues such as the wording of official communications.[38] But Pak was inactive at this
time, a minister without portfolio. Two incumbent state
councilors—Second State Councilor Yi Ch'oe-ŭng and
Third State Councilor Kim Pyŏng-guk—recommended rejection of the Japanese notes. They considered the wording
improper and use of Sino-Japanese script unacceptable.
Moreover, they were outraged by Sō's "unilateral" discard-

36. *Ibid.,* vol. 11, 49–53; TNS, vol. 1, 359–363.

37. For a detailed account of the Moriyama-Hyŏn talks during May-September
1875, see Palais, "Korea on the Eve of the Kanghwa Treaty," 629–657.

38. For Pak's views, see his letter to the Taewŏn'gun in Pak Kyu-su, *Hwanjaejip*
(Collected works of Pak Kyu-su), 11.1a–3b.

ing of his Korean seal. Kojong took the position that "errors" in the Japanese notes should be pointed out, but it
would not be an act of sincerity and goodwill for Korea to
reject the Japanese approach outright. Accordingly, on
March 16 the State Council instructed Hwang Chŏng-nyŏn,
new prefect of Tongnae, to receive Moriyama formally but
to turn down the Japanese notes, pointing out "errors" in
their wording. If the "errors" were corrected, Hwang was
told, he should immediately inform Moriyama of the Korean government's agreement to full restoration of relations
between the two countries.[39]

Hwang scheduled a formal reception for Moriyama for
late March. Almost immediately a dispute broke out over
protocol. The Koreans wanted a traditional ceremony
under the rules that had governed reception of the
Tsushima envoys, including the wearing of traditional
ceremonial dress. The Japanese insisted on a modern reception, at which they would wear the new Western ceremonial
dress. When Hwang referred the matter to Seoul, he was
told that a traditional reception must be held according to
protocol.[40] Moriyama was equally adamant, arguing that he
was an "envoy of Great Japan," not a lowly retainer of the
Tsushima daimyo, and that to dictate to him on what to
wear was an "infringement upon Japanese sovereignty."[41]

Moriyama regarded Korea's new intransigence as a sign
of weakness and confusion. He reported to Tokyo that the
Korean government had been shaken lately by the "death of
the Ch'ing [T'ung-chih] emperor in the west, and by the
arrival of our mission from the east." He also believed that
the uncompromising position of Korea reflected growing
political instability caused by the resurgent influence of the
Taewŏn'gun and the resultant power struggle between the
Taewŏn'gun and his supporters, on the one hand, and
Queen Min and her relatives, on the other. In a report
taken to Tokyo by Hirotsu in April, Moriyama argued that

39. ISN-JK, 12/2/5, 12/2/9; KJS, 12.8a–10a.
40. ISN-KJ, 12/3/4; KJS, 12.15b.
41. TNS, vol. 1, 369–370.

the best time for an effective demonstration of force would be before the Taewŏn'gun and his anti-foreign supporters regained power. The dispatch of a warship or two to waters near Pusan, he said, would expedite the negotiations and enable him to obtain more favorable terms. Agreeing with Moriyama in principle, Terashima instructed him to continue his diplomatic efforts at Pusan.[42]

Further haggling between the two sides took place at Pusan. At a meeting on May 15, Hyŏn pleaded for a compromise. He told Moriyama that Hwang recognized the validity of Moriyama's arguments; however, he regarded the proposed reception as an occasion for extending official greetings to the Japanese envoy, not for inaugurating change in protocol between the two countries. This should be deferred until after a formal restoration of relations. Hyŏn explained further that Hwang wanted a traditional-style reception to avoid further delay, for if new protocol were to be instituted he would have to refer every detail to Seoul for approval. Rejecting Hyŏn's plea, Moriyama charged that the Korean position was a breach of faith, an interference in Japan's internal affairs, and an insult to its national dignity and honor.[43]

When Moriyama's adamant attitude was reported to Seoul, Kojong summoned some thirty top government leaders to an emergency court conference on June 13. Former Chief State Councilor Kim Pyŏng-hak and his brother, Third State Councilor Kim Pyŏng-guk, took a hard line. They argued that, in view of the improper wording of the Japanese notes, Moriyama should not be received at all—let alone changing protocol to accommodate him. Agreeing with the Kim brothers in principle, Second State Councilor Yi Ch'oe-ŭng expressed the fear that rejection of the Japanese notes might lead to open conflict with Japan. He suggested that the terminology used by the Japanese might be treated as an internal Japanese matter. Pak Kyu-su

42. For Moriyama's recommendations and Terashima's instructions, see NGB, vol. 11, 70–73.
43. *Ibid.*, 86–89; TNS, vol. 1, 374–379.

argued forthrightly that the Japanese notes should be accepted and the Japanese envoy received. He pointed out
that Japan had been calling its ruler "emperor" for
thousands of years and that Japan might resort to arms if its
notes were rejected. Deputy Director of Royal House Administration Hong Sun-mok expressed similar but somewhat equivocal views. However, all but two of the remaining
officials at the conference opposed acceptance of the
Japanese notes.[44]

When he took over the reins of government from his
father, Kojong did so with youthful self-confidence and enthusiasm, ready to put into practice Confucian ideals and
precepts which had been drilled into him by his tutors for
more than a decade. After assuming power, however, his
naive and inept approach brought the government to the
brink of financial bankruptcy and compounded rather than
reduced inefficiency and corruption within the bureaucracy.
His refusal to adopt the measures recommended by the
literati disappointed or alienated most of them; his policy of
reconciliation with Japan failed to appease the Japanese and
aroused strong domestic opposition. All this apparently
weakened Kojong's faith in himself, in the efficacy of Confucian precepts of government, and in his own ability to
lead. When his conciliatory approach toward Japan, based
on the traditional Confucian belief that relations between
states—like those between individuals—could be har-
monized by mutual goodwill and courtesy, proved insufficient and ineffectual, Kojong became uncertain about what
to do next. Facing divided counsel from his ministers, the
young monarch was unable to decide the issue. He ordered
the ministers to discuss the matter further and recommend
a solution.[45]

In the absence of royal leadership, the hard line prevailed. The officials recommended cancellation of the
proposed reception for Moriyama. In order to avoid a com-

44. ISN-KJ, 12/5/10; KJS, 12.19a–b.
45. Palais, *Traditional Korea*, 235–236. For Kojong's early Confucian education,
see *ibid.*, 32–35.

plete breakdown in negotiations, they recommended that a special interpreter be dispatched to Pusan to explain to the Japanese the government's position and its sincere desire for a mutually satisfactory solution. Kojong approved the recommendations; pertinent instructions were sent to the prefect of Tongnae.[46]

On June 24 Hyŏn informed Moriyama of the decision of the Seoul government. Concluding that it was no longer possible to carry out his original instructions, Moriyama decided to send his deputy, Hirotsu, back to Tokyo for new instructions. Moriyama's own recommendation was to withdraw his mission from Pusan and take drastic measures to break the impasse. In late July, when the special interpreter arrived from Seoul, Moriyama refused to see him, insisting that he would not meet with a Korean official unless the dress issue was resolved. He informed the special interpreter through an aide that his deputy had left Korea and that he himself had been ordered to return to Tokyo.[47]

When the matter was reported to Seoul, Kojong again called an emergency court conference of top officials, on August 9. There was even greater pressure against compromise this time. Earlier, on July 24, the Taewŏn'gun had left his mountain retreat suddenly and returned to Seoul, amid a rising clamor among the literati for his leadership. The literati had played an important role in forcing his retirement, but they were now displeased with Kojong's "weak" policy toward Japan. His mere presence in the capital served as a subtle but powerful check on anyone inclined toward compromise with Japan. The assembled officials repeated their earlier recommendations. Instructions were sent to the prefect of Tongnae to "reason" with Moriyama.[48] Unable to carry out his instructions, Prefect Hwang was relieved of his post on September 5, at his own request. On September 20, Moriyama received an order from Tokyo to break off the negotiations and return home. Rejecting

46. ISN-KJ, 12/5/10, 12/5/25; KJS, 12.19b, 12.21b.
47. For details, see TNS, vol. 1, 386–388.
48. ISN-KJ, 12/7/9; KJS, 12.26a–b.

Hyŏn's plea to delay his departure until after the arrival of the new prefect, Moriyama left Pusan the following day.[49]

In his monumental study of modern Japanese-Korean relations, late Professor Tabohashi Kiyoshi blamed Moriyama and Hirotsu for the breakdown of the negotiations at this time. Were it not for their intransigence, born of ignorance of contemporary Korean politics, he observed, accord might have been reached between the two countries in 1875, which would have made it unnecessary for Japan to resort to a threat of force, as it subsequently did.[50] It is difficult to accept the view that these two minor officials, who had been in reasonably close contact with Tokyo, were chiefly responsible for the lost opportunity. Regardless of their personal views and inclinations, it is unlikely that they deliberately subverted their government's policy and decisions regarding Korea. They seem to have acted strictly in accord with the position of the Japanese government toward Korea, which had shifted from compromise to intransigence in the wake of the successful settlement of the Taiwan and Sakhalin questions. It was a shift that pointed to Japan's readiness to use Western-style gunboat diplomacy in dealing with Korea.

THE KANGHWADO *(UNYŌ)* INCIDENT: KOREA AND JAPANESE DOMESTIC POLITICS

While Moriyama was wrangling with Korean officials at Pusan, the Japanese government was taking steps toward the "more drastic action," which he had urged, in Korea. The Taiwan expedition had been a great success outwardly, but Ōkubo knew how dangerous it was to undertake a hasty and ill-prepared foreign venture, especially when the domestic situation was unstable.[51] Before taking drastic action in Korea, therefore, Ōkubo took steps to strengthen

49. NGB, vol. 11, 116–118.
50. TNS, vol. 1, 390.
51. For instance, in a talk with British Minister Harry S. Parkes in January 1875, Iwakura, denying the rumor of an impending Japanese invasion of Korea, said that Japan had learned a lesson from its Taiwan expedition. See Hirose, "Kōka-tō jiken," 29.

the government's position at home: he invited Kido, who had resigned in protest against the Taiwan venture, to rejoin the government. Through the efforts of two Chōshū men, Itō Hirobumi and Inoue Kaoru, the Ōkubo-Kido reconciliation was consummated at a conference in Ōsaka in February 1875. Apparently in a move to strengthen his position in the new coalition, Kido proposed that Itagaki, leader of the Tosa faction who left the government with Saigō, also be invited back. Ōkubo agreed. The principal condition set by Kido and Itagaki for rejoining the government, and accepted by Ōkubo, was the introduction of reforms to transform the government into a more representative national structure. Although Itagaki urged speedy introduction of such reforms, he accepted Kido's doctrine of "gradualism."[52]

Having established a new Satsuma-Chōshū-Tosa coalition at home, Ōkubo and his colleagues proceeded to the settlement of the Sakhalin question with Russia, a prerequisite for "drastic action" toward Korea. In late March Enomoto reached full agreement with the Russians on the terms of a settlement. On April 17 Foreign Minister Terashima wired to Enomoto the Tokyo government's final approval of the draft treaty, which the latter had negotiated with the Russians. At this point Hirotsu returned to Tokyo from Pusan with the request for the dispatch of warships to Korean waters. Instructing Moriyama and Hirotsu to continue their diplomatic efforts at Pusan, Terashima, with approval from Sanjō and Iwakura, arranged with Acting Minister of the Navy Admiral Kawamura Sumiyoshi for the dispatch of three warships to Korea.[53]

Japan's lingering fear of Russian intervention in its action in Korea apparently was dispelled by the settlement of the Sakhalin question with the signing of a treaty in St. Petersburg on May 7, 1875. Moreover, China's fresh dispute with Britain, over the murder of British Vice Consul Augus-

52. For the Ōsaka conference, see Andrew Fraser, "The Ōsaka Conference of 1875," *Journal of Asian Studies* 26.4 (August 1967), 589–610; Iwata Masakazu, *Ōkubo Toshimichi: The Bismarck of Japan*, 227–228.

53. TNS, vol. 1, 395.

tus Margary the previous March, seemed to have greatly
reduced the likelihood of Chinese intervention in such action. At any rate, within a few days of the signing of the
Russian treaty, three Japanese warships sailed for Korean
waters under a cloak of secrecy.

On May 25 one of the warships, the *Unyō*, arrived at Pusan, without warning. It was joined by another a fortnight
later. When the Koreans protested, Moriyama replied that
the ships had brought orders from Tokyo instructing him to
speed up the negotiations. On June 14, when Hyŏn and his
aides wanted to inspect the ships, Moriyama, in consultation
with the commanders, permitted the Koreans to board the
ships. While the visitors were aboard, to their great consternation and discomfort, both craft commenced a gunnery
exercise. Roars of the guns shook the entire harbor. Having
thus demonstrated Japan's growing modern naval power in
a most effective fashion, the *Unyō* left Pusan on June 20. It
sailed north along the east coast of Korea to the Yŏnghŭng
Bay, and back to Pusan for a brief stop, returning to Nagasaki on July 1. Other Japanese naval vessels took soundings
elsewhere along the Korean coast.[54]

Other activities, though not directly related to Korea,
might have had some indirect bearing upon Japan's future
action toward Korea. With Russian goodwill seemingly assured, Japan moved to test China's attitude. In late May
1875 the Japanese government ordered Liu-ch'iu to cease
sending tributary envoys to China; in July it ordered all
Liu-ch'iuan relations with China terminated.[55] A logical
follow-up of the Taiwan expedition, these actions represented another major step toward the complete alienation
of Liu-ch'iu from the Chinese tribute system and its absorption into Japan. There was no immediate Chinese protest
against these moves.

When the Japanese naval demonstrations in Korea failed
to soften the Korean stand, as he had hoped, Moriyama
urged more "drastic action" in his communications to the

54. For an account of the *Unyō*'s visit to Pusan, see NGB, vol. 11, 92–94.
55. *Ibid.*, 325–326, 332–333.

Foreign Ministry during July and August.[56] Meanwhile, absence of Chinese protest against its action in Liu-ch'iu could have only emboldened the Ōkubo government with regard to Korea. In late July, when British Minister Parkes asked Terashima and other cabinet members about Japan's intentions toward Korea, most of them stated that war with Korea would be difficult to avoid. One confided that, before taking decisive action toward Korea, Japan must carefully consider possible Chinese and Russian reactions. Parkes reported to London that the Japanese did not seem to be worried about Russia. He observed that Russian assurance of non-interference in Japanese action in Korea, which Soejima sought in 1873, must have been secured in the spring of 1875. He added that the Japanese government was apparently convinced that China would not actively aid Korea in the event of war between Japan and Korea.[57]

While "favorable" events abroad tended to encourage bolder Japanese action toward Korea, it was domestic political exigencies that seem to have prompted Ōkubo and his colleagues to take such action. Shortly after Kido and Itagaki rejoined the government, Ōkubo partially honored his promise by creating the Senate and the Supreme Court in April and the Prefectural Governors' Conference the following month. Ōkubo, however, put off another measure agreed upon at the Ōsaka conference: separation of the ministries from the Council of State. Ostensibly designed to prevent imperial councilors from holding concurrent ministerial posts, the measure was, in fact, aimed specifically at cutting down the power of Ōkubo, whose position as an imperial councilor holding concurrently the key post of home affairs minister enabled him to control virtually all domestic policies. Ōkubo resisted this and was supported by Sanjō. While Kido was willing to move slowly, Itagaki pressed for immediate adoption of the measure, accusing Ōkubo of bad faith. In his opposition to Ōkubo, the pro-

56. See Moriyama's reports to Terashima, dated July 21 and 25, August 18, and September 3, 1875, in NGB, vol. 11, 109–116.
57. Hirose, "Kōka-tō jiken," 33.

gressive Tosa leader found a strange bedfellow: Minister of
the Left Shimazu Hisamitsu, father of the former Satsuma
lord who wanted a partial restoration of the feudal order.
The combined opposition of the impatient progressive and
the disgruntled reactionary grew in intensity during July and
August, threatening the precarious equilibrium of the coalition.[58] Faced with new domestic political crisis, Ōkubo and
his associates apparently conceived a scheme that would enable them to "kill two birds with one stone"—to achieve Japan's long-sought objectives in Korea and to neutralize
political opposition at home.

During late August and early September, Ōkubo met frequently with Foreign Minister Terashima.[59] There is no record of what they discussed, but it is inconceivable that they
did not discuss Korea. Terashima's order to Moriyama to
break off the negotiations and return home, dated September 3, was undoubtedly issued in consultation with
Ōkubo. Also, precisely at this time, the Ministry of the Navy
ordered the *Unyō* to Korea again, ostensibly to survey waters
between southwestern Korea and southern Manchuria. It
does not seem to be a coincidence that, in addition to
Ōkubo and Terashima, Acting Navy Minister Kawamura
and Commander Inoue Yoshika, the *Unyō's* skipper, were all
Satsuma men.

Meanwhile, there were other indications pointing to impending Japanese action in Korea. In early September,
when it was rumored that Britain and China had settled
their dispute over the Margary affair, no less important
figures than Chancellor Sanjō and Foreign Minister
Terashima personally visited Parkes, in turn, apparently to
ascertain the accuracy of the report. Parkes reported to
London that his visitors did not appear delighted with the

58. For the post-Ōsaka conference dispute between Ōkubo and Itagaki, see
Iwata, *Ōkubo Toshimichi,* 230–234. For the connection between the dispute and the
Unyō incident, see P'eng Tse-chou (Hō Taku-shū), *Meiji shoki Nik-Kan-Shin kankei no
kenkyū* (Studies on Japanese-Korean-Chinese relations in the early Meiji period),
160–165.
59. Ōkubo Toshimichi, *Ōkubo Toshimichi nikki,* vol. 2, 424–427 indicates that
Ōkubo and Terashima met on August 21 and 26 and September 1 and 6, 1875.

prospect of an early Sino-British détente, adding that, if Japan planned an expedition to Korea, naturally it would be happy if China remained enmeshed in its own difficulties and problems.[60] It is impossible to gauge precisely the effect contemporary events in China had on any Japanese decision with regard to Korea at this time, other than to point out that the Sino-British crisis over the Margary affair continued in September 1875; Britain and China did not settle their dispute until the following year. On September 12— within a few days of Parkes' talks with Sanjō and Terashima—the *Unyō* sailed from Nagasaki for Korean waters.[61]

After spending several days off the southwestern Korean coast, on September 20—the day when Moriyama received his orders at Pusan to return home—the *Unyō* reached the Han River estuary in the Kanghwa Bay, the area where the French and American ships had been fired upon before by Korean shore batteries. Although Commander Inoue knew that the area was off-limits to foreign ships, he set off for the shore in a small boat, ostensibly in search of potable water. Predictably, the boat was fired upon by Korean shore batteries. In the ensuing exchange of fire, the *Unyō* easily silenced the shore guns. The *Unyō* then left the area and headed for the open sea. When it reached the waters near Yŏngjong Island off Inch'ŏn, Inoue decided to attack a small fort on the island "in retaliation." Opening fire without warning, the *Unyō* destroyed the fort's guns. Taken by surprise, the defenders offered little effective resistance. Dozens of marines and sailors from the ship quickly overran the fort, killing or wounding scores of Koreans. After looting and burning, they returned to their ship with much booty. The *Unyō* headed for home; it reached Nagasaki on September 28.[62]

The incident was not an accident or a case of poor judgment on the part of the naval commander, although he may·

60. Hirose, "Kōka-tō jiken," 37.
61. P'eng, *Nik-Kan-Shin kankei,* 167.
62. On the *Unyō* incident, see Commander Inoue's report in NGB, vol. 11, 129–132; Yi Sŏn-gŭn, *Han'guksa ch'oegŭnse,* 376–378; Palais, "Korea on the Eve of the Kanghwa Treaty," 667–674; TNS, vol. 1, 398–402.

or may not have knowingly violated the restricted waters of a foreign country. On the basis of available evidence, mostly circumstantial, the incident was deliberately planned as provocation by a Japanese government that was searching for a pretext for "drastic action" in Korea.[63] It was, in fact, part of a scheme by the Ōkubo faction to create a situation to be used to its own political advantage at home and to diplomatic advantage in Korea. Hearing the news of the incident, Saigō Takamori, who undoubtedly knew Ōkubo better than most people, remarked that it was a "desperate plot" of the government to avert its collapse at home.[64] Yamagata Aritomo, minister of war at the time of the incident, was quoted by his biographer, Tokutomi Sohō, as saying that the incident was plotted by the Satsuma clique within the Ministry of the Navy.[65] At any rate, it was precisely the kind of "drastic action" Moriyama had been urging throughout the preceding summer.

The Tokyo government received Commander Inoue's report on the Kanghwa (*Unyō*) incident on the evening of September 28. The following morning Chancellor Sanjō called an emergency cabinet meeting to discuss the incident in the presence of the emperor. At the meeting it was decided to dispatch warships to Pusan to protect the Japanese residents there.[66] Meanwhile, Moriyama, who had learned of the incident upon his arrival at Nagasaki from Pusan on September 30, wired request for permission to return to Pusan. Granting his request, the Foreign Ministry arranged the use of a warship for the trip. Leaving Nagasaki aboard the war-

63. P'eng, *Nik-Kan-Shin kankei*, 170; Yamabe Kentarō, *Nikkan heigō shōshi* (A short history of the Japanese annexation of Korea), 25–26; Fujimura Michio, "Chōsen ni okeru Nihon tokubetsu kyoryūchi no kigen" (Origins of the Japanese concessions in Korea), *Nagoya daigaku bungakubu kenkyū ronshū* 35 (March 1965), 32; Yamada Shōji, "Sei-Kan ron, jiyū-minken ron, bummei-kaika ron" (The proposal for the subjugation of Korea, the advocacy of freedom and people's rights, and the call for civilization and enlightenment), *Chōsenshi kenkyūkai ronbunshū* 7 (June 1970), 120–122; Nakajima Shōzō, "Kōka-tō jiken" (The Kanghwa island incident), *Kokugakuin hōgaku* 8.3 (March 1971), 337–338.

64. Saigo Takamori, *Dai Saigō zenshu*, vol. 1, 842–844.

65. Tokutomi Iichirō, *Kōshaku Yamagata Aritomo den* (A biography of Prince Yamagata Aritomo), vol. 2, 412–413.

66. Tada, ed., *Iwakura kō jikki*, vol. 3, 306–307.

ship *Kasuga* on October 2, Moriyama reached Pusan the following day. His instructions were to take appropriate action, in consultation with the commander of the *Kasuga,* for the protection of the Japanese mission and residents, and to keep Tokyo posted of developments in Korea.[67]

Having taken these initial steps, Ōkubo and his associates proceeded to deal with the domestic political opposition by taking advantage of the "national emergency" created by the incident. At the next cabinet meeting, on October 3, also held in the imperial presence to discuss the Korean situation, Chancellor Sanjō proposed that the intended separation of imperial councilors from the ministries be postponed indefinitely. He argued that such a step would create disruption in government administration at a time when national emergency demanded a close liaison between the Council of State and the ministries. To no one's surprise, Iwakura and Ōkubo supported Sanjō; Itagaki and Shimazu registered strong opposition.[68] In these circumstances, Kido's attitude was crucial in determining whether or not Ōkubo and his associates could push through their scheme without crippling the government once again.

Kido had been critical of both Ōkubo and Itagaki, the former for reneging an explicit pledge made at the Ōsaka conference, the latter for breaking his promise to proceed gradually in introducing reforms. Disgusted with both men, Kido threatened to leave the government but was dissuaded from doing so by Ōkubo.[69] Upon learning of the Kanghwa incident, Kido changed his mind overnight. In his eagerness to undertake the task of settling the Korean question—in which he had always been keenly interested—Kido decided to remain in the government and to support Ōkubo. At a crucial cabinet meeting on October 9, Sanjō's proposal was supported by every imperial councilor except Itagaki. On October 19 the emperor announced that, in view of the Ko-

67. NGB, vol. 11, 119–120, 132.
68. Tada, ed., *Iwakura kō jikki*, vol. 3, 276; Ōkubo, *Ōkubo Toshimichi nikki*, vol. 2, 435; P'eng, *Nik-Kan-Shin kankei*, 161.
69. Kido Takayoshi, *Kido Takayoshi nikki*, vol. 3, 232–233; Iwata, *Ōkubo Toshimichi*, 233; P'eng, *Nik-Kan-Shin kankei*, 160.

rean crisis, there would be no major cabinet reform at this time. On October 27 Itagaki and Shimazu resigned from the government.[70] Their departure did not weaken the government seriously. As the leader of the minority Tosa faction, Itagaki had never held a dominant position in the government; despite his former lordly status, Shimazu had been a figurehead. Kido's decision preserved the all-important Satsuma-Chōshū partnership in the coalition.

It should be noted that Itagaki's resignation did not imply his opposition to the government's Korean policy. In 1873 Itagaki had advocated *sei-Kan* with Saigō Takamori. His protest and anger at this time were directed at what he considered a perfidious maneuver by Ōkubo and his associates. They deliberately provoked an incident in Korea, despite their earlier anti-*sei-Kan* stand, and they were using the incident to sidestep and bury promised domestic reform. Itagaki did not criticize the government's stand toward Korea; he argued that the proposed cabinet reform was essential if discipline, without which no major enterprise abroad could be successfully undertaken, was to be established in the government.[71] In his decision to remain in the government, Kido was motivated equally by factional considerations. In the context of the Satsuma-Chōshū rivalry, Korea was regarded as a Chōshū preserve, while Taiwan was considered that of Satsuma. Apart from his long-standing personal interest in Korea, Kido apparently felt that, since the Taiwan question had been successfully settled by the Satsuma faction under Ōkubo's leadership, it was Chōshū's turn to play the leading role in settling the Korean question. It would be oversimplification, however, to say that, in taking their respective positions, Ōkubo, Kido, and Itagaki had been motivated solely by factional considerations. While not above personal ambition or factional interest, all were patriotic men dedicated to the enhancement

70. For detailed accounts of the event, see Tada, ed., *Iwakura kō jikki*, vol. 3, 275–293; P'eng, *Nik-Kan-Shin kankei*, 161–165.
71. Tada, ed., *Iwakura kō jikki*, vol. 3, 276–278; P'eng, *Nik-Kan-Shin kankei*, 163–165.

of Japan's national prestige; they shared the dream of Japanese expansion, which had grown in Japan since the late Tokugawa period. They believed that, sooner or later, Japan must establish its influence or control over the Korean peninsula. Their disagreement over Korean policy concerned timing and method, not objective.

Apart from Japan's top political leaders, its diplomatic and military officials—whose views should have been less partisan—were all eager to seize the opportunity created by the incident to fulfill Japan's ambitions in Korea. Writing to Foreign Minister Terashima from St. Petersburg, in October 1875, Minister to Russia Enomoto urged that, instead of sending a diplomatic mission, Japan seize an area or island near Pusan and present the Korean government with an ultimatum. He repeated his earlier assurance that Russia would not interfere in such a Japanese action.[72] In another letter to Terashima, the following February, Enomoto emphasized that the seizure of Pusan was a "strategic necessity" for Japan.[73] Although Minister of War Yamagata went along with the peaceful approach taken by Kido and Ōkubo, he, too, was prepared to take military action and was disappointed when such action proved unnecessary.[74]

Immediately after the September 29 cabinet meeting, Kido informed Sanjō and Ōkubo of his desire to go to Korea as chief Japanese negotiator. After consulting his Chōshū friends and followers, such as Itō Hirobumi, Yamagata Aritomo, and Inoue Kaoru, Kido submitted a lengthy memorial to the emperor on October 5; he spelled out his views on the Korean situation and requested that he be given the task of negotiation. While insisting that Korea must be "punished" for its attack on the *Unyō*, Kido opposed outright military action and advocated a peaceful approach. Cognizant of Chinese suzerainty over Korea, Kido said that Japan should ask China if it would accept responsibility for Korea's action. If China refused, Japan should

72. NGB, vol. 11, 127–129.
73. *Ibid.*, vol. 12, 79–80; Yamabe, *Nikkan heigō shōshi*, 36–38.
74. Tokutomi, *Yamagata Aritomo den*, vol. 2, 429–430.

deal directly with Korea and demand an apology. Kido recommended that Japan take punitive measures based on a
careful assessment of its own resources and capabilities only
if Korea failed to comply.[75]

Despite Kido's appeals, Sanjō and Ōkubo refused to make
a major decision with regard to Korea while they were dealing with domestic opposition. Terashima alone took steps
aimed at securing the treaty powers' support for future
Japanese action toward Korea. On October 9 he briefed the
British and French representatives in Tokyo on the *Unyō*
incident, blaming it entirely on the Koreans. On October 17
he sent a formal note to the same effect to all foreign diplomatic representatives in the capital.[76] Meanwhile, the
Foreign Ministry ordered Moriyama to return home to
make a full report on the situation at Pusan. It also ordered
two warships to relieve the *Kasuga* at Pusan. Under the
command of Rear Admiral Nakamuda Kuranosuke, the
ships reached Pusan on October 27. Two days later
Moriyama left Pusan aboard the *Kasuga;* he returned to
Tokyo on November 3.

The following day Moriyama and Hirotsu jointly recommended measures similar to those proposed by Kido. While
stern measures must be taken in retaliation for the attack
on the *Unyō,* they argued, the principal issue was Korea's
"breach of faith" in the negotiations. A plenipotentiary
should be sent directly to Kanghwa to demand an apology,
the punishment of those responsible for the attack on the
Unyō, and a treaty of friendship between the two countries
to prevent similar incidents in the future.[77]

By the end of October, due largely to Kido's decision to
remain in the government, Sanjō and Ōkubo succeeded in
disposing of Itagaki's demand for cabinet reform, without
creating a serious political crisis. Although until then they
had refused to consider Kido's requests to go to Korea,
under the pretext that the domestic political situation re-

75. NGB, vol. 10, 124–125; Tada, ed., *Iwakura kō jikki,* vol. 3, 307–309.
76. NGB, vol. 11, 126–127, 129–130.
77. *Ibid.,* 133–137.

quired his presence at home, they were now ready to grant him his wish. However, Kido suffered a stroke on November 13, and he was forced to abandon his plan. A fight ensued between the Satsuma and Chōshū factions for the top position in the projected mission to Korea. Satsuma was victorious. On December 9 the Satsuma candidate, Lieutenant General Kuroda Kiyotaka, director of the Office of Colonization, was appointed minister extraordinary and plenipotentiary to Korea. To ensure Satsuma-Chōshū cooperation, Chōshū's Inoue Kaoru was appointed deputy minister extraordinary and plenipotentiary to Korea.[78]

CHINA AND THE JAPANESE-KOREAN SETTLEMENT

On November 10, Mori Arinori, former envoy to the United States, was appointed minister to China. Mori was to be resident minister in Peking; his appointment came as a result of Kido's recommendation that Japan should take up the *Unyō* incident with the Chinese authorities before sending a mission to Korea. Son of a Satsuma samurai and educated in England and the United States, Mori was once described by his friend, Itō Hirobumi, as a "Westerner born of Japan."[79] His views on international relations were thoroughly Western, and Mori advised Sanjō and other leaders to regard Korea as independent. Japan would be ill-advised, he told them, to make Korea's refusal to enter into treaty relations with Japan or its attack on the *Unyō* a major issue; as an independent state Korea was free to have or not to have relations with any country, and Korea was not alone to blame for the *Unyō* incident. In settling the dispute with Korea, said Mori, Japan must seek the cooperation of China, not as Korea's suzerain, but as its neighbor—to open Korea before it was seized by a Western power, which would be disastrous to both China and Japan.[80] Refresh-

78. P'eng, *Nik-Kan-Shin kankei*, 172–177.
79. For a biography of Mori, see Ivan Parker Hall, *Mori Arinori.*
80. *Ibid.*, 275; TNS, vol. 1, 529–530.

ingly free of prejudice, Mori took the most enlightened
approach toward Korea among Japanese leaders and officials
of this time.

Mori arrived in Peking early in January 1876. On January 10 he presented a note briefly recounting Korea's
past refusal to receive Japanese communications and its recent attack on the *Unyō* to the Tsungli Yamen. Although
public opinion in Japan had been inflamed by the incident,
Mori continued, the government was for peace. It was sending a mission to Korea with a military escort, solely to guard
the envoys. Japan wished to be sincere and candid with
China and was therefore informing China of its action.
Should Korea receive the mission with courtesy, there would
be peace and friendship between Japan and Korea. Otherwise, Mori warned, Korea would be courting disaster.[81]
Three days later the Yamen replied to Mori, defending the
Korean action and urging moderation. The Yamen said that
Korea had done nothing wrong: it had not invaded
Japanese territory, and Japan was not the only country with
which Korea refused to have treaty relations. Although
China could not interfere in Korean affairs, said the Yamen,
it was concerned for Korea's safety. It hoped that Mori
would inform his government not to use force against
Korea and to conduct negotiations with Korea by mutual
consent and in accordance with the non-aggression clause
of the 1871 Sino-Japanese treaty.[82]

Certain irreconcilable differences emerged between the
Yamen and Mori in the course of further exchanges. The
Yamen maintained that, although Korea was autonomous
with regard to its internal and external affairs, it was a
tributary of China and was covered by the Sino-Japanese
treaty, for Korea acknowledged Chinese suzerainty and its
king received investiture from the Ch'ing emperor. Mori
argued that, whatever its relations with China, Korea must
be regarded as an independent state under international

81. NGB, vol. 12, 142–144; CJHK, vol. 2, 264–265. For Mori's own account of
his talks with the Tsungli Yamen, see NGB, vol. 12, 145–151.
82. NGB, vol. 12, 164–165.

law because it was sovereign in its affairs, and the Sino-Japanese treaty had nothing to do with Korea.[83] Anxious to find a way to break the impasse, Mori requested a meeting with Li Hung-chang, who he hoped might influence the Yamen to change its mind.

Mori journeyed to Paoting, Li's winter headquarters, in late January. Li received his young visitor graciously and held cordial talks with him on January 24 and 25. Their meeting was symbolic. In his early fifties, Li was an imposing figure, with long experience and extensive knowledge of the arts of politics, diplomacy, and warfare. Despite his pragmatism, which had made him the foremost leader of China's contemporary effort to strengthen itself through the introduction of Western science and technology,[84] Li was aware that the tribute system was traditionally the foundation of Chinese supremacy in East Asia. Beneath his dignified and unruffled exterior, he was deeply concerned about external dangers facing China, particularly the growing Russian and Japanese threats. Not yet thirty, Mori was a rising star in the Japanese Foreign Ministry. Thoroughly Western in intellectual orientation, he had rejected Japan's inherited culture and was prepared to challenge traditional Chinese supremacy. Full of youthful enthusiasm and nationalistic zeal, he was confident of his country's future. Li personified the mature wisdom and grandeur of the declining Ch'ing empire; Mori represented the youthful ambitions and vigor of a rising new Japan.

Mori told Li that his mission was to secure China's good offices in order to preserve the peace between Japan and Korea. Defending the Yamen's position, Li replied that China could not help Japan in Korea; if it did, the Western

83. *Ibid.,* 165; *Ch'ing Kuang-hsü ch'ao Chung-Jih chiao-she shih-liao* (Historical materials on Sino-Japanese relations in the Kuang-hsü reign) (hereafter cited as CKCJ), 1.4b–5a; Hilary Conroy, *The Japanese Seizure of Korea, 1868–1910,* 65–66; Frederick Foo Chien, *The Opening of Korea: A Study of Chinese Diplomacy, 1876–1885,* 32–35.

84. On Li Hung-chang's leadership role in the self-strengthening movement, see Kwang-Ching Liu, "Li Hung-chang in Chihli: The Emergence of a Policy, 1870–1875," in Albert Feuerwerker, et al., eds., *Approaches to Modern Chinese History,* 68–104.

powers would seek the same service from China. Counseling patience, Li warned that, should Japan attack Korea, China and Russia would send forces to Korea. Mori emphasized that China must use its influence with Korea if peace between Japan and Korea was to be preserved; Li said that he would see what he could do to help.[85]

Following his return to Peking, Mori resumed his talks with the Yamen. Pressed for a clear statement of Chinese responsibility in Korea, on February 12 the Yamen told Mori that the responsibilities China assumed for Korea were "to relieve Korea's difficulties, to settle its disputes, and to insure its safety." With obvious irritation, the Yamen added that, if there was anything China should do to protect Korea's safety, it would be done without a reminder. Regarding this as China's acceptance of responsibility for Korea, Mori terminated his talks with the Yamen.

While not conclusive, the Yamen-Mori talks established two points: (1) although Korea was autonomous in internal and external affairs and possessed all the powers of an independent state, it was nevertheless a tributary of China; (2) while the Korean king was not answerable to the Ch'ing emperor for the governance of his kingdom, China assumed moral responsibility for Korea's safety. This was clearly at variance with the principles of international law, to which the Japanese government now subscribed fully. Japan's decision not to pursue the matter further amounted to tacit recognition of the Chinese position. This was consistent with the pragmatic foreign policy of the Ōkubo government, which realized that the historic Sino-Korean relationship was a fact that could not be ignored.

Mori failed to secure formal Chinese good offices in Korea; however, his mission was largely successful, for the Chinese authorities advised the Korean government to be friendly toward Japan, which facilitated Japan's next move. On January 9—two weeks before Mori's visit with Li—Li

85. For Chinese and Japanese accounts of the Li-Mori talks, see LWCK, *Tsungli Yamen Letters*, 4.33b–38a; CKCJ, 1.7a–9b; CJHK, vol. 2, 282–288; NGB, vol. 12, 170–181.

received a personal letter from Yi Yu-wŏn, former Korean chief state councilor, who was returning home after a visit to Peking as a special envoy. Outwardly, Yi's letter was no more than a gesture of courtesy and respect toward China's leading statesman. As will be related, Yi was in fact seeking Li's support and advice on foreign policy. On his part, Li, who was concerned about the Japanese-Korean dispute and the possibility of Russian intervention in Korea in the event of a Japanese-Korean conflict, welcomed an opportunity to offer such advice. Replying to Yi, Li immediately conveyed his concern about Korea's relations with Japan and for Korea's safety in a world in which seclusion was no longer possible, for Korea or China. Li believed that Japan's intentions toward Korea were essentially peaceful at this time, nevertheless he feared possible conflict between the two countries. He knew that China would have no alternative but to defend Korea (as it had during the Hideyoshi invasions) if Japan or Russia attacked Korea, and Li was deeply worried about China's military weakness. In a letter of January 19 to the Tsungli Yamen, Li expressed fear that China's treaty with Japan alone would not be an effective deterrent to a Japanese invasion of Korea, which in his opinion would result in the Japanese domination of Korea and a serious threat to Manchuria. He urged the Yamen to advise the Korean government to be forbearing and courteous toward Japan and, perhaps, to send an envoy to Japan to explain the *Unyō* incident to prevent further trouble. Reporting his correspondence with Yi, Li added that he was confident that the Korean government would heed the Yamen's advice.[86]

Two days before Li wrote to the Yamen, the throne approved the Yamen's memorial, which recommended the Board of Rites advise the Korean government not to go to extremes with Japan.[87] On the day Li wrote his letter, the Board sent such a communication to Korea; the letter reached Seoul on February 5—six days before the Japanese

86. LWCK, *Tsungli Yamen Letters*, 4.30a–32a; CJHK, vol. 2, 276–278.
87. CJHK, vol. 2, 270–271; CKCJ, 1.1a–b.

and Korean negotiators were to begin the full-scale negotiations. At the urging of the Yamen, the Board sent a second note to Korea on February 24; this note, however, did not reach Seoul until after Korea signed a treaty with Japan.[88] Meanwhile, sharing Li's fear that Russia might intervene in Korea in the event of war between Japan and Korea, the Yamen wrote to the military governors at Mukden, Kirin, and Heilungkiang, asking them to guard against Russian military activities.[89]

While Mori was conducting his talks with the Chinese authorities in Peking, the Japanese government proceeded to prepare for the Kuroda mission. Early in December 1875, Hirotsu Hironobu was sent to Pusan to announce the impending arrival of the Kuroda mission. On January 13 Kuroda and his party assembled at Tsushima. In addition to dozens of civilian aides and army and navy officers, Kuroda and Inoue were escorted by some 250 soldiers and marines and three warships. Altogether, the mission consisted of more than 800 men and six ships.[90]

Despite its ominous appearance, the Kuroda mission was essentially peaceful in intent. Insisting on a formal apology from Korea for the *Unyō* incident, the Japanese government told Kuroda and Inoue that their primary task was to seek a peaceful settlement. Korea's acceptance of regular relations and an expanded trade with Japan might be considered adequate compensation for the "damage" caused by the attack on the *Unyō*. Kuroda and Inoue were told further that, in their effort to establish new relations with Korea, they should not be bound by Tokugawa precedent. They should demand: (1) a treaty of friendship based on the equality of the two countries; (2) freedom of navigation and surveying in Korean waters for Japanese vessels; and (3) an open port in the Kanghwa area.

Kuroda and Inoue were also given tactical instructions. If subjected to insult or violence, they were to withdraw to

88. CJHK, vol. 2, 280, 298–299. For the Korean acknowledgment of the Board of Rites note, see *ibid.*, 316–317; CKCJ, 1.10a–11a, 11b–12a.
89. CJHK, vol. 2, 294, 298, 300–301, 302–303.
90. The figures are based on data contained in NGB, vol. 12, 3–4.

Tsushima and request further instructions from Tokyo. If they were not received and their communications remained unanswered, they were to lodge a strong protest with the Koreans and request new instructions from Tokyo, without leaving Korean soil. Should the Koreans wish to consult China before granting the Japanese demands, Kuroda and Inoue were to point out that historically China had never interfered in Japanese-Korean relations. Moreover, the envoys should demand to know if recent Korean actions toward Japan, including the attack on the *Unyō*, had Chinese approval. Should the Koreans insist on consulting China, Kuroda and Inoue were to demand the right to station Japanese troops in Seoul and on Kanghwa until receipt of a Chinese reply. Finally, should the Koreans reject the Japanese demands with "false arguments," Kuroda and Inoue were to break off negotiations and return home, but only after warning the Koreans that the Japanese government would take "appropriate action" later.[91]

Unlike the Taewŏn'gun's resolute stand during the French and American invasions, the response of Kojong's government to the *Unyō* incident was tardy, timid, and confused. During the spring and summer of 1875, Pak Kyu-su, the only articulate and forthright advocate of rapprochement with Japan, argued at court for acceptance of the Japanese communications and wrote letters to the Taewŏn'gun and his brother, Second State Councilor Yi Ch'oe-ŭng, urging immediate restoration of relations with Japan. He argued that Japan's new diplomatic terminology and protocol did not affect Korean national dignity and honor. At any rate, he said, these were trivial matters—not important enough to risk war with Japan at a time when Japan was apparently "in collusion with the West" against Korea and when Korea was utterly unprepared for foreign invasion.[92] When the confused and irresolute Kojong proved himself incapable of providing leadership, Pak

91. *Ibid.*, vol. 11, 145–149; TNS, vol. 1, 432–435; Conroy, *Japanese Seizure of Korea*, 63–64; Martina Deuchler, *Confucian Gentlemen and Barbarian Envoys*, 35–36.

92. Palais, *Traditional Korea*, 260–261. For Pak's letter to the Taewŏn'gun and Yi Ch'oe-ŭng, see Pak Kyu-su, *Hwanjaejip*, 11.3b–17a.

turned to the Taewŏn'gun, imploring him to return to the capital, to provide direction and leadership, and then to go back to his mountain retreat again if he so wished.[93] Pak's plea to the Taewŏn'gun was an exercise in futility. Nor could Pak prod the government into positive action, at least until after the *Unyō* incident.

The Japanese government's long silence following the *Unyō* incident both mystified and worried the Korean government. The Seoul government at first feigned ignorance of the national identity of the intruding vessel, but the fear of "retaliatory" Japanese action led Yi Ch'oe-ŭng to follow Pak's advice. On December 12 Yi recommended that the government reverse its previous decision and accept the Japanese communications. Kojong approved and instructions to that effect were sent to Pusan.[94] At Pusan, meanwhile, confusion and indecision on the part of Korean officials invited outrageous behavior on the part of Japanese. On December 13 some sixty Japanese marines illegally marched out of the Japanese compound at Pusan. When stopped by Korean officials, they opened fire and charged into the crowd with fixed bayonets, wounding a dozen Koreans.[95] Yet no effective protest was lodged by Korean authorities. When Hirotsu arrived several days later with advance notice of the Kuroda mission, Hyŏn told him that the Korean government would accept the Japanese notes and the Japanese envoys might dress as they wished. In return for this "concession," Hyŏn requested the Japanese government to call off the Kuroda mission. Hirotsu apparently conveyed this request to Kuroda and Inoue when he met them on Tsushima a few days later.[96] By this time, however, it was out of the question for the two envoys to consider such a request.

The Kuroda mission arrived at Pusan on January 15, 1876, and immediately notified the local Korean officials

93. Pak Kyu-su, *Hwanjaejip*, 11.6a–b; Palais, *Traditional Korea*, 261.
94. ISN-KJ, 12/11/15; KJS, 12.39b–40a.
95. ISN-KJS, 12/11/29; KJS, 12.42a–b; TNS, vol. 1, 405–406.
96. TNS, vol. 1, 407–409.

that it would proceed to Kanghwa Island within a week. If not met by responsible ministers, the Japanese envoys said, they would proceed directly to Seoul.[97] Meanwhile, both Kuroda and Inoue felt that, in view of reportedly fortified Korean defenses in the Kanghwa area, their forces might not be adequate to cope with hostile Korean action. Therefore they sent an urgent request to Tokyo for reinforcement of two battalions. The Tokyo government turned down the request, partly because the dispatch of additional troops would violate its assurance to the Western representatives that the Kuroda mission would not be accompanied by combat troops.[98] However, it ordered Minister of War Yamagata to go to Shimonoseki immediately and make the necessary arrangements for shipping troops to Korea should hostilities break out.[99]

When the Kuroda mission reached the Kanghwa area, in late January, it was contacted by Korean language officers from Seoul. The Japanese declared their intention to land on Kanghwa Island and to go to Seoul, if necessary. Confronted by formidable Japanese strength and determination, the Korean court decided reluctantly to negotiate. On January 30 it appointed General Sin Hŏn, commander of the Royal Guard, as chief negotiator and Yun Cha-sŭng, minister of rites, as deputy negotiator.[100] Preliminary talks followed to select a parley site. During the talks the Koreans tried, in vain, to keep the Japanese away from the strategic island of Kanghwa. On February 10, without Korean consent, Kuroda and Inoue landed on the island with 400 troops; they established their headquarters in the city of Kanghwa. Full-scale negotiations commenced the following day.

Kuroda seized the initiative and denounced Korea's refusal to receive Japanese communications for the past several years and its attack on the *Unyō*. He demanded an

97. *Ibid.*, 435–436; ISN-KJ, 13/1/2; KJS, 13.2a–b.
98. TNS, vol. 1, 437–438.
99. Tokutomi, *Yamagata Aritomo den*, vol. 2, 426–428.
100. ISN-KJ, 13/1/5; KJS, 13.2b–3b.

apology and the punishment of those responsible for the at-tack. Following tactics recommended earlier by Pak Kyu-su, Sin replied that rumors of Japanese invasion spread by Hachinohe in 1867 created a deep suspicion of the Japanese among the Korean officials, which led them to reject sub-sequent Japanese communications. Sin declared that the at-tack on the *Unyō* had been fully justified since the vessel had violated a restricted area.[101] After lengthy but inconclusive exchanges between the two sides, the Japanese delegation put forward a thirteen-article draft treaty, stating that the best way to promote friendship and to prevent misun-derstanding was to sign a treaty. Inoue made a special effort to explain that the draft was based on "international law" and that, under international law, Korea was an "indepen-dent state enjoying the same rights as Japan"—with implied emphasis on Korean independence from China.

Exhibiting complete ignorance of Western international law and of the modern concept of interstate relations, Sin asked the Japanese what they meant by "treaty" (*jōyaku* in Japanese, *choyak* in Korean). When Kuroda explained that a treaty would lay down rules whereby Japan and Korea would open ports and trade with each other, Sin replied that he did not see why the two countries should sign a treaty now; they had traded with each other for three cen-turies without one. Kuroda explained further that all coun-tries wishing to engage in foreign commerce must sign treaties with one another, and that Japan had done so with many countries. Sin countered that Korea, a poor country with little surplus produce, had no desire to engage in foreign trade. Moreover, he said, the Korean people did not like new regulations, and expanded trade between the two countries would cause discord and conflict. The best thing for both countries therefore was to continue the existing trade at Pusan, without change. Kuroda persisted in his ar-

101. KJS, 13.5b–7a; NGB, vol. 12, 80–87. On Pak Kyu-su's suggestion, see Pak Kyu-su, *Hwanjaejip*, 11.15b. For details on the Kuroda-Sin exchanges, see TNS, vol. 1, 455–469; Yi Sŏn-gŭn, *Han'guksa ch'oegŭnse;* 387–394; Deuchler, *Confucian Gentlemen*, 38–42.

gument, and Sin said that he must refer the matter to Seoul. Kuroda demanded a reply within ten days.[102]

Kuroda repeated his warning the following day. Referring to a Japanese supply ship, which had just arrived, he told the Koreans the ship brought additional troops to join the 4,000 (actually 800) already in Korea and reinforcements would follow soon. If Korea rejected the proposed treaty, Japanese soldiers, joined by civilian radicals, might land on Korean soil, and the Japanese government would be unable to control them. Sin rebuked him with the rejoinder that it was highly improper of Kuroda to talk of an invasion when he should be discussing restoration of the old friendship between the two countries.[103]

In Seoul, meanwhile, the Korean government discussed how to proceed in dealing with the Kuroda mission. At a court conference on February 14, Yi Yu-wŏn, Kim Pyŏng-hak, Kim Pyŏng-guk, Hong Sun-mok, and Yi Ch'oe-ŭng agreed that Kuroda's arrival with warships was proof that Japan was seeking war, not friendship. Deploring Korea's unpreparedness, which had invited this Japanese outrage, Pak Kyu-su counseled patience and urged accommodation inasmuch as Japan was at least professing a desire for peace. This time none of the top officials, including those who persistently opposed compromise with Japan, advocated a war policy. None, however, came forward with concrete recommendations.[104]

Even as it faced the bluffing Japanese, the Korean government faced the redoubtable Taewŏn'gun and the militant literati at home, who vehemently opposed any compromise or accommodation with Japan. For the first time since his retirement, the Taewŏn'gun publicly stated his views, in a strongly worded letter to the State Council on February 12. He charged that the government had invited willful and massive Japanese intrusions by taking a weak-kneed stand, and it was about to submit to outrageous

102. KJS, 13.7a–9a; NGB, vol. 12, 87–95.
103. KJS, 13.10a–b.
104. *Ibid.*, 13.9a–b; Palais, *Traditional Korea*, 263–264.

Japanese demands, which, if accepted, would surely lead to national ruination.[105] On February 17, after submitting a fiery memorial imploring the king to reject the Japanese demands and to punish any official recommending their acceptance with death, Ch'oe Ik-hyŏn led a group of fifty literati in a vigil in front of the Kyŏngbok Palace. Each carried an ax in a symbolic gesture to indicate his willingness to face execution if the action incurred royal displeasure. The men prostrated themselves on the palace ground through a long, piercingly cold winter night.[106] The government immediately banished Ch'oe to a remote island, but others were ready to follow his example of protest.

Despite the strong domestic opposition, the government decided on accommodation. It had no practical alternative since Korea was unprepared for war at this time. Neither Kojong nor any of his ministers had a policy other than their commitment to maintain peace with Japan. In addition, other important factors contributed to the decision. First and foremost was Japan's growing military strength and its apparent readiness to use it. Presence of a powerful Japanese squadron in the Kanghwa Bay, with 4,000 men reportedly aboard, was a fact that the Koreans could ignore only at the risk of an instant invasion. The recent Japanese invasion of Taiwan was well known to the Korean authorities. Not adequate for full-scale invasion of the mainland, the troops accompanying Kuroda—400 of whom were on Kanghwa Island with him—could have occupied the whole island and held it indefinitely. The Japanese government might have done precisely this had the negotiations broken down, for it would have blockaded the sea and river routes upon which Seoul depended for its food supplies from the southern provinces.

Another, less obvious but equally important, factor was the attitude of China. The significance of China's new relations with Japan was apparent to the Koreans. For instance, the Ch'ing government did not object to the use of the term

---

105. Palais, *Traditional Korea*, 262–263; Deuchler, *Confucian Gentlemen*, 42.
106. Palais, *Traditional Korea*, 265–267; Deuchler, *Confucian Gentlemen*, 43–44.

"emperor" for the Japanese ruler and the Ch'ing emperor received Japanese envoys wearing Western dress; therefore, it made little sense for Korea to continue to oppose such practices.[107] More importantly, the Chinese authorities explicitly advised the Korean government to be friendly toward Japan. While Korea was told that ultimately it was free to make whatever decision it wished, no Korean ruler or government could or would lightly reject explicit Chinese advice, especially when Korea faced, as at this time, a serious external threat. In this connection, in 1876 the investiture of Kojong's infant son as heir to the throne seems to have provided a rare opportunity for the Chinese authorities to impress the wisdom and necessity of accommodation with Japan upon the Korean court.

After the death of her first son, Queen Min gave birth to another son in March 1874. A year later, in 1875, the Korean court decided to seek investiture for the infant prince as heir to the throne from Peking. Kojong was in his robust twenties and the boy was not yet one year old; there was no objective justification for such haste in selecting a royal heir. Behind this move, however, was an emerging power struggle between Queen Min and her relatives and the Taewŏn'gun and his supporters, a struggle that had crucial implications because of Kojong's proven inability to lead.

Events subsequent to the Taewŏn'gun's retirement, such as the assassination of Min Sŭng-ho, Queen Min's adoptive brother, in January 1875, deepened hostility and suspicion between the queen and her father-in-law. Although there was no clear evidence of the Taewŏn'gun's complicity in the incident, the queen believed that he was behind her brother's death.[108] Meanwhile, rising clamor in the country for the Taewŏn'gun's leadership made his return to power a distinct possibility. This posed a serious threat to the young queen and her relatives, whose appetites for power were

107. In 1873 the Ch'ing and Japanese rulers addressed each other as "great emperor" (*ta-huang-ti* in Chinese; *daikōtei* in Japanese) in official messages. See IWSM-TC, 90.7b–8a; 90.2b–3a; NGB, vol. 9, 140–141, 224.

108. Yi Sŏn-gŭn, *Han'guksa ch'oegŭnse*, 359–360; Palais, *Traditional Korea*, 242–244.

developing, too. In the circumstances, investiture from the Ch'ing court would legitimize the infant's position as future king and strengthen the position of the queen, virtually ensuring her continuation in power in the future. The situation was rendered doubly urgent for the queen and her relatives by the presence of Prince Wanhwa, an older potential candidate for the throne, apparently favored by the Taewŏn'gun.[109]

Traditionally the Ch'ing court had never denied a Korean request for investiture. However, it could do so under unusual circumstances. The Korean request in this instance, though legitimate, was unusual, for the reigning king was young and in good health and his heir-designate was less than a year old. Therefore, the queen and her relatives were extremely careful in preparing their move; a mere delay by the Ch'ing court in granting the request would seriously weaken their position in the domestic power struggle. Having put themselves in this position, it would hardly be prudent for the queen and her relatives to disregard the wishes or advice of the Chinese authorities.

Securing this all-important investiture was a task entrusted to Yi Yu-wŏn, who had resigned as chief state councilor under attack by a Taewŏn'gun supporter. On August 30, 1875—one month after the Taewŏn'gun returned to the capital—Yi left Seoul on his crucial mission to Peking. During an audience prior to his departure, Kojong emphasized the importance of Yi's mission and presented his trusted envoy with a poem he had written for him.[110]

To ensure the success of his mission, Yi was reputedly instructed to seek support from influential Chinese officials. His earlier-mentioned "personal" letter to Li Hung-chang, the most influential voice within the Chinese government at this time on Korean affairs, seems to have been part of this strategy.[111] Since individual contacts of a private or personal nature between China and Korea were discouraged, if not

109. Yi Sŏn-gŭn, *Han'guksa ch'oegŭnse,* 345–360.
110. ISN-KJ, 12/7/30; KJS, 12.28b.
111. TNS, vol. 1, 550.

banned, during the Ch'ing period, it is not likely that Yi wrote to Li on his own initiative. In fact, Yi was to remain an "unofficial" channel of communication between Li and the Korean government for years thereafter. This was a convenient and useful device for both countries: for China, it avoided the appearance of interference in the affairs of a tributary state, and, for Korea, it did not set an institutional precedent that might enable China to intervene in Korea's affairs.

Yi wished to see Li when he passed through Tientsin, but the latter was at his winter headquarters in Paoting. Therefore, Yi talked with one of Li's close associates, Yu Chih-k'ai, prefect of Yingping, a county in Chihli astride the travel route of Korean tributary embassies to and from Peking. Yu subsequently forwarded Yi's letter to Li. The fact that Li expressed concern in his reply to Yi about Korea's relations with Japan—an action without precedent in the history of Ch'ing-Korean relations—strongly suggests that Yi and Yu discussed the subject, during which time Yu had an opportunity to impart both his own and Li's views to Yi.[112] During his stop at Mukden, Yi also talked with Ch'ung-shih, an influential Manchu official who was military governor of Shengching. Expressing concern over Japan's rapid acquisition of Western arms and technology, Ch'ung-shih inquired about the steps Korea was taking to cope with the growing Japanese threat.[113] Yi returned to Seoul on February 12, the day after the Japanese-Korean negotiations began on Kanghwa. His report on the views and attitudes of Li and other Chinese officials undoubtedly influenced Kojong and his ministers and sustained them in their subsequent decision in favor of accommodation with Japan, in the face of opposition from the Taewŏn'gun and his supporters.[114]

The visit a few days later of the Ch'ing envoys bearing the imperial edict of investiture for the heir to the throne

112. *Ibid.*, 551–552. For Yi's letter to Li and the latter's reply, see LWCK, *Tsungli Yamen Letters*, 4.30a–32a; CJHK, vol. 2, 276–278.
113. ISN-KJ, 12/12/16; CJHK, vol. 2, 300.
114. TNS, vol. 1, 555.

further reinforced their resolve. When the envoys, Chi-ho
and Hsi-ch'ung-a, arrived in Seoul, who were said to have
brought Li Hung-chang's reply to Yi Yu-wŏn, Kojong asked
the Korean officer in charge of reception if the imperial
envoys were aware of the Japanese squadron at Kanghwa.
The officer replied that he had explained to the envoys that
the dispute with Japan stemmed from Japan's insistence on
the use of preposterous terminology in official communications.[115] During a visit with the envoys on February 17,
Kojong, disregarding the tradition that discouraged the discussion of political matters on such an occasion, brought up
the Japanese-Korean dispute. He expressed his gratitude
for the Tsungli Yamen's advice; the envoys replied that they
were concerned about the matter and expressed the hope
that Korea would take steps to avoid trouble with Japan.[116]
Two days later, as the imperial envoys left Seoul, the Korean government sent final instructions to its negotiators at
Kanghwa, authorizing them to accept the Japanese demands.[117] One week later, on February 27, the two countries formally signed a treaty.

   The twelve-article treaty began with a preamble expressing the desire of both countries to renew and strengthen
their traditional friendship. The terms "emperor of Japan"
and "king of Korea" in the original Japanese draft were replaced with the "government of Japan" and the "government of Korea" at the insistence of the Korean delegation,
which considered the reference to the Japanese ruler unacceptable. Article I declared that Korea was an "autonomous
[*tzu-chu* in Chinese; *jishu* in Japanese; *chaju* in Korean] state
enjoying the same rights as Japan." The treaty terminated
traditional Japanese-Korean relations and Tsushima's intermediary role between the two countries. It set forth
provisions governing the new relations between the two
countries, whereby Korea agreed: (1) to open two more
ports in addition to Pusan; (2) to grant Japan consular

115. ISN-KJ, 13/1/23; P'eng, *Nik-Kan-Shin kankei*, 69–70.
116. ISN-KJ, 13/1/23.
117. *Ibid.*, 13/1/25; KJS, 13.11b.

jurisdiction at the trade ports; and (3) to permit Japanese ships to survey the Korean coastal waters.[118]

The Treaty of Kanghwa represented a major breakthrough for Japan in its drive for diplomatic reform. Although it failed in its earlier attempt to revise the treaty with China and was making little headway in its efforts to revise unequal treaties with Western powers, Japan succeeded in imposing upon Korea an "unequal" treaty, one similar to those imposed upon China and Japan by Western powers. This meant that Japan established the same privileged position in Korea as that held by the Western treaty powers in China and Japan, precisely the goal Japan set for itself under its diplomatic reform program in the early 1870s. The Meiji government's initial "restoration diplomacy" failed to establish Japan's titular superiority over Korea based on the traditional East Asian concept of interstate relations; its drive for diplomatic reform succeeded in securing Japan's privileged position as an "advanced nation" vis-à-vis Korea based on the Western concept of international diplomacy.

The treaty had epoch-making significance in the history of Japanese-Korean relations and far-reaching implications for future international relations in East Asia.[119] It was Western in concept and form, based essentially on the principle of the equal sovereignty of all states. By redefining Japanese-Korean relations in terms of Western international law, the treaty brought Korea, at least partially, into the framework of the Western international system. Although leaders of the Korean government failed to understand its true significance, the treaty represented a repudiation of the traditional East Asian concept of hierarchical interstate relations. It drove a major institutional wedge into the surviving traditional world order in East Asia and challenged, if it did not openly reject, China's suzerainty over the peninsular kingdom.

118. For the text of the treaty, see KJS, 13.15b–17b; NGB, vol. 12, 114–119.
119. For appraisals of the treaty, Palais, "Korea on the Eve of the Kanghwa Treaty," 782–788; Chien, *Opening of Korea,* 46–48; Deuchler, *Confucian Gentlemen,* 48–50.

Although the Chinese government urged Korea to accept
a treaty with Japan, Chinese leaders were not obtuse; they
realized the long-term implications of such a treaty for traditional Sino-Korean relations as well as for China's future
position in Korea. Any other alternative, however, involved
risk of war between Japan and Korea, which would compel
China to come to the aid of Korea. Faced with internal and
external problems—Muslim rebellions in the northwest and
the dispute with Britain over the Margary affair—China
was ill-prepared for war with Japan at this time. The situation was made particularly alarming by the very real possibility of Russian military intervention in Korea, in the event
of war between Korea and Japan. Thus a Japanese-Korean
treaty, whatever its long-term implications, was a necessity
for China if it was to preserve peace on the peninsula.

Japanese policy toward Korea during the early 1870s, as
in other periods, was inspired by a chauvinistic desire for
aggrandizement abroad and growing zeal to enhance Japan's prestige by emulating the West in international diplomacy. Japan's fear of Russian encroachment in Korea as well
as in Japan and complex Japanese domestic politics were
the twin sources of Japanese adventurism overseas in this
period. In pursuing solution of the Korean problem (*Chōsen
mondai*), the Ōkubo government strove to secure Japan's
strategic advantage against Russia and its diplomatic advantage against China in Korea, while it sought political advantage for itself at home. Combining caution with decisiveness
and logic with calculation, Ōkubo orchestrated bold diplomatic and military activities abroad with shrewd political
maneuvers at home to achieve these goals. Unwavering in
his aims, he was flexible in his tactics. Ōkubo firmly and
almost contemptuously rejected the *sei-Kan* advocates' shrill
cries for war with Korea, but he deliberately provoked an
incident with Korea, and he proceeded to use it to his political advantage at home as well as to Japan's diplomatic advantage in Korea. He opposed a hasty resort to force
against Korea by the *sei-Kan* advocates, but did not hesitate
to use force in Taiwan and was ready to use it in Korea,

albeit on a limited scale, when he judged it to be in his political interest and in Japan's national interest to do so. All in all, Ōkubo's handling of the Korean question demonstrates Japan's mastery of predatory Western diplomatic tactics and provides a classic example of *realpolitik*. Japan's new East Asian diplomacy, as symbolized by the Treaty of Kanghwa, represented a major institutional challenge to the continued survival of the old East Asian world order; Japan's growing strength and ambitions posed a more immediate threat to China's traditional hegemony in East Asia.

CHAPTER VII

Treaty System Diplomacy: China's New Policy in Korea

Contrary to the expectations entertained by most Japanese, the Treaty of Kanghwa did not lead immediately to the establishment of full diplomatic relations between Japan and Korea. Nor did it result in the opening of the hermit kingdom to the outside world. Not comprehending the significance of a modern treaty or the nature of Western international relations, the Korean government regarded the treaty as a step toward restoring traditional relations with Japan, which were limited to regulated trade at Pusan and occasional dispatch of Korean envoys to the bakufu. Apart from this basic misunderstanding, xenophobic agitation in Korea, intensified by the growing Japanese presence, would have made it difficult for the Korean government to broaden relations with Japan, even if it wished to do so.

During the same period, a series of samurai rebellions and peasant uprisings, in several parts of Japan, culminated in the Satsuma Rebellion of 1877. Subsequent assassination of Ōkubo, probably the ablest of the early Meiji leaders, in May 1878, along with the death of Kido the previous year, deprived the Meiji government of its most powerful leaders and created a vacuum in leadership that could not readily be filled. Therefore, Japan was not able to pursue its policy in Korea in the post-Kanghwa years with its earlier vigor and decisiveness.

Even though Japan was unable to expand its diplomatic and commercial gains in Korea as rapidly as it had hoped, leaders of the Chinese government, particularly Li Hung-chang, became increasingly concerned over growing Japanese ambitions toward Korea. They were disturbed, too, by the danger of Russian encroachment on the peninsula. During the mid- and late 1870s, China's concern over the Japanese and Russian threats, as well as its changing views on international relations, caused it to evolve a new policy toward Korea, which was a departure from China's traditional non-interference in Korean affairs. Under Chinese encouragement and tutelage, Korea finally joined the modern international system brought into East Asia by the West. China introduced a multi-state treaty system, similar to the one that had helped preserve peace in China itself since 1861, to Korea. Yet China also sought to assert its suzerainty over Korea, in fact going beyond its relationship with that country since 1644.

POST-KANGHWA KOREA: VACILLATION AND DRIFT

Immediately after the formal signing of the Treaty of Kanghwa, Miyamoto Okazu, who served as Kuroda's senior aide during the negotiations, repeated Kuroda's suggestion that Korea send a goodwill mission to Japan. Now that friendly relations had been restored between the two countries largely by the Japanese initiative, said Miyamoto, it would be gracious of Korea to send a goodwill mission to Japan. Such a mission would help Korea gain a better understanding of new Japan. Miyamoto emphasized the importance of national wealth and military strength for survival in the modern world and Japan's progress in agriculture and armament. He suggested that the proposed mission be sent before the two countries began their talks on a supplementary treaty and trade regulations, which were scheduled to commence within six months of the signature of the main treaty.[1] Sin Hŏn was impressed by

---

1. On the Miyamoto-Sin conversation, see NGB, 12, 122–129.

Miyamoto's arguments, and he recommended acceptance to Kojong during an audience on March 2. Royal approval of the recommendation led to the appointment of Kim Ki-su, third minister of rites, as "friendship envoy" to Japan.[2]

Kojong's decision did not stem from a desire to broaden relations with Japan, as the Japanese hoped. Two days after signing the new treaty, Kojong reassured his officials, who were worried about anti-treaty agitation in the country, that the treaty was no more than a step toward restoring traditional relations with Japan. He regarded Kim's mission to be the same in nature and function as the Korean embassies to Edo had been during the Tokugawa period. He reported his decision dutifully to the Ch'ing Board of Rites.[3]

On May 22, 1876, Kim and his entourage of some eighty men departed from Pusan aboard a Japanese steamship. To avoid the issue of titular precedence between the rulers of the two countries, Korea used the same formula as Japan employed when it sent the Kuroda mission: Kim carried no formal state message, rather an official note from the Korean minister of rites to the Japanese foreign minister. Kim had no specific diplomatic assignment other than "promoting friendship and goodwill" between the two countries.[4] A conservative scholar-official, he had little knowledge of the outside world. Before his departure, his friends and colleagues warned him that the Japanese were "devilish and treacherous" and that they had lately become "lackeys of the Western barbarians." Only aging Pak Kyu-su wrote to Kim to emphasize the importance of the mission, indicating that, if he had been younger, he would have volunteered for it.[5] Full of trepidation, Kim embarked on his mission with grim determination. After a week-long journey, he and his party reached Tokyo on May 29.

Kim's visit in the Japanese capital began with a meeting

2. INS-KJ, 13/2/6, 13/2/22; KJS, 13.19b–20a, 21a–b.
3. INS-KJ, 13/3/2; KJS, 13.23b.
4. For the text of the message Kim carried, see Kim Ki-su, *Iltong kiyu* (Account of a mission to Japan), in Kuksa p'yŏnch'an wiwŏnhoe, ed., *Susinsa kirok* (Records of friendship envoys), 83–84; NGB, vol. 12, 198–199.
5. Kim Ki-su, *Iltong kiyu*, 1–2.

with Foreign Minister Terashima on May 30, followed by an imperial audience on June 1. Uneasy over protocol, Kim at first declined the invitation to meet the emperor, pleading that he had brought no formal message to the mikado. His hosts, however, told him that the emperor had been looking forward eagerly to meeting him. It was agreed that Kim should perform the same form of obeisance toward the Japanese ruler as he did toward his own monarch.[6] The remainder of Kim's visit was devoted to meetings with Japanese leaders, including Chancellor Sanjō, and visits to government offices and educational, military, and industrial facilities. He and members of his party were entertained lavishly at numerous official and private receptions, including a formal banquet given by Sanjō. Kim's party left Tokyo on June 18 and returned to Seoul on July 21.[7]

While Kim and his aides enjoyed Japanese hospitality, they gained little practical information or knowledge. When Kojong asked about Japan's new industrial and military facilities, Kim replied that he had seen only a few of them and that he did not understand well what he had seen. He further stated that, since it had been his intention to make clear to the Japanese that his mission had been undertaken reluctantly and at their insistence, he had refrained deliberately from inquiring about Japan's new institutions.[8] When Inoue Kaoru told Kim that Korea should adopt new weapons and train more troops to ward off the Russian threat, Kim proudly replied that Korea "will always adhere to the way of the Sages" and "will never seek excellence in clever skills and evil arts."[9] Kim and his aides avoided contact with Westerners while in Japan.

On July 26—less than one week after Kim's return to Seoul—Miyamoto arrived at Inch'ŏn with a retinue of a

---

6. *Ibid.*, 21, 46.

7. For the details of the Kim Ki-su mission, see TNS, vol. 1, 557–577; Sin Kuk-chu, *Kŭndae Chosŏn oegyosa yŏn'gu* (Studies on modern Korean foreign relations), 83–102; Cho Hang-nae, *Kaehanggi tae-Il kwan'gyesa yŏn'gu* (Studies on the history of relations with Japan during the period of opening ports), 13–79.

8. ISN-KJ, 13/6/1.

9. Kim Ki-su, *Iltong kiyu*, 51.

dozen aides. He came as commissioner to negotiate a
supplementary treaty and trade regulations. He and his
party reached Seoul on July 30—the first Japanese officials
to visit the Korean capital since the Hideyoshi invasions. Although his arrival was not welcome, Miyamoto was received
in audience by Kojong on August 1, apparently in return
for the courtesy extended to Kim in Tokyo, and allowed to
perform his obeisance to the king according to the West-
ernized protocol of the Japanese court. Afterwards, both
Kojong and Yi Yu-wŏn expressed their concern about the
portents of Miyamoto's visit for the future and hope that
the visitor would not stay long.[10] Negotiations between
Miyamoto and his Korean counterpart, Cho In-hŭi, began
on August 5. Serious differences emerged between the two
sides almost immediately.

Article II of the Treaty of Kanghwa stated: "The Government of Japan, at any time after fifteen months from the
date of the signature of this Treaty, shall have the right to
send an envoy to the Korean capital, where he shall confer
with the minister of rites on matters of a diplomatic nature.
Whether said envoy will remain in the capital for an extended or short period shall be determined by need and
circumstances." Regarding this as an authorization for permanent Japanese diplomatic representation in Korea, the
Japanese government wished to station an envoy with his
family and staff in Seoul. Korea wished to avoid the exchange of formal state messages between the rulers of the
two countries, and Japan was willing, for the time being, to
station only a chargé d'affaires, who would not be accred-
ited formally to the Korean court. The Japanese government also requested the right of its diplomatic and consular
personnel to travel to the Korean interior, including travel
by land between Peking and Seoul.[11]

The Korean government flatly rejected the Japanese de-

10. For Miyamoto's account of the audience with Kojong, see NGB, vol. 12,
226–228; for Kojong's and Yi Yu-wŏn's remarks, see ISN-KJ, 13/6/12.
    11. TNS, vol. 1, 590–594.

mands. Cho contended that a Japanese envoy would be free to stay in Seoul as long as he wished, but the treaty did not authorize him to reside there permanently. Nor did it authorize him or his aides to bring their families. Japanese envoys must travel to and from Seoul by a route specified by the Korean government. As for the right to Peking-Seoul land travel, the question was moot since no Japanese personnel were to be permanently stationed in Seoul. Moreover, it was not a matter that Korea could decide alone. Another point of contention was the size of the area in Pusan and other trading ports within which Japanese nationals were to be permitted free movement and travel. The Japanese government wanted an area ten Japanese *ri* in radius; the Korean government insisted that it should be ten Korean *ri* in radius, which was equivalent to one Japanese *ri* (approximately four kilometers).[12]

Facing adamant Korean opposition, Miyamoto withdrew the demand for permanent diplomatic representation in Seoul, apparently in the hope of winning concessions on other matters. But the eleven-article supplementary treaty, signed after three weeks of hard bargaining, fell far short of original Japanese demands. It denied Japanese diplomats the right to travel to the interior and it restricted free movement and travel by Japanese at Pusan to an area ten Korean *ri* from the port, with an additional privilege of free travel to the city of Tongnae. Korean ignorance enabled Miyamoto to fare better on other issues. He secured the right of Japanese merchants to use Japanese currency in business transactions at Korean trading ports. Another significant Japanese gain was an agreement whereby Korea was to turn over shipwrecked aliens to the Japanese representatives at trading ports for repatriation to their homelands. Japan thus assumed, at least on paper, the responsibility traditionally exercised by China as Korea's suzerain.[13] Anxious to publicize its newly gained "authority"

12. *Ibid.*, 595–598.
13. For the text of the supplementary treaty, see KJS, 13.34a–36a; NGB, vol. 12, 275–279.

in Korea, the Japanese Foreign Ministry lost no time in notifying the Western representatives in Tokyo of this new arrangement; the latter expressed their deep appreciation of Japan's humanitarian concern.

At Cho's request, Miyamoto signed a memorandum stating that the two countries might send envoys to each other's capitals only to conduct diplomatic business, leaving trade matters to be handled by consular personnel at trading ports. The memorandum stated further that Japanese envoys might travel to and from the Korean capital by the route used by Miyamoto. Miyamoto added that, since he had no authority either to accept or reject such conditions, he would send his final answer after his return to Tokyo. Cho, however, believed that Miyamoto had agreed to the conditions, subject to approval by Tokyo.[14]

As for Japanese-Korean Trade Regulations, Korea accepted the Japanese draft without change; it contained no tariff provisions. Miyamoto had been instructed to accept a 5 percent ad valorem duty on Japanese goods entering Korea. Ignorant of the practices of modern international trade, Cho agreed readily to Miyamoto's proposal that both countries exempt import and export duties for several years in order to promote trade between them.[15] This made the Japanese-Korean treaty worse on the whole than the unequal treaties imposed upon China or Japan by Western powers.

Leaving Seoul on August 25, Miyamoto and his party returned to Tokyo on September 21. The Japanese government ratified the Supplementary Treaty and Trade Regulations, but it rejected Miyamoto's memorandum. Meanwhile, in early September, the Korean minister of rites sent a letter to the Japanese foreign minister, requesting that the

14. TNS, vol. 1, 614–615.
15. For Miyamoto's instructions, see NGB, vol. 12, 219–220. For the Cho-Miyamoto negotiations on the trade issue, see Kim Kyŏng-t'ae, "Kaehang chikhu ŭi kwansekwŏn hoebok munje," *Han'guksa yŏn'gu* 8 (September 1872), 82–85; Ch'oe T'ae-ho, *Kaehang chon'gi ŭi Han'guk kwanse chedo*, 18–24. For the text of the Japanese-Korean Trade Regulations, see KHOM, vol. 1, 8–10; NGB, vol. 12, 279–283.

Miyamoto memorandum be ratified and included in the Supplementary Treaty as an article. Cho repeated the request in a separate letter to Miyamoto.[16] The Japanese government, however, had no intention of acceding to this request. On November 13 Miyamoto, following instructions from Terashima, sent a letter to Cho rejecting the Korean demand. Miyamoto argued that, since Japan and Korea were close neighbors, it was essential the two countries station envoys in each other's capitals. Moreover, Japanese envoys must be permitted to travel to and from Seoul by any route they wished, for Korean envoys were to be given a similar right in Japan.[17]

Miffed by repudiation of the Miyamoto memorandum, the Korean government accused Japan of confusing trade and diplomatic matters. In his rebuttal to Miyamoto, dated December 27, Cho contended that, precisely because Japan and Korea were such close neighbors, there was no need to station permanent envoys in each other's capitals. By traveling by a specified route, Japanese envoys would spare the Korean government a great deal of expense. Even imperial envoys from China, he added, traveled a route designated by the Korean government.[18]

Realizing the difficulty of reaching an agreement on the issue of resident minister, the Japanese government took an interim step in early November, appointing Kondō Masuki its representative at Pusan. Although Kondō's responsibilities were those of a consul, he carried the temporary title of commissioner in order to perform diplomatic duties as the principal Japanese official in Korea until such time as a Japanese legation was established.[19] In early December the Korean government responded by elevating Hyŏn Sŏg-un's rank to serve as Kondō's counterpart.[20] During the next few years, despite the new treaty, relations between the two countries were conducted essentially in the same man-

16. NGB, vol. 12, 288–289.
17. *Ibid.*, 318–321; KHOM, vol. 1, 12–15.
18. NGB, vol. 12, 339–341.
19. *Ibid.*, 314–317.
20. ISN-KJ, 13/10/22; KJS, 13.53b.

ner as before: by and through representatives at Pusan. The arrangement was satisfactory to the Korean government, which regarded Kondō simply as successor to the Tsushima factor of earlier days.

Reforms introduced in Japan following the abolition of the domains and the creation of the prefectural system — such as the disestablishment of the samurai class, the introduction of conscription, and changes in land ownership and taxation — created widespread samurai discontent and peasant unrest. Sporadic uprisings and rebellions occurred in various parts of the country during 1876; the anger and resentment of the Satsuma samurai, led by Saigō Takamori, which had smoldered since his defeat in the 1873 *sei-Kan* dispute, exploded into armed rebellion in January 1877. Through most of that year, the Japanese government was occupied with the task of suppressing the rebellion. Despite repeated requests from the Foreign Ministry, the Japanese navy was unable to undertake the survey of the Korean coast necessary for the selection of two additional ports to be opened under the new treaty. Not until September 1877 when the Satsuma Rebellion had virtually ended did the Foreign Ministry decide to resume negotiations with Korea.

The Ministry selected Hanabusa Yoshimoto for the task. In the fall of 1876 Hanabusa returned home from a three-year tour as secretary of the Japanese legation in Russia, where he had assisted Enomoto in negotiating the Sakhalin settlement. Hanabusa learned of the *Unyō* incident in St. Petersburg. He agreed with Enomoto: Japan should seize the incident as a *casus belli* and take decisive action, both military and diplomatic, to attain its objectives in Korea. As his Russian tour neared its end, Hanabusa wanted a new assignment in Korea. Partly in support of Hanabusa's wish, Enomoto addressed his earlier-mentioned letter to Tera-shima, in February 1876, in which he urged Japanese seizure of Pusan. Along with this "strategic necessity," said Enomoto, it was a "political necessity" for Japan to "station a diplomatic agent in Seoul" in order to expand its influence in the peninsula. He recommended Hanabusa as ideally qualified for such an assignment.[21]

Upon his return from Russia, Hanabusa was appointed Japanese chargé d'affaires in Korea; he visited Pusan briefly in November 1876 to supervise Kondō's takeover of the Japanese mission there.[22] His appointment marked a significant shift in Japanese interest in the peninsula. In the past Japan's primary objective had been to establish new relations with Korea based on Western international law. That objective had been attained, and Japan now began actively pursuing its "strategic" interests in the peninsula.

Hanabusa and his party left Tokyo on September 26 and reached Seoul on November 25. His mission was to select the two new ports to be opened and to persuade the Korean government to accept a Japanese legation in Korea. Although the permanent site of the legation must be Seoul, Hanabusa was told, he might select a temporary site somewhere between Kanghwa and Inch'ŏn if the Koreans did not agree to Seoul. While Japanese envoys must be free to travel to and from Seoul by any route, for the first few years they might travel by a specified route. Hanabusa was to negotiate with the Koreans for two months, and, if there was no result, he was to return home quietly and try again the following spring.[23]

Prior to Hanabusa's arrival, some Korean officials argued that, inasmuch as the Japanese government had not answered Cho's letter to Miyamoto of the previous December, regarding the issue of resident minister, the Japanese envoy should not be permitted to enter Seoul. This would obviously jeopardize the new relations with Japan. Therefore the Korean government decided to receive him.[24] On November 27 Hanabusa presented his letter of credence to Minister of Rites Cho Yŏng-ha. Hanabusa

21. NGB, vol. 12, 79–80.
22. *Ibid.*, 314.
23. Hilary Conroy, *The Japanese Seizure of Korea, 1868–1910,* 89. For Hanabusa's instructions, see NGB, vol. 13, 222–225.
24. ISN-KJ, 14/10/12; KJS, 14.33b–34a.

wanted to negotiate with Cho, but he was compelled to deal with Cho's subordinate, Hong U-ch'ang, former prefect of Tongnae, whom the government appointed as chief negotiator. Talks between Hanabusa and Hong began on December 1.

Hanabusa proposed Munch'ŏn—which the Russians had named Port Lazareff—in the Yŏnghŭng Bay on the east coast as one of the two new ports to be opened. Japan's interest in Munch'ŏn dated from earlier days; its opening was suggested first during the treaty negotiations at Kanghwa. At his meeting with Sin Hŏn after signing the treaty, Miyamoto spoke of the danger of Russian encroachment upon Korean territory, citing the Russian "encroachment" upon Sakhalin; he warned that, in their search for an ice-free port, the Russians had an eye on Munch'ŏn. Opening Munch'ŏn to Japanese commerce, said Miyamoto, would promote trade between Japan and Korea and forestall Russian designs on it. The Koreans refused to consider Miyamoto's suggestion on the ground that the tombs of the royal progenitors were in the vicinity of Munch'ŏn.[25] They rejected Hanabusa's proposal on the same ground. As an alternative site, they proposed Pukch'ŏng, farther in the north, but Hanabusa rejected this suggestion.[26]

The Koreans again turned down the Japanese demand for permanent diplomatic representation. Moreover, complaining that frequent visits by Japanese envoys to Seoul were "costly and bothersome," they proposed that future negotiations between the two countries be conducted by correspondence or by representatives at Pusan. Hanabusa argued that, as diplomatic and commercial relations increased between the two countries, it would be essential for Japan to have a resident envoy in Seoul. He warned that Korea had become a focal point of attention from Western powers, particularly Britain and Russia, both of whom coveted Ullŭng Island and a port in the Yŏnghŭng Bay. Should a crisis develop between Korea and one of these

25. NGB, vol. 12, 127–129.
26. ISN-KJ, 14/11/17; KJS, 14.38a. For Hanabusa's report on the port issue, see NGB, vol. 13, 294–296. For details, see Conroy, *Japanese Seizure of Korea,* 91–95.

powers, Hanabusa emphasized, a resident Japanese minister in Seoul could "nip the trouble in the bud," with timely intervention or mediation. The Koreans were not impressed by his arguments.[27]

Although Hanabusa was instructed to accept a compromise on the issue of resident minister by agreeing to a temporary site for the proposed legation, he did not suggest such a compromise. As he confided later, he considered the opening of Munch'ŏn vital to Japanese interests, and he was determined not to compromise on the issue of resident minister until the Koreans agreed to open Munch'ŏn.[28] Northeast Korea was backward economically; there was little actual or prospective trade between this region and Japan at this time. Hanabusa's position was dictated chiefly by a strategy of preemptive action against Russia's interest in Munch'ŏn. For the broadening of relations with Korea, a permanent legation in Korea was obviously essential to Japan. Yet at this time Hanabusa considered it less important to Japan than the opening of Munch'ŏn.

On December 17 Hanabusa addressed a long letter to Minister of Rites Cho, taking pain to explain the differences between the old Japanese-Korean relations based on the traditional East Asian concept of interstate relations and the new relations based on Western international law. He said that even China now subscribed to international law. As evidence, he presented Cho with two copies of Martin's translation, *Wan-kuo kung-fa*, published by the Peking T'ung-wen Kuan (Interpreters' College). Neither the book nor Hanabusa's letter impressed Cho and his colleagues. Two days later Cho sent a short reply to Hanabusa, thanking him for the book, but merely promising further discussion on the resident minister issue at a future date.[29] Hanabusa, however, gained an important concession: he secured an agreement whereby Japan was permitted to build coaling stations on the Korean coast during a twelve-month period commencing in April 1878.[30] With this limited achievement, Hanabusa and

27. TNS, vol. 1, 620–625.
28. *Ibid.*, 625.
29. NGB, vol. 13, 300–304.
30. For the text of the agreement, see *ibid.*, 296–297; KHOM, vol. 1, 23–24.

268   *Last Phase of the East Asian World Order*

his party left Seoul on December 20 and returned to Tokyo on January 10, 1878.

The Korean government, meanwhile, decided to take steps to stop further visits by Japanese envoys to Seoul. A week after Hanabusa's departure, Minister of Rites Cho wrote a letter to Foreign Minister Terashima, repeating the earlier request for approval of the Miyamoto memorandum and its inclusion in the Supplementary Treaty. On April 26, 1878, Terashima replied to Cho, reiterating the reasons for a Japanese resident envoy in Seoul and explaining why such an envoy must be free to travel to and from the Korean capital by any route.[31]

During the spring and summer of 1878, at the request of the Foreign Ministry the Japanese navy conducted an extensive survey of the Korean coast. On the basis of its findings the Japanese government chose Wŏnsan, another fishing port in the Yŏnghŭng Bay, and Inch'ŏn, on the west coast, as the additional ports to be opened under the Treaty of Kanghwa. At this point, a tariff dispute broke out between the two countries, at Pusan.

Although the Korean government accepted the Japanese proposal for a mutual exemption of tariff, it realized its mistake as it gained knowledge and experience in foreign trade. Instead of seeking a revision of the tariff clause through negotiation, however, the Korean government decided simply to introduce a tax that would apply only to Korean merchants engaged in Japanese trade. The new tax went into effect on September 28, 1878.[32] It brought a virtual standstill to the trade at Pusan. The majority of the Japanese traders at Pusan at this time were small Tsushima merchants with limited resources, and this had a crippling effect on their business. On October 9 a group of 135 Japanese merchants marched on Tongnae to appeal to the prefect, Yun Ch'i-hwa, for the repeal of the tax. Yun sum-

    31. KHOM, vol. 1, 25–28.
    32. ISN-KJ, 15/8/10; KJS, 15.26a–b; Kim Kyŏng-t'ae. "Kwansekwŏn hoebok," 99–100; Ch'oe T'ae-ho, *Han'guk kwanse chedo,* 36–37.

marily dismissed them, declaring that the Japanese had no cause to complain for the tax was "in accord with the practice of all nations" and it applied only to Koreans.[33] Possibly this was the first time that a Korean official invoked "international law" in defense of his government's action.

Regardless of whether the tax was legal or otherwise justified, this was a case of deliberate subversion of the trade regulations between the two countries; the Japanese government could not ignore or tolerate such action without protest. In mid-November it ordered Hanabusa to go to Pusan immediately, aboard a warship, to demand repeal of the tax. Should the Korean authorities fail to comply with his demand within a specified time limit, Hanabusa was to seek compliance by "appropriate use of the warship," short of seizure or destruction of the Korean customs house.[34]

Hanabusa reached Pusan aboard the warship *Hiei* on November 29. At his direction, Yamanoshiro Sukenaga, chief of the Japanese mission, sent a bluntly worded note to Yun on December 2, demanding immediate repeal of the tax. Yamanoshiro warned that rejection "might result in war." The Japanese backed their verbal threat with a show of force. On December 4 two squads of marines from the *Hiei* staged a maneuver near the customs house, while the ship conducted a gunnery exercise.[35] Surprised by the vehemence of the Japanese protest, Yun asked Seoul for instructions. The Seoul government, alarmed by the situation, retreated: it ordered Yun to suspend the tax until further notice. The decision was conveyed to Yamanoshiro on December 26.[36] The following day a triumphant Hanabusa sent a letter to the Korean minister of rites, stating that the matter had been settled, but the question of "compensation"

33. Kim Kyŏng-t'ae, "Kwansekwŏn hoebok," 103–104; Ch'oe T'ae-ho, *Han'guk kwanse chedo*, 37–38; TNS, vol. 1, 655.
34. TNS, vol. 1, 655–656. For Hanabusa's instructions, see NGB, vol. 14, 305–307.
35. NGB, vol. 14, 308–311; Kim Kyŏng-t'ae, "Kwansekwŏn hoebok," 106–108; Ch'oe T'ae-ho, *Han'guk kwanse chedo*, 39–41.
36. Kim Kyŏng-t'ae, "Kwansekwŏn hoebok," 108; Ch'oe T'ae-ho, *Han'guk kwanse chedo*, 41.

for the damage suffered by the Japanese traders would be taken up by a Japanese envoy in Seoul at a future date.[37]

While the dispute was quickly settled by Korean retreat, it dramatized the need for early settlement of the issues pending between the two countries. Two months later, in March, the Japanese government ordered Hanabusa to return to Korea to resume negotiations. Hanabusa and his party left Tokyo aboard the warship *Takao* on March 31. En route to Inch'ŏn, the *Takao* and another ship undertook an extensive survey of the Korean west coast, ostensibly in search of a potential trading port. It was not until June 13 that Hanabusa and his party reached Seoul.

Although Hanabusa's mission had several purposes, its chief objective was to secure the opening of Wŏnsan and Inch'ŏn. With regard to Wŏnsan, his instructions emphasized its "strategic importance to both Korea and Japan" in view of the "military preparations of a neighboring country [Russia]." The importance which the Japanese government attached to opening the port was underscored by the fact that this time Hanabusa was not even instructed to bring up the issue of resident minister. As for the tariff question, Hanabusa was to inform the Korean government that should Korea levy import and export duties, the Japanese government would not necessarily object, but it would insist on being consulted in advance regarding the rate. This reasonable position was completely offset by the sweeping demands Hanabusa was to make in connection with the damage allegedly caused by Korea's brief imposition of "duties" at Pusan.

Hanabusa was instructed to demand a formal apology and compensation for the aggrieved Japanese merchants. However, since Japan did not wish to use a monetary issue as means of preserving friendship between the two countries, he was to withdraw the demand if the Korean government would agree to the following: (1) permission for Japanese to engage in business in the free-movement and travel zone, as well as at Pusan and Tongnae; (2) use of

37. NGB, vol. 14, 313–314.

Japanese and Korean currencies in trade between Japan and Korea; (3) employment of Japanese vessels by Koreans in trade, not only between Japanese and Korean trading ports but also between open and non-open ports within Korea; (4) permission for Koreans to travel to Japan to trade, study, or sightsee; (5) permission for Japanese to trade at public market places within the free-movement and travel zone; (6) permission for Japanese scholars and scientists to travel to the Korean interior; and (7) permission for Japanese merchants to participate in the semi-annual herb fair in Taegu, the inland capital of Kyŏngsang Province.[38] Far exceeding privileges guaranteed under the existing treaty or trade regulations, these concessions, if granted, would give the Japanese the right to engage in trade between Japan and Korea and in retail and wholesale business within Korea, as well. Moreover, they would guarantee the Japanese freedom of travel to virtually any part of Korea.

In Seoul, Hanabusa was even less welcome than before. He wished to negotiate directly with the minister of rites but was forced to deal again with his previous counterpart, Hong U-ch'ang. Negotiations between the two commenced on June 18 with the discussion of the port issue. Hong rejected Hanabusa's demand for the opening of Wŏnsan and Inch'ŏn—the former because it was too close to the tombs of the royal ancestors, the latter because it was too close to the royal capital. Weeks went by with neither side showing any sign of compromise. The Korean authorities realized that, if they were to keep the intruding Japanese away from strategically important Inch'ŏn, they would have to give in on Wŏnsan. On July 12 the State Council, therefore, obtained Kojong's approval for the opening of Wŏnsan. Despite Hanabusa's persistent demand, the Council refused to open Inch'ŏn. Finally, amid strong literati opposition, an agreement was reached late in August and formally signed in early October, to open Wŏnsan after May 1880.[39]

38. *Ibid.*, vol. 15, 212–214.
39. TNS, vol. 1, 693–714; Martina Deuchler, *Confucian Gentlemen and Barbarian Envoys*, 78–81. For the text of the agreement on the opening of Wŏnsan, see KJS, 16.27a–28a; NGB, vol. 15, 221–222.

The Korean government refused to permit Japanese scholars and scientists to travel to the Korean interior or to permit Japanese merchants to participate in the herb fair in Taegu. But it indicated willingness to grant, with certain modifications, the remaining five requests, plus a new one for the construction of lighthouses and buoys in harbors and along the coast. In return for these concessions, Hanabusa withdrew the demand for compensation of trade losses allegedly suffered by Japanese merchants at Pusan.[40] Neither side brought up the resident minister issue during the negotiations.

Wŏnsan was formally opened to Japanese commerce in May 1880. Japan obtained, among other privileges, a permanent lease on large tracts of land at Pusan and Wŏnsan as special concessions, similar to those established in China by Western powers, where Japanese nationals were to enjoy the privilege of extraterritoriality.[41] With the opening of Wŏnsan Japan acquired two major footholds on the Korean peninsula, Pusan and Wŏnsan, which were important strategically as well as commercially. Japan's immediate "strategic objectives" in Korea, as defined by men such as Enomoto and Hanabusa, had now been attained.

During the years just reviewed, Korea saw a reemergence of the "rule of the consort clans." In the continued absence of effective royal leadership, decision-making authority within the government was exercised largely by the State Council, which was presided over nominally by Yi Ch'oe-ŭng during most of these years, but actually came increasingly under the influence of Queen Min and her relatives, such as Min T'ae-ho and Min Kyu-ho. Of mediocre endowment, Yi was virtually ignored by his gifted younger brother, the Taewŏn'gun, when the latter was in power. But his position as the king's uncle was useful to the queen and her relatives in their power struggle against the

40. NGB, vol. 15, 218–221.

41. For the Japanese concessions at Pusan and Wŏnsan, see Fujimura Michio, "Chōsen in okeru Nihon tokubetsu kyoryūchi no kigen," *Nagoya daigaku bungakubu kenkyū ronshū* 35 (March 1965), 18–31; Yi Hyŏn-jong, *Han'guk kaehangjang yŏn'gu* (Studies on the trade ports in Korea), 193–203.

Taewŏn'gun, which was becoming intensive and bitter. Exploiting his resentment against the Taewŏn'gun, the Mins gave Yi the trappings of a high position and power but little substance; they used him largely as a figurehead. In the meantime, the Mins themselves had no firm views or clear goals in either domestic or foreign policy, other than perpetuation of their own power. Without conviction or direction, the Korean government vacillated and drifted in its relations with Japan; it refused to come to grips with changing reality in the world and accepted change grudgingly and only under the threat of force.

LI HUNG-CHANG AND CHINA'S NEW KOREAN POLICY

Article I of the Treaty of Kanghwa declared that Korea was an "autonomous state, enjoying the same rights as does Japan." The clause, inserted by the Japanese with the aim of establishing Korean independence from China, was intended to carry far-reaching political implications. As far as the Koreans were concerned, however, it was a simple reaffirmation of historical fact. As we have seen, Korea accepted without reservation Chinese titular superiority and moral authority under the tribute system although it functioned autonomously with little political supervision or interference by its suzerain. Moreover, it was always equal to Japan in status under the traditional world order in East Asia. Korea's political independence from China and its titular equality with Japan were entirely consistent with its titular inferiority and ceremonial submission to China. When the Korean State Council examined the clause in the draft, it simply noted: "no particular objection."[42]

Nor was the clause questioned by the Chinese authorities when they received a copy of the treaty from the Japanese legation, in late April 1876. Since the term "*tzu-chu*" could be interpreted "autonomous" rather than "independent,"

42. TNS, vol. 1, 472.

and since China had considered Korea "autonomous" in the management of its own affairs, neither the Tsungli Yamen nor the court took exception to the clause. Even Li Hung-chang and his associates, with all their diplomatic acumen, did not consider the wording serious enough to justify a protest. Perhaps China felt assured of Korea's allegiance; so long as Korea remained loyal to China, a mere treaty with Japan would not significantly affect China's traditional position in Korea. This belief was not entirely mistaken, as was proven by subsequent events.

The day after signing of the treaty, Kojong sent a note to the Ch'ing Board of Rites, giving a brief account of the negotiations and the gist of the treaty. In a subsequent note to the Board, the king stated that use by Japan of "questionable terms" in reference to its ruler would cause Korea to conduct relations with Japan through communication between the officials of the two countries, not rulers. He thanked the Chinese authorities for their concern for Korea. Expressing gratitude for Li's effort in defense of the Korean position and his warning to the Japanese during his talks with Mori, the king said that a Korean could not have done more for his country.[43]

Contrary to Japan's hope, there was not a noticeable change in Sino-Korean relations following the signing of the Treaty of Kanghwa. If anything, in the face of the growing Japanese and Russian threats, Korea drew closer to China. Not only did Korea continue to discharge all its tributary duties faithfully, as before, it communicated more frequently with China. The Korean government reported everything that took place between Japan and Korea, the Kim Ki-su mission, the signing of the Supplementary Treaty and Trade Regulations, the negotiations on the resident minister issue, and the decision to open Wŏnsan.[44] An obscure but interesting episode will serve to illustrate the attitudes of China, Japan, and Korea toward one another in this period.

43. CKCJ, 1.10a–11a, 11b–12a.
44. For Korean communications to the Ch'ing Board of Rites on these matters, see CJHK, vol. 2, documents nos. 266, 269, 279, 287, 290, and 293.

In May 1878 the Tsungli Yamen received a request from French Chargé d'Affaires Brenier that the Chinese government use its influence with Korea to secure the release of Father Felix-Clair Ridel, who had been arrested by the Korean authorities early that year while attempting to smuggle himself into the country again. In response to a letter from the Ch'ing Board of Rites in early June, the Korean government released the French priest and delivered him to the Chinese authorities.[45] A month later, it received a letter from Foreign Minister Terashima appealing for the release of Ridel in the custody of the Japanese representative at Pusan. To his chagrin, Terashima learned that, at the "direction" of China, the French priest had been released and delivered to the Chinese authorities. Terashima was further mortified by Korea's reference to China as "superior country" (*jōkoku* in Japanese; *sangguk* in Korean). A piqued Terashima refused to receive the Korean note, on the ground that its wording was "improper." In October Hanabusa returned the note to Seoul, along with a letter of protest accusing Korea of violating diplomatic propriety, in general, and Article I of the Treaty of Kanghwa, in particular. When we were negotiating the treaty, said Hanabusa, "your country declared itself an independent state; our government accepted your word. But if your country has a superior country and follows its direction, it is a dependency of that country and does not deserve to be called independent."[46]

In turn, the Korean government found Hanabusa's letter "highly improper and intolerable." Reprimanding the prefect of Tongnae for having accepted the Hanabusa letter, it ordered him to send a rebuttal to Japan immediately.[47] Reporting the incident to the Ch'ing Board of Rites, the Korean government stated that the whole world knew of Korea's submission to China. As for Korea being an "inde-

45. CJHK, vol. 2, 343–345; ISN-KJ, 15/5/4; KJS, 15.12b–13a.
46. For Terashima's and Hanabusa's letters, see KHOM, vol. 1, 30–33; for the Korean reply, see ISN-KJ, 15/6/6; KJS, 15.17b–18a.
47. ISN-KJ, 15/10/26; KJS, 15.35b–36a.

pendent state," the Korean government said that it was the
Japanese who insisted on such a statement.[48] The Chinese
authorities received the Korean report with satisfaction. On
February 8, 1879, the Tsungli Yamen memorialized the
throne to the effect that the Board of Rites be ordered to
advise Korea to handle the matter as it saw fit. So ordered,
the Board sent a note to Seoul two days later. It also advised
Korea to handle the Japanese demand for the opening of
Wŏnsan on its own.[49]

Thus, three years after the signing of the Treaty of
Kanghwa, China maintained its traditional policy of non-
interference in Korea. This, however, did not mean that the
Chinese leaders were complacent about the situation. On
the contrary, Li Hung-chang and his associates grew increasingly worried over the Japanese and Russian threats to the
peninsula. As governor-general of the metropolitan province and imperial commissioner for the northern treaty
ports, Li had vast responsibilities in foreign affairs, in trade
matters, and in the defense of north China. Korea controlled by a hostile power or a potential enemy would be a
direct threat to north China and the imperial homeland of
Manchuria; therefore Li considered Korea more important
strategically to the Ch'ing state than coastal provinces such
as Kiangsu or Chekiang.[50] He was determined to prevent
Korea from falling under Japanese or Russian domination.
From the mid-1870s, Li directed his main effort under the
self-strengthening programs toward the creation of a modern navy, with the aim of checking Japan's expansionist designs on Korea.

Although war was averted by the treaty between Japan
and Korea, Li faced the problem of formulating a long-
range policy that would insure the safety of Korea from
Japanese and Russian aggression. By late 1876 he developed the view that Korea could best ward off the threat
from Japan and Russia by entering into diplomatic and

48. CJHK, vol. 2, 351–353.
49. *Ibid.*, 353–355.
50. LWCK, *Tsungli Yamen Letters*, 1.49a.

commercial relations with those Western powers whose interest in East Asia was chiefly in trade, not in territorial aggrandizement. We call this a "treaty-system policy." The balance of interests among several Western powers with treaty relations with China, as Li found out in the summer of 1876 during his negotiations at Chefoo for the settlement of the Margary affair, might even serve to restrain the demands of so dominant a power as Britain.[51] In view of China's traditional non-interference in Korea, however, the question remained as to how the principle of the balance of power could be applied to Korea. Influential as he was, Li did not have and could not readily obtain the authority to communicate directly with the Korean government. This was a prerogative of the Board of Rites. In the circumstances, his personal correspondence with Yi Yu-wŏn, which had begun in early 1876, proved convenient and valuable.

In late 1876, when he replied to a letter from Yi Yu-wŏn, Li took the opportunity to point out the advantages of having treaty relations with Western powers to Korea.[52] A year later when his friend, Ho Ju-chang, was leaving for Tokyo as China's first minister to Japan, Li asked him to keep Korea in mind and to take timely action to mediate, if necessary, between Japan and Korea. Even as he worried about Japan's ambitions toward Korea, Li grew concerned over Russian intentions toward the peninsula. In 1878, during the Sino-Russian dispute over Ili, Li feared that, with the termination of the Russo-Turkish War early that year, Russia might turn next toward Korea. Answering a letter from Yi in September 1878, Li reiterated that, while powers such as Britain and the United States were interested chiefly in trade, Russia constantly encroached upon and annexed adjacent territories. Suspecting Russia was trying to isolate Korea with the aim of seizing it at an opportune moment,

51. On Li's role in the negotiation of the Chefoo agreement, see S. T. Wang, *The Margary Affair and the Chefoo Agreement*.
52. Hsüeh Fu-ch'eng, Li's private secretary, wrote the letter to Yi Yu-wŏn. See Hsüeh Fu-ch'eng, *Hsüeh Fu-ch'eng ch'üan-chi* (Complete works of Hsüeh Fu-ch'eng), vol. 3, 3.38a–39a.

he suggested that Korea open Wŏnsan to Japanese commerce and accept British overtures for a treaty as means of
forestalling Russian designs.[53]

Li's policy may also be viewed in the light of the ancient
Chinese strategem of "using barbarians to control barbarians" (*i-i chih-i*), but he was undoubtedly inspired chiefly by
China's contemporary experience and his own knowledge of
international politics. He realized that it was the combined
interest of a number of Western powers having treaty relations with China that helped to stabilize China's position in
this period. In addition, he was acquainted with the European balance-of-power concept. In the summer of 1878, Ma
Chien-chung, Li's protégé, who had gone to France the previous year to study international politics, wrote from Paris
expounding the balance-of-power principle, which he said
Western nations endeavored to maintain in the conduct of
international relations. Ma did this in response to a request
from a "friend," who urged him to present his foreign policy views to the Tsungli Yamen.[54] Li and Ma were both impressed by British intervention in the Russo-Turkish War
and the subsequent Berlin Congress, which not only saved
the Ottoman Empire from dismemberment but helped preserve the balance-of-power in Europe.

While fully aware of Japan's growing ambitions toward
Korea, through most of the 1870s Li continued to entertain
hope of Sino-Japanese cooperation against Western powers.
He believed that, with its continuing domestic unrest and
huge financial deficits, Japan was in no position to undertake a new venture abroad. He was also aware of Japan's
Russophobia. In November 1876 Li was visited by two
prominent Japanese: Minister to China Mori and former
Foreign Minister Soejima. Expressing concern over Russian

53. *Ibid.*, 3.39a–b.
54. Ma Chien-chung, *Shih-k'o-chai chi-yen chi-hsing* (Essays and travel accounts
of Ma Chien-chung), 2.7b–20a; Banno Masataka, "Furansu ryūgaku jidai no Ba
Ken-chū" (Ma Chien-chung during his days of study in France), *Kokkagakkai zasshi*
84.5–6 (July 1971), 276–278; Ch'en San-ching, "Lüeh-lun Ma Chien-chung ti
wai-chiao ssu-hsiang" (A brief discussion of Ma Chien-chung's foreign policy
ideas), *Bulletin of the Institute of Modern History, Academia Sinica* 3.2 (December
1972), 548.

expansionism, the visitors told Li of Japan's desire for cooperation with China and Korea in warding off the Russian threat. Soejima intimated that disaffected samurai in Japan might rise in revolt against the government.[55] Although it is not likely that Li was lulled into complacency by Japan's professed desire for cooperation, at this time he had not yet abandoned his hope that Japan could be persuaded to remain friendly to China, in the event of the latter's dispute with Western powers. In 1877, when the Satsuma Rebellion broke out in Japan, Li readily loaned 100,000 cartridges to the Japanese government.[56] Subsequently Japan joined in the international relief efforts during the great Shansi famine in China. However, the era of Sino-Japanese cordiality ended abruptly with Japan's annexation of Liu-ch'iu in 1879.

After Japan forced Liu-ch'iu to terminate its tributary ties with China in the summer of 1875, its king secretly sent emissaries to Peking to seek Chinese protection. Faced with more serious internal and external problems elsewhere, however, China could do little more than verbally protest the Japanese action. On its part, the Japanese government preferred not to discuss Liu-ch'iu with China. In February 1876, in reply to an inquiry from Mori, who was then engaged in talks with the Tsungli Yamen in Peking on the status of Korea, Foreign Minister Terashima instructed him to avoid any discussion on Liu-ch'iu.[57] Meanwhile, a considerable segment of the Japanese public opposed the "costly" takeover of the tiny and poor island kingdom, which "disliked" Japan and "remained loyal to China."[58] Preoccupied with other problems, such as the suppression of samurai rebellions and peasant uprisings at home, the Japanese government did not take further action with regard to Liu-ch'iu.

55. LWCK, *Tsungli Yamen Letters,* 6.31a–32a.
56. *Ibid.,* 7.3b–4a.
57. NGB, vol. 12, 471–472.
58. Fujimura Michio, "Ryūkyū buntō kōshō to tai-Ajia seisaku no tenkan" (Negotiations for the partition of the Ryūkyūs and a shift in policy toward Asia), *Rekishigaku kenkyū* 373 (March 1971), 3–4.

In the summer of 1877, Mori brought an article printed in a London journal the previous year to the attention of Minister of the Right Iwakura. It urged Britain to seize Liu-ch'iu in order to strengthen its military position in East Asia.[59] Japan's ultimate objective in Liu-ch'iu was annexation, and manifestation of British interest in the archipelago alarmed the Japanese government enough to convince it that it must act soon. Accordingly, in late 1878, when the domestic situation regained stability after the assassination of Ōkubo, Minister of Home Affairs Itō Hirobumi, who had inherited Ōkubo's mantle as the principal figure in the government, ordered a study of the ultimate disposition of Liu-ch'iu. On the basis of that study, in March 1879 the Japanese government dispatched a force of 400 infantrymen and 150 policemen to the islands. In early April the troops seized Shuri, the Liu-ch'iuan capital, abolished the island kingdom, and established the new Prefecture of Okinawa as an integral part of Japan.[60]

Japanese annexation of Liu-ch'iu came at a time when the Sino-Japanese jurisdictional dispute over the islands was still unresolved. The Japanese action was timed to coincide with China's embroilment with Russia over Ili. The Chinese authorities were angered particularly by the fact that Japanese action was carried out in disregard of their repeated protests and requests for negotiation. Many Chinese officials, especially a group of young, idealistic scholar-officials in Peking known as the *ch'ing-liu* (purity) group —who took a militant stand against any concession to Russia over Ili— demanded a showdown with Japan over Liu-ch'iu. Most Western diplomats in China were critical of the Japanese action. Characterizing it as an act based solely on force, British Minister Wade said that China should contest it, by force if necessary. German Minister Maximilian von Brandt said that Japanese diplomacy toward China often bordered on treachery.[61]

59. NGB, vol. 13, 194–198.
60. For the steps taken by the Meiji government leading to the annexation of Ryūkyū, see Kinjō Seitoku, *Ryūkyū shobunron* (A discussion of the disposition of Ryūkyū), 238–256.
61. Fujimura, "Ryūkyū buntō kōshō," 6–7.

Though a tributary of China for centuries, Liu-ch'iu had never actually been controlled by China. Nor had China ever considered the small island kingdom important. China was aware that Liu-ch'iu, closer geographically to Japan than to China, had been under Satsuma domination. Therefore China might have acquiesced and accepted the takeover by Japan had it been carried out in a manner that recognized or otherwise respected Chinese suzerainty over the islands. The unilateral and arbitrary character of the Japanese action rendered this impossible. The retention of Liu-ch'iu as tributary was not so much at stake as the integrity of the entire tribute system, which China was trying to preserve. Specifically, rather than the loss of Liu-ch'iu itself, the Chinese authorities were concerned about its possible effect upon other, more important territories and tributaries, such as Taiwan, Vietnam, and, particularly, Korea. This concern prompted Ho Ju-chang to urge his government repeatedly to take an uncompromising stand on Liu-ch'iu, warning that Japan, if unchecked now, would surely do to Korea what it did to Liu-ch'iu.[62]

While Ho's position represented the views of a number of Peking officials at this time, Li Hung-chang took a more realistic position. When consulted by the Tsungli Yamen, Li pointed out that Liu-ch'iu was a small kingdom whose tribute to China was merely a symbol, and that it would be vain for China to go to war over a symbol. Although Liu-ch'iu itself was insignificant, Li, too, feared that Japanese aggression unchecked there might encourage future aggression in Korea. He recommended negotiation to seek a compromise solution under the mutual non-aggression clause of the 1871 treaty with Japan.[63] Japan refused to negotiate, declaring that the Liu-ch'iuan settlement was an internal affair of Japan.

Former U.S. President Ulysses S. Grant arrived in China in May 1879 on a global tour, and Prince Kung and Li ap-

62. See Ho's letters to the Tsungli Yamen in Wen T'ing-ching, ed., *Ch'a-yang san-chia wen-ch'ao* (Writings of three scholars from Ch'a-yang), 45–71; his letter to Li Hung-chang in LWCK, *Tsungli Yamen Letters,* 8.2a–4b.
63. LWCK, *Tsungli Yamen Letters,* 8.1a–2a, 4b–6a.

pealed to him to mediate the Sino-Japanese dispute over Liu-ch'iu. Grant urged a peaceful settlement, suggesting partition of the Liu-ch'iuan archipelago between China and Japan, by direct negotiation without third-party interference. His suggestion formed the basis for protracted negotiations between the two countries during the following months. In October 1880 a tentative agreement was reached for partition of the island between China and Japan, with the proviso that the two countries would grant most-favored-nation treatment to each other.[64] The Tsungli Yamen wished to sign the agreement, hoping that it would prevent a Japanese-Russian alignment against China. This aroused strong opposition from members of the *ch'ing-liu* group.

In a lengthly memorial reaching the throne on November 29, 1880, Ch'en Pao-ch'en, junior supervisor of instructions, attacked the Yamen's position. Ch'en argued that, judging from past behavior in Taiwan and Liu-ch'iu, Japan could not be trusted to abide by an agreement; it would side with the stronger country in the dispute between China and Russia. Elucidating the potential implications of a Chinese concession in Liu-ch'iu, Ch'en emphasized that China's failure to protect Liu-ch'iu from Japan, a small, weak, debt-ridden country, could only encourage Russia's designs on a far more important tributary: Korea. He asserted that war against Japan would be the turning point, of success or failure, in China's contemporary self-strengthening efforts.[65] A few days thereafter Chang Chih-tung, another member of the group, followed with an equally powerful memorial, assailing the Yamen's position and asserting that China's weak, vacillating foreign policy had invited the Japanese challenge.[66]

64. For Grant's mediation role, see Kublin, "the Liu-ch'iu Controversy," 225–228; T. F. Tsiang, "Sino-Japanese Diplomatic Relations, 1870–1894," *Chinese Social and Political Science Review* 17.1 (April 1933), 40–49; Mikuniya Hiroshi, "Ryūkyū kizoku ni kansuru Guranto no chōtei" (Grant's mediation concerning the subjection of Ryūkyū), *Tōhō gakuhō* (Kyoto) 10.3 (October 1939), 29–64.

65. CKCJ, 2.10b–13a.

66. Chang Chih-tung, *Chang Wen-hsiang-kung ch'üan-chi* (Complete works of Chang Chih-tung), 3.22b–24b.

In the face of such opposition from the militant young officials, the throne referred the matter to Li Hung-chang. Li earlier had advocated a policy of placating Japan in the hope of winning its friendship and goodwill in China's struggle against Western powers; apparently he no longer entertained such hope. He agreed with the young officials that Japan's future attitude toward China would depend on China's own strength, not on any agreement. Unlike the young officials, however, Li took the pragmatic position that partition of Liu-ch'iu might be accepted simply to end the controversy. Li was flexible regarding the integrity of the traditional tribute system, but he firmly opposed granting most-favored-nation treatment to Japan.[67]

Leaders of the Japanese government considered Liu-ch'iu an integral part of Japan. Protection of its inhabitants was the principal justification for Japan's expedition to Taiwan in 1874. Japanese willingness to give up a part of the islands in exchange for most-favored-nation treatment in China was a measure of their desire to establish diplomatic and commercial parity with Western powers in China. Li was fully aware of this Japanese desire. Willing to accept a compromise over Liu-ch'iu, he was not about to grant Japan such status in China; an overriding issue of principle in Sino-Japanese relations was at stake. In the circumstances, the negotiations broke down and no agreement was signed. Although the Japanese attempt to strike a diplomatic bonanza in China failed, annexation of Liu-ch'iu, hereafter to be referred to as Ryūkyū, its Japanese name, became a *fait accompli*. The island kingdom became the first East Asian state whose ancient tributary ties with China were forcibly terminated by Japanese expansion in modern times.

Seizure of Ryūkyū heightened Chinese vigilance against Japanese designs on Korea. On August 21, 1879, four months after the incident, the Tsungli Yamen submitted an important memorial that marked the emergence of a new Chinese policy toward Korea, a policy representing a depar-

---

67. See Li's memorial in CKCJ, 2.14b–17a.

ture from China's traditional non-interference in Korean affairs. The Yamen memorial was a follow-up on a similar one submitted earlier by Ting Jih-ch'ang, former governor of Kiangsu and of Fukien and a close friend of Li's. Ting argued in his memorial that Korea should be encouraged to enter into treaty relations with Western powers so that their combined interests would serve to check Japanese designs on Korea. British Minister Wade made a similar suggestion to the Yamen, warning that, unless Korea established relations with Western countries, it would surely follow Ryūkyū's fate. The Yamen requested that the throne order Li to undertake the task of persuading and guiding Korea. The request was approved by the throne; Li was so ordered the same day.[68]

His responsibility for the defense of north China, his rapport with several grand councilors, his vast experience in diplomacy, including negotiations with Japanese envoys, made Li a logical choice for the assignment. The role of tutor and guardian that Li undertook for Korea was without precedent under the tribute system; the Ch'ing government still wished to preserve the appearance of non-interference in Korea's affairs. The imperial edict to Li stated that "since it is difficult for China to force upon Korea what Korea does not want, the court finds it inconvenient to indicate explicitly its intentions toward Korea." Li had already communicated with an envoy of Korea, and he was to "convey [former] Governor Ting's proposal to Korea as his own."[69] Li guided Korean foreign policy through his "personal correspondence" with Yi Yu-wŏn, a device which enabled the Ch'ing government to implement its new Korean policy "without officially interfering" in Korea's affairs. Moreover, Korea being a tributary state and not a "foreign country," it would have been improper for the Tsungli Yamen to handle its affairs.

68. See the Tsungli Yamen memorial in CKCJ, 1.31b–32b.
69. CKCJ, 1.32b; CJHK, vol. 2, 361; Deuchler, *Confucian Gentlemen*, 86–87; Kwŏn Sŏk-pong, "Yi Hong-jang ŭi tae-Chosŏn yŏlguk ibyak kwŏndoch'aek e taehayŏ" (On Li Hung-chang's policy of inducing Korea to sign treaties with powers), *Yŏksa hakpo* 21 (August 1963), 107–109.

On August 26—five days after he had received his new assignment—Li addressed a long letter to Yi Yu-wŏn, in which he painstakingly explained why it was imperative for Korea to enter into treaty relations with Western countries. Citing the seizure of Ryūkyū as an example of Japanese aggression, Li expressed fear that Korea, a nation of literary tradition, would be no match for Japan and that, while China would extend aid to Korea, it might not reach the peninsula in time. Pointing out the possibility of Japanese-Western collusion against Korea, Li said that the trend toward global intercourse was irreversible and not in man's power to check. Inasmuch as Korea had signed a treaty with Japan, it should make treaties with Western powers so that their concern, based on commercial interests, would check Japanese designs on Korea. Li mentioned the effective British intervention in the Russo-Turkish War, which had saved Turkey from total catastrophe. Extolling the efficacy of international law, he cited Belgium, Denmark, and Turkey as small or weak nations protected by it. Treaties with Britain, Germany, and the United States, he argued, would be the best guarantee for Korea's safety from Russian and Japanese aggression. In a cordial, almost pleading, tone, Li continued: "Your country's worries are China's worries. That is why I do not hesitate to go beyond my duties to plan on your country's behalf and state my inner feelings. It is hoped that you will present my suggestion to your king for him to examine, to assemble all ministers, and to let them carefully deliberate, ponder, and secretly discuss its feasibility. If you consider my words not in error, please so indicate in general in your reply." Li added that Korea might obtain better terms from Western powers if it negotiated with them in peace.[70]

Five days later, Li memorialized the throne to report on his letter to Yi and on his future plans for Korea. In view of Korea's lack of familiarity with the treaty system and Western customs, said Li, should Korea decide to discuss treaties

70. CJHK, vol. 2, 366–369.

with Western countries, China must, of necessity, negotiate on Korea's behalf and serve as mediator in order to forestall trouble.[71]

Li's letter reached Yi in early October. The political situation in Korea at this time was not as favorable as Li hoped; since signing the treaty with Japan, xenophobia and exclusionist sentiment had increased rather than decreased. Identifying Japan with the West, the literati were more vehemently opposed than ever to broadening relations with Japan and opening intercourse with the West. Ch'oe Ikhyŏn, the fiery leader who had been exiled for his opposition to the Japanese treaty in 1876, was pardoned in March 1879. However, he and his followers were not appeased; they turned against the government's foreign policy and were making common cause with the Taewŏn'gun, whose brooding presence was a continuing threat to Queen Min and her relatives. Growing aggressiveness that was characteristic of the Japanese attitude alarmed the officials and strengthened their exclusionist sentiments.

Meanwhile, the Korean government was dominated increasingly by the queen and her relatives; in the continued absence of effective royal leadership, it vacillated and drifted. The death of Pak Kyu-su, in 1877, removed from the top council of government the single official of stature sufficient to have responded positively to Li's advice. The former and incumbent state councilors and other top officials, including advocates of rapprochement with Japan, categorically opposed intercourse with the West. Preoccupied with the perpetuation of their own power, the queen and her relatives did nothing that might further inflame the diehard literati. Ironically for China, investiture of her son, while strengthening the position of the queen and her relatives, probably reduced their immediate dependence on Chinese support in the domestic power struggle.

During the spring and summer of 1879, Japanese surveying activities along the Korean coast, Hanabusa's long sojourn in Seoul, and his demand for the opening of Wŏn-

71. *Ibid.*, 373–374.

san and Inch'ŏn caused widespread anti-Japanese agitation. The decision to open Wŏnsan aroused strong local opposition. When the literati of three neighboring districts addressed a joint memorial to the king, the government was compelled to exile their leaders in order to silence the protest.[72] As Hanabusa pressed for the opening of Inch'ŏn in addition to Wŏnsan, Inch'ŏn's proximity to the capital alarmed many officials and aroused opposition from within the government.

Yi Yu-wŏn was in semi-retirement at this time, holding only a sinecure as first minister without portfolio. While he continued to enjoy the favor of the court, he was not as influential in governmental affairs as Li believed him to be. Although he had earlier advocated rapprochement with Japan, Yi wished merely to restore traditional relations with that country. He had become alarmed over Japan's growing aggressiveness and its insatiable demand for "concessions," such as the opening of Inch'ŏn. His own role in the rapprochement with Japan was well known, and Yi apparently became uneasy over the new upsurge of anti-Japanese sentiment in the country. On August 4 suddenly he submitted a memorial to Kojong, in which he pictured himself as a staunch opponent of "concession" to Japan. Stating his firm opposition to the opening of Inch'ŏn, Yi insinuated that disagreement and equivocation among top government leaders had encouraged Hanabusa to persist in his preposterous demands. This infuriated his colleagues. On September 3 former and incumbent state councilors submitted a joint memorial to Kojong to refute Yi. Declaring their unanimous opposition to the opening of Inch'ŏn, they said they were "greatly bewildered" by Yi's insinuation, for "there has not been the slightest difference" between their position and that of Yi. The king soothed their ruffled feelings and asked for understanding even though there were some ill-chosen words in Yi's memorial.[73] One month after this episode Yi received Li's letter of August 26.

72. ISN-KJ, 16/5/28; KJS, 16.21b.
73. See Yi's memorial in ISN-KJ, 16/6/17; KJS, 16.22a–b; for other councilors' countermemorial, see ISN-KJ, 16/7/16; KJS, 16.28a–b.

Over the years Li's correspondence had little positive effect on Yi's thinking about the West. Even if it had, having thus ostracized himself from his colleagues, it would have been difficult for Yi to take the lead in inaugurating a new policy, which would be revolutionary in significance in the history of Korea's relations with the outside world. On October 7 Yi wrote his reply to Li and sent it to Yu Chih-k'ai to be forwarded to Li. While thanking Li for his concern, Yi made no reference to his foreign policy suggestion. In a separate letter to Yu, Yi confided that Korea did not wish to have relations with other countries and that the opening of ports to Japanese commerce was an unwelcome step, dictated by necessity. Pleading for understanding, Yi said that, although he had reported Li's suggestion to the court, he had been "unable to argue for it strongly," because he had been "relieved of office and returned to his native village." In a letter to the Tsungli Yamen, Li noted that there seemed to be reason behind Yi's ambiguous reply, which Yi was apparently not at liberty to reveal. In late December Li replied to Yi graciously, without repeating his earlier suggestion.[74]

After sending his short reply to Li, Yi apparently felt that he owed him a fuller explanation. On December 24 he addressed another letter to Li. Thanking Li profusely for his efforts to protect Korea from Japan and Russia, Yi proceeded to argue politely as to why Korea could not enter into treaty relations with Western countries. He cited Korea's traditional seclusion and its aversion to Christianity as the fundamental reasons. As for the strategem of "using an enemy to control an enemy" (*i-ti chih-ti*), which Li suggested, Yi said that it might work for a larger country; it would not work for a small country, like Korea, which might be destroyed before it could manage to use an enemy. Yi did not have faith in international law since it had not saved Ryūkyū. Nor was he convinced of the advantage of foreign trade, for it had nearly bankrupted, instead of enriching, Japan. Yi clinched his argument by saying that Korea could

74. LWCK, *Tsungli Yamen Letters*, 10.15b–16b; CJHK, vol. 2, 394–396.

always count on Chinese protection in time of need. Since "neither Japan nor the West dare behave with license before your excellency's imposing power," he said, "our inferior country places eternal reliance upon your great virtue."[75]

Whether Yi consulted the government before writing his letter is not known. In view of the nature of his correspondence and of the gravity of the subject, it is inconceivable that Yi said anything contrary to, or at variance with, the views of those in power. His letter can therefore be regarded as accurately reflecting the Korean government's position on the subject. By polite but firm rejection of Li's advice, the Korean government asserted its traditional political independence from China. Moreover, Li's reaction showed his respect for such independence.

Li received Yi's letter on March 5, 1880. Reporting it to the Tsungli Yamen four days later, Li observed with obvious disappointment that, still imprisoned in tradition, Korea could not appreciate careful plans made by China on its behalf. Expressing the belief that Yi was constrained by opinion at home, Li lamented that leading Korea into the arena of international life was a "task that cannot be accomplished overnight."[76] Though disappointed, Li was not disheartened. He did not have to wait long before an opportunity for him to implement the new Chinese policy toward Korea presented itself.

CHINA'S "STRATEGY FOR KOREA"

Following the signing of the Treaty of Kanghwa, Japanese-Korean trade increased rapidly. Although precise statistical information is lacking, the total value of the trade at Pusan increased several fold during the second half of the 1870s.[77] It was expected to rise even more rapidly with the opening of Wŏnsan. As the volume of the trade in-

75. CJHK, vol. 2, 398–401.

76. *Ibid.*, 397; LWCK, *Tsungli Yamen Letters*, 10.23a–b.

77. On the Japanese-Korean trade in the immediate post-Kanghwa period, see Ch'oe Yu-gil, "Yijo kaehang chikhu ŭi Han-Il muyŏk ŭi tonghyang" (The trend in Korean-Japanese trade immediately after the opening of ports by Yi Korea), *Asea yŏn'gu* 15.3 (September 1972), 175–221.

creased, the Korean government, whose chronic shortage of revenue had been aggravated by Kojong's bungling in fiscal policy and by Queen Min's growing extravagance, became more and more anxious to tap this new source of revenue. Meanwhile, Japan's willingness to accept a reasonable tariff had been confirmed by Hanabusa during his visit to Seoul in the summer of 1879.[78] Shortly after the opening of Wŏn-san in May 1880, the Korean government therefore decided to dispatch a mission to Japan to seek a tariff agreement. It appointed Kim Hong-jip to head the mission.

Kim was a talented official with a perceptive mind, thirty-nine *sui* old at this time. He was not closely identified with the Mins or with the supporters of the Taewŏn'gun. Though by no means persuaded that Korea should open its doors to the West, Kim was nevertheless eager to learn about the outside world.[79] He and his party of some sixty men left Seoul in July 1880. Departing from Pusan aboard a Japanese steamship, they reached Tokyo on August 11. The new mission was little different in composition from the Kim Ki-su mission four years earlier; in appearance both missions were similar, except in size, to the Korean embassies to Edo during the Tokugawa period. Bearing the title of "friendship envoy" as had Kim Ki-su, Kim Hong-jip carried an official letter from the Korean minister of rites to the Japanese foreign minister. It simply stated that Kim was being sent to Japan in return for the several visits of Japanese envoys to Korea in recent years. Its postscript indicated Kim's real mission. Recalling the exemption of duties at Pusan was a provisional measure, it expressed the hope that tariff regulations would be negotiated between the two countries under the applicable provisions of the Treaty of Kanghwa.[80]

78. KHOM, vol. 1, 37–38; NGB, vol. 15. 219.

79. On Kim Hong-jip's life and career, see Towŏn sanggong kiryŏmsaŏp ch'ujin wiwŏnhoe, comp., *Kaehwagi ŭi Kim ch'ongni* (Prime minister Kim during the period of enlightenment).

80. Kim Hong-jip, *Kim Hong-jip yugo* (Writings of Kim Hong-jip), 261; Yamabe Kentarō, *Nihon no Kankoku heigō* (Japan's annexation of Korea), 46–47. Kim told Chinese Minister Ho that the tariff issue was the only important business he

Kim's activities in Tokyo confirmed that tariff negotiations, not a general broadening of relations, were the objective of his trip. When informed that he would be received in audience by the Japanese emperor, Kim at first declined the honor. He reluctantly accepted it when he was told that Ho Ju-chang, Chinese minister to Japan, had been received by the emperor and that refusal would hurt the relations between the two countries. It was not until August 30—three weeks after his arrival and after a visit to the Confucian shrine in the capital—that Kim went to the imperial palace for an audience.[81]

Korea's ignorance of modern international diplomacy and its readiness to follow China's example became apparent immediately upon Kim's arrival in Tokyo. During his first visit to the Japanese Foreign Ministry on August 13, Kim brought up the tariff issue for discussion. When asked if he had a draft agreement, Kim replied that he had neither a draft nor authority to negotiate an agreement. Once the two governments agreed on the introduction of a tariff, he said, their representatives at Pusan could negotiate a formal agreement. Japanese Vice Foreign Minister Ueno Kagenori explained that a tariff was an important matter that should be discussed only by the duly authorized plenipotentiaries of the two countries. Kim then suggested that Japan and Korea sign an agreement identical to the one existing between China and Japan. Replying that the proposed agreement could not be the same as the Sino-Japanese agreement, Ueno suggested that Kim discuss the matter with Hanabusa.[82]

In his subsequent talks with Foreign Ministry officials, Kim was at first ready to accept a five-percent ad valorem duty on all imports and exports. But Chinese Minister Ho informed him that Japan was at this time negotiating with

---

wished to discuss with the Japanese. See Kim Hong-jip, *Susinsa ilgi* (Diary of a friendship envoy), in Kuksa p'yŏn-ch'an wiwŏnhoe, ed., *Susinsa kirok* (Records of friendship envoys), 173–174.

81. Kim Hong-jip, *Susinsa ilgi*, 50.
82. *Ibid.*, 150.

the Western treaty powers for a higher tariff. Acting on
Ho's advice, Kim told the Japanese that it would be only fair
for Japan to apply the same rate to Korea as to Western
nations. While agreeing in principle, the Japanese lamely
argued that it would be impractical to do so, because the
distance between Japan and Korea was far shorter than that
between either country and the West.[83] Although further
discussions were held, no agreement was reached, partly because Kim followed Ho's advice not to conclude any agreement in haste.

Kim showed no inclination to discuss the issues of new
ports and resident minister. On their part, the Japanese did
not raise these issues until the last minute. On September 8,
as Kim was leaving Tokyo, Foreign Minister Inoue Kaoru
told him that a Japanese envoy would leave for Korea
within a fortnight in order to resume negotiations on these
issues. Kim asked Inoue to postpone the envoy's departure
so that the Korean government would have time to study
the issues on the basis of his own report. Inoue, however,
replied that his government considered it extremely urgent
to station an envoy in Seoul. He added that, although the
Japanese government was aware of the Korean government's position on these matters, in view of the current
Sino-Russian crisis over Ili, it could not remain "complacent" about Korea, even though Korea itself was "uncon-
cerned about things beyond its own borders."[84]

Inoue had taken over the helm at the Foreign Ministry in
September 1879, after public outcry over a smuggling case
involving a British merchant had forced Terashima's resignation. Thus the change of foreign ministers did not represent change in Japanese policy toward Korea. Japan's goals
in Korea at this time were to expand its influence in the
peninsula and to forestall Russian encroachment. Aware of
its own weakness, Japan, like China, was willing to bring
Western powers into Korea as a means of checking Russian
ambition there. At a meeting with Kim on August 16, Inoue

83. *Ibid.*, 175–176.
84. Yamabe, *Kankoku heigō*, 56.

told him that Japanese leaders had learned from personal experience that exclusionism was no longer a viable policy for any country and that Korea should open its doors to Western nations.[85] When Kim called to bid Inoue farewell on September 7, Inoue told him that Russia had assembled sixteen warships at Vladivostok, just north of the Korean border. Should Russia decide to seek an ice-free port for the fleet, in preparation for naval action against China, Korea would be a logical place to look. Since Korea had no treaties with Western countries and since it did not subscribe to international law, it would be difficult for any country to intervene if Korea were attacked by another country. Therefore, Inoue urged Korea to respond in a friendly manner should a Western power approach it for a treaty. Inoue had the United States in mind when he said this. Thanking Inoue for his advice, Kim asked him if he would put it in writing so that he, Kim, could show it to his government upon his return home. Inoue promptly complied.[86] Although Japan's goals in Korea ran counter to those of China, in the face of a common threat from Russia, the two rival powers adopted an identical strategy: to persuade Korea to enter into treaty relations with Western powers to check Russian designs on the peninsula.

Given Korea's deep-seated distrust of Japan, it is unlikely that Kim was convinced of Inoue's sincerity. There is little doubt, however, that Kim was deeply influenced by similar advice given him by two Chinese diplomats in Tokyo: Minister Ho and Counselor Huang Tsun-hsien. When Kim arrived in the Japanese capital, his hosts urged him to meet with Western diplomats. He made no effort to meet Westerners, but met with Ho and Huang more than half a dozen times during his month-long sojourn in Tokyo.[87] Equally eager to meet Kim, Ho and Huang told him that, "after mingling with people of different kinds" for years, meeting

85. *Ibid.*, 49; TNS, vol. 1, 743.

86. Yamabe, *Kankoku heigō*, 54–56. For Inoue's letter to the Korean minister of rites, see KHOM, vol. 1, 53–54; Kim Hong-jip, *Susinsa ilgi*, 159–160.

87. See Kim's own account of his talks with Ho and Huang in Kim Hong-jip, *Kim Hong-jip yugo*, 314–324; Kim Hong-jip, *Susinsa ilgi*, 171–189.

him was "like meeting a fellow countryman away from home." The three held cordial "talks," conducted on pieces of paper in literary Chinese, in which Kim, like other Korean officials of the time, was thoroughly trained. Kim confided everything to Ho and Huang and sought their advice; the two Chinese officials were delighted to help him.

On the tariff issue, Ho and Huang cautioned against hasty agreement with Japan. Advising Korea to await the outcome of Japan's tariff negotiations with Western countries, they emphasized that it was essential for Korea to retain autonomy in tariff matters. While both Ho and Huang said that the opening of Inch'ŏn and the establishment of a Japanese legation in Seoul would be inevitable, they did not consider either issue urgent.[88] On the other hand, they regarded the Russian threat as the most serious danger facing Korea. They sought to impress upon Kim how urgent it was for Korea to take steps to ward off that threat. Huang told Kim that "the world situation today is without precedent in 4,000 years—one which even Yao, Shun, Yü, and T'ang [ancient Chinese sage emperors] had not anticipated—and that it is no longer possible to cure today's ills with ancient remedies." In response to Kim's question as to how Korea could ward off the Russian threat, Ho suggested the "balance of power" principle, a strategy practiced by Western nations whereby a country threatened by a powerful neighbor would ally itself with other countries in order to create a balance of power. Kim said that he had seen the term "balance of power" in Martin's *Wan-kuo kung-fa* and that he would convey Ho's advice to the Korean court.[89]

Warning Kim against Russia's naval buildup at Vladivostok and its "unfathomable" intentions, Ho asked how opinion at the Korean court had reacted to Li Hung-chang's advice in his letter to Yi Yu-wŏn the previous winter. Kim replied that, while the whole country admired and respected Li, the Koreans still only knew how to adhere to the ancient teachings and were unable to change over-

88. Kim Hong-jip, *Susinsa ilgi*, 187.   89. *Ibid.*, 172, 177.

night. Kim took the opportunity to tell Ho how Korea was indebted to him for his keen observations and timely warnings from Tokyo regarding Japanese intentions toward Korea, which Li had transmitted to Korea in his correspondence with Yi. Repeatedly emphasizing the gravity of the Russian threat, Ho urged that Korea should sign a treaty with the United States, "the only Western power that has never sought selfish gains."[90]

It is unlikely that Ho and Huang really trusted the Japanese, but they believed Japan's desire for cooperation with Korea against Russia to be genuine, partly because they believed that Japan was incapable of carrying out its own designs on Korea. They thought Korea should be friendly toward Japan and wished that Kim would remain in Tokyo as resident minister. On September 6—two days before Kim's departure from Tokyo—Huang presented Kim with a manuscript entitled "A Strategy for Korea" (*Chao-hsien t'se-lüeh*), which he himself had written. Huang explained that Ho and he had pondered Korea's problems, and that it was impossible for them to present their views in a meeting or two before Kim's departure; therefore he had spent the past few days putting them down in writing for Kim's perusal later. Thanking Huang profusely, Kim promised that he would take the treatise home and let his countrymen know "how deeply and sincerely officials of the superior country were solicitous" of Korea.[91]

Opening his treatise with a brief reference to Russia's eastward expansion, Huang declared that, because of its pivotal geographical position in East Asia, Korea had become the primary target of Russian territorial aggrandizement in the region. To meet this threat, Korea must "be intimate with China, unite with Japan, and ally with the United States, and promote its own self-strengthening." He proceeded to expound his reasons: China has always protected Korea; if the whole world were made aware that China and Korea were like members of one family, Russia

90. *Ibid.*, 179, 180, 188.   91. *Ibid.*, 182.

would realize that Korea did not stand alone and would exercise self-restraint toward Korea. Japan and Korea are so close to each other that if either country were seized by Russia, the other would not be able to survive; therefore Korea should overcome its minor misgivings about Japan and promote great plans with Japan. As for the United States, Huang stated that it "has always upheld justice" and "never permitted the European powers to freely perpetrate their evil deeds." Britain, Germany, France, and Italy would follow its lead if the United States signed a treaty with Korea; then, if Russia attacked Korea, it would not be able to achieve its aggressive ambitions, for other Western powers would not permit it.

As for Korea's diplomatic modernization and self-strengthening, Huang urged that Korea start by stationing officials permanently in Peking and envoys in Tokyo and Washington. Korea should invite Chinese merchants to Pusan, Inch'ŏn, and Wŏnsan to prevent a Japanese monopoly of trade at these ports. It should send Korean nationals to Japan to study foreign trade. It should adopt the Ch'ing imperial colors and standard for the Korean army and navy. Korea should send students to the Peking T'ung-wen Kuan to study Western languages, to the Anhwei Army for military training, to the Kiangnan Arsenal to learn weapon manufacturing, to the Foochow Navy Yard to study shipbuilding, and to similar establishments in Japan to study Western science and technology. It should open new schools at Pusan and elsewhere, invite Western instructors, and expand its armaments.[92] Huang's treatise was a clear exposition of China's new "strategy for Korea," which was aimed at creating a counterbalance against what appeared to be a dangerous and growing preponderance of Russian power threatening Korea. It embodied the ideas and spirit of Ho and Huang, and of Li Huang-chang and his associates, who were leading China's contemporary self-strengthening efforts at home and diplomatic modernization abroad.

92. For the text of Huang's treatise, see *ibid.*, 160–171; NGB, vol. 16, 389–394.

Moreover, it may be noted that some of Huang's ideas clearly pointed toward a gradual integration of Korea into the Ch'ing imperial administration—an idea that was to be advocated by some Chinese officials in subsequent periods.

Huang's treatise showed that at this particular time Li and his associates considered Russia a more immediate threat than Japan.[93] No doubt this view was inspired by China's crisis with Russia over Ili. More fundamentally, it stemmed from intimate knowledge of the long history of Russian territorial encroachment along China's frontiers. Since cession of the Maritime Provinces to Russia in 1860, the Ch'ing government had been aware of the growing danger to Korea as well as Manchuria created by Russian colonization and military buildup of the region. Although there had been few instances of Russian military intrusion into Korean territory, Russia's desire for an ice-free port on the Korean east coast was a constant source of concern to China and Japan as well as Korea. The Korean government was concerned even more with the continuing flight of Korean peasants into Russian territory under Russian encouragement and even enticement, which was considered evidence of a Russian intention of future territorial encroachment. By the late 1870s, the number of "renegade" Koreans had reputedly reached 20,000 to 30,000.[94]

Prior to Kim's departure from Tokyo, he discussed with Ho and Huang means by which they would communicate with each other in the future. Before parting, Ho took Kim's hand into his and, again through "pen-talk" (*pi-t'an*), told him what Inoue had told him earlier: a large Russian fleet, commanded personally by the Russian navy minister and anchored near Vladivostok, might move to Korea in search of an ice-free base. Emphasizing "American fairness," he again urged that Korea sign a treaty with the United States.[95] Upon his return to Seoul on October 2, Kim pre-

---

93. See Ho's report to the Tsungli Yamen in CJHK, vol. 2, 403–404.

94. The figures were supplied to Ho by Japanese Foreign Minister Terashima. See *ibid.*, 405.

95. See Ho's report to the Tsungli Yamen *ibid.*, 437–439.

sented Huang's manuscript to Kojong, along with his own report. The document was to prove singularly important in influencing the attitudes of the king and his ministers toward Japan and the West; it stimulated in them an incipient interest in reform and modernization.

Kojong remained an ineffectual ruler, but a subtle change occurred in his attitude around this time. Perhaps as a result of his disillusionment with the top government leadership as well as of his natural youthful inclinations, the young monarch became less receptive to the conservative influence of the senior officials who dominated him in the past. He became more inclined to listen to younger officials, who began to question the practicality, if not the wisdom, of Korea's continued isolation in a changing world. As Korea's contacts with the outside world increased, so did the king's interest in and knowledge of Japan and Western countries. His appointment of Kim, a young and relatively junior official, to head the new mission to Japan and his instructions to Kim were indicative of this change in royal attitude. In addition to the discussion of the tariff issue, Kojong told Kim to obtain as much information about Japan as possible.[96]

Kojong was pleased with the outcome of Kim's mission. He was gratified by the kindred spirit and warm hospitality shown Kim by the Chinese minister in Japan. In response to royal inquiries, Kim described Ho as a man of great talent and wide learning, who was sincerely concerned about Korea. The king was further pleased to learn that he and Ho held the identical view that, while basically untrustworthy, the Japanese nevertheless genuinely desired cooperation with Korea against Russia.[97]

At a court conference of top government leaders on October 11, Kojong asked for comments on Huang's treatise. Chief State Councilor Yi Ch'oe-ŭng stated that many of Huang's ideas coincided with his own and that some of Huang's suggestions might be adopted. With regard to the

96. Kim Hong-jip, *Kim Hong-jip yugo*, 261.
97. *Ibid.*, 262; Kim Hong-jip, *Susinsa ilgi*, 156–157.

West, Yi said that, while its "evil religion" must be rejected, "this should not necessarily lead to quarrels" with the West. At royal command, the assembled officials deliberated further and recommended: (1) no change in policy toward China was necessary since relations with China were already "intimate"; (2) while the Japanese demands for the opening of Inch'ŏn and a permanent legation in Seoul should not be granted, final decisions should be deferred until after the arrival of a Japanese envoy; and (3) since it was not "bad policy to sign a treaty with the United States," should the Americans again send a message, "a friendly reply will be given."[98] Prompt royal approval of these recommendations marked the inauguration of an epoch-making new policy that was to end Korea's isolation and bring about revolutionary changes in its foreign relations, including those with China. Japan was an immediate beneficiary of this policy.

In October 1880, one month after Kim's departure from Tokyo, the Japanese government ordered Hanabusa to go to Seoul again. His mission was to secure Korean consent to the opening of Inch'ŏn and the establishment of a Japanese legation in Seoul. Determined to settle the question of diplomatic accreditation and the resident minister issue, the Japanese government promoted Hanabusa from the rank of chargé d'affaires to minister. As an imperial appointee, Hanabusa carried a letter of accreditation from the Japanese emperor to the Korean king, rather than from the Japanese foreign minister to the Korean minister of rites.[99] This was sure to revive the dispute over diplomatic terminology and titular precedence between the rulers of the two countries. Leaving Tokyo on November 24, Hanabusa and his party reached Seoul on December 17. He immediately requested a royal audience to present his letter of accreditation to the king.

98. KJS, 17.25b–26b. For the reputed gist of the discussions at the court conference, supplied to Ho by a Korean agent, see CJHK, vol. 2, 442–447; NGB, vol. 16, 394–396.
99. Upon his return from Japan, Kim Hong-jip warned Kojong that the elevation of Hanabusa's rank indicated that the Japanese envoy would bring an imperial message. See Kim Hong-jip, *Kim Hong-jip yugo*, 264.

In the message which Hanabusa carried, the Japanese ruler referred to himself as "great emperor"(*dai kōtei* in Japanese; *tae hwang je* in Korean) and addressed the Korean ruler as "great king"(*dai ō* in Japanese; *tae wang* in Korean).[100] The wording of the message provoked heated debate among the top leaders of the Korean government, which resulted in the resignation of two ministers of rites in three days. The debate was no longer over whether the Japanese message should be accepted; the issue was in what form the message should be answered. After several days of inconclusive debate, Kojong announced on December 24 that he would personally accept the Japanese message. On December 27 Hanabusa was received in audience by the king and allowed to present the message. He and his staff thereafter proceeded to settle down in Seoul indefinitely, thus solving the resident minister issue. Not formally acknowledging the establishment of a Japanese legation, the Korean government acquiesced to it as a *fait accompli.*[101] This was a breakthrough for Japan in its long effort to modernize relations with Korea and to expand its influence in the peninsula. Ironically, Chinese influence upon Korea was an important, if not decisive, factor that made this possible. Persuaded by the Chinese that closer ties with Japan would contribute to the security of Korea from the Russian threat, the king became more favorably disposed toward Japan.

100. NGB, vol. 16, 425–428.

101. Kim Hong-jip tried in vain to persuade Hanabusa to reside at Inch'ŏn, instead of Seoul. See *ibid.,* vol. 17, 338. For details concerning these events, see TNS, vol. 1, 630–637.

CHAPTER VIII

The Metamorphosis
of Chinese Authority in Korea

For several years after the inconclusive termination of its naval expedition to Korea in 1871, the United States made no further effort to seek a treaty with that country. Japanese success in a similar effort in 1876 may have revived American interest in Korea. In April 1878 Aaron A. Sargent, U.S. senator from California and chairman of the Senate committee on naval affairs, introduced a draft resolution authorizing the president to appoint a commission to negotiate a treaty with Korea. Although the Sargent resolution did not pass in the Senate, the Department of the Navy in the same year ordered Commodore Robert W. Shufeldt to undertake a diplomatic mission to a number of countries, including Korea. In December 1878 Shufeldt embarked on his mission, aboard the USS *Ticonderoga*. After visiting Africa and the Middle East, Shufeldt arrived in Japan in April 1880 to seek Japanese assistance in establishing initial diplomatic contact with Korea.

Even as Ho Ju-chang, Chinese minister in Tokyo, was establishing a close personal rapport with Kim Hong-jip, which was to prove instrumental in persuading Korean authorities to end their country's isolation, this fortuitous revival of American official interest in Korea provided Li Hung-chang with the first real opportunity to execute his Korean strategy. Going beyond his earlier, indirect approach of urging the Korean government to enter into treaty relations with Western nations, Li decided to mediate directly between Korea and the United States. His initiative and action brought about the first treaty between Korea and a Western state two years later, in 1882; the treaty completed the opening of the hermit kingdom. Unprecedented Chinese intervention in Korean foreign relations was followed by even more unprecedented Chinese intervention in Korean domestic affairs, when a political crisis in Korea suddenly put China's newly inaugurated Korean policy in jeopardy. The opening of Korea thus brought with it a metamorphosis of Chinese relations with Korea, which was to mark the effective end of the traditional world order in East Asia.

THE CHINESE-NEGOTIATED AMERICAN-KOREAN TREATY

Prior to Shufeldt's arrival in Japan, American Minister Bingham, under instructions from Washington, asked Foreign Minister Inoue if he would write official or personal letters to Korean officials "recommending Shufeldt to their favorable consideration." Fearful of jeopardizing Japan's own difficult negotiations with Korea at this time, Inoue turned down the request. He agreed, however, to write a letter introducing Shufeldt to Japanese Consul Kondō at Pusan.[1] Shufeldt left Nagasaki on May 3 and reached Pusan the following day. Kondō took Shufeldt's letter addressed to the Korean king to Sim Tong-sin, prefect of Tongnae, to be transmitted to Seoul. In his letter, Shufeldt stated the peaceful objectives of the United States in seeking a treaty with Korea and requested that the king appoint a plenipotentiary to confer with him at Pusan. Sim refused to take the letter, saying that he had no authority to receive communications from any country other than Japan.[2] Unable to pursue the matter, Shufeldt returned to Japan.

1. NGB, vol. 16, 435–437.
2. ISN-KJ, 17/4/10; KJS, 17.8b–9a; Tyler Dennett, *Americans in Eastern Asia*, 456; Yi Po-hyŏng, "Shufeldt chedok kwa 1880-yŏn ŭi Cho-Mi kyosŏp" (Commodore Shufeldt and Korean-American negotiations in 1880), *Yŏksa hakpo* 15 (September 1961), 68–70.

Following his return to Tokyo in mid-May, Schufeldt succeeded, with Bingham's help, in prevailing upon Inoue to cover his letter to the Korean king with one of Inoue's own and send it to Seoul. Toward the end of May Inoue sent Shufeldt's letter to Korean Minister of Rites Yun Cha-sŭng. In his letter to Yun, Inoue urged that Korea accede to the American request. Emphasizing that he was not trying to interfere in Korea's affairs, Inoue stated that he had persuaded the American envoy not to go to Korea, but to wait for a Korean reply at Nagasaki for sixty days. On July 21, the Shufeldt letter was returned unopened to Kondō, along with Yun's reply to Inoue. Both letters, forwarded to Tokyo by Kondō, reached Inoue in early August. In his reply, Yun told the Japanese foreign minister that he could not accept the American letter, partly because it was improperly addressed, but mainly because his government did not intend to establish relations with any country other than Japan.[3]

Bingham and Shufeldt considered Yun's action offensive and his reply to Inoue evasive. Shufeldt also suspected that the Japanese were not acting in good faith because they wanted to monopolize the Korean trade. Less critical of the Japanese, Bingham merely questioned Kondō's tact and judgment in handling the matter at Pusan. In September, therefore, Bingham asked Inoue again to transmit the Shufeldt letter to the Korean court, through the Japanese envoy in Seoul. Inoue turned down the request, saying that another Korean rebuff would further displease the American government and might jeopardize Japan's position in Korea. Inoue offered to forward the letter once more to the prefect of Tongnae through Kondō. Bingham declined the offer.[4]

Inoue was correct in his assessment of the attitude of the Korean government at this time. Apart from ingrained Korean suspicion of the Japanese, Inoue's effort to help the Americans must have reminded the Korean officials of the warning they received from Li Hung-chang the previous

3. For Inoue's letter to Yun, see KHOM, vol. 1, 48–50; NGB, vol. 16, 445–446. For Yun's reply, see NGB, vol. 16, 449.
4. NGB, vol. 16, 451–456.

October about possible Japanese collusion with the United States or another Western power. Having turned down Li's advice to sign a treaty with the United States a few months earlier, it was inconceivable now for the Korean government to accept similar advice from Japan. One month after the Korean government rejected Inoue's good offices, Yi Yu-wŏn reported the matter to Li, stressing that Korea would not accept communications from any country transmitted by Japan.[5]

Shufeldt's activities in Japan, including his visit to Pusan, were reported to Li by Minister Ho and Chinese Consul Yü Sui at Nagasaki.[6] The news disturbed Li. Although Li had been urging Korea to sign a treaty with the United States, he had no intention of letting Korea do so with Japanese help, for his Korean strategy was directed as much against Japan as against Russia. Li was determined to use Korea's prospective treaties with Western powers to protect, not to weaken, the Chinese position in Korea. He knew that, if modeled on Japan's treaty with Korea, such treaties would surely undermine Chinese authority in Korea. Li's intention all along had been to personally supervise Korea's treaty negotiations with Western countries.[7] On July 23 Li wrote a cordial letter to Shufeldt, inviting the latter to visit him at Tientsin.[8]

Another urgent reason behind Li's action was the imminent danger of war between China and Russia as a result of China's rejection of the Treaty of Livadia, signed in 1879 for the settlement of the dispute over Ili. In response to Chinese action and its preparation for a military showdown, in early 1880 Russia dispatched a fleet under the command of Admiral S. S. Leosovskii to East Asian waters.[9] Virtually everyone in China and Japan, including Western diplomats, agreed that Russia would seek a base for the fleet in Korea.

    5. CJHK, vol. 2, 419–420; Martina Deuchler, *Confucian Gentlemen and Barbarian Envoys*, 113.
    6. CJHK, vol. 2, 411–421; Frederick Foo Chien, *The Opening of Korea*, 76–77.
    7. See Li's memorial reaching the throne on September 3, 1879, in CJHK, vol. 2, 373–374.
    8. Chien, *Opening of Korea*, 77; Dennett, *Americans in Eastern Asia*, 457.
    9. Immanuel C. Y. Hsü, *The Ili Crisis*, 97–98.

Although Li advocated some compromise with regard to the Ili question in the hope of securing Russian cooperation in checking Japanese ambitions toward Korea, he would not acquiesce to Russian encroachment upon the peninsula.[10] In view of China's lack of the modern naval power necessary to protect Korea, Li considered it imperative to bring the United States and other Western powers into Korea at the earliest possible date as a means of forestalling Russian action.

Shufeldt received Li's letter from Consul Yü on August 9. He had heard earlier from Yü of Li's plan to have Korea sign treaties with Western countries, and he therefore accepted Li's invitation. Several days later, Shufeldt learned from Bingham that Korea had again rejected Japanese mediation. He left Nagasaki on August 19 and reached Tientsin six days later. On August 25 he was received cordially by Li.

Shufeldt expressed his hope that China would "use her influence to secure with the Korean government a treaty of amity between Korea and the United States." A long discussion of Korea's strategic position in reference to China, Japan, and Russia followed, during which Shufeldt expressed the fear that Russia might attempt to seize Korea. Li declared that he would "use his influence with the Government of Korea to accede to the friendly request of the United States." He promised that he would inform the American minister in Peking of the Korean government's reactions.[11] Compelled by circumstances, Li decided to abandon his cautious approach toward Korea and to take decisive steps, which would amount to intervention rather than advice in Korean foreign policy. Pleased with the result of his visit, Shufeldt left for home early in September to seek further instructions from Washington.

Subsequent events seemed to favor the implementation of Li's decision. On November 19—two months after Kim

10. *Ibid.*, 100–104.
11. See Li's own account of his talks with Shufeldt in LWCK, *Tsungli Yamen Letters*, 11.28a–b.

Hong-jip's return home—Ho Ju-chang and Huang Tsun-hsien received word in Tokyo that the Korean government had decided to sign a treaty with the United States upon the recommendation of Kim. This was confirmed by a personal letter from Kim.[12] Delighted by the unexpectedly early and positive Korean response, Ho recommended to the Tsungli Yamen that China take over or direct the conduct of Korean foreign policy. "Should China permit Korea to make treaties with other countries on its own," warned Ho, "Chinese suzerainty over Korea would be gone instantly." China "should dispatch an able official experienced in diplomatic matters to Korea to supervise its treaty negotiations with Western countries." Ho further recommended that China "order the Korean king to state in all future treaties that Korea sign them at the command of the Ch'ing court."[13] In late December Ho personally informed American Minister Bingham of the Chinese government's efforts to persuade Korea to sign a treaty with the United States.[14] Although he saw merit in Ho's recommendations, Li Hung-chang opposed them on the ground that such action by China might invite Western objection. Moreover, Li feared that handling of negotiations by Chinese officials might prove disadvantageous to Korea, for Western powers could use it as a pretext for imposing treaties upon Korea similar to those imposed upon China, treaties which China had been forced to accept and which it now wished to revise. As for Ho's misgivings about Chinese suzerainty over Korea, Li was confident that treaties with Western countries would not affect Korean allegiance to China.[15]

Other developments strengthened Li's influence with the Koreans. Though unwilling to end their country's isolation, Korean authorities were not blind to the need for modernizing armaments in order to cope with Japanese and Western threats. Partly out of his desire to learn about Japan's new

12. CJHK, vol. 2, 451–453.
13. *Ibid.*, 439–442.
14. Yi Po-hyŏng, "1880-yŏn ŭi Cho-Mi kyosŏp," 84–85.
15. LWCK, *Tsungli Yamen Letters*, 11.42a–44a; CJHK, vol. 2, 449–450.

military system and weaponry, Sin Hŏn urged acceptance of the Japanese invitation to send a goodwill mission to Japan. Awareness of the need for military modernization grew among Korean officials during the years that followed. In the summer of 1879, the Korean government made plans to train students and apprentices at Li's arsenals at Tientsin. Through Yi Yu-wŏn's correspondence with Li, Korea secured his promise of aid. In August 1880 the Ch'ing Board of Rites received a formal request for imperial approval of the plan. Upon Li's recommendation, the throne approved the plan.[16] When Pyŏn Wŏn-gyu, a Korean liaison officer, visited Tientsin in the fall of that year to discuss details concerning the implementation of the plan, Li took the opportunity to impress upon him the seriousness of the Russian threat and the urgent need for Korea to enter into treaty relations with the United States and other Western powers. Pyŏn promised to convey Li's views to the authorities in Seoul.[17]

Several months later, in February 1881, another Korean liaison officer, Yi Yong-suk, visited Tientsin to seek Li's advice and instructions on issues related to diplomacy and foreign trade as well as the training of Korean apprentices at the Tientsin arsenal. He reported to Li that Korean authorities, particularly the king, definitely favored a treaty with the United States but could not proceed quickly because of strong domestic opposition. Li advised Korea to accept a resident Japanese minister in Seoul and agree to the opening of Inch'ŏn. Foreign trade was a good way to raise revenue, he said, and Korea might use the revenue so raised to expand armaments in defense against external dangers. Li also advised toleration of Japan's use of the term "emperor" in official documents, for, although some Western rulers were called "emperor" and others "king," all were equal in status. Li meant that the Japanese and Korean

16. Kwŏn Sŏk-pong, "Yŏngsŏnsa-haeng e taehan ilgoch'al" (A study of the student-apprentice mission), *Yŏksa hakpo* 17–18 (June 1962), 280–284; Deuchler, *Confucian Gentlemen*, 99–101; Towŏn sanggong kiryŏmsaŏp ch'ujin wiwŏnhoe, comp., *Kaehwagi ŭi Kim ch'ongni*, 93–95.

17. CJHK, vol. 2, 432–436.

rulers were equal in status even though the former was called "emperor" and the latter "king."[18] In no way did he imply that Japan should be accorded titular equality with China in its relations with Korea. Urging early action on behalf of an American treaty, Li handed to Yi the draft of a treaty prepared by Ma Chien-chung, who had returned home after three years of study and travel in Europe and was now serving as Li's assistant in foreign affairs.

Ma was China's leading specialist in international law and diplomacy at this time. It was he who in 1878 expounded the balance-of-power concept in letters to a friend, in all likelihood someone close to Li. Ma's draft treaty, intended as the model for Korea's future treaties with Western nations, is an interesting document; it demonstrates China's growing knowledge of international law as well as China's intention to use it and the treaty system to strengthen traditional Chinese authority and position in Korea. Consisting of ten articles, the draft treaty contained clauses banning merchant consuls and opium trade and provisions designed to ensure Korea's equality with Western powers, particularly its autonomy in tariff matters. On the other hand, it contained no provision for the exchange of diplomatic representatives between Korea and a contracting power. The latter was merely to station a consul-general at a Korean trading port to refer to his country's minister in Peking diplomatic or other matters that he was not empowered to handle himself.[19]

The Korean government, meanwhile, took steps to prepare for opening relations with Western countries. Early in 1881 it created a new office called the "Office for the Supervision of State Administration" (*T'ongni kimu amun*). Modeled on the Ch'ing Tsungli Yamen, it was to exercise broader responsibilities in domestic as well as foreign affairs, including the military "self-strengthening" program being inaugurated with Chinese assistance. Key positions in the new agency were manned by reform-minded junior of-

18. *Ibid.*, 467–470.
19. For the text of Ma's draft treaty, see *ibid.*, 472–475.

ficials such as Kim Hong-jip and others who had returned from an extended inspection tour of Japan the previous year.[20] The decision to open Inch'ŏn made at the end of February 1881, surprised the Japanese, who expected difficult and protracted negotiations.[21] These rapid changes inevitably aroused strong opposition from the xenophobic literati in the country.

The first manifestation of organized opposition appeared in March 1881, when the literati of Yŏngnam (Kyŏngsang Province) submitted to Kojong a collective memorial popularly called the "memorial from ten thousand men in Yŏngnam." It vehemently attacked Huang's "strategy for Korea," which had been copied and widely read. It charged that, although he claimed to be Chinese, Huang was an "apologist for Japan and a faithful agent of Christianity" interested solely in the propagation of this "evil" religion. It urged the king to "burn Huang's treatise" and punish Kim Hong-jip for bringing it home. When neither appeasement nor intimidation succeeded in silencing the signers of the memorial, the government exiled two of the leaders.[22]

The action of the Yŏngnam literati touched off waves of similar protest throughout the country. During the following spring and summer, prominent scholars, mostly disciples and followers of Yi Hang-no and Ch'oe Ik'hyŏn, denounced the government's diplomatic and commercial "concessions" to Japan and its moves to establish relations with Western countries. Condemning the "betrayal" of the *wijŏng ch'ŏksa* principle under Kojong's personal rule in contrast to strict adherence to it under the Taewŏn'gun, one

20. On the new office, see Chun (Chŏn), Hae-jong, "T'ongni kimu amun sŏlch'i kyŏngwi e taehayŏ" (On circumstances leading to the establishment of the Office for the Supervision of State Administration), in Chun Hae-jong, *Tong'a munhwa ŭi pigyosajŏk yŏn'gu*, 204–218. On the inspection tour of Japan, see Chŏng Ok-cha, "Sinsa yuramdan ko" (A study of the gentlemen's sightseeing group), *Yŏksa hakpo* 27 (April 1965), 105–142.

21. See Hanabusa's report to Foreign Minister Inoue, dated February 28, 1881, in NGB, vol. 17, 352–353.

22. ISN-KJ, 18/2/26; KJS, 18.5a–6b; Han Woo-keun (U-gŭn), "Kaehang tangsi ŭi wigi isik kwa kaehwa sasang" (The sense of crisis and enlightenment thought at the time of opening ports), *Han'guksa yŏn'gu* 2 (December 1969), 124–125; Deuchler, *Confucian Gentlemen*, 104–107.

310 *Last Phase of the East Asian World Order*

memorialist, Hong Chae-hak, demanded the death penalty for ministers responsible for the change. The authorities put Hong to death and exiled his mentor and instigator, Kim P'yŏng-muk.[23] When another memorialist singled out Yi Yu-wŏn and Kim Hong-jip for attack—the former for his correspondence with Li Hung-chang—a frightened Yi submitted a countermemorial offering excuses for his action. Angered by Yi's cowardly behavior, Kojong exiled him and his critic.[24]

While it alarmed Queen Min and her relatives, the Taewŏn'gun's growing popularity, particularly among his former critics and foes—the followers of Yi Hang-no and Ch'oe Ik-hyŏn—encouraged him and his supporters. In the summer of 1881, realizing that literati agitation alone would not restore him to power, the Taewŏn'gun and his supporters decided on a military coup to seize power. However, inept planning and their inability to raise a sufficient force foredoomed their plot to failure. The discovery of the plot by the government in September resulted in the swift arrest, imprisonment, and punishment of its leaders. While the Taewŏn'gun's position as father of the reigning monarch spared him open indictment and punishment, Yi Chae-sŏn, his eldest son by a concubine and the king's half-brother, who was allegedly the conspirators' candidate for the throne, was put to death.[25]

Despite its earlier positive response, such internal unrest and opposition prevented the Korean government from taking action on the proposed American treaty. When Shufeldt returned to China in the summer of 1881, Li had not yet received definite word from Seoul. At a meeting with Shufeldt on July 1, Li counseled the commodore to be patient, assuring him that the United States would eventually realize its wishes in Korea. A fortnight later he told Shufeldt that he had sent another letter to Seoul and that he expected a reply within ninety days. He advised Shufeldt

23. Yi Sŏn-gŭn, *Han'guksa ch'oegŭnse p'yŏn*, 451–456.
24. KJS, 18.31a–32b, 34b–35a.
25. For details, see Yi Sŏn-gŭn, *Han'guksa ch'oegŭnse*, 457–461.

to remain in Tientsin. It was not until January 1882, however, that Kim Yun-sik, a Korean envoy, arrived in China with the information for which Li and Shufeldt had been waiting.

A disciple of the late Pak Kyu-su, Kim Yun-sik was one of those young officials, such as Kim Hong-jip, whose moderate reformist views had begun to gain the confidence of Kojong. Kim's mission was ostensibly to lead a group of Korean students and apprentices to be trained at Tientsin, but he was secretly instructed to discuss the proposed United States treaty with Li.[26] After briefing Li on the political situation in Seoul at their first meeting, on January 17 at Li's winter headquarters in Paoting, Kim suggested that to enable the king to overcome domestic opposition to the proposed treaty the Ch'ing court should issue an edict commanding the king to sign it. Li rejected the suggestion on the ground that such an edict would be inappropriate and would leave Korea little room for bargaining with the United States. He instructed Kim to send a secret request to the king to send a high-ranking official with plenipotentiary power to Tientsin to negotiate with Shufeldt.[27] When Li went to Tientsin in mid-March, there was still no word from Seoul; Shufeldt announced his intention to go to Korea for direct talks with Korean authorities. Li thereupon decided to negotiate personally with Shufeldt on behalf of Korea. Negotiations between them began in late March. Although Kim Yun-sik was in Tientsin and was consulted by Li, he remained in the background, not taking part in the talks.

In the month-long negotiations that followed, Li was aided by Chou Fu, customs taotai at Tientsin, and Ma Chien-chung. Shufeldt was assisted by Chester Holcombe, American chargé d'affaires in China. Demonstrating their knowledge of international law and their diplomatic skill, Li and his lieutenants succeeded in obtaining terms for Korea

26. Kwŏn Sŏk-pong. "Yŏngsŏnsa-haeng," 278–279; Deuchler, *Confucian Gentlemen*, 118.

27. Kim Yun-sik, *Ŏmch'ŏngsa* (A diary), 47; LWCK, *Tsungli Yamen Letters*, 13.7b–8a.

better than those in China's treaties with Western powers or Korea's treaty with Japan. But a major disappointment to Li was his failure to persuade Shufeldt to accept a clause recognizing Chinese suzerainty over Korea. Li had previously rejected Ho Ju-chang's proposal that Korea be required to state in its future treaties that it was signing them at Chinese command. He now demanded an article declaring that Korea, "while being a dependent state of the Chinese empire, has nevertheless hitherto exercised her own sovereignty in all matters of internal administration and foreign relations." This was rejected by Shufeldt. Shufeldt agreed to seek instructions from Washington on whether such a declaration should be included in the proposed treaty, but he himself took the position that, as far as the United States was concerned, Korea was a sovereign and independent state, and whatever its relations with China, they had nothing to do with its future relations with the United States. Realizing that Washington was not likely to agree to such a clause, Li proposed a compromise formula whereby the Korean king would make the declaration in a separate note to the American president, should Washington reject its inclusion in the treaty. Shufeldt merely agreed to forward such a note to the president.[28] Although Li was anxious to preserve Chinese suzerainty over Korea under the tribute system, he apparently considered an American treaty with Korea more important at this time than an explicit reference therein to Sino-Korean tributary relations.

On April 16 a Korean emissary arrived in Tientsin with a letter from former Chief State Councilor Yi Ch'oe-ŭng, who was now in charge of the newly created Office for the Supervision of State Administration. This was the first time that Li had received a direct communication from a top Korean official active in governmental affairs since he had undertaken the task of guiding Korean foreign policy. Informing Li that two Korean officials were on their way to

28. LWCK, *Tsungli Yamen Letters*, 13.31a–32b; Chien, *Opening of Korea*, 84–85; Deuchler, *Confucian Gentlemen*, 119.

China to discuss the treaty matter, Yi thanked Li for his past guidance through his correspondence with Yi Yu-wŏn and stated that Korea "relied entirely" upon Li with regard to the proposed treaty. Li immediately wrote his reply, advising Yi that a good treaty between Korea and the United States would check Japanese designs on Korea. If declaration of Korea's status as a tributary of China could not be included in the proposed treaty, Li emphasized it was essential that Korea issue a separate statement affirming its tributary ties with China. Informing Yi that Shufeldt would leave for Korea, Li added that, at the request of Shufeldt and Kim Yun-sik, Ma Chien-chung and Admiral Ting Ju-ch'ang, commander of the Peiyang Navy, would go to Korea to mediate between Shufeldt and Korean officials.[29] Li gave his reply and a copy of the draft treaty to the Korean emissary and had a Chinese warship take him to the estuary of the Yalu River to expedite his return trip. He then obtained the throne's approval for Ma and Ting to go to Korea. Leaving Tientsin on May 3 with three Chinese warships, Ma and Ting reached Inch'ŏn on May 8.

It should be noted that the means by which Li put into execution China's new Korean policy was itself tradition-shattering: modern warships. Less dramatic but equally significant is the fact that for the first time in the history of Ch'ing-Korean relations, the Ch'ing court dispatched Han Chinese, not Manchu, officials as its principal representatives to Korea.

Shufeldt arrived at Inch'ŏn aboard the USS *Swatara* on May 11. Japanese Minister Hanabusa, who had been back to Tokyo for consultation, was anxious to learn what was taking place; he returned to Inch'ŏn a few days before the Chinese officials and the American envoy.

The Korean government, meanwhile, appointed Sin Hŏn and Kim Hong-jip chief and deputy negotiator to meet with Shufeldt. On May 14 Sin and Kim paid their first visit to Ma and Ting. Upon boarding Ting's flagship, the Korean

29. See Yi Ch'oe-ŭng's letter to Li Hung-chang and the latter's reply in LWCK, *Tsungli Yamen Letters,* 13.32b–34b; CJHK, vol. 2, 569–571.

officials performed the kowtow in the direction of the emperor in Peking and extended official greetings to Ma and Ting. Thereafter they went to the USS *Swatara* to greet Shufeldt. In subsequent negotiations, the Koreans proposed no substantial change in the draft treaty except for a ban on the export of rice from Inch'ŏn, which Shufeldt accepted. Declaration of Korea's tributary status vis-à-vis China was dropped from the text of the treaty at American insistence.[30]

The U.S.-Korean Treaty of Amity and Commerce, consisting of fourteen articles, was signed at Inch'ŏn on May 22, 1882. Article I of the treaty declared that, should either contracting party be treated unjustly and oppressively by other powers, the other would extend aid and its services in mediation. The article was included by Li as a check on Japanese and Russian designs on Korea. Article II provided for the mutual exchange of fully empowered diplomatic representatives between the two countries, a clause absent from Ma's original draft. It also provided for the exchange of consular representatives with the proviso that a consul must be a bona fide official and that his exequatur might be revoked if he acted improperly in the conduct of his duties. On the basis of their experience with the Western treaty powers, the Chinese negotiators included the clause to protect Korea from possible abuses by American consular officials. Article IV, while granting the right of extraterritoriality to American citizens in Korea, stated that the privilege would be abolished when necessary judicial reforms were instituted in Korea. Other provisions guaranteed Korea's autonomy in tariff matters, limited trade at open ports, and banned opium traffic and the export of rice through Inch'ŏn. Article XII declared that, the treaty "being the first one negotiated by Korea" and "hence general and incomplete in its provisions," further provisions might be negotiated after an interval of five years. This clause indi-

30. For a detailed account of the Li-Shufeldt negotiations, see Okudaira Takehiko, *Chōsen kaikoku kōshō shimatsu* (A complete account of the negotiations leading to the opening of Korea), 75–144.

cated that China and Korea both considered the treaty with the United States, not the Treaty of Kanghwa with Japan, to be the first step in opening the hermit kingdom to the outside world.[31]

Two days after the signing of the treaty, the Koreans, following Chinese advice, handed Shufeldt a short note from their king to the American president; it read in part: "Cho-sen [Korea] has been a state tributary to China from ancient times. Yet hitherto full sovereignty has been exercised by the king of Cho-sen in all matters of internal administration and foreign relations. Cho-sen and the United States, in establishing now by mutual consent a treaty, are dealing with each other upon a basis of equality. . . . As regards the various duties which devolve upon Cho-sen as a tributary state to China, with these the United States has no concern whatever." Dated May 15, 1882—one week earlier than the signing of the treaty—the note had been prepared by Ma.[32]

On May 27, five days after the signing of the United States-Korean treaty, Vice Admiral George O. J. Willes, commander of Britain's China Station, arrived at Inch'ŏn on a mission to obtain a treaty from Korea on behalf of the British government. He brought instructions from Peking ordering Ma, who was still in Korea, to mediate between Willes and Korean officials. Ma tried unsuccessfully to persuade Willes to accept a treaty which would formally affirm Korea's tributary status vis-à-vis China. On June 6, again with Ma acting as intermediary, the Koreans signed a treaty with Willes which was identical in form and content with the American treaty.[33] Ma left Korea for home two days later. Prior to his departure, he instructed the Koreans that, should other countries approach Korea for a treaty, they were to be told that in view of Korea's unfamiliarity with

31. For the Korean (Chinese) text of the treaty, see KJS, 19.21a–24b; CJHK, vol. 2, 611–616.

32. Ma Chien-chung, *Tung-hsing san-lu* (Record of three journeys to Korea), 17. For various English translations of the note, see M. Frederick Nelson, *Korea and the Old Orders in Eastern Asia*, 145–149; Okudaira, *Chōsen kaikoku kōshō*, 136–139.

33. On the negotiations leading to the signing of the Anglo-Korean treaty, see Okudaira, *Chōsen Kaikoku kōshō*, 145–148; Deuchler, *Confucian Gentlemen*, 122–125.

diplomatic affairs its treaty matters were handled mostly by
China, and anyone wishing to sign a treaty with Korea
should first go to Tientsin and ask the commissioner for the
northern ports to dispatch officials to Korea to supervise
treaty negotiations.[34] Late in June Ma returned to Korea
with German Minister to China Maximilian von Brandt to
mediate the signing of a treaty between Korea and Germany. The German-Korean treaty, also identical in content
to the United States-Korean treaty, was signed on June 30,
1882.[35] After signing the treaties, the Koreans handed the
British and German envoys a note from their king to the
British and German rulers identical to the note of May 15,
affirming Korea's tributary relationship with China.

Signing of these treaties in rapid succession was the
climax of the long and difficult effort to open Korea, an
effort initiated by France and the United States in the late
1860s and early 1870s, pushed forward by Japan in the
early and mid-1870s, and completed by China in the late
1870s and early 1880s. From beginning to end, Korea's first
treaties with Western powers had been masterminded and
negotiated by China under its new "treaty-system policy" for
Korea. Departing from its tradition of non-interference in
Korean affairs, the Ch'ing government intervened in
Korea's foreign affairs and virtually took over the entire
conduct of its foreign policy.

THE KOREAN SOLDIERS' RIOT
AND CHINESE INTERVENTION

With the signing of Korean treaties with the United States,
Britain, and Germany, the new Chinese policy for Korea
appeared to be successfully implemented. Within a few
short weeks, however, a dramatic turn of events in Korea
put Li's laboriously executed Korean strategy in jeopardy.
In mid-July a minor dispute between disgruntled soldiers
and corrupt granary clerks in Seoul resulted in a bloody

    34. Ma Chien-chung, *Tung-hsing san-lu*, 36.
    35. For the negotiations leading to the signing of the German-Korean treaty,
see Okudaira, *Chōsen kaikoku kōshō*, 150–152.

riot by the soldiers, when their appeal was summarily rejected and their leaders were jailed by Min Kyŏm-ho. Min was a relative of Queen Min and director of the Tribute Bureau, which was in charge of the distribution of stipend rice to the troops garrisoned in the capital. Angered by Min's action, the soldiers destroyed his mansion. Fearful of retaliation by the powerful Mins, the leaders of the riot appealed to the Taewŏn'gun for protection. This transformed a spontaneous riot by soldiers angered by officials' ill treatment into a political coup by the Taewŏn'gun and his followers, who were resentful of the queen and her relatives and who were unhappy with the growing Japanese presence in the country and the recent signing of treaties with Western powers.[36]

The Taewŏn'gun seized upon the riot as a long-awaited opportunity to regain power, an opportunity for which he had gone so far as to plot a coup himself only a year earlier. Although there is no record of his instructions to the leaders of the riot when they visited him, it seems obvious that it was at his instigation that they made their next bold moves, aiming at the removal of Queen Min and her relatives from power and the elimination of Japanese influence from the country. On July 23 the rioters, joined by other garrison troops and the mob in Seoul, destroyed several Min residences and burned down the Japanese legation. The following day they stormed the royal palace, looking for Queen Min. Although the mob believed mistakenly they had killed her, the queen managed to escape unharmed. On July 25 the Taewŏn'gun was summoned to the palace and given the task of suppressing the riot and restoring order. On his orders the rioting soldiers returned to their barracks; order was quickly restored in the capital. By a royal edict, which stated that "henceforth all governmental matters, large and small, shall be reported to the Taewŏn'gun for decision," he continued to exercise full powers.[37] Killed during the two-

36. For details concerning the riot, see Kwŏn Sŏk-pong, "Imo gunbyŏn" (The 1882 military riot), in Ch'oe Yŏng-hŭi, et al., eds., *Han'guksa*, vol. 16, 392–441.

37. ISN-KJ, 19/6/9; CJHK, vol. 2, 734–735; Yi Sŏn-gŭn, *Han'guksa ch'oegŭnse*, 479–487.

day rampage were Min Kyŏm-ho; Kim Po-hyŏn, governor of Kyŏnggi Province; and Yi Ch'oe-ŭng, the Taewŏn'gun's brother and former chief state councilor who had collaborated closely with the Mins. The mob also killed several Japanese, including an army second lieutenant who was serving as instructor for a newly created Western-style Korean army unit being trained with Japanese assistance.

When the mob attacked the Japanese legation, Minister Hanabusa and his staff fled to Inch'ŏn for safety. They were again attacked by local troops; six Japanese were killed and five wounded. Some two dozen Japanese managed to escape, were subsequently rescued by a British surveying ship, and reached Nagasaki on July 29. From there Hanabusa cabled his first report on the incident to Tokyo. On July 31 Li Shu-ch'ang, the new Chinese minister in Tokyo, learned of the incident from the Japanese Foreign Ministry. He immediately reported it by cable to Chang Shu-sheng, governor-general of Liang-Kwang and a former Anhwei Army commander, who was at this time acting as governor-general of Chihli and the commissioner for the northern ports.[38] Li Hung-chang had been on leave from these posts since April 1882 and was in Anhwei mourning his mother's death.

Reporting the Japanese government's decision to send warships to Korea in a follow-up cable, Minister Li urged the Chinese government to do the same to investigate the situation in Korea. Both cables reached Chang on August 1. Instructing Admiral Ting to have his warships ready to sail, Chang reported the matter to the Tsungli Yamen and requested approval for dispatch of the warships to Korea, as recommended by Minister Li. At the same time, Chang ordered Tientsin customs taotai Chou Fu to confer with Kim Yun-sik, who was still in Tientsin, to obtain the latter's views. Chou conferred with Kim the evening of August 1 and again the following morning, this time together with Ŏ Yun-jung, another Korean official who had come to China

38. CJHK, vol. 2, 734; P'eng, Tse-chou, *Meiji shoki Nik-Kan-Shin kankei no kenkyū,* 186–187.

earlier in connection with the American-Korean treaty. Although they had no information from Korea, Kim and Ŏ told Chou they were convinced that the Taewŏn'gun and his followers, who had plotted a similar move the year before, were behind the latest violence in Seoul, which caused the Japanese minister to flee the country. Fearful of Japanese retaliation, they urged strongly that China dispatch several warships and 1,000 troops to Korea without delay, in order to suppress the rebels and forestall retaliatory Japanese military action against Korea.[39]

On August 3 Chang Shu-sheng received another cable from Minister Li, reporting the departure of Japanese warships for Korea with "700 soldiers and 700 sailors." Adding that, although the Japanese government had not decided on war with Korea, public opinion had been inflamed and war preparations had started in Japan, Li again urged the dispatch of Chinese warships to Korea. Realizing the gravity of the situation, Chang addressed another message to the Tsungli Yamen, proposing that Admiral Ting be sent to Korea with two warships to observe Japanese activities and to investigate conditions in that country. Chang further proposed that, should the Korean government prove itself incapable of suppressing the rebels, China send an able commander with 2,000 Anhwei Army troops to Korea to do the job. The following day the Yamen gave its full consent to Chang. On August 5 Admiral Ting left Tientsin for Chefoo, where he was to be joined by Ma Chien-chung. On August 9 Ma and Ting, accompanied by Ŏ Yun-jung, departed from Chefoo with three European-built Chinese warships; they reached Inch'ŏn the following night. A Japanese warship had arrived earlier that day.[40]

On the same day that Admiral Ting and Ŏ left Tientsin, Chou Fu and Kim Yun-sik held another meeting to discuss the Korean situation. Kim again stated his belief that the

39. P'eng, *Nik-Kan-Shin kankei*, 187–191. See Kim's own account of his talks with Chou Fu in Kim Yun-sik, *Ŏmch'ŏngsa*, 177–179, and a Chinese and perhaps more accurate account of the same in CJHK, vol. 2, 749–751.
40. CJHK, vol. 2, 748, 766.

Taewŏn'gun was the ringleader of the rebels in Seoul and denounced the latter's character and "past crimes" in strong terms. Chou expressed suspicion that, despite his outward hostility toward the Japanese, the Taewŏn'gun might collaborate with them in order to consolidate his position. Kim rejected this as inconceivable, and he argued that it was unlikely the Taewŏn'gun would accept Japanese terms for settlement of the incident and that the Japanese almost certainly would land troops in Korea in the name of suppressing the rebels. Even after the rebels had been suppressed, the Japanese would go on interfering in Korea's affairs. It was to prevent such an eventuality, Kim emphasized, that he urged China to send warships and troops to Korea; China alone was in a position to deal with the crisis in the peninsula without risking war.[41]

Chou Fu's advice undoubtedly influenced Chang Shusheng's thinking on the crisis. Acting on Chang's communications, the Tsungli Yamen memorialized the throne for approval of the dispatch of warships and troops to Korea, as recommended by Chang. Quoting him, the Yamen ministers stated that Japan had long been seeking to establish control over Korea and that many Koreans had collaborated with the Japanese. Should Japan be allowed to suppress the rebels on behalf of the Korean government, these pro-Japanese Koreans would take advantage of the Japanese action and thereby gain a dominant position in the Korean government. This would certainly raise Japanese influence and damage China's authority in Korea. Therefore China, the memorialists argued, should immediately send ships and troops to Korea to safeguard Korea and to fulfill China's obligations under the treaty of 1871 to protect Japanese in Chinese territory. The throne approved the memorial on August 7 and ordered Chang to proceed with his plans. Taking a very serious view of the situation, the throne also ordered Li Hung-chang to cut short his leave and to return to his post in Tientsin.[42]

41. For accounts of Kim's talks with Chou Fu on August 5, see *ibid*, 769–772; Kim Yun-sik, *Ŏmch'ŏngsa*, 180–183.

42. CKCJ, 3.30b–32b; CJHK, vol. 2, 764–765. For the edict ordering Li to return to his post, see CJHK, vol. 2, 777.

Upon reaching Inch'ŏn on the night of August 10, Ma Chien-chung asked Ŏ Yun-jung to contact a local garrison commander immediately for information. However, Ŏ was unable to obtain specific information. The following morning Ma and Admiral Ting were visited by Kondō Masuki, the Japanese consul who fled to Japan earlier but subsequently returned to Inch'ŏn with an advance Japanese party. Kondō told them Queen Min had been "murdered" by the mob and the Taewŏn'gun had seized power. Ma conferred with Ŏ at length. Condemning the Taewŏn'gun in the same vein as did Kim Yun-sik in his talks with Chou Fu, Ŏ charged that the Taewŏn'gun had constantly schemed to regain power ever since his forced retirement. Taking advantage of his "invulnerable" position as father of the king, he had repeatedly set fire to the royal palace and murdered loyal officials while enticing the "ignorant masses" with anti-foreign slogans. He seized power now, Ŏ went on, by following the scenario which he prepared for his aborted coup the year before—first murdering the king's trusted officials, then attacking the royal palace to eliminate the queen, and, finally, killing Japanese. Though not deposed, the king was but a prisoner in his own palace; officials in charge of foreign relations were killed; and people fled to the mountains. If action was not taken immediately, Ŏ warned, the Japanese would launch massive retaliation; the Taewŏn'gun would mobilize troops in a determined defense, causing untold miseries to the populace and endangering the fate of the Yi dynasty.[43] Ŏ and Kim made these damaging charges against the Taewŏn'gun largely on the basis of conjecture and their own prejudices rather than on the basis of impartial or factual investigation. Ma prepared his initial report to Chang Shu-sheng chiefly on the basis of Ŏ's testimony. Reaching Chang on August 14, the report urged him to take immediate action on his own authority: to memorialize the throne and, at the same time, to issue an order for six Chinese battalions to be sent to Korea on naval ships.[44]

Having decided on a policy of intervention, Chang acted

43. CJHK, vol. 3, 798–804; Ma Chien-chung, *Tung-hsing san-lu*, 56–57.
44. Ma Chien-chung, *Tung-hsing san-lu*, 57–60; CJHK, vol. 3, 789–792.

on the throne's approval granted on August 7 and even before he received Ma's report, Chang contacted General Wu
Ch'ang-ch'ing, commander of the six Anhwei Army battalions stationed in Shantung, and obtained the latter's consent
to go to Korea with his troops. The question remaining was
what to do with the Taewŏn'gun. Kim Yun-sik suggested
that the Chinese troops surround the Taewŏn'gun's residence and obtain an order from Queen Dowager Cho citing
his "crimes" and condemning him to death. Hsüeh Fu-
ch'eng, a member of Li Hung-chang's personal secretariat,
proposed that the Taewŏn'gun be arrested and brought to
China. In a letter to Chang, Hsüeh outlined contingency
plans which might be used by Chinese commanders in
Korea, including one to capture the Taewŏn'gun. Hsüeh,
too, was of the opinion that if the Taewŏn'gun resisted by
force, he might be put to death by order of the queen dowager. Urging swift action, Hsüeh emphasized that it was essential that China forestall the anticipated Japanese move
that might turn Korea into another Ryūkyū.[45] Hsüeh's
recommendation, together with Ma's report from Korea,
virtually sealed the political fate of the Taewŏn'gun.

Meanwhile, Hanabusa returned to Inch'ŏn from Japan
on August 12 to begin talks with the Korean government.
Japanese forces accompanying him consisted of four warships, three transports, and one infantry battalion. Brushing
aside a Korean government request for delay, Hanabusa
proceeded to Seoul on August 16 with a large military
escort. On August 20 he had an audience with Kojong.
Departing from diplomatic protocol, the Japanese envoy
presented a seven-point ultimatum from the Japanese
government directly to the Korean ruler. Included in it
were demands for the punishment of those responsible
for the attacks on the Japanese legation and personnel,
compensation for Japanese lives and property lost during
the riot, and new diplomatic and commercial concessions in
Korea. An answer was demanded in three days. After the

45. Hsüeh Fu-ch'eng, *Hsüeh Fu-ch'eng ch'üan-chi*, vol. 1, 2.33a–35b.

royal audience, Hanabusa met with the Taewŏn'gun, at the latter's request. Apparently the Taewŏn'gun tried to reassure Hanabusa by stating that, in view of the changing times, Korea would not necessarily return to its earlier exclusionist policy.[46]

Waiting for the arrival of Chinese forces at Inch'ŏn, Ma met several times with Ŏ Yun-jung, as well as Cho Yŏng-ha and Kim Hong-jip, whom the Korean government had appointed chief and deputy reception officer to meet with both Chinese and Japanese officials. There is no extant record of the talks between Ma and the two Korean reception officers. But the talks apparently were damaging to the Taewŏn'gun. Ma wrote in his diary that the record of the "pen talks" had been destroyed—presumably to protect the Korean officials from possible leakage—and that after the talks he had become more certain of the "guilt of the rebels."[47] Ma also was visited by Takezoe Shin'ichirō, a Japanese Foreign Ministry official accompanying Hanabusa. Takezoe told Ma that Japanese public opinion had been inflamed by the Korean outrage, but, remembering its own experience two decades earlier when Japan opened its doors to Western nations, the Japanese government wished to settle the matter with Korea peacefully. He assured Ma that the Japanese government had no territorial designs on Korea. Ma stressed that, in view of Korea's poverty and the unsettled conditions in the country, the Japanese government should be forbearing and lenient in dealing with the Korean government.[48]

On August 20 General Wu and Admiral Ting arrived in Korea with 2,000 troops. Kim Yun-sik accompanied them, as their guide. Since there were several Japanese warships at Inch'ŏn, a debarkation point was chosen for the Chinese forces at Namyang, to the south. Upon arrival there, the Chinese commanders were joined by Ma and greeted by Cho Yŏng-ha and Kim Hong-jip. The following day, August

46. TNS, vol. 1, 800–807.
47. Ma Chien-chung, *Tung-hsing san-lu*, 61–64.
48. *Ibid.*, 64–67; TNS, vol. 1, 841–843.

21, Ma received an urgent message from the Taewŏn'gun, informing him of the Japanese ultimatum and requesting Ma's arrival in Seoul to mediate between the Korean government and Hanabusa. Accompanied by Cho, Ma left for Seoul on August 22; he reached there the following day. The Taewŏn'gun personally greeted Ma upon his arrival; the two had a cordial "pen talk."[49]

The following day Ma made a hurried trip to Inch'ŏn to confer with Hanabusa, who had withdrawn there angrily the previous day, when the Korean government requested postponement of the scheduled talks between him and Chief State Councilor Hong Sun-mok. Urging the Japanese envoy to reconsider his hasty action, Ma told him that, as long as the Taewŏn'gun remained in power, there could be no fruitful and binding negotiations with the Korean government; the most urgent thing to do was to restore the king's personal rule. Ma made clear the intention of the Ch'ing government to remove the Taewŏn'gun from power.[50]

On August 25 Ma returned to Seoul. General Wu and Admiral Ting also reached the Korean capital with their troops that day. The Chinese forces encountered no resistance from the Koreans. On August 26, according to carefully made plans, Ma and the two Chinese commanders paid a courtesy visit to the Taewŏn'gun at his residence. They were cordially received. Late that afternoon the Taewŏn'gun returned their call, by visiting them at Chinese headquarters. In the course of another "cordial" talk between him and Ma, the Taewŏn'gun was suddenly accused of usurping power from the king, the only ruler vested with legitimate authority by the Ch'ing emperor. He was told bluntly that he must go to Tientsin immediately and await imperial sanction. He was put forcibly into a sedan chair and whisked away by waiting Chinese soldiers to Namyang, under the cover of night. He was put aboard a Chinese warship the following day and taken to Tientsin.[51]

49. Ma Chien-chung, *Tung-hsing san-lu*, 68–71.

50. *Ibid.*, 71–72; CJHK, vol. 3, 845.

51. On the abduction of the Taewŏn'gun, see Dong Jae Yim, "The Abduction of the Taewŏn'gun, 1882," *Papers on China* 21 (February 1968), 99–130.

In Seoul, meanwhile, the political status quo ante was restored: Kojong resumed his personal rule; the Chinese troops hunted down and executed the ringleaders of the riot; Queen Min returned to Seoul from her country hideout; her surviving relatives regained their increasingly dominant position in the government. Although Japanese representatives refused to negotiate with him directly or officially, it was Ma Chien-chung who masterminded the subsequent negotiations, which quickly led to a Japanese-Korean settlement by the Treaty of Chemulp'o on August 30, 1882.[52]

Using its newly acquired modern warships and weapons and its military strength as compared to Japan, China acted with decisiveness and dispatch. The Ch'ing government decided to intervene in Korean domestic politics within a week of receipt of the first report on the riot in Seoul. Precisely one month after he had been restored to power, the Taewŏn'gun was forcibly taken to China. These unprecedented actions were taken without prior consultation with or a formal request from the Korean government. Although Kim Yun-sik and Ŏ Yun-jung were consulted, neither of them had the proper authority or was of sufficient rank to speak and act for the Korean government. Moreover, although the views of Korean officials no doubt reinforced their own, the Chinese authorities made their decisions independent of the recommendations of the former.

No doubt the Ch'ing government would have preferred to let the Korean government handle the crisis on its own. Some officials, such as Chou Fu, appeared reluctant initially to intervene in Korea, preferring to wait, at least, until the Korean government requested such action. However, the gravity of the crisis, the urgency of the situation, and, especially, the belief that the Korean government could not be fully relied upon to deal with the Japanese in a satisfactory manner prompted China to decisive, unilateral action. The Ch'ing government feared that under the Taewŏn'gun

52. For details concerning the negotiation of the treaty, see TNS, vol. 1, 812–828; P'eng, *Nik-Kan-Shin kankei*, 235–246; Kwŏn Sŏk-pong, "Imo gunbyŏn," 430–441; Deuchler, *Confucian Gentlemen*, 134–138.

Korea would abrogate the newly signed treaties with Western powers and thereby frustrate the new Chinese policy of
protecting Korea and the Chinese position in the peninsula
by a treaty system. Even more, China feared that the impending showdown between Japan and Korea would result
in war or, conceivably, in Japanese-Korean collaboration,
either of which would lead to Japanese ascendancy in the
peninsula, to the detriment of Chinese interests and the
safety of north China and Manchuria.

Viewing the melodrama of July-August 1882 in terms of
a power struggle between the Taewŏn'gun and his supporters on the one hand and Queen Min and her relatives on
the other, some historians have characterized such men as
Kim Yun-sik, Ŏ Yun-jung, Cho Yŏng-ha, and Kim Hong-jip
as partisans supporting the Mins.[53] Yet there is no reason to
doubt that these four Korean officials were patriotic men of
intelligence and integrity. Their views and actions were prej-
udicial to the Taewŏn'gun and contributed to the restoration of the power of the Mins. Still, none of these four men
can be considered a pure Min partisan. Rather, each was a
relatively young official who enjoyed the confidence of the
young Kojong and who played an important role in Korea's
incipient reforms, including the establishment of relations
with Western nations. While they may not have been free of
partisanship, on the whole they acted with the honest conviction that, if restored to power, the Taewŏn'gun would
take the country in a ruinous direction by undoing the new
reforms they had initiated with Kojong's support, by an-
tagonizing Japan again, and by reimposing isolation upon
the country.[54]

Negotiating on Korea's behalf its first treaties with Western powers, China made a major departure from the
tradition of non-interference in Korea's affairs under the
tribute system. The action transformed China's traditional

53. For a summary of scholarly views on these men, see P'eng, *Nik-Kan-Shin
kankei*, 200–204, 208–212.
54. For Kim Yun-sik's views, see CJHK, vol. 2, 771–772; for Ŏ Yun-jung's
views, see Ma Chien-chung, *Tung-hsing san-lu*, 64.

ceremonial authority over Korea into substantive authority. As of May 1882, however, Chinese intervention in Korea's affairs was still limited to an advisory role in the latter country's foreign relations. But the soldiers' riot in Seoul created a real possibility of imminent Japanese intervention and raised the specter of Japanese ascendancy in the peninsula. An unfortunate chain of events ensued. By its unilateral intervention in Korean domestic politics in July-August 1882, China transformed its newly enhanced authority in Korea from an advisory role to a new form of political control. Instead of preserving tradition or the status quo in Sino-Korean relations, the Ch'ing actions in Korea in the summer of 1882 brought about a metamorphosis in China's role as Korea's suzerain. It marked the beginning of a new phase in Sino-Korean relations, an era of Chinese political domination over the court in Seoul.

CHAPTER IX

Conclusion: Toward an
International Order in East Asia

Entry of China and Japan into the Western international
system during the middle decades of the nineteenth century
caused revolutionary changes in international relations in
East Asia. The treaties that each of the East Asian countries
accepted from Western powers, however, did not bring an
immediate end to the ancient world order that had
flourished in that part of the world for some two millennia.
The Western system was superimposed upon the preexist-
ing East Asian system of conducting interstate relations. Initially, the new system applied only to relations between each
of the East Asian countries on the one hand and Western
nations on the other. Relations between East Asian states
and peoples continued to be governed by the traditional
East Asian system based on the ancient Chinese cosmology,
which recognized the Chinese emperor as the Son of
Heaven and suzerain of a universal empire (with the
Japanese emperor sometimes posing as a rival claimant). As
of the 1860s, the Western system, potent as it was, had not
been accepted by all countries of East Asia. Korea, one of
the region's major states, remained outside the new system.
The "long twilight" of the Chinese tribute system[1] gave the
existing world order in East Asia a dualistic character that
was partly Eastern and partly Western, partly traditional

1. John K. Fairbank, "The Early Treaty System in the Chinese World Order,"
in John K. Fairbank, ed., *The Chinese World Order,* 263–269.

328

and partly modern. It was not until the early 1880s that this duality disappeared, though even then not completely. The ultimate demise of the old world order in East Asia came largely as a result of the developments which we have examined in the preceding chapters and of such other events as the French seizure of Vietnam in the mid-1880s.

Korea, the most "Confucian" of East Asian societies outside the Chinese heartland, had long been regarded as China's model tributary. In the middle of the nineteenth century, despite China's acceptance of treaties with Western powers which stipulated equal status between the Son of Heaven and Western heads of state, Korea remained the most loyal of the Ch'ing dynasty's vassal states, sending its annual tributary missions to Peking without fail. The Korean peninsula was, moreover, of prime strategic importance to the security of north China and Manchuria, particularly after the Russian seizure of the land east of the Ussuri River in 1860 and the rise of Meiji Japan a decade later. Yet continued Western expansionism, emulated by the newly unified Japanese state, was to challenge Korea's accustomed isolation and China's authority over the peninsula. The resulting opening of the hermit kingdom — attempted by France in 1866 and by the United States in 1871, pushed forward by Japan in 1876, but consummated only in 1882 by a series of treaties with Western powers negotiated by China—marked the end of a transitional period, the last phase of the East Asian world order.

Korea's transition from a Ch'ing tributary to a member of the international community may be viewed in three phases, each representing a change in the policies of the countries, Western and East Asian, which had an interest in the peninsular kingdom. The first of these phases comprised the events that led to the French expedition to Korea in 1866 and the American expedition in 1871, the same year that saw Japan concluding its first treaty with China, at least partly for the sake of gaining a status superior to Korea. The moves on the part of France, the United States, and Japan must be regarded as no more than probing actions, which left the international situation surrounding Korea largely unchanged. The second phase commenced with Japan's effort, through attempted treaty revision, to attain equal status with Western powers, even vis-à-vis China. Inspired by incipient expansionism, Japan succeeded, by a Perry-like expedition, in wresting from Korea the Treaty of Kanghwa in 1876. During this period, relations between China, Japan, and Korea underwent rapid and vast changes for the first time, largely as a result of the growing Western orientation of Japanese foreign policy and its new expansionism. The following six years, until the signing of Korea's first treaties with the United States, Britain, and Germany in 1882, constituted the third and final phase, during which the Ch'ing empire, in response to a growing threat to Korea from Russia and Japan, developed a new policy toward the peninsula that represented an unprecedented departure from its traditional non-interference in Korea's affairs. This new Chinese policy brought about Korea's entry into the Western international system and ushered in a new international order in East Asia.

During the first stage of Korea's transition, there were no appreciable changes in the existing relations between China, Japan, and Korea. Although China had repeatedly suffered defeat and humiliation at the hands of Western powers, it still remained the Celestial Empire, whose authority and supremacy were not challenged by any East Asian country. Nor did China exhibit any inclination or desire to alter or relinquish its traditional suzerainty over the East Asian world. There is no indication that the Ch'ing government of this period considered China's old relations with East Asian states and peoples under the tribute system incompatible with its new relations with Western nations under the treaty system. Ch'ing "diplomatic adaptability" in this period amounted to little more than growing knowledge and skill in the art of diplomatic accommodation with Western powers. In no way did it indicate a significant change in China's concept of relations with its East Asian tributaries.

The resistance to change was even more complete with Korea. Shackled by cultural chauvinism and ignorant of the growing might of the Western world, Korea clung to the "Confucian dream world" and its centuries-old isolation. To be sure, Christianity managed to defy official persecution for nearly a century, but this defiance merely convinced the Korean government of the danger of the alien faith, which presented a fundamental challenge to the Neo-Confucian socio-political views of the Korean elite. The Korean government was convinced that Christianity was part of a general Western conspiracy to seize Korea either through internal subversion or by external attack. The Korean officials viewed China's accommodation with Western powers with strong disapproval. Influenced by persistent Ming loyalism and anti-Manchu sentiment, they believed that the lamentable state of affairs in China had been brought about by Manchu corruption in general and by Prince Kung's personal depravity in particular. Even more repugnant to them was Japan's effort to emulate the West, which they regarded as proof of Japanese treachery and betrayal of Eastern culture and tradition.[2] They found the new Japanese imperial regime's claim of superiority over Korea preposterous and insulting. Supported by a solid consensus among the ruling elite, the Taewŏn'gun maintained a rigid exclusionist policy against Western nations and an uncompromising stand against Japan. The repulsion of the French and American expeditionary forces strengthened his belief that Korea could expel any Western intruders.

Japan remained equally "traditional" as far as its attitude toward its East Asian neighbors was concerned. While there were some changes in the Japanese views of China and Korea in the 1860s, they were mostly "retrogressive" in nature, inspired chiefly by the spirit of imperial restoration at home. As political authority was restored to Japan's ancient monarchy in the late 1860s, an old indigenous myth gained

2. For the Korean view of the Japanese in this period, see Hatada Takashi, "Kindai ni okeru Chōsenjin no Nihonkan" (The Korean view of the Japanese in modern times), *Shisō* 520 (October 1967), 59–73.

popularity and official sanction. It was asserted that, as a divine land ruled by an unbroken imperial line, Japan rather than China was destined to preside over the world. Influenced, moreover, by the widely held view that the early Korean kingdoms had been tributaries of Yamato Japan, leaders of the new Japanese regime believed that the restoration of imperial rule at home should logically be followed by a restoration of Japan's ancient "overlordship" over Korea. Such a policy created an immediate diplomatic problem for Korea and posed a potential challenge to Chinese authority in the peninsula. Nevertheless, it fell within the traditional East Asian concept of hierarchical interstate relations.

Reflecting the transitional political structure that had come into being with the restoration of imperial rule, initial Meiji policy toward Korea was a mixture of Japan's resurgent imperial tradition and feudal legacy. It was as full of contradictions as it was unrealistic. Despite the lofty position it assumed toward Korea, the new imperial regime could not immediately take over the management of Korean affairs. Implementation of its Korean policy was left almost entirely in the hands of Tsushima. On its part Tsushima wished to retain the diplomatic and trading privileges in Korea which it had traditionally enjoyed as the intermediary in Japanese-Korean relations. Although the retention of these privileges was contingent upon the continuation of its semi-tributary obligations toward Korea, Tsushima renounced these obligations unilaterally because the new Japanese regime would not permit such practices. From the Korean standpoint, neither the new Japanese regime's claim of superiority nor Tsushima's new self-assertion was acceptable. It was not Korea's intransigence and its ignorance of modern international relations alone that were responsible for the Japanese-Korean diplomatic feud that followed the restoration of imperial rule in Japan. The Meiji government's initial "restoration diplomacy" was at least equally responsible, for it was in fact as anachronistic and unrealistic as the contemporary Korean government's insistence that the two countries continue the same form and practice in the conduct of their relations as they had used during the Tokugawa period.[3]

Repeatedly rebuffed by Korea, Japan sought a treaty with China in order to establish its titular equality with the Middle Kingdom, at least partly as the means to secure for itself a status superior to Korea. Although the resultant Sino-Japanese treaty of 1871 had epoch-making significance in the modernization of international relations in East Asia, the traditional East Asian concept of hierarchical relations between states was still implied, since Japan had sought the treaty initially to gain equality with China and thus titular superiority over Korea. Japan's claim of suzerainty over Ryūkyū, to be put forward dramatically three years later, was also based on a hierarchical concept.

Throughout the 1860s there was neither a serious external threat to Korea nor a real challenge to China's traditional authority in the peninsula. Although the French and American expeditions to Korea resulted in armed clashes, they were undertaken largely in retaliation for the Korean maltreatment of French missionaries and American sailors. Neither expedition represented a determined effort to invade Korea or to end its isolation. While France and the United States both demanded from China an intelligible definition of Sino-Korean relations which would be acceptable under Western international law, as of the 1860s neither country rejected outright Chinese suzerainty over Korea. In keeping with the tradition of non-interference in Korea's affairs, the Ch'ing government refused to intervene in Korea's disputes with France and the United States. Nor did the Tsungli Yamen believe at this time that France or the United States posed a real threat to Korea. The East Asian interstate order, though significantly altered, plainly

3. For an analysis of early Meiji policy toward Korea, see Mōri Toshihiko, "Meiji shoki gaikō no Chōsenkan" (The Japanese view of Korea in early Meiji diplomacy), *Kokusai seiji* 51 (1974), 25–42.

remained largely intact in the 1860s. This generalization applies not only to Korea, but also to Ryūkyū and Vietnam, and, in a different geopolitical context, to Inner Asia.[4]

A potential problem for China and Korea, however, was the rise of Japanese continental interest and expansionism. While proposals for sending expeditions to Korea in bakumatsu and early Meiji Japan were no more than rhetoric inspired either by the fear of Western aggression or by domestic political exigencies, they nevertheless reflected a persistent desire to extend Japan's power or influence to the Korean peninsula—and beyond. In contrast to its general complacency toward the Western threat to Korea, the Ch'ing government was alert to any sign of Japanese ambition or interest in the peninsula, as was seen in the Tsungli Yamen's reaction to the Hachinohe affair in 1867. At a time when few considered Japan capable of seriously challenging China, Prince Kung and his associates reacted immediately to the rumors of a Japanese expedition to Korea, going so far as to declare that any Japanese threat to Korea was a threat to China. In 1870 the fear of Japanese-Western collaboration against China was the principal factor that persuaded the Ch'ing government to grant the Japanese demand for a treaty, in spite of strong domestic opposition and misgivings about the consequences of such a treaty for the future of Sino-tributary relations in East Asia.

As Korea's transition entered its second stage, the potential Japanese threat became a real one for China and Korea. Between 1871 and 1876 Japan undertook a series of bold and well-coordinated diplomatic and military ventures in East Asia. It forced Ryūkyū to terminate its tributary missions to China, sent an expedition to Taiwan, and imposed a treaty upon Korea virtually at gunpoint, thereby challenging squarely hitherto undisputed Chinese supremacy in East Asia. As Japan embraced the Western concept and practice in the conduct of international relations, its traditional

---

4. For China's position in Inner Asia in this period, see Joseph Fletcher, "The Heyday of the Ch'ing Order in Mongolia, Sinkiang, and Tibet," in Denis Twitchett and John K. Fairbank, eds., *The Cambridge History of China*, vol. 10, 351–408.

concept of suzerain-vassal relationship gave way to a new impulse for predatory expansion. Leaders of the Meiji government wished to establish a new identity for Japan in the Western mold.[5] They believed that the domestic reforms instituted since the restoration of imperial rule had transformed Japan into an "advanced" modern state and put it in the same category as Western nations. It was their view that in dealing with "backward" countries, such as China and Korea, Japan deserved the status and privileges enjoyed by Western powers. Earlier diplomatic goals, such as titular equality with China and superiority over Korea, were discarded in favor of practical modern advantages, such as extraterritoriality and most-favored-nation treatment. Diplomatic and commercial parity with Western powers became the primary goal of Japanese diplomacy in East Asia. Although Japan's initial attempt to achieve this ambitious goal failed in 1872, when China rejected its demand for the revision of the 1871 treaty between the two countries, Japan achieved the goal in Korea by the Treaty of Kanghwa in 1876.

It should be emphasized that, aside from institutional forms in foreign relations, Japan in this period also emulated European-style expansionism. Partly with Western encouragement, Japan's nascent expansionism went beyond the realm of speculation and rhetoric.[6] It was manifested in concrete action in such events as the *sei-Kan* controversy in 1873, the Taiwan expedition in 1874, the consolidation of exclusive jurisdiction over Ryūkyū in 1875, the *Unyō* incident later that year, and the showdown with Korea early in 1876. While an impulse for expansion was behind these Japanese actions, they were also caused by domestic political exigencies. The correlation between domestic politics and

5. For changes in the Japanese view of foreign relations in this period, see Marius B. Jansen, "Modernization and Foreign Policy in Meiji Japan," in Robert E. Ward, ed., *Political Development in Modern Japan,* 149–188.

6. For the influence of Americans such as Charles LeGendre and Charles E. De Long, see Hilary Conroy, *The Japanese Seizure of Korea, 1868–1910,* 37–41. See also Sandra Caruthers Thomson, "Filibustering to Formosa: General Charles LeGendre and the Japanese," *Pacific Historical Review* 40.4 (November 1971), 442–456.

overseas expansion was nowhere more clearly visible than in early Meiji policy toward Korea.

Many Japanese political leaders in this period regarded Korea more as a Japanese frontier than as a foreign country. They often regarded policy toward Korea as a domestic issue. In times of tension or crisis, politicians in and out of power exploited the "Korean question" for the sake of securing domestic political advantage—as did the early *sei-Kan* advocates in the bakumatsu period, Kido in the immediate post-Restoration days, Saigō and his supporters in 1873, and Ōkubo in 1875. At the root of all this lay the widely held belief, virtually a national consensus, that Japan must extend its power and influence to the Korean peninsula in one way or another if it was to survive as an independent nation in an age of Western expansionism. Hilary Conroy emphasized, in his seminal study of Meiji policy toward Korea, that leaders of the Japanese government in this period had no plot or plan to "seize" Korea.[7] This does not mean that their attitudes, views, and actions were not expansionist toward Korea, for expansion could take different forms and be of varying degrees. Moreover, what the Japanese regarded as their legitimate or enlightened national interest could have been expansionist and predatory in nature, if seen from the Korean or Chinese standpoint. While Conroy's theme of realism versus idealism is valuable, this distinction alone does not seem to explain fully the nature of Meiji Japan's policy toward Korea in its early phase; the seizure of Korea that was to come in 1910 may, in fact, be seen as the culmination of that policy. Korea's role in Japanese domestic politics and its importance to Japanese security interests, along with Japan's ever-present desire to extend influence or control to the peninsula, formed the basic mental framework within which most Japanese political leaders formulated their proposals and made their policies with regard to Korea. Their objectives, plans, and actions at any given time could be determined or changed

---

7. Conroy, *Japanese Seizure of Korea, passim.*

"realistically" or otherwise, depending on the exigencies of domestic politics and international circumstances. However, as seen in the facts presented in this study, a basic Japanese mentality regarding Korea was evident in the 1870s.

The early 1870s saw little change in Korea's own ex-clusionist policy. The American expedition intensified rather than weakened the anti-Western xenophobia of Korean officials and literati. Meanwhile, the suspicion grew among Korean authorities that the Japanese were collaborating with Western powers against Korea. The Taewŏn'gun's anti-Western and anti-Japanese foreign policy continued to enjoy solid support. But his pragmatic approach to government and his domestic reforms, especially those aimed at strengthening royal power and central authority at the expense of the vested interests and privileges of the *yangban* class, caused increasing resentment and oppposition from the more orthodox Confucian literati. Also, his son, King Kojong, developed his own ambitions as ruler as he reached manhood. The king's majority, along with literati discontent, forced the Taewŏn'gun into involuntary retirement at the end of 1873.

Kojong's assumption of personal rule did not bring a change in Korea's exclusionist policy against Western nations. However, there began to be a reduction of official Korean hostility toward Japan. Concerned over the violent *sei-Kan* disturbances in Japan and its expedition to Taiwan, Kojong and his ministers wished to end the running feud with Korea's island neighbor at a time when the peninsular kingdom was facing growing dangers from the West. The fear of a rumored Japanese invasion, reinforced by an official Chinese warning in mid-1874, was the principal factor behind the Korean government's decision to effect a reconciliation with Japan. Nevertheless, the decision did not mean that Kojong's government was ready to accept the Japanese demand for new and broadened relations based on Western international law. It merely indicated the desire of Kojong and his ministers to ameliorate the existing antagonism between the two countries, which they thought had been caused at least partly by the Taewŏn'gun's excessive hostility and intransigence. Kojong and his ministers believed that the Japanese could be mollified and peace could be preserved between the two countries if Korea simply treated Japan with courtesy and goodwill.

Growing anti-Japanese agitation in Korea prevented Kojong's government from proceeding quickly with the actual reconciliation with Japan. Meanwhile, the Korean government's insistence on traditional practice and usage in the conduct of Japanese-Korean diplomacy exasperated the Japanese. Moreover, whatever conciliatory posture Kojong had shown the Japanese merely encouraged intransigence on the part of the Japanese government, which was becoming increasingly confident of its ability to "handle" Korea in the flush of its success in Taiwan. As a result, Japan's Korean policy shifted from the conciliatory approach adopted after the *sei-Kan* crisis of 1873 to intimidatory gunboat diplomacy, which culminated in the *Unyō* incident in September 1875. This tactical shift in Japanese policy and, especially, the timing of the *Unyō* incident were closely linked to the Ōkubo regime's maneuvers for neutralizing domestic political opposition.

The Treaty of Kanghwa was significant in two important respects. First, it was a major institutional wedge driven into the existing world order in East Asia. Japan and Korea, the two East Asian states which had hitherto conducted their relations with each other under the traditional East Asian concept of interstate relations and on the basis of a common acknowledgment of Chinese supremacy, were now to conduct their relations on the basis of treaties and of Western international law. Moreover, by formally declaring Korea's equality with Japan, which had already established its own equality with China, the treaty technically put Korea in the same category as China under Western international law. It represented an indirect Japanese challenge to traditional Chinese suzerainty over Korea under the tribute system. Japan thus took the position of rejecting Chinese authority in Korea while using its own similar authority in

Ryūkyū as the legal basis for placing the island kingdom under Japanese control. Second, quite apart from consideration of the tribute system, the Treaty of Kanghwa threatened China's advantage of having in Korea a stable buffer state. The treaty provided Japan with a solid diplomatic and commercial base from which it could compete and challenge China for influence and control in an area vital to Ch'ing strategic interests

In contrast to the activism and change that characterized Japanese policy toward Korea in the early and mid-1870s, inaction continued to mark Chinese policy toward the peninsula in the same period. There was, however, growing concern behind inaction. Beginning with the Tientsin Massacre of 1870, which destroyed what little had remained of the Western "cooperative policy" toward China, the Ch'ing government faced one crisis after another in its foreign relations. Beset by its own internal and external problems, including the large-scale rebellions in the northwestern provinces and Sinkiang, the Ch'ing court had neither time nor resources to concern itself with Korea. Li Hung-chang, however, remained watchful for any sign of Japanese ambition toward the peninsula. Every expansionist Japanese action elsewhere alerted him to possible similar Japanese action against Korea. Particularly alarming was the Japanese expedition to Taiwan, which revealed Japan's growing ambitions and power and China's appalling weakness in naval strength and coastal defense.

In late 1874 Li's concern prompted him to submit an important memorial to the throne, which touched off within the Ch'ing government the celebrated policy debate over maritime and Inner Asian frontier defense.[8] Emphasizing the gravity of the unprecedented threat to China posed by Japan as well as Western maritime powers, Li argued forcefully and persuasively for a large-scale naval expansion and

8. For details, see Immanuel C. Y. Hsü, "The Great Policy Debate in China, 1874: Maritime vs. Frontier Defense," *Harvard Journal of Asiatic Studies* 25 (1964–65), 212–228; Liu Shih-chi, "Ch'ing-chi hai-fang yü se-fang chih cheng ti yen-chiu" (A study of the late Ch'ing debate over maritime versus Inner Asian frontier defense), *Ku-kung wen-hsien* 2.3 (June 1971), 37–59.

modernization program to meet the threat.[9] Li's arguments, however, were opposed by Tso Tsung-t'ang, leading advocate of a strategy which would, for the moment, assign priority to Inner Asia. In his counter-memorial, Tso argued with equal force and logic for the continuation of his campaign for the recovery of Sinkiang.[10] Although virtually everyone, including Tso himself, recognized the importance of maritime defense, Li's position represented a departure from the traditional Ch'ing strategy by giving naval and coastal defense a clear priority over the Inner Asian frontier. Moreover, there was the compelling fact that all of Sinkiang was in the hands of the Muslim rebels, while the strategic Ili area was occupied by the Russians. Wen-hsiang, the influential Manchu statesman who was as anxious for maritime defense as Li, warned that, if left unchecked, the Muslim revolts, which had affected Outer Mongolia, might spread to Inner Mongolia, thereby posing a direct threat to Peking.[11] The court opted for the continuation of Tso's northwestern campaign, even though it was to cost millions of taels a year. With limited resources at the dynasty's disposal, it became impossible for Li and one or two other like-minded provincial officials to obtain sufficient resources to undertake a new naval program on the scale they had envisioned.

It was against this background of Ch'ing government finances as well as the British threat to make war with China over the Margary affair that Li watched with growing concern the Japanese-Korean confrontation in the Bay of Kanghwa. Unable to take forceful action at this time, China could only exert indirect influence on Japan and Korea. The firm stand taken by the Tsungli Yamen and Li in their talks with Japanese Minister Mori in 1876 must have had a restraining effect upon the Japanese government. At the

9. IWSM-TC, 99.14a–b.

10. Tso Tsung-t'ang, *Tso Wen-hsiang-kung ch'üan-chi* (Complete works of Tso Tsung-t'ang), 46.32a–35b.

11. Kwang-Ching Liu and Richard J. Smith, "The Military Challenge: The Northwest and the Coast," in Twitchett and Fairbank, eds., *The Cambridge History of China*, vol. 11 (forthcoming).

same time, China could not but urge Korea to accept a treaty and thus avoid a disastrous rupture with Japan. Ch'ing advice and support sustained Kojong's government in its difficult decision to sign a treaty with Japan in the face of strong domestic opposition and against its own misgivings.

As the transition of Korea's international position entered its third and final stage, there was a temporary slowdown in Japan's forward policy. Domestic crises such as the Satsuma Rebellion prevented the Japanese government from continuing a vigorous diplomacy in Korea. Nevertheless, Japan wished to strengthen its strategic position in Korea as well as its diplomatic and commercial interests, particularly against the new threat of Russian encroachment from the north. By the early 1880s, Japan had consolidated its position in the peninsula by establishing its legation in Seoul and by opening two ports, Wŏnsan and Inch'ŏn, in addition to Pusan. While officially maintaining a position that rejected Chinese suzerainty over Korea, Japan did little to challenge it. On the contrary, it was willing to follow the Chinese initiative in Korea and to cooperate with China in warding off the Russian threat to the peninsula. The Japanese government realized that, modern international law notwithstanding, Chinese suzerainty over Korea was a historical fact that could not be ignored.

Despite its long-range implications, the Treaty of Kanghwa did little to change Korea's traditional relations with China or its attitude toward foreign relations immediately. Regarding the treaty as a step toward restoring old relations with Japan, the Korean government barred, until the end of 1880, the establishment of a Japanese legation in Seoul. It entertained no desire whatever to establish formal relations with Western countries. The declaration of Korean autonomy in the Kanghwa treaty was simply considered a reaffirmation of what had been true historically under the tribute system. Few Koreans in the 1870s and the early 1880s regarded their country as "equal" to or "independent" of China.

Nevertheless, after signing the Kanghwa treaty, the threat

to Korea from Japan and Russia continued to grow, creating a "situation without precedent in thousands of years," which called for an equally unprecedented response. It was becoming abundantly clear that, if China was to protect Korea and thereby secure its own strategic position in northeast Asia, it must abandon or drastically alter its traditional policy of non-interference in the affairs of the peninsular state and adopt a new activist policy that would be commensurate to the gravity of the situation. As the principal official responsible for the security of the metropolitan region of north China, it was incumbent upon Li Hung-chang to formulate such a policy for the protection of Korea, traditionally regarded as the "eastern shield" of that region. Denied adequate resources for building a large modern navy or a railroad through Manchuria to the Korean border, both necessary for China's defense of Korea, Li had little choice but to rely chiefly on diplomacy. It was in these circumstances that he conceived the idea of using a treaty system to protect the peninsula. If Korea could be induced to enter into treaty relations with Western powers, Li reasoned, and if such powers developed sufficient commercial interests in Korea, they might serve as a check on the Japanese and Russian designs on the peninsula.

Li's new Korean strategy was similar in basic concept to the ancient Chinese strategem of *i-i chih-i,* which China had historically used to maintain its supremacy among the nomadic peoples in and beyond its Inner Asian frontier regions. Under this strategem, China used one or more groups of so-called barbarians of these regions to check other and stronger barbarians, or alternately used a strong group of barbarians to control weaker ones.[12] More directly, Li was inspired by China's contemporary experience in dealing with Western powers. During the negotiations with the British that led to the settlement of the Margary affair in the fall of 1876, he had an opportunity to observe firsthand the

12. Ying-shih Yü, *Trade and Expansion in Han China,* 14–16.

restraint exercised upon Britain by other Western powers.[13] Since China was at this time the beneficiary of an existing balance of power among the Western powers having interests in China, Li hoped to create a similar situation in Korea by cultivating Western commercial interests in the peninsula as a counterweight against Japan and Russia. He was also influenced by the European balance-of-power concept, which had been expounded by men such as his protégé, Ma Chien-chung. Impressed by the British intervention in the Russo-Turkish War, which had saved Turkey from destruction, Li and his associates believed that the same balance-of-power principle could be applied to save Korea from Japan and Russia.

Obviously there were important differences between Li's Korean strategy and the balance-of-power principle operating in contemporary Europe. European practitioners of balance-of-power diplomacy—such as Victorian England or Bismarckian Germany—were powerful states, capable of throwing their weight against any power or group of powers to prevent an enemy from gaining the domination of Europe, the Near East, or Africa. China at this time did not have sufficient power of its own to practice such diplomacy effectively. Moreover, while Western practitioners of the balance-of-power concept under similar circumstances would have sought a formal or informal alliance or entente, Li and his associates neither contemplated nor attempted such arrangements, at least as of the 1870s and the early 1880s. Despite their pragmatism and growing knowledge of modern international diplomacy, Ch'ing policy-makers still thought in terms of "manipulating the Western barbarians," as China had manipulated the "Inner Asian barbarians." Nevertheless, beginning in the summer of 1882, China, while hoping to promote a treaty system in Korea without any formal alliance, did exhibit its military power in Korea.

In any case, Li Hung-chang's Korean policy was not sim-

13. For Li's role in the negotiations, see T. S. Wang, *The Margary Affair and the Chefoo Agreement.*

ply "using barbarians to control barbarians." While often
powerful and unruly, many of the Inner Asian frontier
peoples to whom this strategy was applied acknowledged
Chinese suzerainty or superiority for the sake of trade or
other practical advantages and were usually amenable to
Chinese manipulation and control. The Western powers of
the 1870s, however, not only did not acknowledge Chinese
superiority; they had great advantages over China by virtue
of the unequal treaties. They were beyond Chinese control
and to a very large degree beyond Chinese manipulation.
Li's policy was actually to "manipulate" them by holding out
the incentive of a treaty system in Korea. Inasmuch as the
treaty system was a non-Chinese institution, Li's strategy was
a variant of the *i-i chih-i* principle that went beyond traditional Chinese statecraft.

The very unorthodoxy of Li's Korean strategy called for a
cautious implementation. Li at first had no explicit authority over Korean affairs, which remained in the hands of the
conservative Board of Rites. He was aware of Korea's antipathy toward Western nations. He also knew that to urge a
new policy, foreign or domestic, upon Korea was contrary to
the tradition of non-interference which the Ch'ing dynasty
had scrupulously maintained toward Korea. Unsolicited or
unwelcome Chinese advice, however well meaning, would
be resented and resisted by Korea and defeat its purpose.
Finally, Li was aware that Korea's prospective relations with
Western nations might create difficulties in the Sino-Korean
relations under the tribute system, which remained, after
all, Li's chief hold on Korea. For these reasons, despite the
sense of urgency he felt about the Korean situation, Li
chose an unofficial approach, namely, his personal correspondence with Yi Yu-wŏn, as the means of inducing the
Korean government to enter into treaty relations with Western nations.

Not unexpectedly, the Korean response to Li's indirect
overtures was negative. Our knowledge of the Korean history of this period suggests that, even if Li or the Ch'ing
government had taken a stronger initiative toward Korea,

the result could not have been much different. With its ineffective royal leadership, ultraconservative bureaucracy, and militantly xenophobic literati, it is inconceivable that Korea could have responded positively to Li's suggestion, for to do so would have meant a further unwelcome departure from its tradition of national seclusion—witness the slow implementation of the Kanghwa treaty.

In fact, it took a dual foreign crisis for the Ch'ing government to break its own tradition and initiate a new policy toward Korea: the Sino-Russian dispute over Ili and the Japanese seizure of Ryūkyū in 1879. While the former dramatized the nature of the Russian menace, the latter clearly warned of what Japan might do to Korea in the future. Japan's outright annexation of Ryūkyū, based on its tenuous claim of exclusive suzerainty over the archipelagic kingdom, may have suggested to some Chinese officials what China could or should do with Korea on the basis of its far more authentic suzerainty over the peninsular kingdom.[14] The resulting Ch'ing government decision to persuade Korea to enter into treaty relations with Western nations was without precedent in the history of Sino-Korean relations. Yet the decision unmistakably bore the mark of tradition since even this novel policy was made possible only by expanding the application of Chinese authority under the tribute system. The change in Ch'ing policy developed gradually but unmistakably. In 1879 Li Hung-chang, in his capacity as imperial commissioner for the northern ports, was authorized to deal with the Korean question by bypassing the Board of Rites and the Tsungli Yamen. At first Li was instructed to communicate privately with Yi Yu-wŏn, indicating the Ch'ing government's reluctance to intervene officially in Korea's affairs. But within three years, Li, with the approval of the Ch'ing throne, was to intervene offi-

14. A proposal for the administrative incorporation of Korea into China, made by Chang Chien, who was on General Wu Ch'ang-ch'ing's staff in Korea, seems to have been inspired at least partly by the Japanese annexation of Ryūkyū. A proposal by Chang P'ei-lun, a *Hanlin* compiler, for Chinese takeover of Korean foreign affairs and defense may have been similarly inspired. For the latter proposal, see CKCJ, 4.28a–29b. See also TNS, vol. 1, 861–864.

cially, overstepping the practice of the suzerain's authority in traditional Sino-Korean relations.

It is not surprising, therefore, that Korea initially rejected Li's efforts to guide its foreign policy. However, Korea soon decided to accept Li's advice on foreign relations. This was partly because a number of Korean officials realized the danger of their country's international position. Still, this would have been inconceivable if the advice had come not from China but from, say, Japan. This bespeaks the theoretical absoluteness of the suzerain's authority, as M. Frederick Nelson correctly pointed out.[15]

Chinese intervention in Korea's affairs increased gradually, almost imperceptibly at first. Initially, Li envisioned his role as merely an adviser to the Korean government in negotiating treaties with Western powers. Subsequently, the fear that Japan might cut the ground out from under him by mediating between Korea and the United States made him involve himself directly in negotiations with the Americans. The Korean government's ignorance of modern international diplomacy and its inability to act decisively finally forced him to assume the role of a self-appointed plenipotentiary. He negotiated with the American representatives on his own, with little consultation with the Korean government. Korean authorities concurred or acquiesced in all Li's decisions.

It was thus neither the imminent Western threat nor pressure exerted by Japan, but Chinese initiative and leadership, that proved decisive in persuading the hermit kingdom to end its centuries-old isolation and open its doors to Western nations. Yet the Korean government was not a totally passive participant in these events. In view of Korean chauvinism and xenophobia of the period, especially lingering anti-Manchu sentiment, it is doubtful that Li Hung-chang's initiative alone could have brought about the opening of the peninsula at the particular time and in the peaceful manner in which it was actually accomplished. A small group of young reform-minded Korean officials supported by the youthful Kojong played an important role in

15. M. Frederick Nelson, *Korean and the Old Orders in Eastern Asia, passim.*

making Li's effort successful. Nor should one overlook the effect which rapidly modernizing Japan had on many of these early Korean reformers.[16]

Signing of Korea's treaties with the United States, Britain, and Germany in the early summer of 1882 was the fulfillment of a major goal of China's new Korean policy. Yet Li and his associates tried without success to use these treaties to strengthen China's traditional authority in Korea. Li valued Chinese suzerainty over Korea because it gave China a legitimate basis for intervention in the peninsula's affairs. Li was not doctrinaire concerning China's claims under the tribute system. He was willing to compromise with Japan over Ryūkyū's allegiance in 1874 during the Taiwan crisis and, again, in 1879; later he was to compromise with the French concerning China's claims on Vietnam. But in Korea he sought to safeguard China's traditional suzerainty, the application of which could be expanded flexibly, for it was his principal leverage in influencing Korea's policies. During his negotiations with Shufeldt for an American-Korean treaty, Li at first wanted a clause in the treaty recognizing Korea's tributary relationship with China. After Shufeldt rejected such a clause, Li insisted that China's suzerainty over Korea be stated in a letter from the Korean ruler to the American president. Li's policy called for a treaty system in Korea and preservation of China's traditional hold over Korea.

Li and his associates hoped that Korea's treaties with Western powers would not significantly affect its position as China's vassal state. However, the very fact that these treaties were masterminded and negotiated almost completely by China altered the nature of Chinese suzerainty over Korea. Virtually taking over the conduct of Korean foreign policy, China made an unprecedented departure from the traditional practice of non-interference in Korea's

16. The governmental reforms undertaken in Korea in 1881, including the establishment of relations with Western powers, were initiated by officials such as Kim Hong-jip and Ŏ Yun-jung, who had visited Japan at one time or another. See TNS, vol. 1, 746–747; Chŏng Ok-cha, "Sinsa yuramdan ko," *Yŏksa hakpo,* 139–140; Martina Deuchler, *Confucian Gentlemen and Barbarian Envoys,* 101–102; Towŏn sanggong kiryŏmsaŏp ch'ujin wiwŏnhoe, comp., *Kaehwagi ŭi Kim ch'ongni,* 87–100.

affairs. By its own actions and by Korea's ready acquiescence, China transformed what had been its moral and ceremonial authority into a political authority. Moreover, as a result of the unfortunate army riot in Seoul in July 1882 and the Japanese-Korean tension which ensued, Ch'ing influence in the conduct of Korea's external relations was followed by an imperious Chinese intervention in Korean domestic politics. China sent troops to Korea without prior consultation with the Korean government and, while there, the troops abducted the Taewŏn'gun, who had been installed in office, though under questionable circumstances, as a kind of prime minister, by the legitimate ruler of the country. Such Chinese moves would have been inconceivable a few years before. Circumstances forced China to act in the domineering fashion of a colonial power rather than in the traditional manner, whereby it exercised moral and ceremonial authority over the peninsular kingdom.

Decisive Chinese action forestalled retaliatory Japanese military action against Korea and made sure that the new treaties between Korea and the Western powers were accepted. Yet China and Korea both paid a price for the new "treaty-system" policy, for the Japanese-Korean settlement over Japanese losses during the army riot strengthened the Japanese position in the peninsula. Moreover, the absence of a hoped-for surge in Western interest in Korea compelled China to maintain its military and political control over the peninsula, in order to provide a counterweight to the reinforced Japanese presence. What had been regarded initially as temporary Chinese military intervention turned into a prolonged occupation, which engendered among Koreans resentment against and a yearning for independence from China. The traditional suzerain-vassal relationship between China and Korea gave way to a new type of relationship between imperialist power and colonial dependent. Contrary to Li's fond hope, the United States, which turned out to be the only Western treaty power to open its legation in Korea, refused to recognize Chinese suzerainty over Korea and, instead, encouraged Korean independence from China.[17] Combined with growing Japanese influence in the peninsula, this inspired an anti-Chinese coup by a small band of Japanese-supported radical Korean reformers in December 1884.[18] Although the coup was crushed by Chinese troops, the Sino-Japanese diplomatic settlement reached at Tientsin between Li Hung-chang and Itō Hirobumi the following spring gave Japan virtually the same right of intervention in the peninsula as China. Korea's ancient suzerain was reduced to merely one of the powers seeking its control and domination.[19]

Nelson, the pioneering scholar of the East Asian world order, called Chinese actions in Korea in the post-1882 period "indicia" of traditional Chinese theory of suzerainty over Korea unaffected by Korea's new relations with Western nations.[20] Given the flexibility of the concept of suzerainty under the tribute system, this view is not entirely wrong. What Nelson failed to emphasize, however, is that, in practice, such an exercise of China's suzerain authority was without precedent in the history of Sino-Korean relations, at least since the Mongol domination of the peninsula in the thirteenth and fourteenth centuries. Rather than being indicia of the unchanged Chinese authority over Korea, Ch'ing policy after 1882 represented a fundamental metamorphosis of Chinese authority over the peninsula. The new Chinese policy was made necessary by the exigencies of international circumstances as well as the Taewŏn'gun's anti-foreignism,[21] but it may also be viewed as a kind of forward policy inspired by the Western example in

17. For American policy toward Korea after signing the 1882 treaty, see Tyler Dennett, *Americans in Eastern Asia,* 466–487; Fred Harvey Harrington, *God, Mammon, and the Japanese;* Lee Yur-bok, *Diplomatic Relations between the United States and Korea, 1866–1887.*

18. For the 1884 coup, see TNS, vol. 1, 946–991; Harold F. Cook, *Korea's 1884 Incident;* Yu Hong-nyŏl, "Kapsin chŏngbyŏn" (The 1884 political coup), in Ch'oe Yŏng-hŭi, et al., eds., *Han'guksa,* vol. 16, 500–550.

19. For the Li-Itō convention, see TNS, vol. 1, 1097–1133; Yamabe Kentarō, "Nisshin Tenshin jōyaku ni tsuite" (On the Sino-Japanese Tientsin convention), *Ajia kenkyū* 7.2 (November 1960), 1–46.

20. Nelson, *Korea and the Old Orders,* 152–163.

21. The Taewŏn'gun did, however, indicate, during a meeting with Hanabusa, that he would not return to his earlier, anti-foreign policy. See TNS, vol. 1, 806.

Asia and the Japanese seizure of Ryūkyū. To be sure, the
Sino-Korean tribute system was to survive in outward form;
the Son of Heaven was to be honored ceremoniously by the
Korean court for a dozen years more. But the harmony,
cordiality, and kindred spirit that had characterized Sino-
Korean relations in the past were rapidly replaced by
mutual distrust, suspicion, and even antagonism. Instead of
the Confucian rules of propriety that had regulated traditional Sino-Korean relations, power, greed, and national interest were increasingly to dictate relations between the two
countries.[22] Along with the alienation of Vietnam from the
Chinese tribute system in the mid-1880s, as a result of
the French seizure of Tongking, this metamorphosis of
Sino-Korean relations brought the final demise of the old
world order and ushered in a new international order in
East Asia.

The transition of Korea's international position described
in this volume is not only significant to Korea itself. Korea's
position as "vortex of empires" brought out the tendency
for expansionism on the part of China as well as Japan. In
the case of Japan the expansionist policy was more con-
spicuous, since Japan took the initiative. Chinese forward
policy in Korea was essentially defensive; it was nevertheless
executed with vigor. Among the officers of the gentlemanly
General Wu Ch'ang-ch'ing was the young Yüan Shih-k'ai,
who was to be the Chinese proconsul in Korea after 1885
and who was at least as arrogant as a Hanabusa.[23]

While the impetus and initiative for the opening of Korea
came from Western powers—mainly France and the United
States—the lead was taken over by Japan and China. Unlike
the earlier opening of China and Japan, which represented
an almost passive East Asian response to Western expansionism, the opening of Korea was the result of activism on
the part of Japan and innovation on the part of China, with

22. For the post-1882 Chinese policy, see Lin Ming-te, *Yüan Shih-k'ai yü Chao-
hsien* (Yüan Shih-k'ai and Korea).
23. For Yüan's conduct in Korea, see *ibid.;* Harrington, *God, Mammon, and the
Japanese, passim;* Fujioka Kikuo, "Chōsen jidai no En Sei-gai" (Yüan Shih-k'ai during his days in Korea), *Tōyō gakuhō* 52.4 (March 1973), 1–51.

Korean concurrence to China's decisions. These developments reflect the fact that, by the 1870s and the early 1880s, China and Japan, whatever their respective places in the traditional East Asian world order, were facing the realities of new international circumstances. Korea's fate was to be at the center of regional East Asian power politics. While powers such as Russia, Britain, and the United States were to be involved in the next phase of international rivalry in the Korean peninsula, China was to dominate Korea for the next dozen years and Japan was to win out eventually. The unfolding drama of Sino-Japanese rivalry in Korea must still be viewed in light of the traditional interstate order in East Asia, for certain institutional forms and predilections continued. Nevertheless, with the establishment of the Japanese legation in Seoul in December 1880 and the arrival of Chinese troops there in August 1882, the last phase of the East Asian world order had come to an end. It was to be followed by an international order in which intraregional tensions would take on the new spirit of international power rivalry.

Glossary

An Tong-jun	安東晙
Andō Nobumasa	安藤信正
Ashikaga Yoshimitsu	足利義満
Bansho Shirabedokoro	蕃書調所
Chang Chih-tung	張之洞
Chang P'ei-lun	張佩綸
Chang Shu-sheng	張樹聲
Chao-hsien ts'e-lüeh	朝鮮策略
Ch'en Ch'in	陳欽
Ch'en Pao-ch'en	陳寶琛
Ch'eng-lin	成林
ch'i-fu	欺負
Chi-ho	吉和
Ch'i-ying	耆英
Ch'in Kuai	秦檜
ch'ing-liu	清流
Cho, Queen Dowager	趙大妃
Cho In-hŭi	趙寅熙
Cho Yŏng-ha	趙寧夏
choch'ŏn (ch'ao-t'ien)	朝天
Ch'oe Ik-hyŏn	崔益鉉
Ch'ŏljong, King	哲宗
chonhwa yang'i	尊華攘夷
Chŏng Hyŏn-dŏk	鄭顯德
Chŏng Ki-wŏn	鄭岐源
Chŏngjo, King	正祖
Chōsen mondai	朝鮮問題
Chou Fu	周馥
Chou Wen-mu (James)	周文謨
Ch'ung-cheng	崇禎
Ch'ung-shih	崇實
Chung-wai hsin-wen	中外新聞
Dajōkan	太政官
Date Munenari	伊達宗城

datsu-A	脱亜
Enomoto Takeaki	榎本武揚
Etō shimpei	江藤新平
fudai	譜代
fukoku kyōhei	富国強兵
fuyō	附庸
gaifu	外府
Gotō Shōjirō	後藤象次郎
Hachinohe Junshuku	八戸順叔
Hai-kuo t'u-chih	海國圖誌
han	藩
Han Kye-wŏn	韓啟源
Hanabusa Yoshimoto	花房義質
hanseki hōkan	藩籍奉還
Hashimoto Sanai	橋本左内
hatamoto	旗本
Hayashi Shihei	林子平
Higuchi Tesshirō	樋口鉄四郎
Hirano Kuniomi	平野国臣
Hirayama Takatada	平山敬忠
Hirotsu Hironobu	玄津弘信
Ho Ju-chang	何如璋
Honda Toshiaki	本田利明
Hong Chae-hak	洪在鶴
Hong Sun-mok	洪淳穆
Hong U-ch'ang	洪祐昌
Hŏnjong, King	憲宗
Hsi-ch'ung-a	喜崇阿
Hsüeh Fu-ch'eng	薛福成
Huang Tsun-hsien	黄遵憲
Hwang Chŏng-nyŏn	黄正淵
Hwang Sa-yŏng	黄嗣永
Hyojong, King	孝宗
Hyŏn Sŏg-un	玄昔運
i-i chih-i	以夷制夷
i-ti chih-ti	以敵制敵
Ii Naosuke	井伊直弼
Ikchong	翼宗
Inoue Kaoru	井上馨
Inoue Yoshika	井上良馨
Itagaki Taisuke	板垣退助

Itakura Katsukiyo 板倉勝静
Itō Hirobumi 伊藤博文
Iwakura Tomomi 岩倉具視
jōi 攘夷
kaikoku 開国
Kaikoku heidan 海国兵談
Kanda Takahira 神田孝平
Kang No 姜浩
kangaku 漢学
Katsu Yasuyoshi (Kaishū) 勝安芳（海舟）
Kawamura Sumiyoshi 川村純義
Kido Takayoshi
  (Katsura Kogorō) 木戸孝允（桂小五郎）
Kija (Ch'i-tzu) 箕子
Kim Cho-sun 金祖淳
Kim Hong-jip 金弘（宏）集
Kim Ki-su 金綺秀
Kim Po-hyŏn 金輔鉉
Kim Pyŏng-guk 金炳國
Kim Pyŏng-hak 金炳學
Kim P'yŏng-muk 金平黙
Kim Se-ho 金世鎬
Kim Tae-gŏn (Andrew) 金大建
Kim Yun-sik 金允植
Koga Kin'ichirō 古賀謹一郎
kōgai naikyū no jutsu 攻外内救之術
Kondō Masuki 近藤真鋤
Kojong, King 高宗
kokken gaikō 国権外交
kokugaku 国学
Kung, Prince 恭親王
Kuroda Kiyotaka 黒田清隆
Kusaka Genzui 久坂玄瑞
Kuze Hirochika 久世広親
kyorin 交鄰
li 禮
Li Hung-chang 李鴻章
Li Shu-ch'ang 黎庶昌
Ma Chien-chung 馬建忠
Maki Yasuomi (Izumi) 真木保臣（和泉）
Mandongmyo 萬東廟

Mao Ch'ang-hsi	毛昶熙
Maruyama Sakura	丸山作樂
Matsudaira Yoshinaga	松平慶永
Min, Queen	閔妃
Min Kyŏm-ho	閔謙鎬
Min Kyu-ho	閔奎鎬
Min Sŭng-ho	閔升鎬
Min T'ae-ho	閔台鎬
Miyamoto Okazu	宮本小一
Mori Arinori	森有礼
Mori Sukenobu	森祐信
Mōri Takachika	毛利敬親
Moriyama Shigeru	森山茂
Nakamuda Kuranosuke	中牟田倉之助
na-kung-chih pang	納貢之邦
Namin	南人
Namyŏn, Prince	南延君
Noron	老論
Ŏ Yun-jung	魚允中
Oguri Tadamasa	小栗忠順
Ōki Takatō	大木喬任
Ōkubo Toshimichi	大久保利通
Ōkuma Shigenobu	大隈重信
Ōmura Masujirō	大村益次郎
Ōshima Tomonojō	大島友之允
Paekche	百濟
Pak Che-gwan	朴齊寬
Pak Kyu-su	朴珪壽
P'an Wei	潘霨
pang-t'u (fōdo)	邦土
Pyŏkp'a	僻派
pi-t'an	筆談
Pug'in	北人
Pyŏn Wŏn-gyu	卞元圭
rangaku	蘭學
ri	里
rōjū	老中
Sada Hakubō	佐田白茅
sadae	事大
Sagara Masaki	相良正樹
Saigō Takamori	西鄕隆盛

Saigō Tsugumichi	西郷従道
Saitō Sakae	斉藤栄
Sakamoto Ryōma	坂本竜馬
sakoku	鎖国
Sanjō Sanetomi	三条実美
Sankoku zusetsu tsūran	三国図説通覧
Sasu Iori	佐須伊織
Satō Nobuhiro	佐藤信淵
Sawa Nobuyoshi	沢宣嘉
sei-Kan ron	征韓論
Shen Pao-chen	沈葆楨
Shimazu Hisamitsu	島津久光
Silla	新羅
Sim Tong-sin	沈東臣
Sin Hŏn	申櫶
Sip'a	時派
sirhak	實學
Sō Yoshikazu	宗義和
Sō Shigemasa (Yoshisato)	宗義達 (重正)
Soejima Taneomi	副島種臣
Song Si-yŏl	宋時烈
sonnō	尊王
Sukchong, King	肅宗
Sun Shih-ta	孫士達
sung-Myŏng pan-Ch'ŏng	崇明反清
Sunjo, King	純祖
Taebodan	大報壇
Taewŏn'gun (Yi Ha-ŭng)	大院君 (李昰應)
taikun (taegun)	大君
Takasugi Shinsaku	高杉晋作
Terashima Munenori	寺島宗則
Ting Jih-ch'ang	丁日昌
Ting Ju-ch'ang	丁汝昌
Tokugawa Iemochi (Yoshitomi)	徳川家茂 (慶福)
Tokugawa Nariaki	徳川斉昭
Tokugawa (Hitotsubashi) Yoshinobu	徳川 (一橋) 慶喜
Tokutomi Iichirō (Sohō)	徳富猪一郎 (蘇峰)
T'ongni kimu amun	統理機務衙門
t'ongsinsa	通信使
Toyotomi Hideyoshi	豊臣秀吉

tozama 外様
Tseng Kuo-fan 曾國藩
Tso Tsung-t'ang 左宗棠
Tsuda Masamichi 津田真道
Tung Hsun 董恂
T'ung-chih, Emperor 同治帝
T'ung-wen Kuan 同文館
tzu-chu (chaju, jishu) 自主
T'zu-hsi, Empress Dowager 慈禧
Udai kondō hisaku 宇内混同秘策
Ueno Kagenori 上野景範
Unyō 雲揚
Urase Yutaka 浦瀬裕
Waegwan 倭館
Wan Ch'ing-li 萬青藜
Wan-li, Emperor 萬曆帝
Wan-kuo kung-fa 萬國公法
Wanhwa, Prince 完和君
Wei Yüan 魏源
Wen-hsiang 文祥
wijŏng ch'ŏksa 衛正斥邪
Wu Ch'ang-ch'ing 吳長慶
Yamada Hōkoku 山田方谷
Yamagata Aritomo 山県有朋
Yamanoshiro Sukenaga 山之城祐長
Yanagiwara Sakimitsu 柳原前光
Yi Chae-sŏn 李載先
Yi Ch'oe-ŭng 李最應
Yi Hang-no 李恒老
Yi Ik 李瀷
Yi Sŏng-gye 李成桂
Yi Yong-suk 李容肅
Yi Yu-wŏn 李裕元
Ying-han 英翰
Ying Pao-shih 應寶時
yōgaku 洋学
Yokoyama Shōtarō 横山正太郎
Yŏngnam man'inso 嶺南萬人疏
Yŏnhaeng (Yen-hsing) 燕行
Yoshida Shōin 吉田松陰
Yoshioka Kōki 吉岡弘毅

Yu Chih-k'ai	游智開
Yu Ch'i-sŏn	俞致善
Yü Sui	余瓙
Yüan Shih-k'ai	袁世凱
Yun Cha-sŭng	尹滋承
Yun Ch'i-hwa	尹致和

Works Cited

Abe, Takeo 安部健夫. *Chūgokujin no tenka kannen* 中国人の天下観念 (The Chinese concept of the world). Kyoto: Dōshisa University, 1956.

Asao, Naohiro 朝尾直弘. *Sakoku* 鎖国 (National seclusion). Tokyo: Shōgakkan, 1975.

Banno, Masataka 坂野正高. "Furansu ryūgaku jidai no Ba Ken-chū" フランス留学時代の馬建忠 (Ma Chien-chung during his days of study in France). *Kokkagakkai zasshi* 国家学学会雑誌 84.5–6 (July 1971), 257–293.

Beasley, W. G. *The Meiji Restoration.* Stanford: Stanford University Press, 1972.

Brown, Sidney Devere. "Ōkubo Toshimichi: His Political and Economic Policies in Early Meiji Japan." *Journal of Asian Studies* 21.2 (February 1962), 183–197.

Castel, Albert and Nahm, Andrew C. "Our Little War with the Heathen." *American Heritage* 19.3 (April 1968), 19–23, 72–75.

Ch'a-yang san-chia wen-ch'ao 茶陽三家文鈔 (Writings of three scholars from Ch'a-yang). Wen T'ing-ching 温廷敬, ed. Reprint. Taipei: Wen-hai, 1966.

Chang, Chih-tung 張之洞. *Chang Wen-hsiang-kung ch'üan-chi* 張文襄公全集 (Complete works of Chang Chih-tung), 229 chüan in 6 vols. Wang Shu-nan 王樹柟, ed. Reprint. Taipei, Wen-hai, 1963.

Chang, Ts'un-wu 張存武. "Ch'ing-Han kuan-hsi, 1636–1644" 清韓関係 1636–1644 (Ch'ing-Korean relations, 1636–1644). *Ku-kung wen-hsien* 故宮文獻 4.1 (December 1972), 15–37; 4.2 (March 1973), 15–35.

————. "Ch'ing-tai Chung-kuo tui Chao-hsien wen-hua chih ying-hsiang" 清代中國對朝鮮文化之影響 (Chinese cultural influence on Korea during the Ch'ing period). *Bulletin of the Institute of Modern History, Academia Sinica* 4.2 (December 1974), 551–599.

————. *Ch'ing-Han tsung-fan mou-i, 1637–1894* 清韓宗藩貿易 1637–1894 (Sino-Korean tributary trade, 1637–1894). Taipei: The Institute of Modern History, Academia Sinica, 1978.

Ch'en, San-ching 陳三井. "Lüeh-lun Ma Chien-chung ti wai-chiao ssu-hsiang" 略論馬建忠的外交思想 (A brief discussion of Ma Chien-chung's foreign policy ideas). *Bulletin of the Institute of Modern History, Academia Sinica* 3.2 (December 1972), 546–556.

Chien, Frederick Foo. *The Opening of Korea: A Study of Chinese Diplomacy, 1876–1885.* Hamden, Conn.: Shoe String Press, 1967.

Cho, Hang-nae 趙恒來. *Kaehanggi tae-Il kwan'gyesa yŏn'gu* 開港期對日關係史研究 (Studies on the history of relations with Japan in the period of opening ports). Taegu: Hyŏngsŏl ch'ulp'ansa, 1973.

Choe, Ching Young. *The Rule of the Taewŏn'gun, 1864–1873: Restoration in Yi Korea.* Cambridge, Mass.: Harvard University Press, 1972.

Ch'oe, Ch'ang-gyu 崔昌圭 *Han'gug'in ŭi chŏngch'i isik* 韓國人의政治意識 (The political consciousness of the Koreans). Seoul: Han'guk munhwa yŏn'guso, 1971.

————. "Ch'ŏksaron kwa kŭ sŏngkyŏk" 斥邪論과 그 性格 (The *ch'ŏksa* doctrine and its nature), in Ch'oe Yŏng-hŭi 崔永禧, et al., eds., *Han'guksa* 한국사 (History of Korea), vol. 16, 288–314. Seoul: Kuksa p'yŏnch'an wiwŏnhoe, 1975.

Ch'oe, Sŏg-u 崔奭祐. "Pyŏng'in yang'yo sogo" 丙寅洋擾小攷 (A short study of the 1866 Western invasion). *Yŏksa hakpo* 歷史學報 30 (April 1966), 108–124.

————. "Ch'ŏnjugyo ŭi suyong" 天主敎의受容. (Acceptance of Catholicism), in Ch'oe Yŏng-hŭi 崔永禧, et al., eds., *Han'guksa* 한국사 (History of Korea), vol. 14, 88–123. Seoul: Kuksa p'yŏnch'an wiwŏnhoe, 1975.

Ch'oe, T'ae-ho 崔泰鎬. *Kaehang chŏn'gi ŭi Han'guk kwanse chedo* 開港前期의 韓國關稅制度 (The Korean tariff system in the early period of opening ports). Seoul: Han'guk yŏn'guwŏn, 1976.

Ch'oe, Yu-gil 崔柳吉. "Yijo kaehang chikhu ŭi Han-Il muyŏk ŭi tonghyang" 李朝開港直後의 韓日貿易의動向 (The trend in Korean-Japanese trade immediately after the opening of ports by Yi Korea). *Asea yŏn'gu* 亞細亞研究 15.3 (September 1972), 175–221.

Chŏng, Ok-cha 鄭玉子 "Sinsa yuramdan ko" 紳士游

覽圍考 (A study of the gentlemen's sightseeing group). *Yŏksa hakpo* 歷史學報 27 (April 1965), 105–142.

Chun (chŏn), Hae-jong. "Sino-Korean Tributary Relations during the Ch'ing Period," in John K. Fairbank, ed., *The Chinese World Order*, 90–111. Cambridge, Mass.: Harvard University Press, 1968.

————. *Han-Chung kwan'gyesa yŏn'gu* 韓中関係史研究 (Studies on the history of Korean-Chinese relations). Seoul: Il-chogak, 1970.

————. *Tong'a munhwa ŭi pigyosajŏk yŏn'gu* 東亞文化의比較史的研究 (Comparative historical studies on East Asian culture). Seoul: Ilchogak, 1976.

CJHK: *Ch'ing-chi Chung-Jih-Han kuan-hsi shih-liao* 清季中日韓関係史料 (Historical materials on Sino-Japanese-Korean relations during the late Ch'ing period), 11 vols. Taipei: The Institute of Modern History, Academia Sinica, 1972.

CKCJ: *Ch'ing Kuang-hsü ch'ao Chung-Jih chiao-she shih-liao* 清光緒朝中日交涉史料 (Historical materials on Sino-Japanese relations during the Kuang-hsü reign), 88 chüan in 2 vols. Reprint. Taipei: Wen-hai 1970.

Conroy, Hilary. "Government versus 'Patriot': The Background of Japan's Asiatic Expansion." *Pacific Historical Review* 20.1 (February 1951), 31–42.

————. *The Japanese Seizure of Korea, 1868–1910*. Philadelphia: University of Pennsylvania Press, 1960.

Craig, Albert M. *Chōshū in the Meiji Restoration*. Cambridge, Mass.: Harvard University Press, 1967.

————. "Kido Kōin and Ōkubo Toshimichi: A Psychohistorical Analysis," in Albert M. Craig and Donald H. Shively, eds., *Personality in Japanese History*, 264–308. Berkeley: University of California Press, 1970.

CWS: *Chosŏn wangjo sillok* 朝鮮王朝實録 (The veritable record of the Yi dynasty), 48 vols. Seoul: Kuksa p'yŏnch'an wiwŏnhoe, 1955–58. (Index, 1963).

Dennett, Tyler. *Americans in Eastern Asia: A Critical Study of United States Policy in the Far East in the Nineteenth Century*. Reprint. New York: Barnes & Noble, 1963.

Deuchler, Martina. *Confucian Gentlemen and Barbarian Envoys: The Opening of Korea, 1875–1885*. Seattle: University of Washington Press, 1977.

Ebisawa, Arimichi 海老沢有道. *Nihon Kirishitan shi* 日本キリ

シタン史 (A history of the early Christians in Japan). Tokyo: Hanawa shobō, 1966.

Fairbank, John K. ed., *The Chinese World Order*. Cambridge, Mass.: Harvard University Press, 1968.

———. "The Early Treaty System in the Chinese World Order," in John K. Fairbank, ed., *The Chinese World Order*, 257–275. Cambridge, Mass.: Harvard University Press, 1968.

Fairbank, John K. and Teng, S. Y. "On the Ch'ing Tributary System." *Harvard Journal of Asiatic Studies* 6 (1941), 135–246.

Fletcher, Joseph. "The Heyday of the Ch'ing Order in Mongolia, Sinkiang, and Tibet," in Denis Twitchett and John K. Fairbank, eds., *The Cambridge History of China,* vol. 10, 351–408. Cambridge: Cambridge University Press, 1978.

Fox, Grace. *Britain and Japan, 1858–1883*. London: Oxford University Press, 1969.

Fraser, Andrew. "The Ōsaka Conference of 1875." *Journal of Asian Studies* 26.4 (August 1967), 589–610.

Fujimura, Michio 藤村道生. "Chōsen ni okeru Nihon tokubetsu kyoryūchi no kigen" 朝鮮における日本特別居留地の起源 (Origins of the Japanese concessions in Korea). *Nagoya daigaku bungakubu kenkyū ronshū* 名古屋大学文学部研究論集 35 (March 1965), 21–76.

———. "Meiji shoki ni okeru Nisshin kōshō no ichidammen" 明治初期における日清交渉の一断面 (An aspect of Sino-Japanese relations in the early Meiji period). *Nagoya daigaku bungakubu kenkyū ronshū* 名古屋大学文学部研究論集 47 (March 1967), 1–8.

———. "Meiji shonen ni okeru Ajia seisaku no shūsei to Chūgoku" 明治初年におけるアジア政策の修正と中国 (The revision of Asian policy in the early Meiji years and China). *Nagoya daigaku bungakubu kenkyū ronshū* 名古屋大学文学部研究論集 53 (March 1968), 3–24.

———. "Ryūkyū buntō kōshō to tai-Ajia seisaku no tenkan" 琉球分島交渉と対アジア政策の転換 (Negotiations for the partition of the Ryūkyūs and a shift in Asian policy). *Rekishigaku kenkyū* 歴史学研究 373 (March 1971), 1–13.

Fujioka, Kikuo 藤岡喜久男. "Chōsen jidai no En Sei-gai" 朝鮮時代の袁世凱 (Yüan Shih-k'ai during his days in Korea). *Tōyō gakuhō* 東洋学報 52.4 (March 1973), 1–51.

Fujitsuka, Rin 藤塚鄰. *Shinchō bunka tōden no kenkyū* 清朝文化東伝の研究 (A study of the transmission of Ch'ing culture to Korea). Tokyo: Kokusho kankōkai, 1975.

Gaimushō 外務省, comp. *Nichi-Ro kōshō shi* 日露交涉史 (A history of Japanese-Russian relations). Reprint. Tokyo: Hara shobō, 1968.

Haehaeng ch'ongjae 海行摠載 (Collected accounts of maritime missions), 4 vols. Keijō: Chōsen kosho kankōkai, 1928.

Han, Woo-keun (U-gŭn) 韓沽劤. "Kaehang tangsi ŭi wigi isik kwa kaehwa sasang" 開港當時의危機意識과開化思想 (The sense of crisis and englightenment thought at the time of opening ports). *Han'guksa yŏn'gu* 韓國史研究 2 (December 1969), 105–139.

———. *Han'guk kaehanggi ŭi sang'ŏp yŏn'gu* 韓國開港期의商業研究 (A study of commerce in Korea during the period of opening ports). Seoul: Ilchogak, 1970.

———. *The History of Korea*. Seoul: Eul-Yoo Publishing Co., 1970.

———. *Tonghangnan kiin e kwanhan yŏn'gu* 東學亂起因에關한研究 (A study on the causes of the Tonghak rebellion). Seoul: Han'guk munhwa yŏn'guso, 1971.

Haraguchi, Kiyoshi 原口清. *Nihon kindai kokka no keisei* 日本近代国家の形成 (The formation of the modern Japanese state). Tokyo: Iwanami shoten, 1968.

Harootunian, H. D. *Toward Restoration: The Growth of Political Consciousness in Tokugawa Japan*. Berkeley: University of California Press, 1970.

Harrington, Fred Harvey. *God, Mammon, and the Japanese: Dr. Horace N. Allen and Korean-American Relations, 1884–1905*. Madison: University of Wisconsin Press, 1966.

Hashimoto, Sanai 橋本左内. *Hashimoto Keigaku zenshū* 橋本景岳全集 (Complete works of Hashimoto Sanai), 2 vols. Tokyo: Keigakkai, 1943.

Hatada, Takashi 旗田巍. "Kindai ni okeru Chōsenjin no Nihonkan" 近代における朝鮮人の日本観 (The Korean view of Japan in modern times). *Shisō* 思想 520 (October 1967), 59–73.

———. *Nihonjin no Chōsenkan* 日本人の朝鮮観 (Japanese views on Korea). Tokyo: Keisō shobō, 1969.

Hayashi, Shihei 林子平. *Hayashi Shihei zenshū* 林子平全集 (Complete works of Hayashi Shihei). Yamamoto Yutaka 山本鐃, ed. Tokyo: Seikatsusha, 1943.

Hino, Seizaburō 日野清三郎. *Bakumatsu ni okeru Tsushima to Ei-Ro* 幕末における対馬と英露 (Tsushima, Britain, and Russia in the bakumatsu period). Tokyo: University of Tokyo Press, 1968.

Hirose, Yasuko 広瀬 靖子   "Kōka-tō jiken no shūhen" 江華島事件の 周辺 (Circumstances surrounding the Kanghwa Island incident). *Kokusai seiji* 国際 政治 37 (1967), 23–40.

Hsü, Immanuel C. Y. *China's Entrance into the Family of Nations: The Diplomatic Phase, 1858–1880.* Cambridge, Mass.: Harvard University Press, 1960.

———. *The Ili Crisis: A Study of Sino-Russian Diplomacy.* London: Oxford University Press, 1965.

———. "The Great Policy Debate in China, 1874: Maritime vs. Frontier Defense." *Harvard Journal of Asiatic Studies* 25 (1964–65), 212–228.

Hsü, Shih-chiai (Kyo Sei-kai) 許世楷 . "Taiwan jiken (1871–1874)" 台湾事件 (1871–1874) (The Taiwan incident, 1871–1874). *Kokusai seiji* 国際政治 28 (1964), 38–52.

Hsüeh, Fu-ch'eng 薛 福成 . *Hsüeh Fu-ch'eng ch'üan-chi* 薛福成全集 (Complete works of Hsüeh Fu-ch'eng), 3 vols. Reprint. Taipei: Kwang-wen, 1963.

Ienaga, Saburō 家永三郎 , et al., eds., *Kindai Nihon no sōten* 近代日本の 争点 (Controversies in modern Japan), 3 vols. Tokyo: Mainichi shimbunsha, 1972.

Inaba, Iwakichi 稲葉岩吉 . *Kōkaikun jidai no Man-Sen kankei* 光海君時代の 満鮮関係 (Manchu-Korean relations during Prince Kwanghae's reign). Keijō: Ōsakayagō shoten, 1933.

Inoue, Kiyoshi 井上 清 . *Nihon gendai shi* 日本現代史 (History of modern Japan), 4 vols. Tokyo: University of Tokyo Press, 1951.

———. *Nihon no gunkokushugi* 日本の 軍国主義 (Japanese militarism), 2 vols. Tokyo: University of Tokyo Press, 1953.

———. *Meiji ishin* 明治維新 (The Meiji restoration), vol. 20 in Inoue Mitsusada 井上光貞 , et al., eds., *Nihon no rekishi* 日本の 歴史 (A history of Japan), 26 vols. Tokyo: Chūō kōronsha, 1966.

INS-KJ: *Ilsŏngnok: Kojong p'yŏn* 日省録 高宗篇 (The record of daily reflection: Kojong reign), 44 vols. Seoul: Seoul National University Press, 1967–72.

Iwakura kō jikki 岩倉公実記 (The authentic records of Prince Iwakura), 3 vols. Tada Kōmon 多田好問 , ed. Reprint. Tokyo: Hara shobō, 1968.

Iwakura Tomomi kankei monjo 岩倉具視 関係文書 (Papers related to Iwakura Tomomi), 9 vols. Tokyo: Nihon shiseki kyōkai, 1927–34.

Iwao, Seiichi 岩生成一 . *Sakoku* 鎖国 (National seclusion). Tokyo: Chūō kōronsha, 1966.

Iwata, Masakazu. *Ōkubo Toshimichi: The Bismarck of Japan.* Berkeley: University of California Press, 1964.

IWSM-TC: *Ch'ou-pan i-wu shih-mo: T'ung-chih ch'ao* 籌辦夷務 始末 同治朝 (The complete account of the management of barbarian affairs: the T'ung-chih reign), 100 chüan. Peiping: Palace Museum, 1930.

IWSM-TK: *Ch'ou-pan i-wu shih-mo: Tao-kuang ch'ao* 籌辦夷務 始末 道光朝 (The complete account of the management of barbarian affairs: the Tao-kuang reign), 80 chüan. Peiping: Palace Museum, 1930.

Jansen, Marius B. "Modernization and Foreign Policy in Meiji Japan," in Robert E. Ward, ed., *Political Development in Japan.* 149–188. Princeton: Princeton University Press, 1968.

Kaehwagi ǔi Kim ch'ongni 開化期의 金總理 (Prime minister Kim during the period of enlightenment). Compiled and published by Towǒn sanggong kiryǒmsaǒp ch'ujin wiwǒnhoe 道園相公記念事業推進委員會 . Seoul, 1977.

Kang, Chae-ǒn (Kyō Zai-gen) 姜在彦 *Chōsen kindaishi kenkyū* 朝鮮近代史研究 (Studies on modern Korean history). Tokyo: Nihon hyōronsha, 1970.

———. *Kindai Chōsen no shisō* 近代朝鮮の思想 (Modern Korean thought). Tokyo: Kinokuniya shoten, 1971.

Kang, W. J. "Early Korean Contact with Christianity and Korean Response," in Yung-hwan Jo, ed., *Korea's Response to the West.* 43–56. Kalamazoo: The Korea Research and Publications, Inc., 1971.

Katsu, Yasuyoshi 勝安芳 . *Katsu Kaishū zenshū* 勝海舟 全集 (Complete works of Katsu Kaishū), 22 vols. Etō Jun 江藤淳 , et al., eds. Tokyo: Keisō shobō, 1970–77.

Keene, Donald. *The Japanese Discovery of Europe, 1720–1830.* Stanford: Stanford University, 1969.

Kemuriyama, Sentarō 煙山專太郎 . *Sei-Kan ron jissō* 征韓論實相 (The truth about the *sei-Kan* controversy). Tokyo: Waseda University Press, 1907.

KHOM: *Ku Han'guk oegyo munsǒ* 舊韓國外交文書 (Diplomatic documents of late Yi Korea), 24 vols. Seoul: Koryǒ taehakkyo Asea munje yǒn'guso, 1965–69.

Kido, Takayoshi 木戸孝允. *Kido Takayoshi ibunshū* 木戸孝允遺文集 (Miscellaneous letters of Kido Takayoshi). Tsumaki Chūta 妻木忠太, ed. Tokyo: Taizanbō, 1942.

——. *Kido Takayoshi nikki* 木戸孝允日記 (Diary of Kido Takayoshi), 3 vols. Tokyo: Nihon shiseki kyōkai, 1932–33.

Kido Takayoshi monjo 木戸孝允文書 (Kido Takayoshi papers), 8 vols. Tokyo: Nihon shiscki kyōkai, 1930–31.

Kikuda, Sadao 蒲田貞雄. *Sei-Kan ron no shinsō to sono eikyō* 征韓論の真相とその影響 (The truth about the *sei-Kan* controversy and its effect). Tokyo: Tokyo nichinichi shimbunsha, 1941.

Kim, Chong-wŏn 金鍾圓. "Cho-Chung sangmin suryuk muyŏk changjŏng e taehayŏ" 朝中商民水陸貿易章程에對하여 (On Korean-Chinese private maritime and overland trade regulations). *Yŏksa hakpo* 歷史學報 32 (December 1966), 120–149.

Kim, Hong-jip 金弘集. *Sunsinsa ilgi* 修信使日記 (Diary of a friendship envoy), in Kuksa p'yŏnch'an wiwŏnhoe 國史編纂委員會 ed., *Susinsa kirok* 修信使記錄 (Records of friendship envoys). 113–193. Seoul: T'amgudang, 1971.

——. *Kim Hong-jip yugo* 金弘集遺稿 (Writings of Kim Hong-jip). Koryŏ taehakkyo chung'ang tosŏgwan 高麗大学校中央圖書館, ed. Seoul: Koryŏ University Press, 1976.

Kim, Ki-su 金綺秀. *Iltong kiyu* 日東記游 (Account of a mission to Japan) and *Susinsa ilgi* 修信使日記 (Diary of a friendship envoy), in Kuksa p'yŏnch'an wiwŏnhoe 國史編纂委員會, ed., *Susinsa kirok* 修信使記錄 (Records of friendship envoys), 1–148. Seoul: T'amgudang, 1971.

Kim, Kyŏng-t'ae 金敬泰. "Kaehang chikhu ŭi kwansekwŏn hoebok munje" 開港直後의關稅權回復問題 (The tariff rights recovery issue immediately after the opening of ports). *Han'guksa yŏn'gu* 韓国史研究 8 (September 1972), 81–112.

Kim, Sŏng-ch'il 金聖七. "Yŏnhaeng sogo: Cho-Chung kyosŏp ŭi ilgu" 燕行小攷--朝中交涉의一齣 (A short study of the missions to Peking: An Aspect of Korean-Chinese relations). *Yŏksa hakpo* 歷史學報 12 (May 1960), 1–79.

Kim, Yong-gi 金龍基. "Chosŏn ch'ogi ŭi tae-Myŏng chogong kwan'gye ko" 朝鮮初期의對明朝貢關係考 (A study of tributary relations with the Ming in the early Yi period). *Pusandae nonmunjip* 釜山大論文集 14 (1972), 131–182.

Kinjō, Seitoku 金城正篤. *Ryūkyū shobunron* 琉球処分論 (A discussion of the disposition of the Ryūkyūs). Naha: Okinwa Times, 1978.

KJS: *Kojong Sunjong sillok: Kojong sillok* 高宗純宗實錄高宗實錄 (The veritable record of Kojong and Sunjong: the veritable record of Kojong), 3 vols. Seoul: T'amgudang, 1970.

Kobayashi, Shigeru 小林茂. "Tokugawa jidai ni okeru Chōsen tsūshinshi no jogō mondai: Yodo han no baai" 徳川時代における朝鮮通信使の助郷問題--淀藩の場合 (The question of local support for the Korean communication embassies during the Tokugawa period: the case of the domain of Yodo). *Chōsen gakuhō* 朝鮮学報 43 (May 1967), 49–82.

Kobori, Keiichirō 小堀桂一郎. *Sakoku no shisō* 鎖国の思想 (The concept of national seclusion). Tokyo: Chūō kōronsha, 1974.

Kokubu, Taneyuki 国分亂之. *Gyosui jitsuroku* 魚水実録 (Correspondence between Lord Itakura of Bitchū and his retainers), 2 vols. Tokyo: Kyū-Takahashi han shimbokukai, 1911.

Kublin, Hyman. "The Attitude of China during the Liu-ch'iu Controversy." *Pacific Historical Review* 18.2 (May 1949), 213–231.

Kuno, Yoshi S. *Japanese Expansion on the Asian Continent,* 2 vols. Berkeley: University of California Press, 1940.

Kuo, Ting-yee and Liu, Kwang-Ching. "Self-strengthening: the Pursuit of Western Technology," in Denis Twitchett and John K. Fairbank, eds., *The Cambridge History of China,* vol. 10, 491–542. Cambridge: Cambridge University Press, 1978.

Kwŏn, Sŏk-pong 權錫奉. "Yŏngsŏnsa-haeng e taehan ilgoch'al" 領選使行에對한一考察 (A study of the student-apprentice mission). *Yŏksa hakpo* 歷史學報 17–18 (June 1962), 277–312.

———. "Yi Hong-jang ŭi tae-Chosŏn yŏlguk ibyak kwŏndoch'aek e taehayŏ" 李鴻章의對朝鮮列國立約勸導策에對하여 (On Li Hung-chang's policy of inducing Korea to sign treaties with powers). *Yŏksa hakpo* 歷史學報 21 (August 1963), 101–130.

———. "Imo gunbyŏn" 壬午軍變 (The 1882 military riot), in Ch'oe Yŏng-hŭi 崔承禧, et al., eds., *Han'guksa* 한국사 (History of Korea), vol. 16, 392–441. Seoul: Kuksa p'yŏnch'an wiwŏnhoe, 1975.

Ledyard, Gari. "Korean Travelers in China over Four Hundred Years." *Occasional Papers on Korea* 2 (March 1974), 1–42.

Lee, Yur-Bok. *Diplomatic Relations between the United States and Korea, 1866–1887*. New York: Humanities Press, 1970.

Leung, Pak-Wa (Edwin). "China's Quasi-war with Japan: The Dispute over the Ryūkyū (Liu-ch'iu) Islands, 1871–1881." Ph.D. dissert., University of California, Santa Barbara, 1978.

Liang, Chia-pin 梁嘉彬. "Liu-ch'iu wang-kuo Chung-Jih cheng-ch'ih k'ao-shih" 琉球亡國中日爭持考實 (A factual study of the Sino-Japanese dispute over the demise of the Liu-ch'iuan kingdom). *Ta-lu tsa-chih* 大陸雜誌, pt. 1, 48.5 (May 1974), 193–218; pt. 2, 48.6 (June 1974), 263–290.

Lin, Ming-te 林明德. *Yüan Shih-k'ai yü Chao-hsien* 袁世凱與朝鮮(Yüan Shih-k'ai and Korea). Taipei: The Institute of Modern History, Academia Sinica, 1970.

Liu, Kwang-Ching. "Li Hung-chang in Chihli: The Emergence of a Policy, 1870–1875," in Albert Feuerwerker, et al., eds., *Approaches to Modern History*, 68–104. Berkeley: University of California Press, 1967.

———. "The Ch'ing Restoration," in Denis Twitchett and John K. Fairbank, eds., *The Cambridge History of China*, vol. 10, 409–490. Cambridge: Cambridge University Press, 1978.

Liu, Kwang-Ching and Smith, Richard J. "The Military Challenge: The Northwest and the Coast," in Denis Twitchett and John K. Fairbank, eds., *The Cambridge History of China*, vol. 11. Cambridge: Cambridge University Press (forthcoming in 1979).

Liu, Shih-chi 劉石吉. "Ch'ing-chi hai-fang yü se-fang chih cheng ti yen-chiu" 清季海防與塞防之爭的研究 (A study of the late Ch'ing debate over maritime versus Inner Asian frontier defense). *Ku-kung wen-hsien* 故宮文獻 2.3 (June 1971), 37–59.

LWCK: Li, Hung-chang 李鴻章. *Li Wen-chung-kung ch'üan-shu* 李文忠公全書(Complete works of Li Hung-chang), 100 ts'e. Edited by Wu Ju-lun 吳汝綸 and published by the Li family. Nanking, 1908.

Ma, Chien-chung 馬建忠. *Shih-k'o-chai chi-yen chi-hsing* 適可齋紀言紀行 (Essays and travel accounts of Ma Chien-chung). Reprint. Taipei: Wen-hai, 1968.

———. *Tung-hsing san-lu* 東行三錄 (Record of three journeys to Korea). Reprint. Taipei: Kwang-wen, 1967.

Maruyama, Kanji 丸山幹治. *Soejima Taneomi haku* 副島種臣伯(Count Soejima Taneomi). Tokyo: Dainichisha, 1936.

Masumi, Junnosuke 枡味準之輔 . *Nihon seitō shiron* 日本政党史論 (A historical survey of political parties in Japan), 4 vols. Tokyo: University of Tokyo Press, 1965–68.

Mayo, Marlene J. "The Korean Crisis of 1873 and Early Meiji Foreign Policy." *Journal of Asian Studies* 31.4 (August 1972), 793–819.

McCune, George M. "Korean Relations with China and Japan, 1800–1864." Ph.D. dissert., University of California, Berkeley, 1941.

———. "The Exchange of Envoys between Korea and Japan during the Tokugawa Period." *Far Eastern Quarterly* 5.3 (May 1946), 308–325.

McWilliams, Wayne C. "Soejima Taneomi: Statesman of Early Meiji Japan, 1868–1874." Ph.D. dissert., University of Kansas, 1973.

———. "East Meets West: The Soejima Mission to China, 1873." *Monumenta Nipponica* 30.3 (Autumn 1975), 237–275.

Meiji bunka shiryō sōsho 明治文化資料叢書 (Meiji cultural material series), 13 vols. Tokyo: Meiji bunka shiryō kankōkai, 1962–64.

Meiji bunka zenshū 明治文化全集 (Collected works on Meiji culture), 32 vols. Meiji bunka kenkyūkai 明治文化研究会 , ed. Tokyo: Nihon hyōronsha, 1955–74.

Meng, S. M. *The Tsungli Yamen: Its Organization and Functions.* Cambridge, Mass.: Harvard University Press, 1962.

Mikuniya, Hiroshi 三国谷 宏 . "Ryūkyū kizoku ni kansuru Guranto no chōtei" 琉球帰属に関するグラントの調停 (Grant's mediation concerning the subjection of Ryūkyū). *Tōhō gakuhō* 東方学報 (Kyoto) 10.3 (October 1939), 29–64.

Miyake, Hidetoshi 三宅英利 . "Tokugawa seiken shokai no Chōsen shinshi" 徳川政権初回の 朝鮮信使 (The first Korean embassy to the Tokugawa regime). *Chōsen gakuhō* 朝鮮学報 82 (January 1977), 101–132.

Mōri, Toshihiko 毛利敏彦 . "Meiji shoki gaikō no Chōsenkan" 明治初期外交の朝鮮観 (The Japanese view of Korea in early Meiji diplomacy). *Kokusai seiji* 国際政治 51 (1974), 25–42.

Mukai, Toshio 向井淳郎 . "Bakumatsu ni okeru Shina keiryakuron no hatten to sono seishitsu" 幕末における支那経略論の発展とその性質 (The rise of the proposal for the subjugation of China in the bakumatsu period and its nature).

Shirin 史林 , pt. 1, 25.4 (October 1940), 481–498; pt. 2, 26.1 (June 1941), 103–113.

Nakajima, Shōzō 中島昭三 . "Kōka-tō jiken" 江華島事件 (The Kanghwa Island incident). *Kokugakuin hōgaku* 国学院法学 8.3 (March 1971), 324–359.

Nakamura, Hidetaka 中村栄孝 . *Nissen kankeishi no kenkyū* 日鮮関係史の研究 (Studies on the history of Japanese-Korean relations), 3 vols. Tokyo: Yoshikawa kōbunkan, 1965–69.

Nelson, M. Frederick. *Korea and the Old Orders in Eastern Asia.* Baton Rouge: Louisiana State University Press, 1945.

NGB: *Nihon gaikō bunsho* 日本外交文書 (Diplomatic documents of Japan). Japan. Gaimushō 外務省 , comp. Tokyo: Nihon kokusai kyōkai, 1936–

Nihon rekishi daijiten 日本歴史大辞典 (Great dictionary of Japanese history), 12 vols. Tokyo: Kawade shobō, 1970.

Nish, Ian. *Japanese Foreign Policy, 1869–1942: Kasumigaseki to Miyakezaka.* London: Routledge & Kegan Paul, 1977.

Ōe, Shinobu 大江志乃夫 . *Kido Takayoshi* 木戸孝允 (Kido Takayoshi). Tokyo: Chūō kōronsha, 1968.

Ōkubo, Toshimichi 大久保利通 . *Ōkubo Toshimichi nikki* 大久保利通日記 (Diary of Ōkubo Toshimichi), 2 vols. Tokyo: Nihon shiseki kyōkai, 1927.

Ōkubo Toshimichi monjo 大久保利通文書 (Ōkubo Toshimichi papers), 10 vols. Tokyo: Nihon shiseki kyōkai, 1927–29.

Okudaira, Takehiko 奥平武彦 . *Chōsen kaikoku kōshō shimatsu* 朝鮮開国交渉始末 (A complete account of the negotiations leading to the opening of Korea). Reprint. Tokyo: Tōkō shoin, 1969.

Ōkuma bunsho 大隈文書 (Okuma papers), 5 vols. Tokyo: Waseda daigaku shakaikagaku kenkyūjo, 1958–62.

Pak, Kyu-su 朴珪壽 . *Hwanjaejip* 瓛齋集 (Collected works of Pak Kyu-su), 11 kwŏn in 5 vols. Kim Yun-sik, ed. Dated 1911.

Palais, James B. "Korea on the Eve of the Kanghwa Treaty, 1873–1876." Ph.D. dissert., Harvard University, 1968.

——. *Politics and Policy in Traditional Korea.* Cambridge, Mass.: Harvard University Press, 1975.

P'eng, Tse-chou (Hō Taku-shū) 彭澤周 . *Meiji shoki Nik-Kan-Shin kankei no kenkyū* 明治初期日韓清関係の研究

(Studies on Japanese-Korean-Chinese relations in the early Meiji period). Tokyo: Hanawa shobō, 1969.

Reischauer, Edwin O. and Fairbank, John K. *East Asia: The Great Tradition*. Boston: Houghton Mifflin Co., 1958.

Saigō, Takamori 西鄉隆盛. *Dai Saigō zenshū* 大西鄉全集 (Complete works of Saigō Takamori), 3 vols. Tokyo: Dai Saigō zenshū kankōkai, 1926–27.

Sakai, Robert K. "The Ryūkyū Islands as a Fief of Satsuma," in John K. Fairbank, ed., *The Chinese World Order*. 112–134. Cambridge, Mass.: Harvard University Press, 1968.

Shōgiku Kido kō den 松菊木戶公傳 (A biography of Kido Takayoshi), 2 vols. Tokyo: Kido kō denki hensankai, 1927.

Sin, Ki-sŏk 申基碩. *Hanmal oegyosa yŏn'gu* 韓末外交史研究 (Studies on the history of late Yi Korean foreign relations). Seoul: Ilchogak, 1967.

Sin. Kuk-chu 申國柱. *Kŭndae Chosŏn oegyosa yŏn'gu* 近代朝鮮外交史研究 (Studies on the history of modern Korean foreign relations). Seoul: T'amgudang, 1965.

Sin, Sŏk-ho 申奭鎬. "Chosŏn wangjo kaeguk tangsi ŭi tae-Myŏng kwan'gye" 朝鮮王朝開國當時의對明關係 (Relations with the Ming at the time of founding the Yi dynasty). *Kuksasang ŭi chemunje* 國史上의諸問題 1 (1959), 93–134.

Sohn, Pow-key. "Power versus Status: The Role of Ideology in the Early Yi Dynasty." *Tongbang hakchi* 東方学志 10 (December 1969), 437–444.

Sŏng, Nak-hun 成樂熏. "Han-guk tangjaeng sa" 韓國黨爭史 (A history of Korean factionalism), in *Han'guk munhwasa taegye* 韓國文化史大系 (Grand outline of Korean cultural history), vol. 2, 220–383. Seoul: Kodae minjok munhwa yŏn'guso, 1965.

Steinberg, David I. *Korea: Nexus of East Asia: An Inquiry into Contemporary Korea in Historical Perspective*. New York: American-Asian Educational Exchange, 1968.

Tabohashi, Kiyoshi 田保橋潔. "Nisshi shinkankei no seiritsu, bakumatsu ishinki ni okeru" 日支新関係の成立--幕末維新期における (The establishment of new Sino-Japanese relations during the bakumatsu and restoration periods). *Shigaku zasshi* 史学雑誌, pt. 1, 44.2 (February 1933), 163–199; pt. 2, 44.3 (March 1933), 314–338.

————. *Kindai Nissen kankei no kenkyū* 近代日鮮関係の研究 (Studies on modern Japanese-Korean relations), 2 vols. Keijō: Chōsen sōtokufu, 1940.

Tamamuro, Taijō 圭室 諦成. *Saigō Takamori* 西郷隆盛 (Saigō Takamori). Tokyo: Iwanami shoten, 1960.

Tanaka, Takeo 田中健夫. "Sakoku seiritsuki Nitchō kankei no seikaku" 鎖国成立期 日朝関係の性格 (The nature of Japanese-Korean relations during the development of the national seclusion policy). *Chōsen gakuhō* 朝鮮学報 34 (January 1965), 29–62.

————. *Chūsei taigai kankei shi* 中世対外関係史 (A history of foreign relations during the middle ages). Tokyo: University of Tokyo Press, 1975.

Tei, Nagayasu 鄭永寧. "Soejima taishi teki-Shin gairyaku" 副島大使適清概略 (A general account of Ambassador Soejima's mission to China), in *Meiji bunka zenshū* 明治文化全集 (Collected works on Meiji culture), vol. 11, 61–72. Tokyo: Nihon hyōronsha, 1955–74.

Thomson, Sandra Caruthers. "Filibustering to Formosa: General Charles LeGendre and the Japanese." *Pacific Historical Review* 40.4 (November 1971), 442–456.

TNS: See Tabohashi, Kiyoshi, *Kindai Nissen kankei no kenkyū.*

Toby, Ronald P. "Korean-Japanese Diplomacy in 1711: Sukchong's Court and the Shogun's Title." *Chōsen gakuhō* 朝鮮学報 74 (January 1975), 231–256.

————. "Reopening the Question of *Sakoku.*" *Journal of Japanese Studies* 3.2 (Summer 1977), 323–363.

Tokutomi, Iichirō 徳富猪一郎. *Kōshaku Yamagata Aritomo den* 公爵山県有朋伝 (A biography of Prince Yamagata Aritomo), 3 vols. Reprint. Tokyo: Hara shobō, 1967.

Treat, Payson J. *Diplomatic Relations between the United States and Japan,* 3 vols. Palo Alto: Stanford University Press, 1932–38.

Tsiang, T. F. "Sino-Japanese Diplomatic Relations, 1870–1894." *Chinese Social and Political Science Review* 17.1 (April 1933), 1–106.

Tso, Tsung-t'ang 左宗棠. *Tso Wen-hsiang-kung ch'üan-chi* 左文襄公全集 (Complete works of Tso Tsung-t'ang). Reprint. Taipei: Wen-hai, 1964.

Tsunoda, Ryusaku, et al., eds., *Sources of Japanese Tradition* (paperback), 2 vols. New York: Columbia University Press, 1964.

Walker, Hugh D. "The Yi-Ming Rapprochement: Sino-Korean Relations, 1392–1592." Ph.D. dissert., University of California, Los Angeles, 1971.

Wang, S. T. *The Margary Affair and the Chefoo Agreement.* London: Oxford University Press, 1940.

Ward, Robert E., ed., *Political Development in Japan.* Princeton: Princeton University Press, 1968.

Watsuji, Tetsurō 和辻哲郎. *Sakoku* 鎖国 (National seclusion). Tokyo: Chikuma shobō, 1951.

Weems, Benjamin B. *Reform, Rebellion, and the Heavenly Way.* Tucson: University of Arizona Press, 1964.

Wilson, George M. "The Bakumatsu Intellectual in Action: Hashimoto Sanai in the Political Crisis of 1858," in Albert M. Craig and Donald H. Shively, eds., *Personality in Japanese History,* 234–263. Berkeley: University of California Press, 1970.

Woodside, Alexander B. *Vietnam and the Chinese Model: A Comparative Study of Nguyen and Ch'ing Civil Administration in the First Half of the Nineteenth Century.* Cambridge, Mass.: Harvard University Press, 1971.

Wright, Mary C. "The Adaptability of Ch'ing Diplomacy: The Case of Korea." *Journal of Asian Studies* 17.3 (May 1958), 363–381.

Yamabe, Kentarō 山辺健太郎. *Nikkan heigō shōshi* 日韓併合小史 (A short history of the Japanese annexation of Korea). Tokyo: Iwanami shoten, 1966.

———. *Nihon no Kankoku heigō* 日本の韓国併合 (Japan's annexation of Korea). Tokyo: Taihei Shuppansha, 1966.

———. "Nisshin Tenshin jōyaku ni tsuite" 日清天津条約について (On the Sino-Japanese Convention of Tientsin). *Ajia kenkyū* アジア研究 7.2 (November 1960), 1–46.

Yamada, Hōkoku 山田方谷. *Yamada Hōkoku zenshū* 山田方谷全集 (Complete works of Yamada Hōkoku), 3 vols. Yamada Jun 山田準, ed. Okayama: Yamada Hokōku zenshū kankōkai, 1951.

Yamada, Shōji 山田正次. "Sei-Kan ron, jiyū-minken ron, bummei-kaika ron" 征韓論・自由民権論・文明開化論 (The proposal for the subjugation of Korea, the advocacy of freedom and people's rights; and the call for civilization and enlightenment). *Chōsenshi kenkyūkai rombunshū* 朝鮮史研究会論文集 7 (June 1970), 117–141.

Yamaguchi, Masayuki 山口正之. *Chōsen Seikyō shi: Chōsen Kirisutokyō no bunkashiteki kenkyū* 朝鮮西教史--朝鮮キリスト教の文化史的研究 (A history of Christianity in Korea: a cultural historical study of Korean Christianity). Tokyo: Yūzankaku, 1967.

Yamaji, Aizan 山路愛山. *Katsu Kaishū* 勝海舟 (Katsu Kaishū). Tokyo: Tōadō, 1911.

Yen, Sophia Su-fei. *Taiwan in China's Foreign Relations, 1836–1874.* Hamden, Conn.: Shoe String Press, 1965.

Yi, Hyŏn-jong 李鉉淙. *Han'guk kaehangjang yŏn'gu* 韓國開港場研究 (Studies on the trade ports in Korea). Seoul: Ilchogak, 1975.

Yi Ik, 李瀷. *Sŏngho sasŏl* 星湖僿説 (Miscellaneous essays of Yi Ik), 2 vols. Seoul: Kyŏnghŭi Ch'ulpansa, 1967.

Yi, Kwang-nyin 李光麟. *Han'guk kaehwasa yŏn'gu* 韓國開化史研究 (Studies on the history of modernization in Korea). Seoul: Ilchogak, 1969.

Yi, Nŭng-hwa 李能和. *Chosŏn Kidokkyo kŭp oegyo sa* 朝鮮基督教及外交史 (A history of Christianity and foreign relations in Korea). Reprint. Seoul: Hangmungak, 1968.

Yi, Po-hyŏng 李普珩. "Shufeldt chedok kwa 1880–yŏn ŭi Cho-Mi kyosŏp" Shufeldt 提督과 1880年의朝美交渉 (Commodore Shufeldt and Korean-American negotiations in 1880). *Yŏksa hakpo* 歷史學報 15 (September 1961), 61–91.

Yi, Pyŏng-do 李丙燾. "Kwanghaegun ŭi tae-Hugŭm chŏngch'aek" 光海君의對後金政策 (Prince Kwanghae's policy toward the Manchus). *Kuksasang ŭi chemunje* 國史上의諸問題 1 (1959), 135–175.

Yi, Sang-baek 李相佰. *Han'guksa kŭnse hugi p'yŏn* 韓國史近世後期篇 (History of Korea: late modern period). Seoul: Ŭryu munhwasa, 1965.

Yi, Sŏn-gŭn 李瑄根. *Han'guksa ch'oegŭnse p'yŏn* 韓國史最近世篇 (History of Korea: most recent period). Seoul: Ŭryu munhwasa, 1961.

Yim, Dong-jae. "The Abduction of the Taewŏn'gun, 1882." *Papers on China* 21 (February 1968), 99–130.

Yoshida, Shōin 吉田松陰. *Yoshida Shōin zenshū* 吉田松陰全集 (Complete works of Yoshida Shōin), 10 vols. Tokyo: Yamaguchi-ken kyōikukai, 1934–36.

Yu, Hong-nyŏl 柳洪烈. *Kojong ch'iha ŭi Sŏhak sunan ŭi yŏn'gu*

高宗治下의西學受難의硏究 (A study of Christian ordeals under the rule of King Kojong). Seoul: Ŭryu munhwasa, 1962.

————. *Han'guk Ch'ŏnjugyohoe sa* 韓国天主教會史 (A history of the Roman Catholic Church in Korea). Seoul: K'at'orik ch'ulpansa, 1962.

————. "Kapsin chŏngbyŏn" 甲申政變 (The 1884 political coup), in Ch'oe Yŏng-hŭi 崔永禧, et al., eds., *Han'guksa* 한국사 (History of Korea), vol. 16, 500–550. Seoul: Kuksa p'yŏnch'an wiwŏnhoe, 1975.

Yü, Ying-shih. *Trade and Expansion in Han China: A Study of Sino-Barbarian Economic Relations.* Berkeley: University of California Press, 1967.

Index

Abe Takeo, 1n
Alcock Convention, British refusal to ratify, 143
Alcock, Rutherford, 90, 151
Andō Nobumasa, 90
Andong Kim clan, 32, 43, 44, 207; Christianity tolerated by, 37; power of weakened by the Taewŏn'gun, 205
Anglo-French War against China, 39, 83, 88; and development of the treaty system in East Asia, 39; impact on Korean security, 41–42, 44
Anglo-Satsuma war in 1863, 100, 188
Anhwei Army, 296, 318, 319, 322
Ansei Purge of 1859, 85, 86, 88
An Tong-jun, 158; response to Japanese restoration diplomacy, 118–120, 121, 122; views of the Taewŏn'gun represented by, 119; negotiations with Sagara Masaki, 163–164; charges against, 211; arrested, 212; executed, 213
Asao Naohiro, 24n
Ashikaga Japan, viii, 17; investiture of rulers by the Ming court, 15, 23–24

Bakufu (central government) in Japan, 16, 30; ceremonial diplomacy with Korea, 16–17, 21–22, 72; political prestige gained from formal relations with Korea, 21–22; direct contact with the Korean government terminated, 17, 22, 23; commercial relations with China, 24; aborted intervention in Korea to mediate Korean foreign disputes, 54, 74, 100–109, 112; fall in 1868, 54, 78, 107, 111, 112, 154; alleged plans to invade Korea, 72, 73, 75; and Korean failure to send the quinterrenial tribute to Japan, 72, 73; role in the development of Japanese expansionism, 78, 88–100; and conservative proponents of Japanese continental expansion, 81, 83–84, 85–87, 98, 107; declining authority of, 88, 98, 106; proposal to take over Tsushima, 91, 95; daimyo of Tsushima changed by, 93; military and economic aid promised to Tsushima, 96, 97; war with Chōshū, 97, 99, 100–101, 106, 112; military weakness of, 100–101, 106
Balance-of-power concept, in Chinese "treaty-system policy," 277, 278, 294, 308, 343
Bannerman (hatamoto), 94
Banno Masataka, 278n
Bansho Shirabedokoro, 146
Beasley, W. G., 86n
Belcher, Edward, 40
Belgium, 285
Bellonet, Henri de, 49, 71n; punitive expedition to Korea sent by, 47–48
Berlin Congress, 278
Berneux, Bishop Simon-François, 45–46
Berthemy, French minister in China, 46

Korea (*continued*)
    Japanese-Korean relations;
    Sei-Kan-ron; Treaty of Kanghwa;
    "Treaty system policy"
    Taewŏn'gun
Korea, domestic politics in: power
    struggles and social unrest, 31–33,
    207–208, 209, 249, 272–273, 286,
    317, 321, 326; rule of the consort
    clans, 32–33, 44, 205, 272;
    Christianity in, 32–38, 44–47, 49,
    50; role in Korean-Japanese
    rapprochement, 210–211, 212–213,
    222–223, 224–225, 247–248,
    249–252, 337–338; literati
    opposition to the opening of
    Korea, 225, 247–248, 271, 286,
    287, 309, 317, 337; relative to
    Japanese achievement of its
    strategic objectives, 272–273; and
    Chinese efforts to impose treaty
    system diplomacy on Korea,
    286–287, 289, 298, 316–327
Korea, exclusionist policy of, x–xi;
    promoted by the Taewŏn'gun,
    xi–xii, 44, 53, 61, 67, 205, 326,
    331; intensified by the Korean
    "victory" in the French invasion,
    50–51, 65; vs. tradition of treating
    shipwrecked aliens kindly, 51, 58,
    62; rigidity of, 62–68, 107; militant
    cultural chauvinism in, 63, 65,
    331; relative to the Treaty of
    Kanghwa, 256; promoted by
    Japanese expansionism, 286; and
    initial rejection of treaty relations
    with Western powers, 288; end of,
    298–299, 337
Korea, exclusionist policy of, origins
    of, x, 25–38, 62–63; invasions of
    Korea, 25–27; genesis and effect
    of Ming loyalism on, 27–29;
    distrust of Japan, 29–31; cultural
    chauvinism, 30–31, 37, 63; *yangban*
    factions and bureaucratic

corruption, 31–33; threat posed by
    the spread of Christianity, 33–38,
    49, 50
Korea, King of: manipulated by the
    yangban class, x, 31; shrines to
    honor the Ming built by, xi, 28;
    investiture by the Chinese
    emperor, 6–7, 8–9, 12, 15, 238,
    249–252, 324; term used for in
    Japanese diplomatic messages,
    116, 300, 307–308; reference to
    deleted in the Treaty of Kanghwa,
    252. *See also* Kojong, King
Korea, opening of: major studies of,
    xxi–xxii; phases of relative to
    changing East Asian and Western
    policies, 257, 269, 298–300, 301,
    302, 315, 329–351; completed by
    the U.S.-Korean treaty (1882),
    302, 330; resulting from Japanese
    activism and Chinese innovation,
    350–351. *See also* "Treaty system
    policy" of China toward Korea
Korea, opening of, role of Japan in,
    xxi, xxii, 329, 330; Korean ports
    opened to Japanese commerce,
    252, 264–268, 271–272, 287, 288,
    292, 341; and establishment of a
    Japanese legation in Seoul,
    260–261, 263–267, 268, 270, 292,
    294, 299–300, 351. *See also* Treaty
    of Kanghwa
Korea, opening of: role of Western
    nations in, xxi, 39–76, 329–330,
    350; initial British and French
    efforts to trade with Korea, 40;
    foreign commerce rejected by
    Korea, 40, 52, 59, 62, 67; French
    proposed seizure of Korea, 41;
    Catholic purges and the French
    invasion of Korea, 45–51, 329,
    331, 333; American expedition to
    Korea, 51–62, 329, 331, 333, 337
Korea, security of: under the
    traditional Chinese tribute system,

Ports, Korean (*continued*)
  264–268, 270, 271–272, 287, 288,
  292, 341; Russia's need for an
  ice-free port in Korea, 293, 297,
  304
Possadonick, Russian warship, visit to
  Tsushima, 89–90; impact on initial
  Japanese proposals to invade
  Korea, 91, 93, 95, 105
Predatory Western tactics, used by
  Japan, 155, 255
Prefectural Governors' Conference,
  creation of, 229
Prefecture of Okinawa,
  establishment of, 280
Price, Don C., xxiii, xxiv
Prussia, treaty with China, 146–147
Pukch-ŏng, 266
P'ung'yang Cho clan in Korea, 32,
  36, 43, 207
Pusan, 103, 118, 119, 125, 159;
  Japanese representatives not
  allowed beyond, 17, 19, 30;
  German warship in, 122; illegal
  trade at, 177; riot of Japanese
  marines at, 244; restricted rights
  of Japanese to travel in, 261; tariff
  dispute at, 268–270; privileges
  and concessions of Japan in, 272.
  See also Japan House
Pyŏkp'a, faction in Korea, 32
Pyŏn Wŏn-gyu, 307

Queen Min. *See* Min, Queen

Reischauer, Edwin O., 32n
Restoration diplomacy of Japan, xiii,
  75, 110–153; and myth of Japan's
  destiny to preside over the world,
  xiii, 82, 131, 331–332; issue of
  titular superiority over Korea in,
  75, 111–123, 155, 165, 253; role of
  Kido Takayoshi in, 112–113, 115,
  123–124, 125–126, 132–133,
  134–135, 137; ideological

framework outlined in Lord Sō's
  memorial, 113–115; efforts to
  establish diplomatic relations with
  Korea based on Korea's ancient
  tributary status to Japan, 113, 115,
  120, 123, 124, 128, 131; notification
  to Korea of the imperial
  restoration, 115, 116–117; and use
  of Korean seals, 116, 117, 118, 121;
  rejected by Korea, 118–123;
  diplomatic disputes with Korea,
  118–121, 332–333; impact of the
  Brandt incident on, 121–123;
  invasion of Korea as a solution for
  Japanese domestic politics,
  123–136; position of the Foreign
  Ministry in, 127–128, 131, 134;
  traditional East Asian concept of
  hierarchical relations in, 127–128,
  131, 153, 220, 331–333; role of
  Moriyama Shigeru in, 128, 129,
  216; and Sino-Japanese Treaty of
  1871, 130–131, 136-153; goals to
  establish titular equality with
  China to gain titular superiority
  over Korea, 137, 138, 140, 147, 149,
  151, 152, 153, 155, 333; achieved
  goals of, 152; compared to later
  developments in Japanese foreign
  policy, 155, 157, 220, 335
Ridel, Father Felix-Clair, 47, 275
Ritual, in traditional East Asian
  relations, ix, 6, 7, 8
Roches, Leon, 102
Rodgers, John: role in U.S. invasion
  of Korea, 56, 58, 59, 60, 61
Roman Catholic Church in Korea,
  34–37; as a tool of the French
  government, 37, 45–47, 50, 212.
  See also Christianity in Korea
Roze, Pierre-Gustave: punitive
  expedition against Korea led by,
  49–50; unauthorized by the
  French government, 49, 54;
  withdrawal from Korea, 50

Compositor: Viking Typographics
Printer: Braun-Brumfield
Binder: Braun-Brumfield
Text: VIP Baskerville
Display: VIP Baskerville
Paper: 50 lb. P&S Offset Vellum